JOIN US ON THE INTERNET

WWW: http://www.thomson.com
EMAIL: findit@kiosk.thomson.com   A service of I(T)P®

South-Western Educational Publishing

an International Thomson Publishing company I(T)P®

Cincinnati • Albany, NY • Belmont, CA • Bonn • Boston • Detroit • Johannesburg • London • Madrid
Melbourne • Mexico City • New York • Paris • Singapore • Tokyo • Toronto • Washington

QBasic™
Second Edition

Susan K. Baumann
Steven L. Mandell

South-Western Educational Publishing
an International Thomson Publishing company I(T)P®

Cincinnati • Albany, NY • Belmont, CA • Bonn • Boston • Detroit • Johannesburg • London • Madrid
Melbourne • Mexico City • New York • Paris • Singapore • Tokyo • Toronto • Washington

Copyeditor: Loretta Palagi
Composition: Martin Arthur, Atelier 88
Technical Review: Colleen Kobe

Photo credits follow the index.

ISBN 0-314-20547-0 (hard cover)

4 5 BN 00 99

Printed in the United States of America

I(T)P
International Thomson Publishing

South-Western Educational Publishing is a division of International Thomson Publishing, Inc. The ITP trademark is used under license.

Contents-in-Brief

Contents

vii

Preface

Since the mid-1960s, when Drs. John Kemeny and Thomas Kurtz first developed BASIC, it has been a commonly taught introductory programming language. Over the years, many different dialects have evolved. As structured programming became the widely accepted methodology, the shortcomings of traditional BASICs became more and more obvious. In recent years, structured BASICs have become available. These BASICs encourage the development of well-designed, reliable programs that have readily apparent logic and are easy to maintain. They provide a wide variety of control structures and simplify program modularization.

The language presented in this text is Microsoft QBasic, a well-structured BASIC used on IBM PCs and PC-compatibles. Because QBasic is very similar to Microsoft QuickBASIC 4.5, the text can also easily be used with Microsoft QuickBASIC 4.5; differences are presented in Appendix D.

Structured problem solving is emphasized throughout the text, and problem solutions are functionally decomposed with the aid of structure charts. Each programming chapter ends with a comprehensive programming problem that ties together new statements and concepts. This comprehensive problem is developed using top-down design and is modularized with the aid of a structure chart.

Each chapter contains a number of pedagogical devices to improve learning. Chapter Outlines, Objectives, and an Introduction give students an overview of chapter content. Learning Checks provide self-testing as the chapter progresses. Programming Hints help students avoid common problems and end-of-chapter Review Questions allow students to demonstrate mastery of the chapter content. Debugging Exercises and Programming

xiii

Problems at the end of the programming chapters provide practice in using new statements and structures.

A number of enhancements have been incorporated into this second edition:

- The discussion of computer hardware in Chapter 1 has been expanded.

- Chapter 1 now includes a section titled "Being a Responsible Computer User," a topic of ongoing importance to all educators.

- The end-of-chapter programming problems are now divided into three levels: Level 1, Level 2, and Challenge Problems. In most instances, the Challenge Problems include exact specifications that the student must achieve. The text provides a mix of general, business, and mathematically-oriented problems.

- There is an increased emphasis on interactive programming.

- Parameters have been added to structure charts. This feature decreases the chances for parameter-passing errors.

- The level of sophistication of the sequential and random-access files chapter has been increased.

- The section on sorting algorithms has been expanded.

- The graphics chapter has been expanded and updated.

Color coding has been used in programming examples as follows:

`Colored shading`	Highlighted Statements (Used to indicate statement currently being discussed)
`Black lettering`	Computer Output
`Colored lettering`	User Response

ACKNOWLEDGEMENTS

Thanks are owed to many professionals for their input to this new edition, including Pam Starkey and Mario Rodriguez for guidance throughout the development and production process, Martin Arthur for page composition and graphics, and Colleen Kobe for technical review. Also, a note of gratitude to Harriette Kisilinsky for preparing the instructional supplements. Finally, a special word of thanks to Denis Ralling for never letting us get too far off track.

We were very fortunate to have had a number of outstanding educators serve as reviewers for this project, and we wish to express our thanks for their help:

Carol Barner
Glendale Community College
Arizona

Earl Cobb
Hilldale High School
Oklahoma

Jonetta Crain
White Deer High School
Texas

Bruce R. Gill
Whitefish Bay High School
Wisconsin

Cheryl Hiller
McCallum High School
Texas

Larry McBride
Las Cruces High School
New Mexico

Derek Merrill
Arizona State University
Arizona

Merle L. Niemiec
Reagan High School
Texas

Robinson Parson
Houston Independent School District
Texas

Mary Ann Ratliff
Clark High School
Texas

                                                                    Susan K. Baumann
                                                                    Steven L. Mandell

QBasic™

Second Edition

Introduction to Computer Systems and QBasic

Outline

Objectives

After studying this chapter, you will be able to:

- List the three kinds of tasks a computer can perform.
- Name the three features that make a computer useful.
- Explain the purpose of the central processing unit and main memory.
- Name and describe the two components of the central processing unit.
- Discuss the different input, output, and secondary storage devices used with computer systems.
- List the four categories of computer systems.
- Explain the purpose of the computer's operating system.
- Access QBasic and identify the different parts of the QBasic screen.
- Explain how to choose options from the QBasic menu bar.
- Explain the difference between the Save and Save As options.
- Enter a simple program, store it on disk, and load it back into the computer's main memory.
- Edit program statements.

■ **Define the term** *computer ethics.*

■ **Discuss the rules for caring for diskettes.**

■ **Explain the differences between commercial software, shareware, and public-domain software.**

INTRODUCTION

Computers have become an important force in our society. People use them to perform an ever-increasing variety of tasks, including banking, locating books in libraries, and making reservations on airline flights. Elementary-school children learn their multiplication tables with the help of computer programs that are entertaining, motivating, and more patient than any human teacher. Everywhere we look, we see fascinating applications for these versatile machines. The uses for computers are limited only by the creativity of the people who control them.

What is it that makes these machines different from the other machines that we use every day, such as cars or typewriters? First, a **computer** is an electronic machine that is capable of processing facts in a wide variety of ways with an extremely high degree of speed and accuracy. In addition, the versatility of the computer is enhanced by its ability to combine many simple operations into a single, integrated whole. A sequence of instructions that work together to allow the computer to solve a specific problem is called a **program**. A language that is used to direct the computer to carry out, or **execute**, these instructions is called a **programming language**.

This textbook will teach you the programming language QBasic. We begin by presenting some information about computers in general. Later in the chapter you begin to learn about the QBasic system.

Computer *An electronic machine capable of processing data in many different ways. Its speed, accuracy, and storage and retrieval capabilities make it extremely useful to people.*

Program *A list of step-by-step instructions that a computer can use to solve a problem.*

Execute *To carry out the instructions in a program.*

Programming language *A language that a programmer can use to give instructions to a computer.*

WHAT COMPUTERS CAN DO

The actual tasks that computer systems are capable of performing can be divided into three categories:

1. Arithmetic operations (addition, subtraction, multiplication, and division).

2. Comparison (or logical) operations (determining whether a given value is greater than, equal to, or less than another value).

3. Storage and retrieval operations (such as saving a program on disk so that it can be used later).

What makes the computer particularly useful to people is its ability to perform these tasks with a high degree of speed and accuracy. With care, a person can add a hundred numbers and find the correct result, but the chances of making an error somewhere along the way are considerable. Also, it is a boring job. This is the kind of task that is well suited to a computer; it can perform the task quickly and accurately, and it will not get bored. Moreover, it can store the result for future use.

THE COMPONENTS OF A COMPUTER SYSTEM

The physical components of a computer system are called the **hardware** (Figure 1-1) and consist of a system unit and peripheral devices.

The System Unit

The main component of the computer system is the **system unit**. The system unit contains the central processing unit and main memory. The **central processing unit** (**CPU**) performs the actual processing and can be thought of as the "brain" of the computer. As shown in Figure 1-2, the CPU consists of two major components: the control unit and the arithmetic/logic unit. In a microcomputer, such as an IBM Personal Computer, the CPU is

Hardware *The physical components of the computer system, such as the central processing unit, printers, and disk drives.*

System unit *The main component of the computer system; it contains the central processing unit, main memory, and possibly other hardware devices.*

Central processing unit (**CPU**) *The "brain" of the computer, composed of two parts: the control unit and the arithmetic/logic unit.*

FIGURE 1-1

The physical components of a computer system are referred to as hardware.

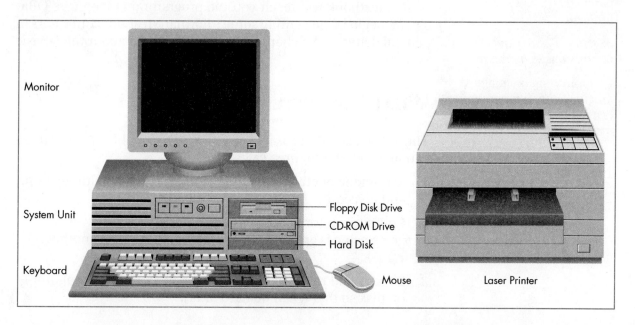

Monitor

System Unit

Keyboard

Floppy Disk Drive
CD-ROM Drive
Hard Disk

Mouse

Laser Printer

FIGURE 1-2

Computer systems are composed of a central processing unit, main memory, and peripheral devices.

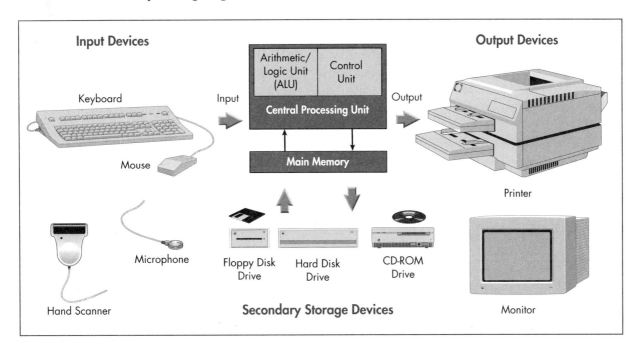

Microprocessor *A single chip that contains an entire central processing unit.*

Control unit *The part of the central processing unit that governs the actions of the various components of the computer.*

contained on a single chip, referred to as a **microprocessor** (Figure 1-3).

The **control unit** is in charge of the activities of the CPU. It does not process or store data; instead, it instructs various parts of the computer to perform these tasks. Instructions given to the computer by the user are interpreted by the control unit, which then tells the computer how to carry out these instructions. It also tells the computer which input device will be used to enter the data, and it keeps track of which parts of a program have been executed. Finally, it collects the output and sends it to the designated output device, such as a monitor screen or a printer.

FIGURE 1-3

In a microcomputer, the CPU is on a single chip called a microprocessor.

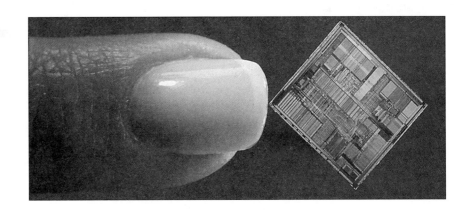

Arithmetic/logic unit (ALU) *The part of the central processing unit that performs arithmetic and logical operations.*

The **arithmetic/logic unit** (ALU) performs mathematical computations and logical operations. A logical operation instructs the computer to make a comparison. For example, a program statement might tell the computer to determine whether number X is greater than number Y and to print X if this condition is true. If the condition is false, the program might specify another course of action, such as printing Y.

Main memory *The component of the central processing unit that temporarily stores programs, data, and results.*

The **main memory** (also referred to as **main storage** or **primary storage**) holds program instructions, data, and the intermediate and final results of processing. It consists of many storage locations, each of which can hold a single unit of information. Each storage location is assigned a unique address. This address allows the computer to locate items that have been stored in its memory. Computers can have millions of storage locations.

Peripheral Devices

Peripheral devices allow the CPU to communicate with the outside world. For example, keyboards allow the user to type data into the computer and printers provide program results. A single computer system can have many different peripheral devices. Peripheral devices are typically attached to the system unit by cables. The peripheral devices discussed here can be divided into three categories: input devices, output devices, and secondary storage devices. Figure 1-2 illustrates some commonly used peripheral devices.

Input *Data that is entered into the computer to be processed.*

Data *Facts that have not been organized in a meaningful way.*

Information *Data that has been processed to make it meaningful.*

Input Devices. Programs and data entered into the computer to be processed are called **input**. The word **data** refers to facts that have not been organized in any meaningful way. When data is processed, or changed into a meaningful form, the result is **information**. For example, in a national election, the records of all the votes cast for the office of president are data. When these votes are tabulated and the final totals are determined, the result is information.

Cursor *The blinking rectangle of light on the screen indicating where typing will appear on the screen.*

Input devices such as those shown in Figure 1-4 allow data to be entered into the computer. The most commonly used input device is the keyboard. Other input devices include mice, graphics tablets, light pens, and scanners. A mouse is a hand-movable device that fits into the user's palm. When it is slid across a flat surface such as a table top, signals are sent through a cable to the computer, and the **cursor** (the block of light indicating where input will appear on the screen) moves in the same direction. Graphics tablets are flat, board-like pads on which the user draws, using a special pen or a finger. The images traced on the pad appear on the monitor screen. A light pen is a pen-shaped object with a light-sensitive cell at its end. To enter data into the com-

FIGURE 1-4

There are many different types of input devices.
(**a**) Keyboard (**b**) Mice (**c**) Digitizing tablet (**d**) Scanner

a

b

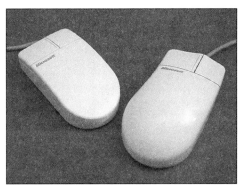

c

d

puter, the user touches the screen with the device. Scanners change images on paper into a digital form that can be stored in the computer. The images can then be displayed on the screen and manipulated.

Output Devices. As with input devices, a single computer system can have many different output devices. For example, a programmer may opt to print the results of a program on paper or display them on a screen. Output displayed on a monitor screen is referred to as **soft copy**. This is a fast, convenient way for the user to examine program results, but soft copy is lost as soon as something else replaces it on the screen. Printing the results on paper saves this information permanently for later reference. Printed output is called **hard copy**. Figure 1-5 shows an example of a monitor screen and a printer.

Soft copy *Output displayed on a monitor screen.*

Hard copy *Output printed on paper.*

Secondary Storage Devices. Computers have only a limited amount of storage space in main memory. Programs, information, and data that need to be saved for later use can be transferred to **secondary storage** (also called **auxiliary storage**). Diskettes (also called *floppy disks*) and hard disks are commonly used types of secondary storage (see Figure 1-6). Notice that the parts of the diskette are labeled. When the computer needs to process something in secondary storage, it is transferred back into the computer's main memory. The devices used to transfer data from secondary storage to main memory are called **secondary storage devices**. Although it takes more time to access items in secondary storage than those in main memory, secondary storage can store large quantities of data at reasonable cost. Expanding secondary storage can be as easy as going to the store and buying a new diskette.

> **Secondary storage** *Storage that is supplementary to the primary storage unit. It can be easily expanded. The secondary storage most commonly used with microcomputers is floppy or hard disks.*
>
> **Secondary storage device** *A device used to copy data to and from secondary storage.*

Diskettes come in 3½-inch and 5¼-inch sizes. The 3½-inch size is most commonly used with today's microcomputers because it can store more data and is sturdier than the 5¼-inch size. Hard disks are widely used because they can store large quantities of data. Unlike diskettes, most hard disks remain permanently mounted in the computer's hard disk drive. Diskette and hard disk drives can be either internal or external. Internal disk drives are contained within the system unit, whereas external disk drives are contained in their own housings.

FIGURE 1-5

A monitor screen displays soft copy whereas a printer provides hard copy. **(a)** Monitor **(b)** Hewlett-Packard LaserJet

a

b

FIGURE 1-6

Types of Disks Commonly Used with Microcomputers
(a) 3½-Inch Diskette (b) Hard Disk

a

Metallic Shutter (when disk is inserted into drive, the shutter slides over to expose the read/write window)

MF2HD

— Recording Window
— Hard Plastic Cover

— Label

— High-Density Hole

Write-Protect Tab (slide up to protect contents of disk)

b

Byte *The amount of space required to store a single character.*

Storage space is measured in **bytes**, with a single byte being the amount of space required to store a single character, such as the letter *m*. Common measurements used for secondary storage media are explained in Table 1-1. Most 3½-inch diskettes can store approximately 1.44 megabytes (MB) of data. Hard disk drives typically have storage capacities from 500MB to several gigabytes.

CD-ROM drives are another type of secondary storage device. CD-ROMs (see Figure 1-7) can store large quantities of data (typically 680MB) on small discs similar to the CDs used for musical records. CD-ROMs are relatively inexpensive and are used to store games, encyclopedias, and other items that require large amounts of storage space. Relatively expensive special equipment is required to write (or "burn") data onto a CD-ROM. Once data is stored on a CD-ROM, it typically cannot be altered. However, the CD-ROM drives needed to read the discs are inexpensive and come with most computer systems sold today.

TABLE 1-1 MEMORY MEASUREMENTS

Quantity	Abbreviation	Approximately Equal To
Byte	B	amount of memory required to store 1 character
Kilobyte	KB	1 thousand bytes
Megabyte	MB	1 million bytes
Gigabyte	GB	1 billion bytes
Terabyte	TB	1 trillion bytes

Learning Check 1-1

1. The three characteristics that make computers different from other machines are their _____, _____, and _____.

2. Name two types of secondary storage devices.

3. _____ consists of facts that have not been organized in any meaningful way.

4. Keyboards, disk drives, and mice are all examples of _____.

5. Output that is printed on paper is called _____.

THE CATEGORIES OF COMPUTER SYSTEMS

Computers are categorized by size, capability, price range, and speed of operation. It is becoming more and more difficult to distinguish among the different classifications of computers, however, because smaller computers have increasingly larger memories and faster operating speeds. Nonetheless, categorizng

FIGURE 1-7

CD-ROMs can typically store 680 MB of data.

computer systems is useful when making general comparisons. The four major categories of computer systems are supercomputers, mainframes, minicomputers, and microcomputers.

Supercomputers

Supercomputer *The fastest type of computer currently available, it is very expensive and primarily used for tasks that involve large quantities of numerical processing.*

Supercomputers are the largest, fastest, and most expensive computers made. They can perform hundreds of billions of arithmetic operations every second and are so fast that their chips often must be surrounded by a liquid coolant to prevent them from melting. Some supercomputers contain hundreds of microprocessors, all working together. These systems are typically used for figuring lengthy and complex calculations. Most organizations have no need for supercomputers, nor can they justify the large cost of the hardware and software. Software development for supercomputers is much more complex and expensive because the design of the machines is so different from the design of less powerful computers. Still, the demand for supercomputers is increasing. Scientists use them in weather forecasting, oil exploration, energy conservation, seismology, artificial intelligence, and cryptography (developing and breaking codes). Figure 1-8a shows the Cray Research CRAY T90 supercomputer.

Mainframes

Mainframe *A large computer system capable of quickly processing enormous quantities of data.*

While not as powerful or expensive as supercomputers, **mainframes** operate at high speeds and can support many input and output devices that also operate very rapidly. Mainframes are used chiefly by businesses, hospitals, universities, and banks (see Figure 1-8b). Mainframes can be subdivided into small, medium, and large systems, and most are manufactured as "families" of computers. A family consists of several mainframe models varying in size and power. An organization can purchase or lease a small mainframe, and if its processing needs expand, upgrade to a medium or large system. Mainframes typically require special installation and maintenance procedures; they create a fair amount of heat, so special cooling systems are usually needed. All these factors add to the cost of using a mainframe.

Minicomputers

Minicomputer *A computer that has many of the capabilities of a mainframe, but is typically slower, has less memory, and is somewhat less expensive.*

Minicomputers were developed in the 1960s and, generally speaking, are smaller and less expensive than mainframes and have slower processing speeds. The more powerful minicomputers are called *superminis*. Minicomputers are easier to install and operate than mainframe computers. They may fit on a desk or they may be as large as a file cabinet. Figure 1-8c shows a minicomputer. They typically require few special environmental conditions (in fact, they often do not require air conditioning) and they can be plugged into standard electrical outlets.

Microcomputer *The smallest and least expensive type of computer currently available; it is generally designed to be used by only one person at a time. The CPU typically is contained on a single chip, called the* microprocessor.

Microcomputers

As previously mentioned, a **microcomputer** (see Figure 1-8d) is a computer in which the CPU is contained on a single computer chip, called the *microprocessor*. This is the type of computer you will be using in this course. They are small and relatively inexpensive. The larger systems previously discussed are designed to be used simultaneously by many users, whereas microcomputers are

FIGURE 1-8

There are four basic categories of computers.
(a) Supercomputer (b) Mainframe (c) Minicomputer
(d) Microcomputer

a

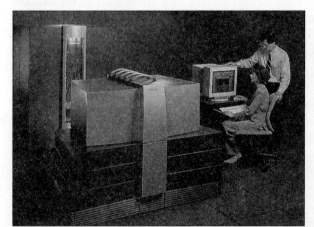

b

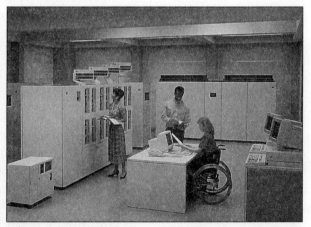

c

d

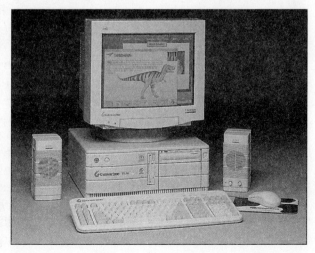

Network *To join computer hardware components so that hardware, software, and e-mail can be shared.*

E-mail *Messages that are sent electronically from one computer system to another.*

typically used by a single person at a time. Microcomputers currently are the most popular type of computers and the demand continues to increase. One fact that has led to this widespread popularity is the enormous supply of inexpensive software that is available. In addition, microcomputers are often **networked**, or joined together, so that software and hardware can be shared. Networking allows users to send electronic mail (**e-mail**) to one another.

Learning Check 1-2

1. True or False? The software currently available for microcomputers is expensive and there is a limited amount of it available.

2. _____ are less expensive than supercomputers, but are capable of processing the enormous quantities of data necessary to run large businesses such as banks.

3. _____ are very expensive and require special software, but are the fastest machines currently available.

4. When computers are joined together so that hardware, software, and e-mail can be shared, they are _____.

GETTING STARTED

This textbook teaches the programming language QBasic. QBasic is used on IBM Personal Computers and IBM PC-compatibles. IBM PC-compatibles work in the same way as IBM PCs and can run the same kinds of software.

Operating system (OS) *A collection of programs that manages system resources, runs other software, and provides the user interface.*

User interface *The part of a program such as an operating system that allows the user to interact with the system.*

Command-line user interface *A user interface that requires the user to type in commands.*

The Disk Operating System

To function efficiently, computers use a special collection of programs called an **operating system** (**OS**). The operating system acts as an interface between the computer hardware and software programs such as QBasic. The operating system manages the peripheral devices and directs the system's resources to perform the tasks necessary to meet the user's needs. Many types of operating systems are available. Examples include Microsoft's MS-DOS, Windows 95, IBM's OS/2 Warp, and the Macintosh Operating System.

The part of the operating system that allows the user to give the system instructions is called the **user interface**. User interfaces can be divided into two broad categories: **command-line user**

Graphical user interface (GUI) *A visually oriented interface that allows the user to interact with the system by manipulating icons and selecting commands from menus. Typically a mouse is used to perform these actions.*

interfaces and **graphical user interfaces,** or **GUIs** (pronounced *gooeys*). Command-line interfaces require the user to use the keyboard to type in commands. For example, you might have to enter *DIR* to see a list of all the files stored on a disk. Graphical user interfaces allow the user to manipulate on-screen icons (graphical symbols that represent files, disks, and other objects). Because GUIs do not require the user to memorize and type in commands, most users find them easier to work with. The Macintosh OS, IBM's OS/2 Warp, and Microsoft's Windows 3.1 and Windows 95 systems all use GUIs.

The operating system typically used to run QBasic on an IBM PC-compatible is called MS-DOS or simply DOS for short. DOS is a command-line interface, although it has simple menu systems that make it somewhat easier to use. Over the years, there have been many versions of DOS, each one an improvement over the previous version. A recent version is DOS 6.22. DOS allows you to perform many tasks that involve manipulating data stored on disks. For example, it allows you to prepare a diskette to have data stored on it, copy a file from one disk to another, and erase a file from a disk.

Using QBasic

BASIC, an acronym for *B*eginner's *A*ll-purpose *S*ymbolic *I*nstruction *C*ode, was developed in the mid-1960s at Dartmouth College by professors John Kemeny and Thomas Kurtz to teach programming to their students. It uses English-like words and statements such as LET, READ, and PRINT. It is easy to learn and is considered a general-purpose programming language because it can be used for a wide variety of tasks.

QBasic is a well-designed version (or *dialect*) of BASIC developed by Microsoft Corporation. It has many advantages over older versions of BASIC. A major advantage is that it is menu driven. This means that commands are chosen from a list, or menu. This simplifies the learning of QBasic because you do not need to memorize commands; the menu helps you remember each command's name.

Another advantage is that QBasic has online help. Online help consists of instructions and information that are part of the QBasic software program itself, rather than a separate printed manual. You can access online help right at the computer. It is explained in Chapter 3.

In addition to the major features just mentioned, QBasic, unlike most older versions of BASIC, is a structured programming language. The importance of structured languages is explained in Chapter 2.

The Opening Screen

You can start QBasic by typing *qbasic* at the DOS prompt and pressing [Enter ←]. When QBasic is started, the opening screen appears. The largest part of this screen is the View window. As you type in programs, they will appear in the View window. When you first start QBasic, the View window contains some general information. As indicated, if you wish to see the Survival Guide, press [Enter ←]. The Survival Guide provides some basic information about using QBasic. You will probably want to read it the first time you use QBasic. To bypass the Survival Guide, press [Esc]; the screen then appears as shown in Figure 1-9. QBasic is now ready for you to enter a program.

The Menu Bar

The menu bar shows the menus that are available to you. When you open a menu, the menu "drops down," displaying a list of available options. You can use either the keyboard or a mouse to open a menu.

To use a mouse to open a menu, just click on the menu; the menu then opens (see Figure 1-10) and you can click on the

FIGURE 1-9

QBasic Opening Screen

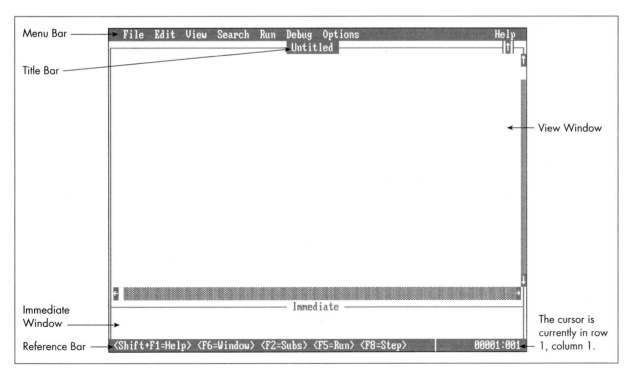

option you want. If your mouse has more than one button, you typically should click the leftmost one. To use the keyboard to access a menu, press [Alt] and then press the first letter of the menu you wish to open. For example, pressing [Alt][F] accesses the File menu. You can use the down arrow key ([↓])to highlight the desired command, then press [Enter ↵] to execute it.

Let's take a moment to discuss the manner in which key sequences will be indicated in this text. If the keys are separated by commas (for example, [Alt],[Tab],[⇧ Shift]), the keys should be pressed one after the other. However, if there is no comma (for example, [⇧ Shift][PrtScr]), the keys must be held down simultaneously. In this example, this means that [PrtScr] must be pressed while [⇧ Shift] is being held down.

If you wish to close a menu without making a selection, press [Esc]; the menu closes and the cursor reappears in the View window. Some commonly used QBasic commands are discussed later in this chapter; other commands are discussed in subsequent chapters.

The Title Bar

The title bar shows the name (or title) of the program currently in the View window. When a new program is being entered and has not yet been saved on disk, its name is "Untitled." Once you have saved it on disk, the name you assigned will appear in the title bar.

FIGURE 1-10

The File Menu

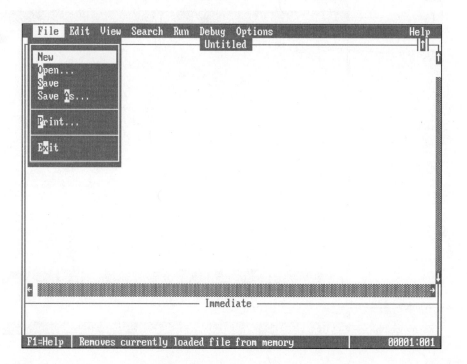

The Reference Bar

The reference bar is at the bottom of the screen, below the Immediate window (refer back to Figure 1-9). It provides quick information. For example, when a menu option is highlighted, the reference bar contains a brief explanation of it. It also tells you which row and column currently contain the cursor and whether the CapsLock and NumLock keys are depressed.

The Immediate Window

The Immediate window allows you to execute commands quickly, without placing them in a program. This window's use is discussed in Chapter 3.

Learning Check 1-3

1. A(n) _____ is a collection of programs that allows a computer to manage its resources efficiently.

2. The part of the operating system with which the user interacts is called the _____.

3. The _____ window is the portion of the QBasic screen in which programs are entered.

4. The _____ bar indicates the row and column currently containing the cursor.

5. What key can be pressed to access the menu bar?

The File Menu

The File menu (refer to Figure 1-10) contains options that can be used to manipulate programs. The commonly used commands are explained below.

New. This command erases any program currently in main memory and prepares the computer to accept a new program.

Open. Notice in Figure 1-10 that this command is followed by three dots (...), called *ellipses*. When ellipses follow any command, this indicates that a dialog box is displayed when that command is chosen. Dialog boxes provide the programmer with information and require that the programmer enter a response. For example, when Open is selected, the screen shown in Figure 1-11 appears. Type in the name of the program you want placed into main memory and press Enter↵. The program then appears on the screen.

It is possible to specify a disk drive. For example, if you wish to open a program named SAMPLE1.BAS on the disk in drive A, type the drive name (A:) in front of the file name: A:SAMPLE1. As discussed in the next section, it is not necessary to enter the ".BAS" part of the name; QBasic supplies it automatically. You also can select a program from the list in the Files box. Just position the mouse pointer on the program's name and click the mouse button.

Save and Save As. The Save and Save As options are used to save the current program on disk. If you have a program in the View menu that has not previously been saved on a disk, choose Save from the File menu. A dialog box appears, allowing you to give the program a name. For example, if you type in

SAMPLE1 Enter ↵

the program will be saved under SAMPLE1.BAS on the current disk. QBasic automatically adds the ".BAS" extension to program files so that you can readily identify them.

The difference between the Save and the Save As options is seen when you wish to save a modified program on disk. Let's assume you have added 10 new lines to an existing program and now wish to save it. If you choose the Save option, the previous

FIGURE 1-11

The Open Dialog Box

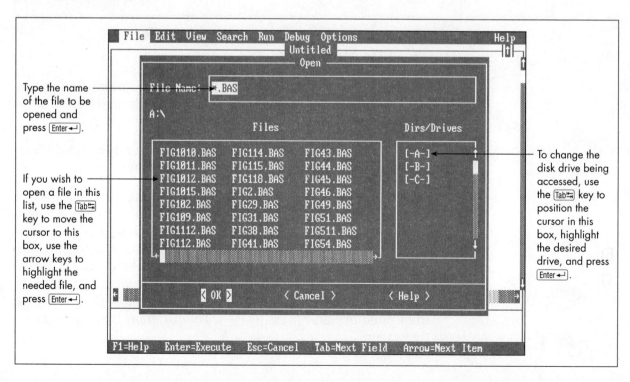

program will be overwritten with the new version. The previous version is lost. Often, this is fine because you no longer wish to save the original program. There may be times, however, when you want both the previous version and the new one saved on disk. You can accomplish this by using Save As. When you use Save As to save an existing program, the Save As dialog box appears, allowing you to assign a different name to the modified program. For example, if your original program was named SUMUP1 you might name the new version SUMUP2. This way, you can access either version of the program, as needed.

When naming a file, you can use any combination of letters or numbers; however, the first character must be a letter. File names have a base part (the part to the left of the period) with up to eight characters and an extension (the part to the right of the period) with up to three characters. If you do not specify an extension for a file containing a QBasic program, ".BAS" will be added automatically. If you enter any lowercase letters, the computer will convert them to uppercase. File names should describe what is stored in them. Below are some valid QBasic file names:

INVENTRY.BAS

CLASS.BAS

SALES.BAS

Print. The Print command allows you to print the program that is currently opened. A printer must be properly connected to your computer and it must be turned on. When the Print command is selected, the dialog box shown in Figure 1-12 appears. To print the current contents of the View window, select "Current Window." If you wish to print the whole program, choose "Entire Program." Use the up and down arrow keys to highlight the desired option and press Enter ↵ to begin printing. Choose Cancel or press Esc if you change your mind.

Exit. Use this command to leave QBasic. If you have not saved the program in the View window, QBasic will ask you whether you wish to save it. Respond with "Yes" to save the program or "No" to leave QBasic without saving it.

FIGURE 1-12

The Print Dialog Box

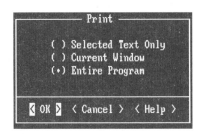

Learning Check 1-4

1. What is the purpose of the New option in the File menu?

2. If you want to save a modified program under a new name so that the previous version will not be overwritten, be sure to use the _____ option in the File menu.

3. If you save a program under the name SKB, QBasic will automatically add the extension _____ to the file name.

4. To obtain a hard copy of your program, choose _____ from the File menu.

5. The _____ option allows you to leave QBasic.

The View Menu

When the View menu is opened, the options shown in Figure 1-13 are displayed. Only one of these options is discussed here: the Output Screen command. The SUBs command is discussed in Chapter 6.

Output Screen. This option causes QBasic to switch to the output screen. The output screen displays the results of the most recently executed program. This allows you to refer to program output whenever needed while debugging a program. Press any key to return to the View window.

FIGURE 1-13

The View Menu

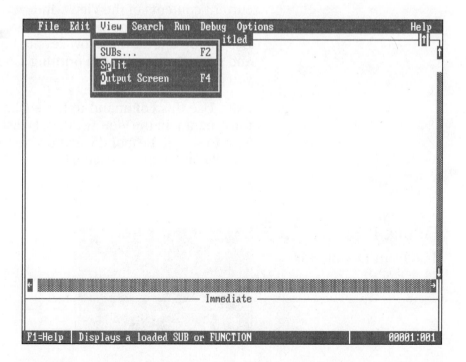

The Run Menu

This menu controls the execution of programs. Its options are shown in Figure 1-14. Only two of these commands are covered here: the Start command and the Continue command.

Start. Choose Start to execute a program in main memory. The output screen will appear. For example, if the program segment

```
CLS
PRINT "HI, MOM!"
```

is executed, the screen appears as shown in Figure 1-15. The CLS command clears the screen before the new output is displayed; it is discussed in detail later. The PRINT statement causes the characters in quotation marks to be displayed. If you follow the command at the bottom of the screen and press any key, you will return to the View window.

Some commands can be carried out by using the keyboard's function keys. On most keyboards these keys are labeled F1 through F10 or F1 through F12. For example, you can execute a program by simply pressing ⇧ Shift F5. If you are in the View window and want to switch to the output screen, press F4.

Continue. When a program is executing, the execution can be halted by pressing Ctrl Break. Use Continue to resume execution where it left off. You also can resume execution of a halted program by pressing F5.

FIGURE 1-14

The Run Menu

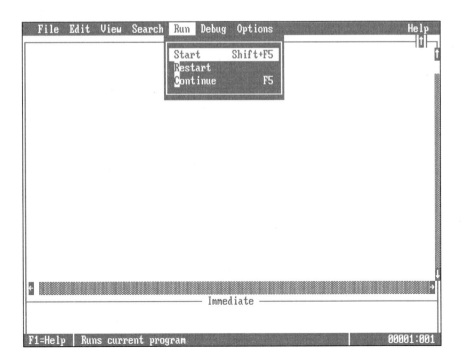

FIGURE 1-15

The Output Window

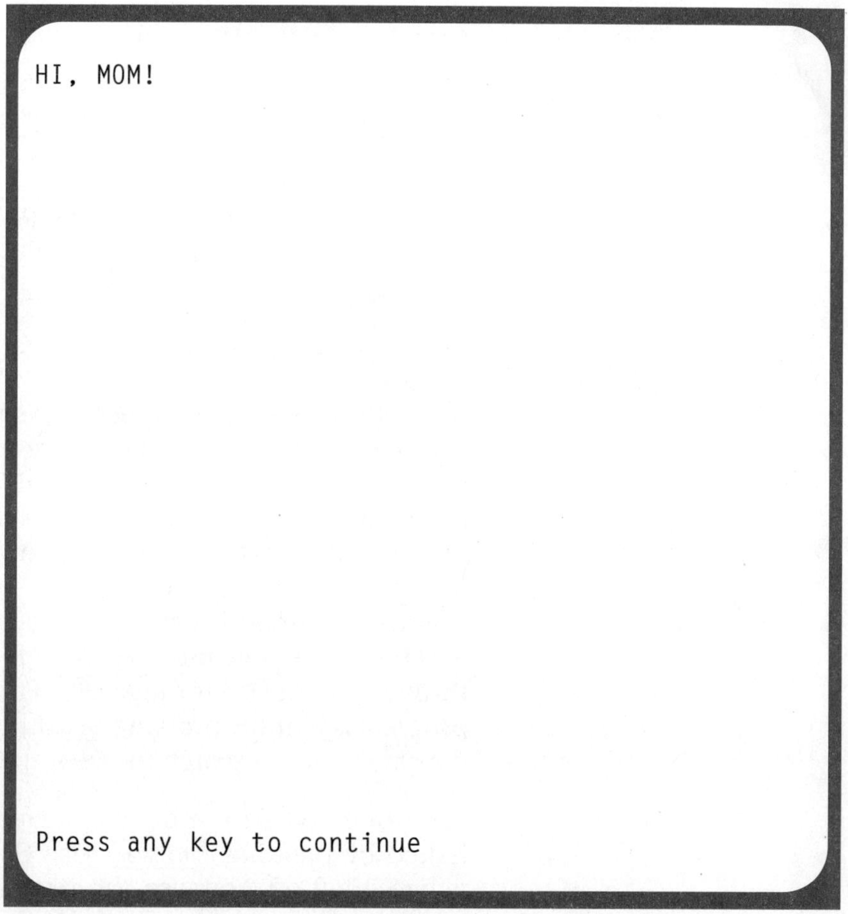

```
HI, MOM!




















Press any key to continue
```

Entering and Editing Programs

As previously mentioned, programs are entered in the View window. Enter your programs a line at a time, pressing (Enter ◄┘) at the end of each statement. QBasic programs can be edited in a variety of ways. Table 1-2 shows some of the keys that are useful when editing programs. The next section allows you to practice using some of these keys to enter, execute, and save a short program.

As previously mentioned, the active window is the one with the highlighted title. The (F6) key can be used to move from one window to another. If you are using a mouse, you can position the mouse pointer in the window you wish to activate and click the mouse button. This window will be activated and the cursor will appear in it.

Sometimes a program has so many lines that the entire program cannot be displayed on the screen at once. If only the top half of a program is on the screen and you wish to view the bottom portion, position the mouse pointer on the down scroll arrow (see Figure 1-16) and hold down the mouse button until the program segment you need appears on the screen. This process is

Scroll *To change the portion of a document that is currently visible so that you can see items that were previously hidden from view.*

referred to as **scrolling**. Likewise, hold down the up scroll arrow to go back toward the top of the program. The scroll box allows you to move even more quickly around the program. Position the pointer on the scroll box and then slide the scroll box up and down the scroll bar. You can scroll horizontally (left or right) by using the scroll arrows at the bottom of the screen. You also can use the directional arrow keys on the keyboard to move around the screen. For example, pressing [↑] twice will move you up two lines in your program.

TABLE 1-2 EDITING AND CURSOR MOVEMENT KEYS

Key(s)	Name of Key	Action
[Enter ↵]	Enter	Moves the cursor to the next line.
[← Bksp]	Backspace	Located above the [Enter ↵] key; moves the cursor one position left and erases that character, and moves any characters to the right of the cursor one character left.
[⇧ Shift] [PrintScreen] *†	Shift-Print Screen	When [PrintScreen] is pressed while holding down [⇧ Shift], whatever appears on the screen will be sent to the printer. On some computer keyboards, this key is labeled [PrtScr].
[←]	Left Arrow	Moves the cursor to the left one space.
[→]	Right Arrow	Moves the cursor to the right one space.
[↑]	Up Arrow	Moves the cursor up one line.
[↓]	Down Arrow	Moves the cursor down one line.
[PgUp]	Page Up	Moves the cursor up one whole screen.
[PgDn]	Page Down	Moves the cursor down one whole screen.
[Insert]	Insert	Toggles between insert and overstrike modes.
[Del]	Delete	Deletes the character at the current cursor position, and drags all characters to the right of the cursor one character left.
[Tab ⇆]	Tab	Moves the cursor to the next tab stop.
[⇧ Shift]	Shift	On letter keys, causes capital letters to be output. On keys containing numbers or special symbols, the symbol on the top half of the key is displayed (for example, pressing [⇧ Shift][3] causes "#" to be displayed).
[CapsLock]	Caps Lock	Causes capital letters to be output; however, nonalphabetic keys remain unchanged.
[Ctrl][Y] *	Delete Line	Causes the line containing the cursor to be deleted (this is a convenient way of erasing an entire line).
[Home]	Home	Moves the cursor to the beginning of the current line.
[End]	End	Moves the cursor to the end of the current line.
[Ctrl][Home]*	Control-Home	Moves the cursor to the beginning of the program.
[Ctrl][End]*	Control-End	Moves the cursor to the end of the program.

* When two keys appear next to one another (for example, [⇧ Shift][PrtScr]), you should hold down the first key while pressing the second one.

† This command may not work on your system, particularly if you are using a network.

FIGURE 1-16

Scrolling Through a Program

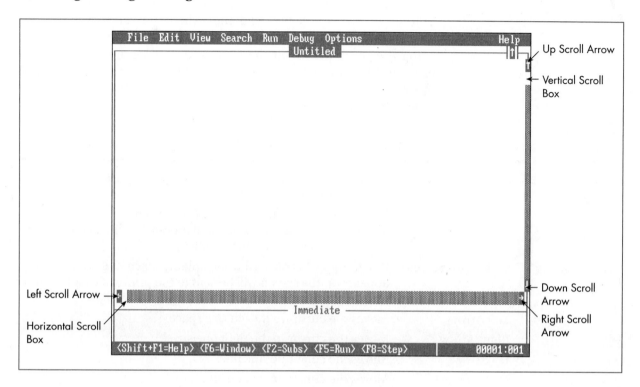

A Practice Program

This section allows you to practice some of the QBasic commands introduced in this chapter. Access the QBasic system. Enter the following statements exactly as they appear:

```
CLS
INPUT "Enter your name"; Nme$
INPUT "Enter the time of this class (for example, 8:30)"; Tim$
PRINT Nme$; " has computer programming at "; Tim$
END
```

Carefully proofread your program before continuing. Now choose Start from the Run menu to begin execution of the program. The following will appear:

```
Enter your name?
```

Type in your name and press [Enter⏎]. The next question will appear:

```
Enter the time of this class (for example, 8:30)?
```

Once again, answer the question and press [Enter ↵]. The program output will appear; for example:

```
Sue Baumann has computer programming at 10:30
```

Now let's save it so that you can access it later. Press any key to return to the View window. From the File menu, choose Save, and then type in *PROGRAM1*. The program will be saved on disk under the file name PROGRAM1.BAS. Choose Exit from the File menu to leave QBasic. Note that the program output appears on the screen. Type *QBasic* again to return to QBasic and from the File menu choose Open. Type in *PROGRAM1* for the file name and your program is again displayed.

We are now going to edit this program. Position the cursor at the end of the third line and press [Enter ↵]. A blank line will be inserted. Add the following statement in this space:

```
INPUT "Enter your instructor's name"; Instructor$
```

Next, place the cursor on the next line, over the letter *c* in *computer*. Press the [Ins] key to cause the existing characters to be overwritten. When you press [Ins] once, text is overwritten; pressing it again causes new text to be inserted, pushing any existing text to the right. Change the line so that it reads as follows:

```
PRINT Nme$; " has "; Instructor$; " for computer programming at "; Tim$
```

Execute the program again to see that it has been altered. Even though the new version of the program is on the screen, it is important to realize that the old version is still on disk; to save the new version, from the File menu, choose Save. The new version automatically overwrites the old one on disk. Leave QBasic and you are done with this practice program.

Learning Check 1-5

1. What menu option will execute the program currently in the View window?

2. What is the purpose of the Continue command in the Run menu?

3. The _____ key allows you to switch between overwriting and inserting text.

4. To display a program on the screen that has previously been saved on a disk, use the _____ option in the File menu.

BEING A RESPONSIBLE COMPUTER USER

We live in an information society. Much of the work we do involves the manipulation of information. It is important that this information be treated in an ethical and safe manner. By design, access to information is simplified when computer files replace paper documents as storage media. Unfortunately, this easier access has allowed some individuals to use information illegally and destructively. Inevitably, control of access and the rights of individual privacy have become major concerns.

Business and government can implement many security measures to protect computers and their data, but the security of systems most frequently depends on the ethics of the individual user. **Computer ethics** is a term that refers to the standard of moral conduct in computer use. Ethics govern an individual's attitude toward computer use on the job, at school, and at home, and toward the copying of commercial software.

Computer ethics *The standard of moral conduct applied to computer use.*

Using Hardware Properly

Proper treatment of hardware means that everyone will have more computer time because machines are less likely to be damaged. Always be sure to follow any rules that have been established by your computer lab or your instructor. Never place any drinks or other liquids near computer equipment. Always leave the computer system as you have been instructed.

In business and industry, employees generally undergo special training on the proper use of computer hardware and software. Many problems can be avoided by providing proper training, performing routine maintenance on equipment, and backing up data that is being kept in secondary storage. A **backup** is a duplicate copy of data for use in case the original is damaged or destroyed. Businesses are very careful to follow regular schedules when creating backups. These backups are often stored in a locked vault away from the location where the actual processing takes place.

Backup *A duplicate copy of data for use in case the original is damaged or destroyed.*

In this course, you may be storing your programs and data on diskettes. The following rules will reduce the chances of having the data stored on your diskettes lost or damaged:

- Always keep diskettes away from magnetic fields, such as those contained in computer monitors, televisions, and speakers. Diskettes store data magnetically and their contents can be wiped out when placed too close to a magnetic field.

- Store diskettes in a dry place at room temperature. Diskettes, like most plastic items, can be damaged by extreme heat and cold. Never leave a diskette in an automobile because the windshield can magnify the sun's rays, and temperatures inside a car can be much higher than outside.

• It is best to store diskettes vertically (on end) rather than flat or in horizontal stacks.

• If you need to write on a label that is already on a diskette, use a felt-tip pen and try not to press too hard.

• If you are using 5¼-inch diskettes, keep them in their protective sleeves when not in use.

• When inserting a diskette, place your thumb on the top of the label and slide the diskette into the drive slowly (see Figure 1-17). Be careful not to bend the disk when you are inserting it. On 3½-inch drives you will hear a metallic click when the disk is properly positioned. On 5¼-inch drives, you generally must close a lever after the disk is inside the drive. You will hear a whirring sound. When a diskette is being accessed, the drive indicator light is lit.

• Never try to remove a diskette from a drive when the drive indicator light is lit.

Even with the best of care, diskettes occasionally become damaged. You should get in the habit of always making backups of your diskettes. Store the backups in a different place from the originals. For example, you may choose to keep your original diskettes with you and leave your backups at home.

Ethical Software Use

Commercial software *Software developed with the intent of making a profit. The user must agree to follow the licensing agreement that comes with the software.*

There are three basic categories of software licensing. The first category is **commercial software**, which is copyrighted and has been developed with the intent of making a profit. The software

FIGURE 1-17

Properly Inserting a Diskette

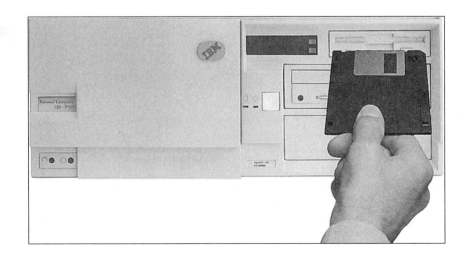

packages that you purchase at a computer store or through the mail fall into this category. They contain a licensing agreement (see Figure 1-18) that the user must follow. After you have installed a commercial package on your computer system, you typically are reminded that the software is copyrighted each time you start the program. The license states the conditions under which the software may be used. For example, you may be allowed to make one backup copy of the software for your protection; however, it is illegal to make copies for friends to use on their computers.

The second category of software licensing is **shareware**. The author holds the copyright on the shareware, but makes it readily available to anyone. If users like the software and plan to use it, they are requested to send money (often in the $20 to $50 range)

Shareware *Software that is copyrighted but can be distributed free of charge to anyone. If, after trying out the software, an individual plans to use it on a regular basis, the program's author expects a nominal payment for the software.*

FIGURE 1-18

An Example of a Software License

IMPORTANT: PLEASE READ BEFORE OPENING PACKAGE.
THIS SOFTWARE IS NOT RETURNABLE IF SEAL IS BROKEN.

SunBurst Software Company
1026 Tejon Avenue
Colorado Springs, CO 80901

PERSONNA™
Personal Information Manager
LIMITED USE LICENSE

Read the following terms and conditions carefully before opening this CD-ROM package. Breaking the seal on the CD-ROM jewel box indicates your agreement to the license terms. If you do not agree, promptly return this package unopened to SunBurst Software Company ("SunBurst") for a full refund.

By accepting this license, you have the right to use Personna (the "Software"), but you do not become the owner of these materials.

This copy of Personna is licensed to you for use only under the following conditions:

1. PERMITTED USES
You are granted a non-exclusive limited license to use the Software under the terms and conditions stated in this License. You may:

    a. Use the Software on a single computer.

    b. Transfer this copy of the Software to another user if the other user agrees to accept the terms and conditions of this License. Transfer of this copy of the Software automatically terminates this License as it applies to you.

2. PROHIBITED USES
You may not use, copy, modify, distribute, or transfer this Software or any copy, in whole or in part, except as expressly permitted in this License.

3. TERM
This License is effective when you break the seal on the CD-ROM jewel box and remains in effect until terminated. You may terminate this License at any time by ceasing all use of the Software and destroying this copy and any copies you have made of all or part of the material included on this CD-ROM. The License will also terminate automatically if you fail to comply with the terms of this License. Upon termination, you agree to cease all use of this Software and to destroy any copies of material contained on this CD-ROM.

4. DISCLAIMER OF WARRANTY
Except as stated herein, this Software is licensed "as is" without warranty of any kind, express or implied, including warranties of merchantability or fitness for a particular purpose. SunBurst Software Company does not warrant the performance nor the results that may be obtained with this Software. We do warrant that the media upon which this Software is provided will be free from defects in materials and workmanship under normal use for a period of 90 days from the date of delivery to you as evidenced by a receipt.

Some states do not allow the exclusion of implied warranties so the above exclusion may not apply to you. This warranty gives you specific legal rights. You may also have other rights which vary from state to state.

5. LIMITATION OF LIABILITY
Your exclusive remedy for breach by SunBurst Software Company of its limited warranty shall be replacement of any defective media upon its return to SunBurst at the above address, together with a copy of the receipt, within the warranty period. If SunBurst Software Company is unable to provide you with a replacement CD-ROM that is free of defects in material and workmanship, you may terminate this License by returning the Software, and the license fee paid hereunder will be refunded to you. In no event will SunBurst be liable for any lost profits or other damages including direct, indirect, incidental, special, consequential or any other type of damages arising out of the use or inability to use this Software even if SunBurst has been advised of the possibility of such damages.

6. GOVERNING LAW
This Agreement will be governed by the laws of the State of Colorado.

You acknowledge that you have read this License and agree to its terms and conditions. You also agree that this License is the entire and exclusive agreement between you and SunBurst and supersedes any prior understanding or agreement, oral or written, relating to the subject matter of this agreement.

to the author. Many young programmers got their start developing shareware and much shareware is well written. Many people like shareware because they can test it before paying for it.

Public-domain software is freely available to anyone, for any legal purpose. You can give copies to your friends, for example, or place the software on a computer bulletin board. Public-domain software often consists of games, small utility programs that perform specialized functions, and simple word processing and spreadsheet programs.

Public-domain software
Software that is made available to the public for use by anyone without paying a fee.

Controlling System Access

Using a computer system without authorization is just as illegal as breaking into someone's home or business. Companies have developed a number of methods for controlling unauthorized access. Often, it is necessary to enter a user name and a password before you can obtain access to a computer system or a network. As shown in Figure 1-19, the password does not appear on the screen, eliminating the possibility that an onlooker might view it. If the user name and password correspond to the same account, the user is allowed to access the system; if not, the user typically is allowed several more chances before being locked out of the system. Passwords are especially important when systems are accessed remotely, for example, by using a modem.

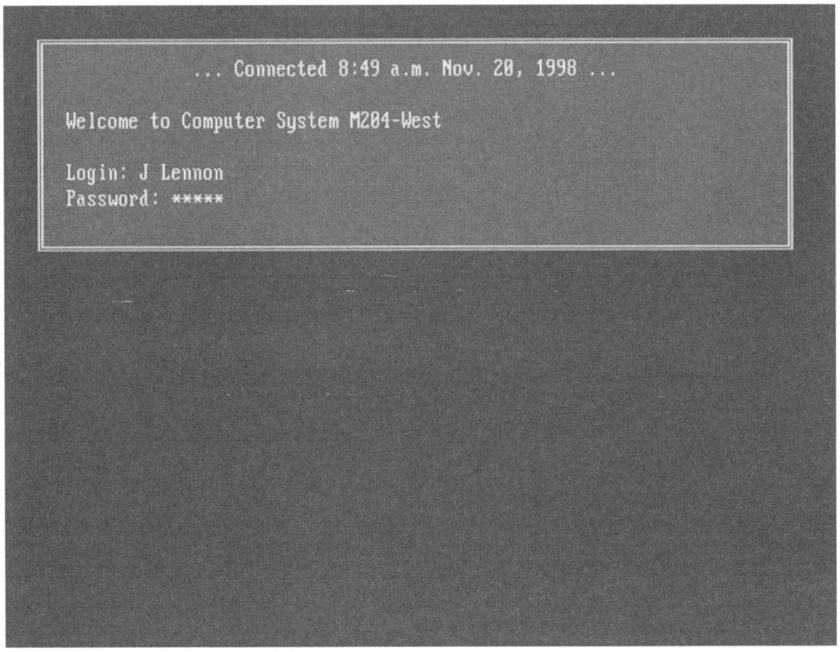

FIGURE 1-19

Requiring users to enter a user name and a password is an important method of controlling access.

```
        ... Connected 8:49 a.m. Nov. 20, 1998 ...
Welcome to Computer System M204-West

Login: J Lennon
Password: *****
```

Learning Check 1-6

1. The data and programs on disks should always be _____ in case the original disks are destroyed, lost, or damaged.

2. Computer _____ refers to the standard of moral conduct in computer use.

3. One way to control system access is to require potential users to enter a user name and a(n) _____ before being allowed access.

4. _____ is software that can be used for any legal purpose, without paying for it.

SUMMARY POINTS

▌ A computer is an electronic machine that can process data with great speed and accuracy.

▌ A program is a series of instructions that a computer uses to solve a problem; it must be written in a programming language.

▌ Tasks performed by computers can be divided into three categories: arithmetic operations, comparison operations, and storage and retrieval operations.

▌ The system unit contains the central processing unit and main memory.

▌ The CPU can be thought of as the "brain" of the computer and consists of the control unit and the arithmetic/logic unit. Main memory is used to store data and processing results.

▌ Peripheral devices can be divided into input devices, such as the keyboard; output devices, such as printers and monitor screens; and secondary storage devices, such as disk and tape drives.

▌ Operating systems consist of collections of programs that allow computers to run application software and manage their resources efficiently.

▌ QBasic is a version of BASIC that is easy to use but also has many advanced features. The operating system typically used with QBasic is MS-DOS, which is a command-line interface.

▌ The QBasic screen is divided into a number of parts, including a View window, which shows the program currently in main memory.

▌ The menu bar allows the user to select commands that are to be executed.

▌ The File menu contains commands to manipulate programs, such as preparing for a new program, opening a program previously stored on disk, and saving a program on disk.

▌ The View menu has several commands including Output Screen, which allows the user to examine program results.

▌ The Run menu allows the programmer to execute a program and resume program execution after it has been halted. Program execution can be halted by holding down the Ctrl key and pressing Break.

▌ Computer ethics is a term used to refer to the standard of moral conduct applied to computer use. Proper training helps employees to use hardware correctly. Regular backups should be made of all programs and data.

▌ Diskettes should be treated with care and kept in dry, room-temperature locations away from magnetic fields.

▌ The three categories of software licensing are commercial software, shareware, and public-domain software. When you purchase commercial software, you agree to follow the licensing agreement that comes with it. Shareware authors request a donation if you plan to continue using the product, whereas public-domain software can be freely used for any legal purpose.

▌ Unauthorized access of a computer system is illegal. Organizations attempt to control access by requiring users to enter account names and passwords.

KEY TERMS

Arithmetic/logic unit (ALU) – 6
Backup – 26
Byte – 9
Central processing unit (CPU) – 4
Command-line user interface – 13
Commercial software – 27
Computer – 3
Computer ethics – 26
Control unit – 5
Cursor – 6
Data – 6
E-mail – 13
Execute – 3
Graphical user interface (GUI) – 14
Hard copy – 7
Hardware – 4
Information – 6

REVIEW QUESTIONS

1. Into what three categories can all functions performed by the computer be divided?

2. Into which of the three categories of computer functions would each of the following be placed?

   a. Finding the square of a number.

   b. Storing a program so that it can be run at a later time.

   c. Determining which of two letters comes first alphabetically.

   d. Calculating a paycheck by multiplying the hours worked by the hourly pay rate.

3. List the two parts of the central processing unit, and tell what each does.

4. What is the difference between data and information?

5. Name several common input and output devices.

6. What are the advantages of using secondary storage rather than main memory? What is a disadvantage? What kind of secondary storage does your computer system use?

7. What is the purpose of the computer's operating system? What is the purpose of the user interface?

8. Explain the purpose of the title bar. What appears in the title bar when a new program is being entered? What appears when a program in secondary storage is loaded into main memory?

9. List and briefly explain each option under the File menu.

10. What is the purpose of scrolling? How can you scroll through a program?

11. Explain the steps in executing a program currently in the View window.

12. What is the output screen? How can you switch between the View window and the output screen?

13. Why is it important to make backup copies of data and programs?

14. List the rules for properly caring for diskettes.

15. How is commercial software different from shareware and public-domain software?

CHAPTER 2

Introduction to Structured Programming and Problem Solving

Outline

Objectives

After studying this chapter, you will be able to:

▮ Describe the three levels of programming languages.

▮ Discuss why structured programming was developed.

▮ Explain why structured programs are divided into modules.

▮ Discuss the history of the BASIC language.

▮ List the four steps used in problem solving.

▮ Determine the needed input and output for simple programming problems.

▮ Define the term *algorithm* and develop algorithms for problem solutions.

▮ List the three basic control structures.

▮ Draw structure charts for simple programming problem solutions.

▮ Define top-down design and list three of its advantages.

▮ Define the terms *flowchart* and *pseudocode*.

▮ List and explain the purpose of the five flowcharting symbols discussed in this chapter.

▮ Explain how the three basic control structures are represented in flowcharts.

INTRODUCTION

The first part of Chapter 1 focused on computer hardware, which consists of the physical components of the system. This chapter focuses on **software**, the programs that the hardware executes. Without software, the hardware is unusable. The software allows the user to tell the computer what tasks to perform. In this chapter, you will learn about the history of software development and a method of problem solving that encourages the writing of well-designed software.

Software *A program or a group of related programs.*

PROGRAMMING LANGUAGES

A computer cannot carry out instructions unless they are written in a programming language. This section presents a brief overview of programming languages and how they have changed since the early days of computing. There are three broad categories: machine languages, assembly languages, and high-level languages.

Machine Language

Machine language *The only instructions that the computer is able to execute directly; consists of combinations of 0's and 1's that represent high and low electrical voltages.*

Machine language is the only language that the computer can execute directly. Programs written in any other type of language must be translated into machine language by the computer before they can be executed. Machine-language statements consist of series of 1's and 0's representing "high" and "low" electrical voltages. A programmer can specify a "high" state with a one (1) and a "low" state with a zero (0). Every operation that the computer is capable of performing (such as addition or storing a value in a given memory location) is indicated by a specific binary code (a sequence of 1's and 0's). The programmer must use the proper code for each operation. In addition, memory locations must be accessed by listing their storage address in binary code.

Because the 1's and 0's have no intrinsic meaning to humans, writing machine language instructions is very difficult. The programmer must carefully keep track of which values have been stored in which storage locations. It is easy to accidentally reference a wrong location or to store a new value in a location that has already been used for something else, thereby losing the previous contents.

Examples of machine language statements are shown in Figure 2-1. The equivalent QBasic statement is shown at the top of the figure. These statements perform the task of adding the contents of one storage location to the contents of another. The resulting sum is then stored in a third location.

FIGURE 2-1

A QBasic Statement and
Its Machine-Language
Equivalent

High-Level Language (QBasic)

LET C = A + B

Machine Language (MOS-TECH 6502 machine language)

```
1010   0000   0000   0000   0000   1101
1010   1101   0000   1110   0000   1101
0111   1001   0110   0000 . 0000   1100
1101   1000
1000   1101   0011   1111   0000   1100
```

Because machine language is different for each type of computer, it is necessary for the programmer to be familiar with the particular computer that will execute the program. Although such programs are tedious to write, they allow the programmer to use the computer's potential fully, because he or she is interacting directly with the computer hardware.

When computers were first developed, machine language was the only way to program them. Programmers quickly realized that this method often led to errors and was extremely time consuming. Assembly languages were developed in an attempt to correct these problems.

Assembly Language

Assembly language *A programming language that uses symbolic names instead of the 1's and 0's of machine language. It falls between machine language and high-level languages in difficulty.*

Assembly languages allow the programmer to use symbolic names (rather than 1's and 0's) to specify various machine operations. For example, the word ADD might be used to instruct the computer to add the contents of two storage locations. Names are used to represent storage locations; the programmer does not need to know the address of the storage location in which a particular value is kept.

In general, assembly language instructions have a one-to-one correspondence with machine language instructions. The assembly language instructions to add two numbers might look like this:

```
LOAD A
ADD B
STORE C
```

These instructions tell the computer to add the value stored in location B to the value stored in location A and to place the sum in location C.

As with machine languages, assembly languages are different for each type of computer. Although assembly language is easier for people to understand than machine language, it is still very difficult and time consuming to use. Another major difficulty with assembly language, as with machine language, is that it is different for different types of computers.

High-Level Languages

Although it is simpler to write a program in assembly language than in machine language, considerable knowledge of the internal operation of the computer is still required. To simplify programming further, other languages have been developed that more closely resemble "natural languages" such as English. These languages do not require the programmer to understand the technical details of the hardware. Because they are oriented toward the programmer rather than the computer, they are termed **high-level languages**. Even a person who does not know a particular high-level language can often determine the general purpose of the program statements. Consider the following statement:

> **High-level language** *A programming language that uses English-like statements that must be translated into machine language before execution.*

```
LET C = A + B
```

Even a nonprogrammer would have little difficulty understanding that this statement adds the value of A to B and stores the result in C.

Programs written in high-level languages are usually portable. This means that they can be run on different types of computers with only minor modifications. For example, QBasic programs can be executed, with minor differences, on either IBM or Macintosh computers. It is important to remember, however, that programs written in high-level languages must be translated into machine language before they can be executed. The QBasic software performs this task automatically before runing a program. A single high-level language statement may translate into many machine language statements.

Some of the more popular high-level languages are C, COBOL, Ada, and BASIC. Individual high-level languages can have many different versions, commonly called *dialects*. For example, QBasic and Visual Basic are both dialects of the BASIC programming language.

STRUCTURED PROGRAMMING

When high-level languages were first developed, programs written in them often consisted of long lists of instructions with little organization. We might compare them to a textbook that had no structure or form, no paragraphs or chapters, no introductions or summaries, no table of contents or index. It would be a time-consuming task for the reader to locate a section dealing with a specific topic in such a book. Likewise, it was difficult for anyone but the original programmer to understand early programs. If changes had to be made at a later date (as they almost always do), it was difficult to locate the section of the program to be altered.

To correct these problems, computer scientists came up with a method of writing programs called **structured programming**. Structured programming encourages the development of programs with easy-to-follow logic. This is accomplished by dividing programs into **modules** and using only the three basic control structures. These two techniques are discussed next. Other characteristics of structured programming are presented throughout this textbook.

Structured programming *A method of programming in which programs are constructed with easy-to-follow logic, attempt to use only the three basic control structures, and are divided into modules.*

Module *A subpart within a program designed to perform a specific task.*

Using Modules

A structured program is divided into modules, each of which performs a specific task. In QBasic, these modules are referred to as *procedures*. Each module is like a program within a program and can be compared to a chapter in a textbook. In a textbook, each chapter deals with a specific topic and has specific goals. The chapters are combined to present a unified whole. Dividing a program into modules makes the program's logic easier to follow, just as dividing a book into chapters (and subsections within those chapters) makes the facts and ideas presented easier to understand. Programs developed in this manner tend to have fewer errors than unstructured programs because the logic is readily apparent. Dividing a program into modules is a very important concept of structured programming and is explained in Chapter 6.

The Three Basic Control Structures

Computer scientists have determined that any programming problem can be solved by using the needed combination of three basic control structures: the sequence, the decision structure, and the loop structure.

A **sequence** is merely a series of statements that the computer executes in the order in which they occur in the program. A program that converts feet to miles is a sequence. It determines the number of feet, divides this number by 5,280, and prints the number of miles.

Sequence *A group of statements that are executed in the order in which they occur in the program.*

When a program contains a decision structure or a loop structure, the program statements are no longer executed in the order in which they occur in the program. For example, certain statements may be skipped, or a group of statements may be repeated

Decision structure *A structure in which a condition is tested. The action taken next depends on the result of this test.*

Loop structure *A structure that allows a series of instructions to be executed as many times as needed.*

many times. In a **decision structure**, a comparison is made; what happens next depends on the result of this comparison. The decision structure is similar to decisions people make every day. For example, when you get up in the morning, you may decide to take one action (stay in bed) if it is a weekend and another action (get ready for class) if it is a weekday. An example of a decision that a computer might make would be to determine the percentage of income tax a person must pay based on his or her earnings during the last year.

Loop structures involve the performance of repetitive tasks. When you do 50 pushups in physical education class, you are executing a loop structure—you are repeatedly performing the same action. Loops are very useful in computer programs for performing tasks such as reading a list of names or adding a series of numbers. A loop structure allows a series of instructions to be executed as many times as needed. Loop structures are discussed in Chapter 7.

Structured Programming Languages

Structured programming languages allow the programmer to efficiently implement the concepts of structured programming. Virtually all modern programming languages are structured languages. Because BASIC was originally developed before the concepts of structured programming were thoroughly understood, early versions of this language were not structured. However, the newer versions, such as QBasic, implement these principles.

Learning Check 2-1

1. _____ consists of the programs that are executed by the computer's hardware.

2. The only language that computers can execute directly is _____.

3. Of the three levels of programming languages discussed here, the most English-like one is _____.

4. In structured programming, programs are divided into _____, each of which performs a specific task.

THE PROGRAMMING PROCESS

People solve problems every day of their lives. Most problems have a number of possible solutions, and usually there is more than one way to arrive at an acceptable answer to a problem.

Think of how many ways are there to clean a room. For example, either window washing or furniture dusting can be done first. The floor can be cleaned by sweeping it with a broom or with a vacuum cleaner.

The same is true in designing computer programs. There may be many paths that lead to the same solution. Your job will be to find the most practical way to get there.

People who are good programmers are also good problem solvers. Writing a program is a way of using a computer to solve a problem. The last half of this chapter examines problem-solving methods that can help you arrive at solutions in an efficient, logical manner.

To use the computer effectively as a problem-solving tool, the programmer performs several steps, which together are called the **programming process**:

Programming process *The steps used to develop a solution to a programming problem.*

1. Define and document the problem.

2. Design and document a solution.

3. Write and document the program.

4. Debug and test the program, revising the documentation if necessary.

Figure 2-2 illustrates these steps. Each step includes **documentation**, which consists of the instructions or statements written to explain a program to humans. These statements may be in the program itself or separate from the program.

Documentation *Written statements or instructions explaining programs to humans.*

Defining and Documenting the Problem

It is virtually impossible to get somewhere if you do not know where you are going. Likewise, in programming, a clear and concise statement of the problem is necessary before anything else is done. Many programming disasters have occurred because this step was ignored. In business, the person who writes the program is generally not the same person who will be using it, and these people (or groups of people) may not have the same understanding of how the program should work. Therefore, before the programmer begins work, the problem must be clearly defined and documented in writing. Documentation is very important, because people often believe they understand how a task is to be performed, but when they take time to write it down, they realize that certain steps are missing. This documentation of the problem definition must be agreed on by all parties involved. It includes a description of the program input and output:

1. What data is necessary to obtain the desired output? Where will this data be obtained? How will this data be entered? The programmer should make it as easy as possible for the user

FIGURE 2-2

The Steps in the
Programming Process

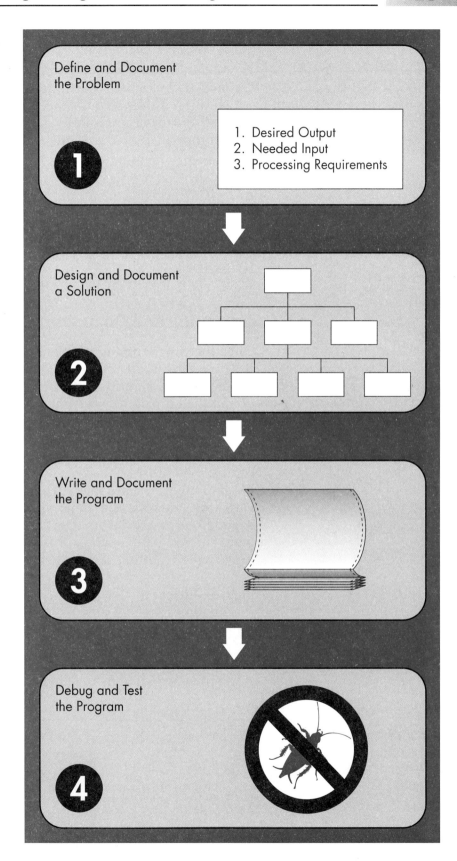

programmer should make it as easy as possible for the user to enter the needed data.

2. All output and the manner in which it is to be formatted must be described. Formatting refers to the way in which the output is displayed or printed to make it easy for the user to read and use. For example, placing output in columns with appropriate headings is one way of formatting it.

Let's practice defining and documenting a simple problem. Suppose you need a program to convert a given number of feet to miles. The output is the number of miles in the stated number of feet. The input is the number of feet to be converted. In addition, you need to know the conversion formula (that is, how many feet there are in one mile). The input and output are graphically illustrated in Figure 2-3, where the Processing box represents the steps necessary to obtain the needed output from the input.

Designing and Documenting a Solution

Once the programming problem is thoroughly understood and the necessary input and output have been determined, it is time to develop an **algorithm** that consists of the steps needed to obtain the correct output from the input. In an algorithm, each step must be listed in the order in which it is to be performed.

Algorithm *The sequence of steps needed to solve a problem. Each step must be listed in the order in which it is to be performed.*

Developing an algorithm is an important step in all programming. In fact, computers are machines designed to execute algorithms. Algorithms, however, are not only used in computer programming—we use them in all areas of our lives. In chemistry class, for example, the steps you follow when conducting an experiment constitute an algorithm. If you have ever bought an unassembled item, such as a bicycle, the instructions you followed when putting it together were an algorithm. Everyone knows how frustrating it is when these instructions are incomplete or unclear.

Sometimes you are able to figure out what needs to be done even if the instructions are not precise. This is because humans are capable of drawing on past experiences to determine how to perform a task. For example, if the first step in assembling a bike is to screw two sections together, you know that a screwdriver is

FIGURE 2-3

Input and Output for Converting Feet to Miles

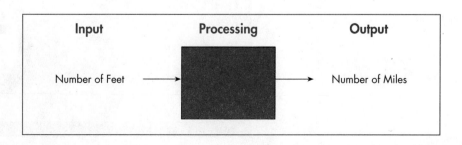

needed. You can even determine whether you need a regular or a Philips screwdriver. You also know how to use the screwdriver to insert the screw properly. Computers, on the other hand, cannot make assumptions or draw on past experiences as humans can. Therefore, when developing an algorithm for a computer to follow, be careful not to skip any steps.

Let's develop an algorithm for the problem of converting feet to miles. The steps could be stated like this:

1. Enter the number of feet to be converted to miles.

2. Find the number of miles by dividing the number of feet by 5,280 (the number of feet in one mile).

3. Output the number of miles.

The importance of taking time to carefully design a solution cannot be overemphasized. A well-designed solution can save countless hours in writing a program and correcting errors. We next examine some specific techniques for designing and documenting solutions.

Learning Check 2-2

1. True or False? Any given problem has only one correct solution.

2. What is the first step in solving a problem?

3. What is the second step in solving a problem?

4. A(n) _____ is a sequence of steps needed to solve a problem.

5. True or False? The steps in an algorithm can be listed in any order.

Top-Down Design. The most difficult aspect of programming is learning to organize solutions in a clear, concise way. Structured programming uses **top-down design**, which proceeds from the general to the specific, attempting to solve the major problems first and worrying about the details later. This process of gradually dividing a problem into smaller and smaller subproblems is often referred to as the divide-and-conquer method, because it is easier to deal with a large job by completing it a small step at a time. Top-down design prevents the programmer from becoming overwhelmed by the size of the job.

Top-down design can be applied to tasks people perform every day, such as cleaning a car. Figure 2-4 illustrates the input and output for this task. The box labeled Processing would contain all of the tasks necessary to complete the job. A basic algorithm might be stated as follows:

Top-down design *A method of solving a problem that proceeds from the general to the specific. The major problems are dealt with first, and the details are left until later.*

FIGURE 2-4

Input and Output for
Cleaning a Car

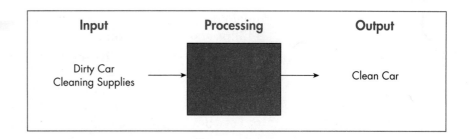

1. Collect cleaning supplies.
2. Clean interior of car.
3. Clean exterior of car.
4. Put away supplies.

This algorithm can be further subdivided by breaking each step into smaller substeps. For example, Step 3 (clean exterior of car) could be divided like this:

a. Wash body and tires.

b. Clean windows.

c. Clean chrome.

Even these steps could be divided further. For example, Step *a* (wash body and tires) contains many substeps. The box labeled Processing would contain all of the tasks necessary to complete the job.

FIGURE 2-5

Structure Chart for Cleaning a Car

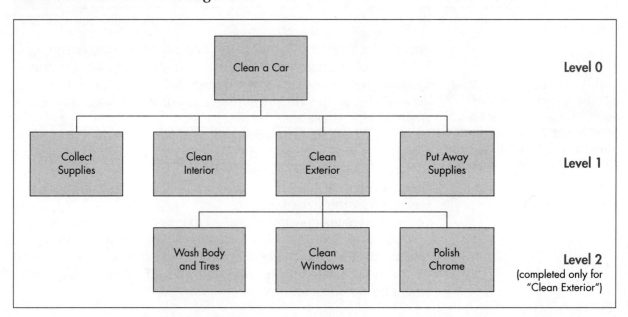

Structure chart *A diagram that visually illustrates how a problem solution has been divided into subparts.*

Figure 2-5 shows a **structure chart**, which graphically illustrates the results of the top-down design process. Each level represents a further subdividing of the tasks into smaller subtasks. Level 0 contains the general statement of the problem, and Level 1 contains the first-level subtasks. In Figure 2-5, only one step in Level 1, Clean Exterior, has been broken down further. Of course, each of these steps could be further subdivided.

The structure chart for the problem of converting feet to miles is shown in Figure 2-6. The three subtasks are the same as the steps listed in the algorithm. Because each subtask is fairly simple, there is no need to have more than one level in the structure chart.

Flowchart *A graphic representation of the solution to a programming problem.*

Flowcharts. One way of graphically representing the steps needed to solve a programming problem is by using a **flowchart**. A flowchart shows the actual flow of the logic of a solution, whereas a structure chart simply shows how the problem can be divided into subtasks. The following list shows several flowcharting symbols and their meanings:

▬	Process symbol	Represents calculations or other processing steps.
▬	Input/output symbol	Indicates inputting data or outputting program results.
⬭	Terminal symbol	Indicates the beginning or end of a program.
◆	Decision symbol	Represents a comparison. The action taken next depends on the result of the comparison.
●	Connection symbol	Indicates entry from or to another part of the flowchart.

Additional symbols are explained throughout this textbook as they are needed.

FIGURE 2-6

Structure Chart for Converting Feet to Miles

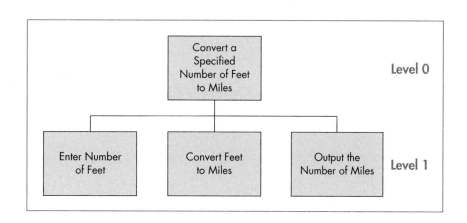

FIGURE 2-7

The Three Basic Control Structures

1. Sequence
One statement after another is executed in order (A, then B).

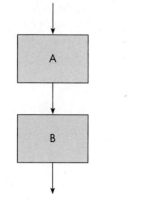

2. Decision Structure
It requires making a comparison and, depending on the result of the comparison, one of two paths is taken. For instance: IF comparison A is true THEN execute statement B; ELSE execute statement C.

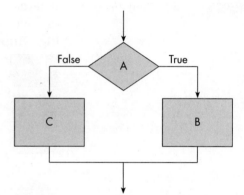

3. Loop Structure
Execution of statements E and F continued as long as D is true. If D is false, the loop is exited, and E and F are not executed.

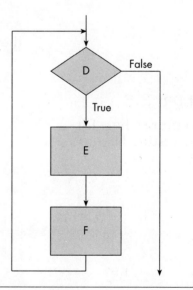

FIGURE 2-8

Flowchart for
Converting Feet to
Miles

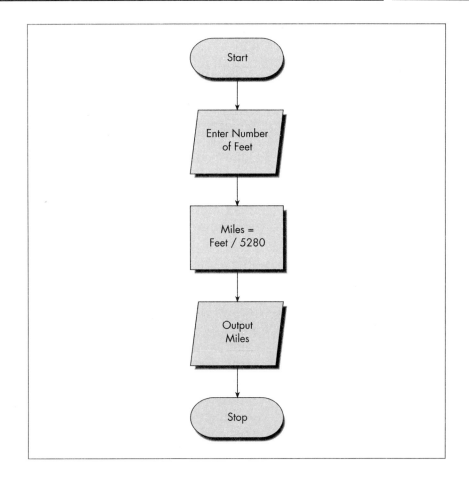

Figure 2-7 explains how the three basic control structures can be represented using flowchart symbols. The flowchart for the problem of converting feet to miles is shown in Figure 2-8. It begins and ends with the terminal symbol. Two input/output symbols are used: one when the number of feet is entered and another when the number of miles is printed. A processing symbol indicates the arithmetic step of dividing the feet by 5,280.

Pseudocode *An English-like description of a program's logic.*

Pseudocode. **Pseudocode** is an English-like description of the logic of a programming problem solution. The prefix *pseudo* means "similar to." Therefore, pseudocode is similar to the actual statements (or code) in the program. It is a type of algorithm in that all steps needed to solve the problem must be listed. However, algorithms can be written to solve all types of problems, whereas pseudocode is used specifically for programming problems. The pseudocode for the problem of converting feet to miles could be written as follows:

Begin
Enter the number of feet
Miles = feet/5,280

Print the number of miles
End

There are no rigid rules for writing pseudocode. However, once you have developed a style, you should use it consistently.

Writing and Documenting a Program

Code *To write a problem solution in a programming language.*

Desk check *To trace through a program by hand in an attempt to locate any errors.*

Once a solution to a programming problem has been developed and documented with a structure chart, flowchart, and/or pseudocode, you should find it fairly simple to actually write, or **code**, the solution in a programming language. Before entering it into the computer, the programmer should spend some time **desk checking** the program, that is, making sure each statement follows the syntax rules of the language. This book explains the syntax of QBasic. These rules may be hard to understand at first, like the rules of any foreign language, but they will quickly become second nature to you. When a programmer desk checks a program, he or she also traces through the program to determine whether the logic is correct. This simple process often locates many errors that can easily be corrected before the program is entered into the computer.

Like the original problem, the program must be thoroughly documented. This type of documentation consists of remarks placed within the program to explain it to humans; the computer simply ignores these remarks. Documenting a program thoroughly is especially important in business, where many different programmers may have to modify, or alter, the program over a period of time.

Figure 2-9 shows the final program that converts feet into miles. Don't worry if you do not completely understand it at this point. However, notice the similarity between the final program and the pseudocode for this problem.

Debugging and Testing a Program

Structured programming techniques encourage the development of programs with easy-to-follow logic and fewer errors than unstructured programs. Nonetheless, programs of any significant length virtually always contain errors, and correcting them can account for a large portion of time spent in program development.

Debug *To locate and correct program errors.*

Syntax error *A violation of the grammatical rules of a language.*

Debugging is the process of locating and correcting program errors. The most common errors made by a beginning programmer are **syntax errors**, which occur when the programmer violates the grammatical rules of the language (which are stricter than those of English). Most syntax errors are caused by simple typing mistakes, for example, by typing *INUPT* instead of *INPUT*.

FIGURE 2-9

Program to Convert Feet to Miles

```
***              Program Feet to Miles              ***

'*** This program prompts the user to enter a       ***
'*** specific number of feet and then converts      ***
'*** it to miles.                                    ***

CLS
PRINT "This program converts feet to miles."
PRINT
INPUT "Enter number of feet to be converted: ", Feet
LET Miles = Feet / 5280
PRINT "There are"; Miles; "miles in"; Feet; "feet."
```

```
This program converts feet to miles.

Enter number of feet to be converted: 10560
There are 2 miles in 10560 feet.
```

Run-time error *An error that causes a program to stop executing before its end is reached.*

If a syntax error is made, an error message is usually displayed when the programmer attempts to execute the program. This type of error can be prevented by careful proofreading. A second type of error is the **run-time error**, which causes a program to stop executing before it has reached the end. Attempting to perform an illegal operation, such as trying to divide a number by zero, will cause a run-time error.

Logic error *An error caused by a flaw in a program's algorithm.*

Once the computer is able to run your program, you will need to test it with a variety of data to determine whether the results are always correct. **Logic errors**, which are caused by a flaw in the algorithm used to create the program, can mean that the program will execute properly but, at least some of the time, will yield incorrect results. Once errors are corrected, the programmer must remember to revise any corresponding documentation.

Learning Check 2-3

1. _____ is the process of writing a problem solution in a programming language.

2. Tracing through a program by hand, attempting to locate errors, is called _____.

3. A violation of the grammatical rules of a programming language generally results in a(n) _____ error.

4. _____ is the process of locating and correcting program errors.

5. True or False? The computer uses documentation to tell it how to execute a program.

SUMMARY POINTS

▌ Software consists of the programs that are executed on computer hardware.

▌ The three levels of programming languages are machine languages, assembly languages, and high-level languages.

▌ Machine language is the only language that the computer can execute directly and is different for each type of computer. All other languages must be translated into machine language before execution.

▌ High-level languages are the most English-like, and assembly language is between machine languages and high-level languages.

▌ Structured programming was developed to encourage the development of easy-to-understand, more error-free programs. A structured program is divided into modules, each of which performs a specific task.

▌ BASIC was developed in the mid-1960s by Professors John Kemeny and Thomas Kurtz.

▌ QBasic is a version of BASIC that incorporates structured programming techniques.

▌ There are four basic steps in the programming process:

1. Define and document the program.
2. Design and document a solution.
3. Write and document the program.
4. Debug and test the program, revising the documentation if necessary.

▌ Before a problem can be solved, it must be thoroughly understood. A clear statement of the problem is written, including the needed input and output.

▌ An algorithm is developed that lists all steps necessary to solve the problem.

▌ Top-down design is an efficient way of developing a problem solution. This method proceeds from the general to the specific. Thus, the programmer can concentrate on major problems first and leave the details until later.

▌ Structure charts graphically represent how a problem solution has been broken down into subtasks.

▌ Flowcharts graphically represent the logic flow of a solution to a programming problem.

▌ Pseudocode is an English-like description of a solution to a programming problem.

▌ The actual process of writing a program is called *coding*. Coding should be fairly simple if the programmer has already developed a clear solution. After a program is coded, it should be desk checked.

▌ Debugging is the process of finding and correcting program errors. After a program is running, it must be executed with a wide variety of data to determine whether the program always yields correct results.

KEY TERMS

Algorithm – 44
Assembly language – 38
Code – 50
Debug – 50
Decision structure – 41
Desk check – 50
Documentation – 42
Flowchart – 47
High-level language – 39
Logic error – 51
Loop structure – 41
Machine language – 37
Module – 40
Programming process – 42
Pseudocode – 49
Run-time error – 51
Sequence – 40
Software – 37
Structure chart – 47
Structured programming – 40
Syntax error – 50
Top-down design – 45

REVIEW QUESTIONS

1. Explain why computer hardware is of little use without software.

2. Give two reasons why writing programs in machine language is a difficult process. What is an advantage of using machine language?

3. What were some early difficulties in writing programs that led to the development of structured programming?

4. Think of a task you perform every day, such as brushing your teeth. What input is needed to complete this task? What is the output? Develop an algorithm for the task.

5. The first step in the programming process is to define and document the problem. What is meant by defining the problem?

6. Give an example of each of the three basic control structures.

7. Write an algorithm that will evaluate the following expression:

$$\frac{14 + 8}{2} \times \frac{3}{16}$$

8. How is top-down design used in developing a programming problem solution?

9. Explain how you might write a term paper for a class using top-down design. Create a structure chart for the problem.

10. List and explain the purpose of the flowchart symbols discussed in this chapter.

11. Draw a flowchart to illustrate the steps needed to start up QBasic on your computer.

12. Write the pseudocode needed to start up QBasic on your computer.

13. If the programmer has properly followed the steps listed in the programming process, why should the actual coding of the program be fairly simple (assuming the programmer is familiar with the programming language being used)?

14. Why is it important to test a program by executing it with a wide variety of data?

15. Refer to the structure chart in Figure 2-5. Complete Level 2 for the Clean Interior step.

Fundamental Statements

Outline

Objectives

After studying this chapter, you will be able to:

▌ Differentiate between numeric and character string constants and give examples of each.

▌ Use numeric and character string constants correctly in programs.

▌ Explain how variables are used to store values in the computer's main memory.

▌ List the rules for naming variables.

▌ Define the term *keyword*.

▌ Correctly document programs.

▌ Assign values to variables.

▌ Perform arithmetic operations using both constants and variables.

▌ Evaluate arithmetic expressions according to the hierarchy of operations.

▌ Display program output on the monitor screen.

▌ Use the Immediate window to execute statements in immediate mode.

▌ Use the various forms of help available with QBasic.

INTRODUCTION

Chapter 1 discussed how to use QBasic to enter, edit, and save programs. This chapter begins to teach you how to actually write programs. Five statements are covered here: CLS, REM, LET, PRINT, and END. You also will learn how to write statements that perform arithmetic operations.

QBASIC STATEMENT COMPONENTS

A program is a sequence of instructions that tells the computer how to solve a problem. Figure 3-1 is an example of a program that calculates the gross pay of an employee who worked 40 hours at $7.50 per hour. This program has eight statements. All QBasic statements are composed of programming commands, called *keywords*, that have special meanings to QBasic, and other language elements. These statement components are discussed here.

Constants

Constant *A value that does not change during program execution.*

Constants are values that do not change during the execution of a program. There are two kinds: numeric constants and character string constants.

FIGURE 3-1

Program to Calculate an Employee's Gross Pay

```
'*** This program computes an employee's gross pay.  ***

CLS                             'Clear the output screen.
LET Hours = 40
LET Rate = 7.5
LET Pay = Hours * Rate          'Calculate the total pay.
LET Heading$ = "Gross pay is"
PRINT Heading$, Pay             'Display the result.

END
```

```
Gross pay is    300
```

Numeric constant *A number contained in a statement.*

Numeric Constants. A number included in a statement is called a **numeric constant**. Numeric constants can be real numbers, which include decimal points, or integers, which are numbers without decimal points. Below are some examples of real constants:

```
6.0        6.782
.95        0.58
-7.234     10024.91
```

Here are some *invalid* real constants:

```
14,005.5   (No commas allowed)
6.8%       (% not allowed)
1 86.94    (No blank spaces allowed)
```

The following numbers are integer constants:

```
29         123912
3432       3910
2          39
```

Some *invalid* integer constants follow:

```
16.05      (Decimal portion not allowed)
38&        (& not allowed)
```

When using numbers, remember these rules:

1. No commas can be included in numbers when entering them into the computer. The computer interprets the digits before and after a comma as two separate numbers. For example, the computer would interpret 3,751 as the number 3 *and* the number 751. The valid form of the number is 3751.
2. If a number has no sign, the computer assumes it is positive. For example, 386 is the same as +386.
3. If a number is negative, the negative sign must precede the digits, as in –21.
4. Fractions must be written in decimal form. For example, 2.75 is the correct representation for 2¾.

QBasic uses *exponential notation* (or *scientific notation*) to represent very large or very small numbers. For example, QBasic represents the number 12641109243291515 as

```
1.2641109243291515D+16
```

The *D+16* portion of the number indicates that the decimal point should be moved 16 places to the right. A very small decimal number, such as 0.00000000000000012, is represented as:

```
1.2D-16
```

In this example, the decimal point must be moved 16 places to the left. The general format used in exponential notation is

$\pm x.xxxxD\pm n$. Each part of the number is explained in the following list:

- The symbol $\pm$ represents the sign of the number, positive or negative. The plus sign is optional with positive numbers, but the minus sign is mandatory for negative numbers.

- $x.xxxx$ is the *mantissa* and represents the digits of the number.

- The letter D indicates this is a double-precision number. QBasic uses double-precision numbers when storing large values. They are explained in detail in Chapter 10.

- $\pm n$ is the positive or negative exponential value. For example, D–17 indicates that the decimal point should be moved seventeen places to the left and D+19 indicates that it should be moved nineteen places to the right.

Character string constant *A group of alphanumeric data consisting of any type of symbols.*

Alphanumeric data *Any combination of letters, numbers, or special characters.*

Character String Constants. A **character string** (or **string** for short) **constant** is a collection of symbols called **alphanumeric data**. A string can include any combination of letters, numbers, and special characters including dashes, commas, blanks, and so forth. The character string must be enclosed in double quotation marks. You can include single quotation marks within a string that is contained within double quotation marks. The following are examples of valid character strings:

```
"A rose by any other name"
"She said, 'What is his name?'"
"Gary's tennis racket."
```

The following character string constant is invalid:

```
"The letter "A" is a vowel."
```

The system will recognize the double quotation marks before the letter *A* as indicating the end of the string. Actually, the quotation mark at the end of the line is supposed to indicate the end of the string. This string would be valid if single quotation marks had been used around the letter *A*.

The length of a string is determined by counting all its characters. Here is a character string nine characters long:

```
"TOUCHDOWN"
```

The following string is 11 characters long because it has two blank spaces at the end:

```
"TOUCHDOWN  "
```

The computer can store a blank just as it can store any other character.

The maximum length of a string is 32,767 characters.

Variables

Before proceeding any further, it is important that you understand how data is stored in the main memory of the computer. Imagine a block of post office boxes, each with an assigned number that acts as an address for that particular box (see Figure 3-2). The addresses of these boxes always remain the same, but their contents will almost certainly change over a period of time. Similarly, the main memory in a computer is divided into many separate storage locations, each with a specific address. A storage location containing a value that can change during program execution is referred to as a **variable**. A variable can contain only one value at a time; when a new value is assigned to a variable, the old value is lost.

> **Variable** *A storage location whose value can change during program execution.*

These storage locations can be referred to by their addresses, just as post office boxes can be referred to by the numbers assigned to them. In machine language programming, a storage location is always referred to by its actual address. It is a difficult task for the programmer to keep track of these addresses. Fortunately, in QBasic (and other high-level languages) the programmer is allowed to use names for storage locations. Names are much easier to remember than addresses. Hours and Rate are **variable names** in Figure 3-3. The values (or contents) of the locations they identify are 40 and 7.50, respectively.

> **Variable name** *A name used to identify a storage location.*

Variable names can have any number of characters; however, QBasic recognizes only the first 40 characters. This means that if the first 40 characters of two names are identical, QBasic sees the name as being identical, even if the 41st character is different. The first character of the name must be a letter. The remaining characters may be letters, numbers, and periods. QBasic does not differentiate between uppercase and lowercase letters in variable names; therefore, it sees these three names as being identical:

FIGURE 3-2

Variables are similar to post office boxes.

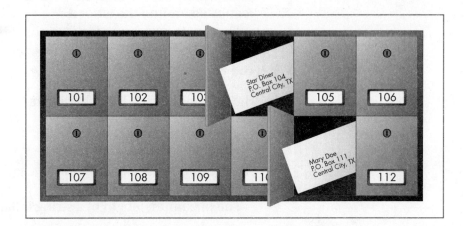

```
FirstDown
FIRSTDOWN
firstdown
```

Many programmers use a combination of uppercase and lowercase letters to improve readability and we will follow this practice here.

Descriptive variable name *A variable name that describes the contents of the storage location it represents.*

Good programming habits include the use of **descriptive variable names**, that is, names that describe the values they identify. Such names make the logic of programs easier to understand. A variable named QuantityOnHand has more meaning than QUAN.

Numeric variable *A variable that stores a number.*

Numeric Variables. **Numeric variables** are used to store numbers that are either supplied to the computer by the programmer or internally calculated during program execution. A numeric variable name must begin with a letter, followed by letters, digits, and periods. It cannot have embedded blanks. The numeric variables in Figure 3-1 are Hours (the number of hours worked), Rate (the hourly pay rate), and Pay (the gross pay for the week). Some additional examples of valid variable names are as follows:

```
BigNumber
TOTAL.PRICE
Warehouse8
CLASS1B
```

The following names are *invalid*:

```
Maximum/Average    (Contains an invalid character)
1stChoice          (Name must start with a letter)
Square Yards       (Blanks are not allowed within the name)
```

There are actually several types of numeric variables; these are discussed in detail in Chapter 10.

FIGURE 3-3

Variables in Storage

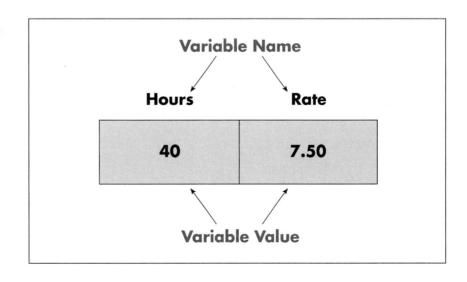

String variable *A variable that stores a character string.*

String Variables.

A **string variable** is used to store a character string, such as a name, an address, or a social security number. As with numeric variables, string variables can store only one value at a time.

A string variable name begins with a letter followed by letters or digits and must be terminated with a dollar sign ($). Some valid string variable names are as follows:

```
Heading$
Employee$
SSNO$
DayOfWeek$
```

Keywords

Keyword *A word that has a predefined meaning to QBasic.*

Certain words have specific meanings to QBasic. These are referred to as **keywords** (or **reserved words**) and cannot be used as variable names. Examples are READ, LIST, PRINT, LET, and END. A complete list is contained in Appendix A.

You can enter keywords in either uppercase or lowercase letters. However, if they are entered in lowercase, QBasic automatically converts them to uppercase.

RULES FOR CREATING VARIABLE NAMES

- Must begin with a letter.
- Can contain letters, numeric digits, and the period.
- Cannot contain blanks.
- Can have any number of characters; however, only the first 40 characters are significant.
- Cannot be a keyword.*
- String variable names must end with the dollar sign ($).

* Keywords are listed in Appendix A.

Learning Check 3-1

1. The two types of constants are _____ constants and _____ constants.
2. A(n) _____ is a storage location whose value can change during program execution.
3. A(n) _____ variable name must have "$" as its last character.
4. Character strings are delimited by _____.
5. Keywords are also referred to as _____.

SIMPLE QBASIC STATEMENTS

This section introduces five programming statements that will be useful in virtually all programs you write: CLS, REM, LET, PRINT, and END.

Clearing the Output Screen

The statement

```
CLS
```

removes any existing text from the Output screen and positions the cursor in the upper-left corner of the screen. It is a good idea always to place CLS at the beginning of a program that will have output displayed on the monitor screen.

Notice the box labeled "The CLS Statement." Each time we introduce a new statement, we will use a format box similar to this one to provide a quick reference on the statement's syntax.

The CLS Statement

Flowchart Symbol	Statement Format
	CLS

Documenting a Program

The REM, or remark statement, provides information for the human half of the programming team. It is ignored by the computer. Statements that are ignored by the computer are referred to as nonexecutable statements and are not included in flowcharts. This information is referred to as **documentation** and its function is to explain the purpose of the program, what variables are used in the program, and anything else of importance. Because documentation does not affect program execution, it can be placed anywhere in the program. As shown below, the keyword REM indicates that the text following it is documentation:

Documentation *Statements that are used to explain a program to humans. Documentation is ignored by QBasic.*

```
REM *** This program computes an employee's gross pay. ***
```

Placing asterisks before and after the remark is optional. The asterisks simply set the documentation apart from the rest of the program. It is also possible to indicate documentation by placing a single quotation mark (') to the left of it:

```
'*** This program computes an employee's gross pay. ***
```

This method is used in Figure 3-1. Remarks can also be placed after a program statement, as follows:

```
LET Pay = Hours * Rate              'Calculate the total pay.
```

This remark explains the statement to its left.

Well-documented programs make it easier not only for the programmer but also for anyone else trying to understand a program. Documentation is particularly useful if a program needs to be changed in the future. It is important to develop the habit of documenting programs as they are written and revising the documentation as the programs are debugged or otherwise changed.

The REM Statement

Flowchart Symbol

Because the REM statement is a nonexecutable statement, it does not have a flowchart symbol.

Statement Format

REM documentation

Note: A single quotation mark (') can be used in place of the keyword REM.

WHY NO LINE NUMBERS?

If you have previously used another version of BASIC that used line numbers, you may be wondering why we have not been using line numbers. The purpose of line numbers is to transfer control to another portion of a program. Because QBasic is a structured language, this type of transfer is not needed. You no longer need to mess with entering line numbers, renumbering them when editing, and so forth.

Assigning Values to Variables

Assignment statement *A statement used to assign a value to a variable.*

The **assignment statement** stores a value in main memory in the location allotted to the stated variable. In a flowchart, the assignment statement is illustrated by a processing symbol (☐). An example appears below:

```
LET Day$ = "SUNDAY"
```

This statement assigns the character string SUNDAY to Day$. The word LET is optional; the statement can also be written as follows:

```
Day$ = "SUNDAY"
```

For simplicity's sake, we will discontinue using LET after this chapter.

The assignment statement can be used to assign values directly to variables or to assign the result of a calculation to a variable. In either case, the expression to the right of the equal sign is assigned to the variable on the left side.

The program in Figure 3-1 has four assignment statements:

```
LET Hours = 40
LET Rate = 7.5
LET Pay = Hours * Rate            'Calculate the total pay.
LET Heading$ = "Gross pay is"
```

The first two assign numeric constants (in this case, the hours worked and the pay rate) to two numeric variables. The third statement assigns the result of an arithmetic calculation to the numeric variable Pay. The last statement assigns an appropriate character string to Heading$.

The same variable name can appear on both sides of the equal sign:

```
LET Count = 10
LET Count = Count + 1
```

The first statement stores the value 10 in Count and the second statement increments Count by 1. Therefore, after the second statement is executed, Count will be equal to 11.

It is possible to assign a number to a string variable if the number is placed in quotation marks:

```
LET ClassSize$ = "35"
```

Because this value is stored as a character string, it is stored exactly as it appears inside the quotation marks. In addition, it cannot be used in arithmetic operations.

The Assignment Statement

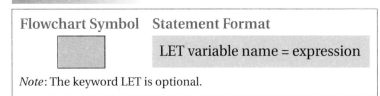

Flowchart Symbol	Statement Format
	LET variable name = expression

Note: The keyword LET is optional.

Arithmetic Operations

In QBasic, arithmetic expressions are composed of numeric constants, numeric variables, and arithmetic operators. The most commonly used arithmetic operations are defined in the following table:

Operator	Operation	BASIC Expression
+	Addition	A + B
−	Subtraction	A − B
/	Division	A / B
*	Multiplication	A * B
^	Exponentiation	A ^ B

For example, in the statement

```
LET X = Y ^ 3
```

Y is cubed, and the result is stored in the location identified by X. Note that a space has been left on each side of the operators. This spacing is not necessary, but it greatly improves the readability of the program. Table 3-1 contains some more samples of statements that use arithmetic operators.

Hierarchy of Operations. When more than one operation is performed in a single arithmetic expression, the computer follows a **hierarchy of operations** to determine the order in which the expressions are to be evaluated. Operations are performed as follows:

Hierarchy of operations
Rules that determine the order in which operations are performed.

Priority	Operation	Symbol
First	Exponentiation	^
Second	Multiplication, division	*, /
Third	Addition, subtraction	+, −
Fourth	Any operations on the same level are performed left to right	

TABLE 3-1 STATEMENTS USING ARITHMETIC OPERATORS

Statement	Result
X = 4 + 5 − 1	X = 8
Y = 5 * 10 + 2	Y = 52
Z = 6 + 4 ^ 2	Z = 22
M = 12 / 4 − 5	M = −2

In the statement

```
LET X = 10 + 4 * 2
```

X is assigned the value of 18 because the multiplication is performed before the addition.

When parentheses are used in an expression, the operations inside the parentheses are performed first. If parentheses are nested (placed inside one another), the operations are performed from the inside out.

Translating arithmetic expressions into QBasic requires care. Consider the following:

$$\frac{A \times B}{N-1} \times \frac{x+y^2}{N+1}$$

The left side could be written

```
A * B / (N - 1)
```

It is not necessary to put A * B in parentheses, but it might help keep things clear. The right side would look like this:

```
(X + Y ^ 2) / (N + 1)
```

Lastly, the two are multiplied together:

```
(A * B / (N -1)) * ((X + Y ^ 2) / (N + 1))
```

Table 3-2 gives some examples of how expressions are evaluated.

Learning Check 3-2

1. The _____ statement is used to erase any previous text on the output screen.

2. What are the two ways in which documentation can be indicated?

3. The keyword _____ is optional in assignment statements.

4. Write an assignment statement to do each of the following:

   a. Assign your age to an appropriate variable.

   b. Assign the value 8 cubed to a numeric variable.

   c. Assign the total calories in your lunch to an appropriate variable. (Assume you had three items for lunch containing 100, 65, and 305 calories.)

Continued on next page

5. Evaluate the following expressions:

a. `3 * 6 - 12 / 3`

b. `4 ^ (8 / 4)`

c. `3 ^ 2 ^ 2`

d. `12 + 6 / (3 * (10 - 9))`

Displaying Results

The PRINT statement is used to display the results of computer processing. It is flowcharted using the input/output symbol (⬜). The output of a PRINT statement can be formatted in many different ways. This topic is discussed in detail in Chapter 4. For now, we use commas, which automatically space the items across the output line.

Displaying the Value of a Variable. You can tell the computer to output the value assigned to a storage location simply by using the keyword PRINT with the variable name after it. In Figure 3-1, the following statement displays the program results on the monitor screen:

```
PRINT Heading$, Pay                    'Display the result
```

TABLE 3-2 EXAMPLES OF HOW EXPRESSIONS ARE EVALUATED

Expression	Evaluation Process
1. Y = 2 * 5 + 1	
First: 2 * 5 = 10	Process highest priority
Second: 10 + 1 = 11	Process next priority
Result: Y = 11	
2. Y = 2 * (5 + 1)	
First: 5 + 1 = 6	Perform processing within parentheses
Second: 2 * 6 = 12	Perform next priority
Result: Y = 12	
3. Y = (3 + (6 + 2) / 4) + 10 ^ 2	
First: 6 + 2 = 8	Process innermost parentheses
Second: 8 / 4 = 2	Perform highest priority operation inside outer parentheses
Third: 3 + 2 = 5	Process rest of outer parentheses
Fourth: 10 ^ 2 = 100	Perform next priority
Fifth: 5 + 100 = 105	Perform lowest priority
Result: Y = 105	

Heading$ displays the character string "Gross pay is" and Pay displays the amount owed. The output appears as follows:

```
Gross pay is    300
```

Printing has no effect on the contents of the storage location being printed. The PRINT statement merely accesses the value of a variable and displays it on the screen.

Displaying Literals. A **literal** is a group of characters containing any combination of alphabetic, numeric, and/or special characters. It is essentially the same as a constant, but the term is applied to constants used in PRINT statements. There are two types: character string and numeric.

A character string literal is a group of letters, numbers, and/or special characters enclosed in quotation marks. Everything inside the quotation marks is displayed exactly as is. For example, when this statement is executed:

```
PRINT "SAMPLE @%OUTPUT 12"
```

the following is output:

```
SAMPLE @%OUTPUT 12
```

Note that the quotation marks are not displayed.

Literals can be used to print headings in output. One method of printing column headings is to put each heading in quotation marks and separate them with commas. Here is an example:

```
PRINT "NAME", "RANK", "SERIAL NUMBER"
```

When this statement is executed, the following appears:

```
NAME            RANK            SERIAL NUMBER
```

Headings can be set off from the rest of the output by underlining and/or by a blank line. One way to underline headings is to include a separate PRINT statement that contains the necessary underscore lines, as follows:

```
PRINT "NAME", "RANK", "SERIAL NUMBER"
PRINT "____", "____", "_____"
```

the output will be

```
NAME            RANK            SERIAL NUMBER

____            ____            _____
```

Note that, because of the separate PRINT statement, the underline is slightly separated from the heading. If desired, a row of

> **Literal** *A group of characters in a PRINT statement that contains any combination of alphabetic, numeric, and/or special characters.*

Note that, because of the separate PRINT statement, the underline is slightly separated from the heading. If desired, a row of hyphens can be used instead of underscores.

Numeric literals also can be placed in PRINT statements. They do not have to be enclosed in quotation marks. The statement

```
PRINT 103
```

will output

```
103
```

Refer to the box with the heading "The PRINT Statement." Notice that "[expression-list]" is in brackets. Any time a section of a format statement is in brackets, that section is optional. PRINT can be used alone to insert a blank line into output to improve readability. For example,

```
PRINT "101 W. Merry"
PRINT
PRINT "East Lansing, MI"
```

displays

```
101 W. Merry

East Lansing, MI
```

The PRINT Statement

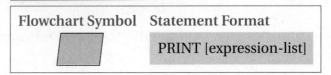

Flowchart Symbol	Statement Format
	PRINT [expression-list]

Displaying the Value of an Expression. QBasic can print not only literals and the values of variables, but also the values of arithmetic expressions. Look at the following program:

```
LET X = 15
LET Y = 5
PRINT (X + Y) / 2, X / Y
END
```

The expression in the third line is evaluated and the result is displayed:

```
10          3
```

The END Statement

The END statement instructs the computer to stop program execution. In a flowchart, it is indicated by the termination symbol (⬭). The END statement is always the last line to be executed in a program.

The END Statement

Flowchart Symbol	Statement Format
⬭	END

THE IMMEDIATE WINDOW

Programming mode The mode in which programs usually are entered and executed. Programs are not executed until the programmer instructs QBasic to execute them.

Immediate mode The mode in which a QBasic statement is executed as soon as Enter↵ is pressed. The statement is entered in the Immediate window.

Programming statements are ordinarily executed in **programming mode**; execution does not begin until you instruct QBasic to start. However, you can use the Immediate window to execute statements as soon as Enter↵ is pressed. This is referred to as **immediate mode.** The Immediate window is at the bottom of the QBasic screen, as shown in Figure 3-4. It is useful when you want

FIGURE 3-4

QBasic Screen with Immediate Window

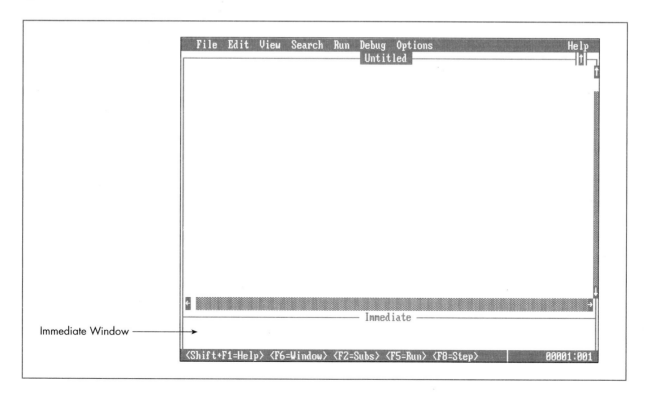

to test a statement quickly or find a result. For example, if you wish quickly to determine the sum of the three numbers 180, 231, and 128, you could enter the following statement in the Immediate window:

```
PRINT 180 + 231 + 128
```

As soon as you press Enter ⏎, the answer will appear in the Output screen. Press any key to return to the Immediate window. To move the cursor from the View window to the Immediate window, press F6 (F6 makes the next window the active window).

GETTING HELP

QBasic contains "online" help. Online help is accessible from within QBasic as compared to printed reference manuals, which are external to the system. The advantage of online help is that it can be referenced right at the computer. The function key F1 allows you to access online help. The function keys can be either on the left side or across the top of the keyboard (some keyboards even have them in both places). For example, if you want help on the New option, simply highlight this option and then press F1. As shown in Figure 3-5, an explanation of New will appear. Likewise, if you need information on using a QBasic keyword, use the arrow keys to position the cursor in the keyword and again press F1. If you are using a mouse, you can press the right mouse but-

FIGURE 3-5

The Help Screen for the
New Command

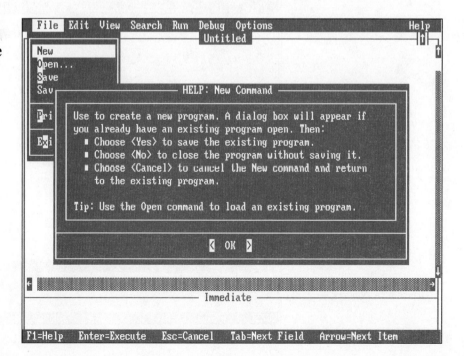

FIGURE **3-6**

The Help Screen for the
Keyword PRINT

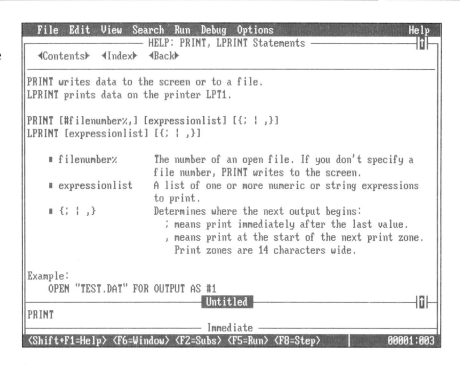

FIGURE **3-6**

The Help Screen for the
Keyword PRINT

ton instead of [F1]. For example, Figure 3-6 shows the help screen
for the keyword PRINT. Press [Esc] to close the help screen. To get a
list of help topics, press [Alt],[H]. Press the highlighted letter to
choose a particular command.

QBasic has a "smart editor." It catches many types of syntax
errors as you are typing in a program. It also offers suggestions for
correcting the error. For example, suppose you attempt to print a
character string but forget to place it in quotation marks:

```
PRINT Tomorrow is Wednesday
```

As soon as you press [Enter ↵], a message will be displayed providing hints on how to correct the error, as shown in Figure 3-7.
Because there is no quotation mark in front of "Tomorrow," the
smart editor thinks it is a variable name. Therefore, the editor says
you need to separate "Tomorrow" from "is" by a comma or a semicolon. Press [Enter ↵] and you will return to the line containing the
error so that you can correct it. At first, you may have some trou-
ble interpreting error messages; however, as you learn to "think
like the computer," they will become simpler to understand.

FIGURE **3-7**

Message Provided by
QBasic's Smart Editor

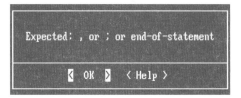

If you forget to insert a closing quotation mark:

```
PRINT "Tomorrow is Wednesday
```

the smart editor automatically adds it:

```
PRINT "Tomorrow is Wednesday"
```

In addition, it automatically capitalizes keywords and inserts spaces after punctuation and around operators. If you type in

```
LET SUM=X+Y+Z
```

The smart editor changes it to

```
LET SUM = X + Y + Z
```

Learning Check 3-3

1. True or False? When a variable is printed, the contents of that variable's storage location are changed.

2. A(n) _____ is an expression consisting of any combination of letters, numbers, or special characters.

3. The _____ statement causes program execution to stop.

4. Write statements to do the following:

    a. Display the headings NAME and ADDRESS.

    b. Underline the headings displayed in part **a**.

    c. Display the values of variables City$ and State$.

    d. Display the result of X + Y * Z.

    e. Display the values of variables A, B, and A ^ B.

5. Indicate whether the following are valid or invalid PRINT statements.

    a. `PRINT Buttons + 1`

    b. `PRINT NAM$ AND AGE`

MASTERING PROGRAM DEVELOPMENT

Problem Definition

The Top Team Sporting Goods Company manufactures leather balls for use in team sports. The cost of manufacturing these balls is as follows:

Baseballs	$11.72
Footballs	$17.64
Soccer balls	$14.80
Softballs	$8.25

The company calculates the wholesale prices of these items by adding on 28 percent of the manufacturing costs. The retail prices are calculated by adding on 62 percent of the wholesale cost. A computer program is needed to calculate the wholesale cost and the retail price of each item. A report, with appropriate headings, should be displayed on the monitor screen.

Solution Design

The tasks this program must perform are as follows:

1. Assign the manufacturing cost of each item to a variable.

2. Add on 28 percent of the manufacturing cost to obtain the wholesale cost.

3. Add on 62 percent of the wholesale cost to obtain the retail cost.

4. Display the price table.

Figure 3-8 shows the structure chart. Notice that Level 1 contains one module for each of the four tasks. Because the last task (Display Price Report Table) is more complex, it has been further subdivided.

The first part of the processing will use assignment statements to assign each of the manufacturing costs to a variable. Each wholesale and retail price can be determined by using simple arithmetic operations. The report headings and values can be displayed using PRINT statements. The flowchart and pseudocode for this solution are shown in Figure 3-9.

The Program

The complete program is contained in Figure 3-10. Examine the documentation in the first section of the program. The top line states the program's title. The next six lines explain the overall pur-

FIGURE 3-8

Structure Chart for Price Report Program

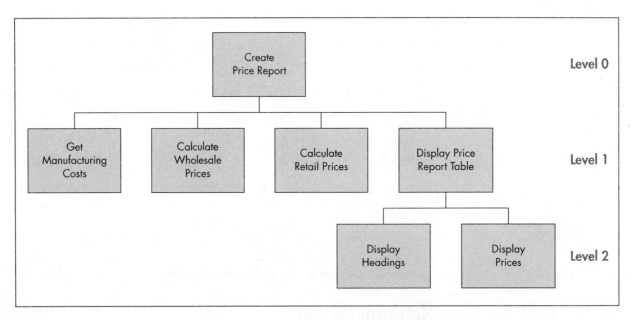

pose of the program. The documentation section concludes with an explanation of the program variables.

A blank line separates the documentation from the part of the program where the work is done. CLS is used to clear the output screen. The remainder of the program is divided into four sections, as indicated by the four remarks. These sections correspond to each of the four modules in Level 2 of the structure chart in Figure 3-8. Assignment statements are used to (1) get the manufacturing costs, (2) calculate the wholesale prices, and (3) calculate the retail prices.

Notice the statements that display the table headings:

```
PRINT "Manufacturing", "Wholesale", "Retail"
PRINT "Cost", "Cost", "Cost"
PRINT "------------------------------------------------"
```

As you can see from the output, the headings line up under one another. A row of hyphens separates the headings from the prices. The cost, wholesale price, and retail price of each item are printed on a separate line. The program concludes with an END statement.

FIGURE 3-9

Flowchart and Pseudocode for Price Report

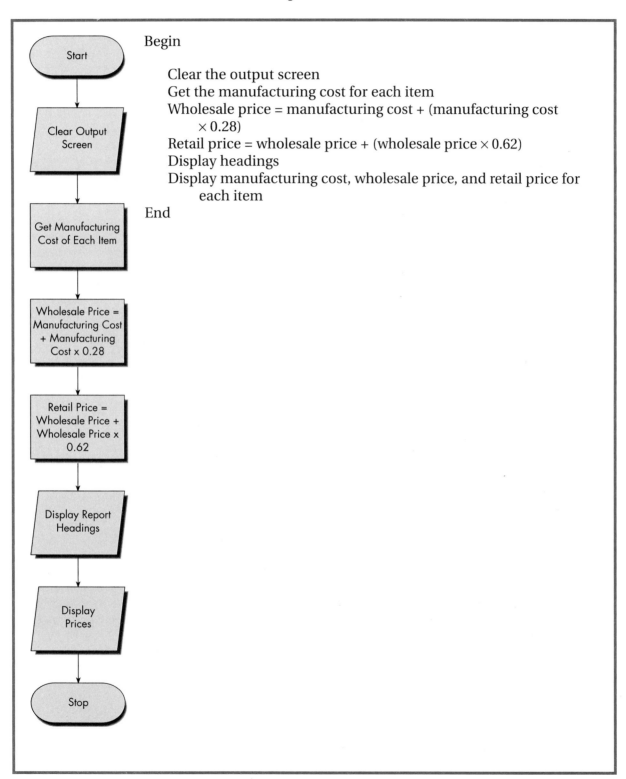

Begin

    Clear the output screen
    Get the manufacturing cost for each item
    Wholesale price = manufacturing cost + (manufacturing cost
        $\times$ 0.28)
    Retail price = wholesale price + (wholesale price $\times$ 0.62)
    Display headings
    Display manufacturing cost, wholesale price, and retail price for
        each item

End

Flowchart elements:

- Start
- Clear Output Screen
- Get Manufacturing Cost of Each Item
- Wholesale Price = Manufacturing Cost + Manufacturing Cost x 0.28
- Retail Price = Wholesale Price + Wholesale Price x 0.62
- Display Report Headings
- Display Prices
- Stop

FIGURE 3-10

Price Report Program

```
'***                        Price Report                    ***

'*** This program calculates the wholesale and retail prices ***
'*** of 4 items. Wholesale prices are calculated by the      ***
'*** formula:                                                ***
'***     Manufacturing cost + (wholesale price * .28)        ***
'*** Retail prices are calculated by the formula:            ***
'***     Wholesale price + (wholesale price * .62)           ***
'*** Major variables:                                        ***
'***     Cost1 - Cost4           Manufacturing cost of each  ***
'***                                    item                 ***
'***     Wholesale1 - Wholesale4 Wholesale price of each item ***
'***     Retail1 - Retail4       Retail cost of each item    ***

CLS                     'Clear the output screen
'*** Get manufacturing cost of each item. ***
LET Cost1 = 11.72
LET Cost2 = 17.64
LET Cost3 = 14.8
LET Cost4 = 8.25


'*** Calculate wholesale price of each item. ***
LET Wholesale1 = Cost1 + (Cost1 * .28)
LET Wholesale2 = Cost2 + (Cost2 * .28)
LET Wholesale3 = Cost3 + (Cost3 * .28)
LET Wholesale4 = Cost4 + (Cost4 * .28)


'*** Calculate retail price of each item. ***
LET Retail1 = Wholesale1 + (Wholesale1 * .62)
LET Retail2 = Wholesale2 + (Wholesale2 * .62)
LET Retail3 = Wholesale3 + (Wholesale3 * .62)
LET Retail4 = Wholesale4 + (Wholesale4 * .62)


'*** Display the price table. ***
PRINT "Manufact.", "Wholesale", "Retail"
PRINT "Cost", "Cost", "Cost"
PRINT "-------------------------------------------"
PRINT Cost1, Wholesale1, Retail1
PRINT Cost2, Wholesale2, Retail2
PRINT Cost3, Wholesale3, Retail3
PRINT Cost4, Wholesale4, Retail4


END
```

FIGURE 3-10

Continued

```
Manufact.      Wholesale      Retail
Cost           Cost           Cost
-------------------------------------
 11.72          15.0016        24.30259
 17.64          22.5792        36.5783
 14.8           18.944         30.68928
  8.25          10.56          17.1072
```

PROGRAMMING HINTS

- It is a good idea always to use the CLS statement to clear the output screen.
- Be careful not to use keywords as variable names.
- Check carefully to make sure that the variable name type matches the value being assigned to it.
- Only variable names can be to the left of the assignment operator.
- Remember to conclude programs with an END statement.
- Always enclose character strings in quotation marks.
- Double-check any mathematical expressions to make certain they will be evaluated correctly. Remember that the computer always follows the hierarchy of operations when evaluating arithmetic expressions.
- When in doubt, add parentheses to arithmetic expressions. Adding parentheses, even when they are not needed, can make the expressions easier for people to understand.

SUMMARY POINTS

- QBasic statements contain keywords, constants, variables, and operators.
- Constants are values that do not change during program execution. A valid numeric constant is any integer or real number. Character strings are alphanumeric data enclosed in quotation marks.

▌ Variable names are programmer-supplied names that identify storage locations where data values may be stored. Numeric variable names represent numbers. String variables contain alphanumeric values; their names are distinguished from numeric names by the $ symbol as the last character.

▌ CLS clears the output screen in preparation for output of the current program.

▌ Documentation provides information for humans; the computer ignores it. It can be indicated by the keyword REM or by placing a single quotation mark (') to the left of the remark.

▌ The assignment statement is used to assign values and results of arithmetic calculations to variables. The keyword LET is optional.

▌ Arithmetic expressions are evaluated according to the following hierarchy of operations: (1) operations in parentheses, (2) exponentiation, (3) multiplication and division, and (4) addition and subtraction. Multiple operations at the same level are evaluated left to right.

▌ The PRINT statement enables the user to see the results of a program. It can be used to print the values of variables, literals, arithmetic expressions, or a combination of these.

▌ The END statement causes program execution to stop.

▌ Statements can be executed in immediate mode by using the Immediate window. Program output is generated as soon as the Enter⏎ key is pressed.

▌ QBasic provides a variety of online help. An easy way of getting help concerning the syntax of a statement is to highlight the keyword and press F1. Instructions for the use of the highlighted keyword will be displayed. QBasic also has a smart editor that checks each statement for syntax errors as it is entered.

KEY TERMS

Alphanumeric data – 59
Assignment statement – 64
Character string constant – 59
Constant – 57
Descriptive variable name – 61
Documentation – 63
Hierarchy of operations – 66
Immediate mode – 71
Keyword – 62

REVIEW QUESTIONS

1. What is a constant? Give an example of each of the two types of constants.

2. What is a variable?

3. How does QBasic distinguish a string variable name from a numeric variable name?

4. Which of the following are illegal variable names and why?
    a. 7$
    b. DOWN.ONE
    c. SB
    d. Quantity@Cost
    e. $FACT
    f. DOWN ONE
    g. Country$
    h. Print

5. What is a keyword? What happens if you attempt to use a keyword as a variable name?

6. How are each of the following statements indicated in a flow-chart?
    a. LET
    b. END
    c. PRINT

7. List the arithmetic operators covered in this chapter. In what order are these operators evaluated?

8. Why is it important for programmers to document programs thoroughly?

9. Convert each of the following arithmetic expressions into a QBasic expression.
    a. $$\frac{9 \times B + 4^2}{5 + A}$$

b. $\dfrac{A+B+C+\left(D\times E\right)}{F}$

c. $\dfrac{X^2}{Y/Z+5}$

d. $A+3C-D^2$

e. $\left(A+4\right)\div6+\left(D\times E\right)$

f. $\dfrac{\left(X^2-4\right)+6}{\left(L\times M\right)N}$

10. What is the output of the following program segment?

```
PRINT "Marie Almato"
PRINT
PRINT
PRINT "Editor-in-Chief"
```

11. Write a valid assignment statement for each of the following problems:

   a. Add two numbers and store the result in a variable named Total.

   b. Store the character string BOOKS in a variable named Item$.

   c. Store the value 3 in a variable location.

   d. Copy the contents of variable Number1 to variable Number2.

Refer to the following program to answer Questions 12 through 14.

```
'***   Add tax onto an item.                        ***
'***   Major variables:                             ***
'***     Price              Price of the item       ***
'***     TaxRate            Percentage of tax        ***
'***     Tax                Amount of tax           ***
'***     Total              Price with tax added     ***
CLS
LET TaxRate = 0.5
LET Price = 115.89
LET Tax = Price * TaxRate
LET Total = Price + Tax
PRINT "Total Cost"
PRINT ----------
PRINT Total
END
```

12. Find and correct the single error in this program.

13. Draw a flowchart to represent this program.

14. Write an appropriate remark to precede the three PRINT statements.

15. In what types of situations might the Immediate window be useful? How can you move to the Immediate window from the View window?

DEBUGGING EXERCISES

Locate any errors in the following programs or program segments and debug them.

1.
```
*** This program prints the name and age of a person. ***
LET A = 21
LET Student$ = "STACY"
PRINT Student$, A
END
```

2.
```
REM *** Print 3 values. ***
LET A = 3 + 1
LET X + Y = B
LET N$ = 54
PRINT N$, A,B
```

3.
```
'*** Find the average of two numbers. ***
LET A = 12
LET 20 = B
PRINT A * B / 2
END
```

4.
```
'*** This program finds the cube of a number. ***
LET X = 5
LET C$ = X ^ 3
PRINT C$
END
```

5.
```
'*** Assign character strings to N$ and L$. ***
LET N$ = NANCY
LET L$ = LINDA
'*** PRINT N$ AND L$
PRINT N$, L$
END
```

Programming Problems

Level 1

1. Write a program to display the following:

First line:	Your name
Second line:	Your age
Third line:	Blank
Fourth line:	Your address

2. Write a program that will display your initials in large block letters. Use X's or other appropriate symbols to create the blocks.

3. Write a program to cube the digits 1 through 9, and display the results with appropriate labels.

4. Write a program that displays the U.S. flag on the monitor screen. Use asterisks and/or other special characters to display the design.

5. WHO Radio is giving away two concert tickets to the fourteenth person to call the station after a special bell is rung. Based on previous contests, you have determined it takes the disc jockey approximately 15 seconds to answer and tally each of the calls before the fourteenth. You also have determined that it takes ten seconds for the radio station's phone to begin ringing after you begin entering the phone number. Write a program that calculates how long you should wait after the bell rings before you begin placing the call. Remember, in order to win the prize, you must be the fourteenth caller.

6. The local sporting goods store has monthly specials on sporting equipment. The manager has asked you to write a program to calculate the total amount of the sales for the following items:

Item	Sales Price	Units Sold
Hockey stick	$9.95	12
Soccer ball	12.95	5
Baseball gloves	$17.95	20

    The program should display the total sales for each item and the total sales for all three items. Be sure to label these results.

Level 2

1. Iceland has approximately 242,000 people and 39,800 square miles. Write a program to determine the number of people per square mile. Display this result with an appropriate label.

2. Johnny Thurn wants to know how much it will cost for gas to drive his car to Miami, Florida, and back home. Miami is 2,340 miles from his home. His car gets 28 miles per gallon, and he estimates that gas will cost an average of $1.21 per gallon. Write a program that produces output similar to the following:

   ```
   DISTANCE              TOTAL COST
    XXXX                  XXX.XX
   ```

3. The Igloo Ice Cream Store would like you to write a program to calculate the quantities of ice cream, nuts, sauce, and cones that are used on a given day. The following is a list of items sold and the quantities of ingredients used in each item:

   Sundaes 8 oz. ice cream
   1 oz. nuts
   2 oz. sauce

   Cones 6 oz. ice cream
   1 cone

   Shakes 10 oz. ice cream
   1 oz. sauce

   On a given day, the store sold 104 sundaes, 94 shakes, and 96 cones. Output should be stated in terms of quarts (32 fluid ounces per quart) of ice cream and sauce, pounds of nuts, and units of cones. Label each item clearly.

4. Frank Mendelle is the father of two teenagers, and lately his telephone bills have been extremely high. To control this expense, he is charging each child $1.00 for every 10 minutes for long-distance calls and $0.25 for every 10 minutes for local calls. During the last month, the following calls were made:

   Tom One 20-minute long-distance call
   Four 30-minute long-distance calls
   Eight 10-minute local calls
   Eleven 20-minute local calls

   Jenny Three 10-minute long distance calls
   One 20-minute long-distance call
   Seven 10-minute local calls
   Three 20-minute local calls
   One 30-minute local call

Compute how much each child owes Frank, and the total for the two children. Assume the telephone bill totaled $73.62. How much of his own money does Frank owe the telephone company?

5. Tuition at Famous University is $4,000 per year, and room and board fees are $9,500 per year. Next fall, tuition is expected to rise by 15 percent; room and board fees by 10 percent. Karl Perry wants to know what the fees will be and whether he will have enough money to cover them. Karl earns approximately $14,000 a year working part time and summers and gets no additional help for his college expenses. Write a program for Karl. The output should have the following format:

```
Tuition   Room/Board   Total   Excess (or Shortage)
XXXX      XXXX         XXXXX   XXX
```

6. The Rainbow Paint Shop would like a program to determine the cost and number of gallons of paint needed to paint one room, based on the room's length, width, and height. Assume that each gallon of paint covers approximately 250 square feet and the cost is $15.95 a gallon. Write a program that assigns the dimensions of a room to variables and then displays the cost of the paint and gallons needed. Use any values you wish for the room's dimensions. All results should be appropriately labeled.

7. When swimming underwater, a person's eardrums experience a water pressure that varies directly with the depth at which he or she is swimming. When a person is at a depth of 10 feet, the pressure on the eardrums is approximately 4.3 pounds per square inch. Pressures of more than 65 pounds per square inch on the eardrums are unsafe for nonprofessional divers. Write a program that calculates how deep such a diver can safely swim. Display this depth with an appropriate label.

Challenge Problems

1. Linda Lomez is considering buying a new sports car. The price of the car is $22,000, to be paid for in five years at 15 percent interest. The down payment is 10 percent of the selling price. Write a program that will calculate her monthly car payments.

Processing requirement:

Calculate the monthly payment for an installment purchase, using the following formula:

$$P = I(T-D)\left[\frac{(1+I)^m}{(1+I)^m - 1}\right]$$

where

P is the monthly payment in dollars,
T is the purchase price in dollars,
D is the down payment in dollars,
I is the monthly interest rate (determine this value by dividing the annual rate by 12), and
M is the number of months.

Output:

Display the amount of the monthly payments on the monitor screen. Be sure that the amount of payment is appropriately labeled.

2. Doughnut Island, a small, uninhabited island in the South Pacific, has a large lagoon in its center and is shaped as shown here:

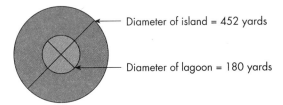

Diameter of island = 452 yards

Diameter of lagoon = 180 yards

The diameter of the island's outer edge is 452 yards; the lagoon's diameter is 180 yards. Write a program that calculates the number of square yards of dry land on the island.

Processing Requirement:

a. Use the formula for the area of a circle (πr^2) to calculate the area of the entire island.

b. Calculate the area of the lagoon.

c. Subtract the area of the lagoon from the total area.

Output:

Display the amount of dry land on the monitor screen. Be sure to label it appropriately.

Input and Output

Outline

Objectives

After studying this chapter, you will be able to:

- Use the INPUT statement to allow data to be entered during program execution.
- Create prompts that provide instructions for entering data.
- Write programs so that the output is formatted in a readable way.
- Use commas and semicolons to format program output.
- Use the TAB and SPC functions to format output.
- Discuss the rules for formatting attractive, readable output.
- Use the LOCATE statement to position output on the monitor screen.
- Use the LPRINT statement to send program output to the printer.
- Explain how the PRINT USING statement works and use it in programs when appropriate.
- Send program output to the printer.
- Use the Edit menu to move or copy portions of a program from one location to another.

INTRODUCTION

The first part of this chapter explains how data can be entered into a program. The INPUT statement asks the user to enter data while the program is running. The data entered is then assigned to variables.

Chapter 3 discussed displaying program results by using the PRINT statement. However, outputting the results of a program is only the beginning. To be truly useful to people, these results must be displayed on the monitor (or printed on paper) in a manner that makes them easy to read and understand, such as in a report or table. This is called *formatting* the output and it is discussed in the second half of this chapter.

STORING DATA IN VARIABLES

Entering Data During Execution

In many programs, the data changes each time the program is executed. For example, think of a program that calculates the gas mileage for your car. Each time you run this program, you will want to be able to enter new values for the number of miles traveled and the amount of gas used. If such a program used assignment statements to assign these values to variables, the statements would have to be rewritten every time you wanted to calculate your gas mileage. A more practical approach to this programming problem is to use the INPUT statement.

The INPUT statement allows the user to enter data at the keyboard while the program is executing. Its format is:

```
INPUT ["prompt";] variable1[, variable2]...
```

Take a minute to study the method used to present the format of this statement. This method will be used whenever a new statement is introduced in this text. Let's look at each part of this format description:

`INPUT`	The statement must begin with the keyword INPUT. (Any uppercase words in a format statement must be placed in the statement exactly as they appear in the format description.)
`["prompt";]`	A prompt is optional. (Anything placed in brackets is optional.) If a prompt is used, it is placed in quotes and may be followed by a semicolon.

variable1   The name of a variable must come next. (Because *variable1* is lowercase, it is used here to represent something else, in this case an actual variable name.)

[, variable2]...   Additional variables are optional. The dots indicate that as many variable names as are needed may be listed in this statement.

Therefore, by examining this format description, we can determine that the following are all valid INPUT statements:

```
INPUT Student$, GPA, Year
INPUT Address$
INPUT Total.Pay, Net.Pay, Tax
INPUT Month$, Day$, Year
```

The following INPUT statements are *invalid*:

```
INPUT CITY$ ST
```
(Variable names must be separated by commas)

```
TABLES, INPUT CHAIR
```
(INPUT must come first)

The programmer places INPUT statements in a program at the point at which user-entered data is needed, as determined by the logic of the program. When an INPUT statement is encountered while a program is running, the program temporarily stops executing and a question mark appears on the monitor screen. The user must then enter the required data and press [Enter ⏎]. After each value entered is stored in its corresponding variable, program execution continues to the next statement. Consider the following program:

```
CLS
INPUT City$
INPUT State$
INPUT People
PRINT City$, State$, People
END
```

A sample execution of this program is shown:

```
? Cedar Rapids
? Iowa
? 125000
Cedar Rapids   Iowa                125000
```

Let's trace through what happens as this program is executing. When QBasic executes the first INPUT statement, it prints a question mark and stops. The user enters the value *Cedar Rapids* and presses Enter ↵ . Execution continues and *Cedar Rapids* is assigned to the character string variable City$. Execution then proceeds to the second INPUT statement, and QBasic again prints a question mark and stops until the user enters a value and presses Enter ↵ . This process is repeated for the last INPUT statement in the program, which assigns the value *125000* to the numeric variable People. The values of these three variables are then displayed by the PRINT statement, and the program ends. Note that quotation marks are not needed when using the INPUT statement to enter character strings.

The three INPUT statements in the program could be combined into a single statement like this:

```
INPUT City$, State$, People
```

Because of the single INPUT statement, only one question mark appears on the screen when the program is run. In this case, the user enters the data in the following format:

```
? Cedar Rapids, Iowa, 125000
```

Note that when more than one data value is entered on a single line, the values must be separated by commas. After the user enters these values and presses Enter ↵ , *Cedar Rapids* is assigned to City$, *Iowa* to State$, and *125000* to People.

The user must enter the exact number of values needed by the INPUT statement. If fewer values are entered than there are variables in the INPUT statement, an error message is printed. For example, if the user enters only two values in response to the previous INPUT statement, the following appears on the screen:

```
? Cedar Rapids, Iowa
Redo from start
?
```

The system prompts the user to reenter the data because not enough data has been entered. The program will continue executing when the user enters the correct data. If too many values are entered, QBasic simply ignores the extra ones.

If the user attempts to enter a character string to a numeric variable, the "Redo from start" message again appears:

```
? Cedar Rapids, Iowa, USA
Redo from start
?
```

QBasic cannot assign the string USA to the numeric variable People, and therefore an error occurs.

QBasic can, however, assign a numeric value to a character string variable. The numeric value is treated as a string of characters and is stored in the corresponding string variable; therefore, ters and is stored in the corresponding string variable; therefore, it cannot be used in arithmetic operations.

The INPUT Statement

Flowchart Symbol	Statement Format
▱	INPUT ["prompt";] variable1[, variable2] ...

Displaying Prompts for the User

In the previous example, when the INPUT statement was executed, only a question mark (?) appeared on the monitor screen when it was time for the user to enter data. The user was not told what type of data or how many data items to enter. To avoid this difficulty, the programmer should include a **prompt** to tell the user what data needs to be entered. Good programming practice requires that prompts be included whenever the user must enter data. A prompt can consist of a PRINT statement, placed before the INPUT statement in the program, which tells the user the type and quantity of data to be entered.

Figure 4-1 shows a short program that calculates the volume of a box. The length, width, and height of the box are entered, and the volume is displayed. Examine the two lines containing prompts in Figure 4-1:

```
PRINT "Enter the length, width, and height of the box."
```

The next line contains an INPUT statement:

```
INPUT Length, Wdth, Height
```

After this INPUT statement is executed, the computer stops and waits for the user to enter the desired length, width, and height. Then execution continues, and the volume of the box is calculated and displayed on the screen.

The prompt can also be contained within the INPUT statement itself. If this were done for the program in Figure 4-1, the PRINT and INPUT statements could be replaced with a single statement:

```
INPUT "Enter the length, width, and height of the box"; Length, Wdth, Height
```

When this program is run, the question mark and the prompt appear on the same line:

```
Enter the length, width, and height of the box? 2.75,4.5,8.2
Volume of the box is  101.475
```

FIGURE 4-1

Program Demonstrating the INPUT Statement

```
' This program uses the INPUT statement to read the      ***
' dimensions of a box and calculate its volume.          ***
' Major variables:                                       ***
'      Length      Length of the box                     ***
'      Wdth        Width of the box                       ***
'      Height      Height of the box                      ***
'      Volume      Volume of the box                      ***

CLS
PRINT "Enter the length, width, and height of the box."
INPUT Length, Wdth, Height

Volume = Length * Wdth * Height
PRINT "Volume of the box is "; Volume

END


    Enter the length, width, and height of the box.
    ? 2.75,4.5,8.2
    Volume of the box is   101.475
```

Using this format simplifies the writing of the program and makes the logic easy to follow. This method of data entry, in which the user enters a response to a prompt displayed on the monitor screen, is called **inquiry-and-response** or **conversational mode**.

Inquiry-and-response mode
A mode of operation in which the system asks a question and the user types in a response.

You may prefer that a question mark not appear at the end of the prompt. You can instruct QBasic not to print the question mark by placing a comma, rather than a semicolon, at the end of the prompt. If the INPUT statement is written like this:

```
INPUT "Enter the length, width, and height of the box: ", Length, Wdth, Height
```

The prompt will look like this when it is executed:

```
Enter the length, width, and height of the box: 2.75,4.5,8.2
```

Spend a moment looking at the previous INPUT statement. Notice that a colon has been placed after the prompt and there is a space after the colon. If no space was left, the user's typing would appear immediately after the colon.

Learning Check 4-1

1. When data must be entered into a program while it is executing, a(n) _____ statement is used.

2. A(n) _____ is used to tell the user what kind of data to enter into a program.

3. True or False? If data will change each time a program is executed, it is better to use LET statements to assign values to variables than to use INPUT statements.

4. When several values are entered in response to an INPUT statement, each must be separated by a(n) _____.

FORMATTING RESULTS

Chapter 3 explained that the PRINT statement lets us display the results of processing on the monitor screen. When more than one item is to be printed on a line, a variety of methods can be used to control the spacing and format of the output.

Semicolon

The semicolon is often used to separate two or more variables in a single PRINT statement. It instructs QBasic to print the next item starting at the next available print position. The following example shows the result when two strings are separated by a semicolon in a PRINT statement.

```
PRINT "John"; "Drake"
```

```
JohnDrake
```

The first string is printed, and then the semicolon indicates that the next item should be printed in the next available print position, which is the next column.

To display these strings with a space between them, you can insert a blank into one of the strings:

```
PRINT "John"; " Drake"
```

```
John Drake
```

When a numeric value is encountered, a preceding space is printed if the number has no sign, such as 104 or 48. If the number has a sign, such as –176 or +32, no preceding space is printed because the sign is printed in that position. In either case, a space is left after the number for greater readability. Therefore, when numeric values are separated by a semicolon, the printed digits are not adjacent the way they are in character strings. The following example demonstrates this point:

```
PRINT 100; -200; 300
```

```
100 -200  300
```

Notice that the output shows only one space before –200. This is because the computer left a space after printing the number 100. But there are two spaces before 300; not only was a space left after –200 was printed, but a space was left for the sign (an assumed positive) of the number 300.

A semicolon appearing after the *last* item in a PRINT statement prevents the output of the next PRINT statement from starting on a new line. Instead, the next item printed will appear on the same line at the next available print position:

```
PRINT 3567;
PRINT "Neil";
PRINT " Patrick"
```

```
3567 Neil Patrick
```

When the second statement is encountered, *Neil* is printed at the first position after the blank that follows *3567*. The third statement prints a single blank space followed by the last name *Patrick*.

Print Zones

Each line of the monitor screen is divided into sections called *print zones*, which are 14 characters wide, with five zones per line. The beginning columns of the print zones are as follows:

Zone 1	Zone 2	Zone 3	Zone 4	Zone 5
Col 1	Col 15	Col 29	Col 43	Col 57

Commas, like semicolons, can be used within a PRINT statement to control the format of output. A comma indicates that the next item to be printed will start at the beginning of the next print zone. The following example shows how this works:

```
PRINT "SEE", "YOU", "LATER"
```

The first item in the PRINT statement is printed at the beginning of the line, which is the start of the first print zone. The comma between SEE and YOU causes QBasic to space over to the next print zone; then YOU is printed. The second comma directs

QBasic to space over to the next zone (Zone 3) and print LATER. The output is as follows:

```
SEE           YOU           LATER
```

If there are more items listed in a PRINT statement than there are print zones in a line, the print zones of the next line are also used, starting with the first zone. Notice the output of the following example:

```
CLS
PRINT "MALE", 19, "Junior", "CS", 18, 2.5
```

```
MALE          19            Junior      CS          18
2.5
```

Note that *2.5* starts in column 2 because it has no sign. If the value to be printed exceeds the width of the print zone, the entire value is printed, regardless of how many zones it occupies. A following comma causes printing to continue in the next print zone, as shown in the following example:

```
Spot$ = "Baghdad"
PRINT "Your next destination will be", Spot$
```

```
Your next destination will be          Baghdad
```

A print zone can be skipped by typing consecutive commas:

```
PRINT "Artist", , "Album"
```

Artist will be printed in Zone 1, the second zone will be blank, and *Album* will be printed in Zone 3:

```
Artist                      Album
```

If a comma appears after the last item in a PRINT statement, the output of the next PRINT statement encountered will begin at the next available print zone. Thus, the statements:

```
PRINT "Shicoff", 32,
PRINT "Male", "Tenor"
```

produce the following output:

```
Shicoff       32           Male        Tenor
```

TAB Function

We have seen that the semicolon causes data to be printed in the next position on the output line and that the comma causes data to be printed according to predefined print zones. Both formats are easy to use, and many reports can be formatted in this fashion. However, there are times when a report should be structured more precisely.

The TAB function allows output to be printed in any column in an output line, thus giving you greater flexibility in formatting. As with the comma and semicolon, one or more TAB functions can be used in a PRINT statement; for example:

```
PRINT TAB(10); "Hi there!"; TAB(25); "Bye!"
```

When this statement is executed, the literal *Hi there!* will be printed beginning in column 10. Then, starting in column 25, the literal *Bye!* is printed:

```
         Hi there!        Bye!
```

The expression in the TAB function may be a numeric constant, a numeric variable, or an arithmetic expression. When a TAB is encountered in a PRINT statement, QBasic spaces over to the column number indicated in the expression. The next variable or literal found in the PRINT statement is printed, starting in that column.

TAB can be used only to advance the print position from left to right; backspacing is not possible. Therefore, if more than one TAB appears in a single PRINT statement, the column number specified should increase from left to right. In the following example, TAB is used correctly:

```
PRINT TAB(5); 3; TAB(15); 4; TAB(25); 5
```

```
       3            4            5
```

However, the following occurs if the TABs do not have increasing values:

```
PRINT TAB(25); 5; TAB(15); 4; TAB(5); 3
```

```
                              5
                 4
       3
```

The program in Figure 4-2 prints a simple table by using the TAB function to place the printed values in columns.

FIGURE 4-2

FIGURE 4-2

Program Demonstrating the TAB Function

```
'***                          Inventory Report              ***

'*** This program displays an inventory report for an       ***
'*** ice cream store.                                       ***
'*** Major variables:                                       ***
'***     Item1$ - Item3$         Name of each item          ***
'***     Quantity1 - Quantity3   Quantity of each item      ***
'
'*** Get the data. ***
CLS
PRINT
INPUT "Enter item and quantity"; Item1$, Quantity1
INPUT "Enter item and quantity"; Item2$, Quantity2
INPUT "Enter item and quantity"; Item3$, Quantity3

'*** Display the report. ***
CLS
PRINT TAB(10); "Inventory Report"
PRINT
PRINT TAB(8); "Item"; TAB(25); "Gallons"
PRINT
PRINT TAB(5); Item1$; TAB(25); Quantity1
PRINT TAB(5); Item2$; TAB(25); Quantity2
PRINT TAB(5); Item3$; TAB(25); Quantity3

END
```

```
Enter item and quantity? Ice Cream,50
Enter item and quantity? Sauce,4
Enter item and quantity? Cherries,1.5
```

```
        Inventory Report

     Item              Gallons

  Ice Cream            50
  Sauce                4
  Cherries             1.5
```

SPC Function

The SPC (an abbreviation for SPACE) function is similar to TAB in that it is used to control output. However, instead of causing output to begin in a specified column, it determines how many spaces the output will be moved over before printing begins. For example,

```
PRINT "WORD"; SPC(10); "LETTER"
WORD          LETTER
```

When this statement is executed, *WORD* appears in columns 1 through 4; then the computer leaves ten blank spaces between the end of *WORD* and the beginning of *LETTER*. Therefore, *LETTER* is printed starting in column 15. Figure 4-3 shows how the program in Figure 4-2 could be rewritten using the SPC function. Notice that the values following SPC vary. This is because SPC causes output to "move over" a specified number of spaces rather than to begin in a specified column.

Learning Check 4-2

1. _____ moves the output over the specified number of columns whereas _____ begins the output in the stated column.

2. A semicolon between items in a PRINT statement tells the computer to skip to the next available _____ to print the next item.

3. The _____ is used in PRINT statements to skip to the beginning of the next print zone.

4. When a PRINT statement ends with a comma or semicolon, the next value output will always begin where?

    a. on the next line

    b. on the next page

    c. on the same line, if there is room

5. In what column will "Ice" begin when the following program segment is executed?
```
PRINT "Middleton"; SPC(10); "Ice Arena"
```

6. Which of the following statements will cause a print zone to be left completely blank?

    a. `PRINT "Yesterday","Today"`

    b. `PRINT "Yesterday",,"Today"`

    c. `PRINT "Yesterday";;"Today"`

FIGURE 4-3

Program Demonstrating the SPC Function

```
'***                        Inventory Report                ***

'*** This program displays an inventory report for an      ***
'*** ice cream store.                                      ***
'*** Major variables:                                      ***
'***     Item1$ - Item3$         Name of each item         ***
'***     Quantity1 - Quantity3   Quantity of each item     ***
'
' *** Get the data. ***
CLS
PRINT
INPUT "Enter item and quantity"; Item1$, Quantity1
INPUT "Enter item and quantity"; Item2$, Quantity2
INPUT "Enter item and quantity"; Item3$, Quantity3

'*** Display the report. ***
CLS
PRINT SPC(14); "Inventory Report"
PRINT
PRINT SPC(8); "Item"; SPC(24); "Gallons"
PRINT
PRINT SPC(5); Item1$; SPC(22); Quantity1
PRINT SPC(5); Item2$; SPC(26); Quantity2
PRINT SPC(5); Item3$; SPC(23); Quantity3

END
```

```
Enter item and quantity? Ice Cream,50
Enter item and quantity? Sauce,4
Enter item and quantity? Cherries,1.5
```

```
                Inventory Report

        Item                      Gallons

     Ice Cream                       50
     Sauce                            4
     Cherries                         1.5
```

LOCATE Statement

The LOCATE statement is used to position the cursor at a specified row and column. The following program segment causes the output to begin at row 10, column 15:

```
LOCATE 10, 15
PRINT "QBasic"
```

The row value must be from 1 through 25 and the column value from 1 through 80.

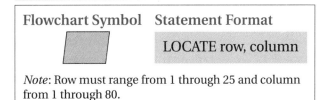

The LOCATE Statement

Flowchart Symbol	Statement Format
	LOCATE row, column

Note: Row must range from 1 through 25 and column from 1 through 80.

More Tips on Formatting Output

It is important to make your program output attractive and easy for the user to read and understand. There are a number of considerations:

1. Clear the screen before displaying the output.

2. Leave blank lines where appropriate to make output more readable.

3. Center headings where appropriate.

   When creating reports, you may wish to center headings above the body of the report. The following steps can be used to center headings:

1. Determine the width of the report (that is, count the number of spaces in the longest line.)

2. Count the number of characters in the heading.

3. Subtract the length of the heading from the entire width of the report.

4. Divide the results of Step 3 by 2.

5. Use this value in a TAB statement to indicate the column where the heading should start.

For example, to center the heading in the inventory report in Figure 4-2, perform the following steps:

1. Determine the width of the report, which is 35 spaces. (This is including four blank spaces on either side of the columns.)
2. Count the number of characters in the heading, which is 16.
3. Subtract 16 from 35, getting 19.
4. Dividing 19 by 2, getting 9.5.
5. The final statement is

```
PRINT TAB (9.5); "INVENTORY REPORT"
```

When a number with a fraction is used in a TAB statement, the number is rounded to the nearest integer. Therefore, in this example, the heading will start in column 10.

When formatting program output, it is often helpful to use a spacing chart, as shown in Figure 4-4. These charts consist of grids of rows and columns. A standard monitor has 80 columns and 25 rows when displaying text. The number of columns and rows you can output when using a printer will depend on the type of printer being used, the size of the type, and so forth.

FIGURE 4-4

Sample Spacing Chart

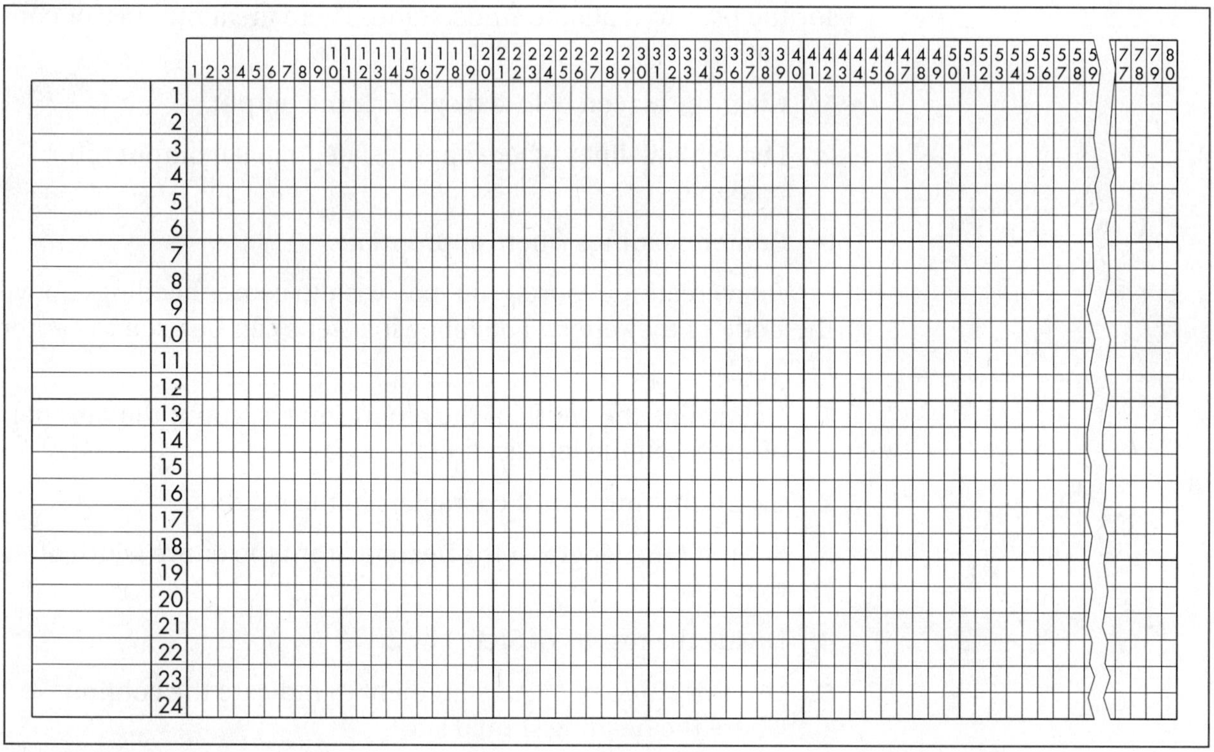

Sending Output to the Printer

There are times when you will want the results of a program printed on paper. You can instruct output to be sent to the printer by using the LPRINT statement. It is used the same way you use the PRINT statement. In this program segment,

```
INPUT "Enter employee's name and salary"; Nme$, Salary
LPRINT "Employee's name is "; Nme$
PRINT "Employee's salary is $"; Salary
```

the second statement is printed on paper whereas the last statement is displayed on the screen. Remember that in order to use the LPRINT statement, your computer must be attached to a printer and the printer must be turned on. If your computer is on a network, LPRINT may not work properly. Check with your instructor if you have problems using it.

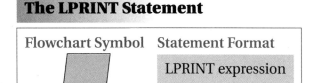

The LPRINT Statement

Flowchart Symbol	Statement Format
	LPRINT expression

The PRINT USING Statement

Another convenient feature for formatting output is the PRINT USING statement. It is especially useful when formatting reports or columns of numbers. Like any PRINT statement, the PRINT USING statement displays the values of expressions, such as variables and constants. However, the PRINT USING statement tells the system to display these values using a specified format. Special control characters are used to indicate the format (see Table 4-1). For example:

```
X = 15.679
PRINT USING "###.##"; X
```

The value of X (15.679) is displayed using the format ###.##. Each number symbol (#) represents a single digit. Because there are only two symbols to the right of the decimal point, the number 15.679 is rounded to two decimal places. When these statements are executed, the output is

```
15.68
```

TABLE 4-1 FORMAT CONTROL CHARACTERS FOR PRINT USING STATEMENT

Character	Explanation	Example
Format Characters for Numeric Values		
#	One symbol is used for each digit to be printed; blanks are added to the left of the number to fill the field.	####.##
$	Dollar sign; printed exactly as is.	$###.##
$$	Causes dollar sign to be printed immediately before first digit.	$$###.##
**	Leading asterisks; prints the asterisks in place of blanks.	**#.##
.	Decimal point; printed exactly as is.	###.##
,	Places a comma in front of each group of three digits to the left of the decimal point.	##,###.##
–	Placed at the end of a formatting field, to print a trailing minus sign for negative numbers only.	###.##–
Format Characters for Character Strings		
\ \	Reserves *n* + 2 spaces for a character string where n is the number of spaces between the slashes.	\ \
&	Causes the entire string to be printed, regardless of its length.	&

One blank space appears at the beginning of the line because the control characters allow for a maximum of three digits to the left of the decimal point.

As shown in the following example, PRINT USING statements are useful for aligning columns of numbers:

```
V1 = 4.562
PRINT USING "####.##"; V1
V2 = 78.907
PRINT USING "####.##"; V2
V3 = 0.03
PRINT USING "####.##"; V3
V4 = 1493
PRINT USING "####.##"; V4
```

```
   4.56
  78.91
   0.03
1493.00
```

The numbers are aligned at the decimal point. When formatting numbers, make certain that you use enough format characters for the largest possible number. For example, ###.## can hold any number up to 999.99.

The following statement places a dollar sign in front of a dollar amount:

```
PRINT USING "$####.##"; Amount
```

If the value of Amount is 3.56, the output is

```
$    3.56
```

Because this number has only one digit to the left of the decimal point, and the format allows for four digits, there are three blank spaces between the dollar sign and the first digit. If you want to have the dollar sign immediately in front of the first digit, you can make it "float" by using two dollar signs ($$):

```
PRINT USING "$$####.##"; Amount
```

Now the output is

```
$3.56
```

A second method of using the PRINT USING statement is to assign the format control characters to a string variable. This variable can then be referred to in the PRINT USING statement. The previous program segment could be rewritten using this method as follows:

```
Format$ = "####.##"
V1 = 4.562
PRINT USING Format$; V1
V2 = 78.907
PRINT USING Format$; V2
V3 = 0.03
PRINT USING Format$; V3
V4 = 1493.0
PRINT USING Format$; V4
```

The first statement assigns the format control characters to the string variable Format$. Format$ is then referenced in each PRINT USING statement. This method is particularly helpful when a number of output lines need to be formatted in the same way.

Another useful control character is the backslash (\), which is used to format character strings. The string will be left-justified in the output field. For example:

```
PRINT USING "\    \ $$####.##"; Item$, Cost
```

There are four spaces between the backslashes. The maximum size of the field is the number of spaces between the backslashes + 2. Therefore, the maximum number of characters that can be output in this field is 4 + 2, or 6. If the string has more than 6 characters it is *truncated* (cut off). If it is any shorter, it is left-justified in the field (that is, the first character of the string is output at the left margin). Any blank spaces are placed at the end of the string. Therefore, if Item$ equals *Bicycle*, and Cost equals *149.50*, the output is

```
Bicycl  $149.50
```

The last letter in *Bicycle* is truncated because the string has more than six characters. However, if the statement is rewritten with 10 spaces between the backslashes (allowing for a 12-character string):

```
PRINT USING "\            \ $$###.##"; Item$, Cost
```

then there will be five blank spaces after *Bicycle* because it is five spaces shorter than the maximum space allowed (12 – 7 = 5):

```
Bicycle        $149.50
```

To make numbers more readable, commas can be inserted between each group of three digits:

```
PRINT USING "##,###.##"; Number
```

If Number equals *1381.80*, the output is

```
1,381.80
```

However, if the number is only *381.80*, no comma is displayed:

```
381.80
```

A minus sign can be put at the end of the field; this sign will be displayed only if the number is negative. For example,

```
PRINT USING "###.##-"; Number
```

If the value of Number is *–174.527*, the following is output:

```
174.53-
```

Whereas if Number is *174.527*, the output is:

```
174.53
```

The LPRINT USING statement works the same as PRINT USING, except that output is sent to the printer.

PLACING MULTIPLE STATEMENTS ON A SINGLE PHYSICAL LINE

It is possible to place several statements on the same line by separating them with colons. For example, the following line actually contains three statements:

```
V1 = 10 : V2 = 20 : V3  = 30
```

However, this can make the logic of the program more difficult to follow. Therefore, it is recommended that you place each statement on a separate line.

THE EDIT MENU

The Edit menu allows portions of a program to be moved from one place to another. It also allows you to delete or copy program segments. You can access the Edit menu by using the mouse to position the cursor on the menu and clicking. You can then click on the option you want. Alternatively, the menu can be opened by pressing [Alt],[E]. The options, shown in Figure 4-5, then appear. Note that the menu lists shortcut keys for each command. For example, Cut can be executed by pressing [⇧ Shift][Del].

FIGURE 4-5

The Edit Menu

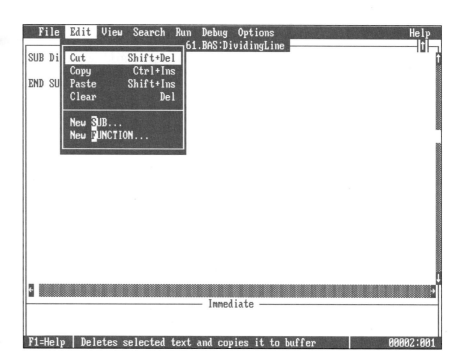

Selecting a Program Segment

Before a program segment can be cut, copied, or deleted, it must be selected. This process tells QBasic exactly what portion of the program you want to manipulate. One selection method is to position the cursor at the beginning of the segment, hold down ⇧Shift while pressing the right arrow key (→) until the entire section is highlighted. If you need to select a large segment, you can use the down arrow key (↓) to select entire lines at a time.

Alternatively, the mouse can be used to select a segment. Position the mouse pointer at the start of the segment and hold down the mouse button while moving the mouse to the end of the segment. Release the mouse button and the segment will be highlighted.

Cut

The Cut option deletes the selected portion of a program and places it on the Clipboard, which is a part of the computer's memory used to store items temporarily. After you have selected the segment to be cut, choose Cut from the Edit menu. The selected segment is deleted from the program and stored on the Clipboard. Remember from Chapter 1 that Ctrl Y is an efficient method of deleting a single line. This line is also placed on the Clipboard.

Copy

The Copy option works in the same manner as Cut, except the selected portion is not deleted. It remains in the program but is also on the Clipboard. Copy is useful when you want the same program segment to appear in two different places.

Paste

To insert the contents of the Clipboard at a new location, position the cursor where you want it and choose Paste from the Edit menu. Program segments can quickly and conveniently be moved to new locations using this method.

Clear

The Clear option is similar to Cut except that the selected portion is not placed on the Clipboard; it is deleted from the computer's memory and cannot be retrieved. Therefore, be very careful when using Clear. Note that after text is selected, the Del key can also be used to erase it.

Learning Check 4-3

1. The _____ statement causes output to be sent to the printer rather than the screen.

2. What is the purpose of the comma (,) control character in the PRINT USING statement?

3. In the LOCATE statement, the _____ is specified first and the _____ second.

4. How will the output of the following statements differ?

```
PRINT USING "$###.##";M
PRINT USING "$$###.##";M
```

5. When using PRINT USING, the format control characters are always placed in _____.

MASTERING PROGRAM DEVELOPMENT

Problem Definition

The Fremont Office Supply Company gives a year-end bonus to all salespeople having total sales of more than $500,000. The sales force is divided into three divisions. The sales manager would like a report showing the percentage of the salespeople in each division who earned the bonus. The program's input will consist of the total number of salespeople in each region and the number in each region who earned the bonus. The output, which should be printed on paper, should contain a report showing the total number of people in each region, the number earning the bonus, and the percentage earning the bonus. Figure 4-6 contains a spacing chart showing how the final report should appear.

Solution Design

The generation of this report can be divided into three subproblems:

1. Prompt user to enter needed data.
2. Calculate percentages of employees earning bonus.
3. Print the report.

Step 1 can be further divided into two steps:

1.A. Prompt user to enter number of salespeople in each region.
1.B. Prompt user to enter number of salespeople earning the bonus in each region.

FIGURE 4-6

Spacing Chart for Sales Bonus Report

		1	2	3	4	5	6	7	8	9	10	11	12	13	14	15	16	17	18	19	20	21	22	23	24	25	26	27	28	29	30	31	32	33	34	35	36	37	38	39	40	41	42	43	44	45	46	47	48	49	50	51	52	53	54	55
1														Fremont Office Supply Company																																									
2																	Bonus Report																																					
3																																																								
4																																																								
5			Region						Salespeople									Bonuses									Percentage																												
6																																																								
7			Region 1								XX									XX								XX.X%																												
8			Region 2								XX									XX								XX.X%																												
9			Region 3								XX									XX								XX.X%																												
10																																																								
11																																																								
12																																																								

Step 2 is fairly straightforward, requiring that the number earning the bonus be divided by the total number of salespeople. Step 3 can be divided as follows:

3.A. Center and print the report headings.

3.B. Print the column headings.

3.C. Print the information for each region.

The structure chart in Figure 4-7 shows how the program can be subdivided by task.

This program should use INPUT statements to allow the user to enter the needed data. The percentages can then be calculated. The most complex part is formatting the table. LPRINT statements will be used to print the table on paper. The major headings (name of company and report title) will be centered above the report body. Rows of hyphens will be used to divide the different parts of the report. The actual data will be properly formatted with LPRINT USING statements. The flowchart and pseudocode showing the logic of the solution are contained in Figure 4-8.

The Program

Figure 4-9 contains the program that prints the bonus report. It begins by prompting the user to enter the total number of salespeople and number receiving bonuses for each of the three regions. A LOCATE statement is used to specify that the first prompt will appear in the sixth row of the screen. Notice that the prompts in the INPUT statements are followed by commas, for example:

FIGURE 4-7

Structure Chart for Sales Bonus Report

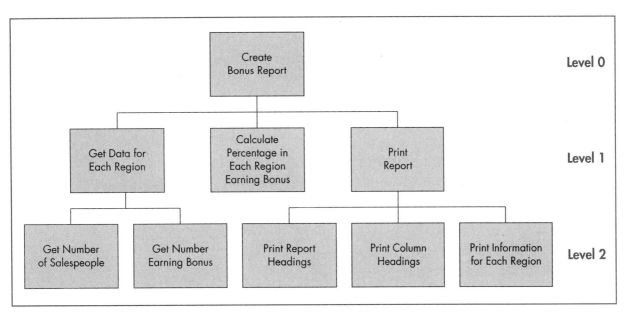

```
INPUT "Enter the number of salespeople in Region 1: ", Region1
```

Using a comma instead of a semicolon means that QBasic will *not* print a question mark at the end of the prompt. The next section of the program calculates the percentages of salespeople receiving bonuses.

Examine the portion of the program where the report is printed. TABs are used in the LPRINT statements to format the headings. However, the actual data is printing using LPRINT USING statements. This allows the numeric data to be properly formatted. Notice that each of the LPRINT USING statements uses the same formatting. This formatting is contained in the following statement:

```
Format$ = "  \          \          ##          ##          ##.#%"
```

The different sections of the report have been divided by rows of hyphens.

FIGURE 4-8

Flowchart and Pseudocode for Sales Bonus Report

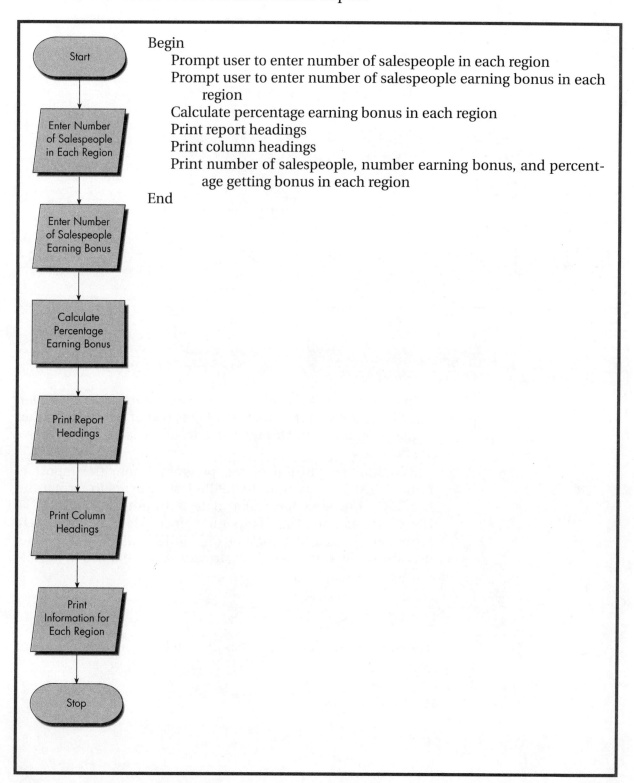

Begin
    Prompt user to enter number of salespeople in each region
    Prompt user to enter number of salespeople earning bonus in each
        region
    Calculate percentage earning bonus in each region
    Print report headings
    Print column headings
    Print number of salespeople, number earning bonus, and percent-
        age getting bonus in each region
End

FIGURE 4-9

Program to Create Sales Bonus Report

```
'***              Fremont Office Supply Bonus Report        ***

'*** This program prompts the user to enter the total number of   ***
'*** salespeople and the number earning bonuses for each sales    ***
'*** region. The percentage of salespeople earning bonuses is     ***
'*** calculated. The results are sent to the printer.             ***

'*** Major variables:                                             ***
'***    Region1 - Region3    Number of salespeople in each region ***
'***    Bonus1 - Bonus3      Number of bonuses in each region     ***
'***    Percent1 - Percent3  Percent earning bonuses in each region ***

'*** Get total number of salespeople in each region.***
CLS
LOCATE 6, 1
INPUT "Enter the number of salespeople in Region 1: ", Region1
INPUT "Enter the number of salespeople in Region 2: ", Region2
INPUT "Enter the number of salespeople in Region 3: ", Region3


'*** Get number earning bonuses in each region. ***
PRINT
INPUT "Enter the number earning bonuses in Region 1: ", Bonus1
INPUT "Enter the number earning bonuses in Region 2: ", Bonus2
INPUT "Enter the number earning bonuses in Region 3: ", Bonus3


'***Calculate percent in each region earning bonus. ***
Percent1 = Bonus1 / Region1 * 100
Percent2 = Bonus2 / Region2 * 100
Percent3 = Bonus3 / Region3 * 100


'*** Print the headings for bonus report. ***
LPRINT TAB(13); "Fremont Office Supply Company"
LPRINT TAB(21); "Bonus Report"
LPRINT ("-----------------------------------------------------------")
LPRINT


'*** Print the body of the report. ***
LPRINT TAB(4); "Region"; TAB(15); "Salespeople"; TAB(30); "Bonuses";
TAB(42); "Percentage"
LPRINT ("-----------------------------------------------------------")
Format$ = "  \      \         ##            ##          ##.#%"
```

Continued on next page

FIGURE 4-9

Continued

```
LPRINT USING Format$; "Region 1"; Region1; Bonus1; Percent1
LPRINT USING Format$; "Region 2"; Region2; Bonus2; Percent2
LPRINT USING Format$; "Region 3"; Region3; Bonus3; Percent3
LPRINT ("-------------------------------------------------------")

END
```

```
Enter the number of salespeople in Region 1: 15
Enter the number of salespeople in Region 2: 21
Enter the number of salespeople in Region 3: 10

Enter the number earning bonuses in Region 1: 7
Enter the number earning bonuses in Region 2: 11
Enter the number earning bonuses in Region 3: 4
```

```
                Fremont Office Supply Company
                        Bonus Report
    ---------------------------------------------------------

       Region      Salespeople     Bonuses      Percentage
    ---------------------------------------------------------

       Region 1         15            7            46.7%
       Region 2         21           11            52.4%
       Region 3         10            4            40.0%
    ---------------------------------------------------------
```

PROGRAMMING HINTS

- Wherever your program contains an INPUT statement, be sure to include a prompt telling the user the number of data values to be entered and the kind of values (numeric or string).

- Remember that if a PRINT statement contains more commas than there are print zones, the print zones of the next line will be used.

- Do not use commas in a TAB statement. TAB will work properly only if the items are separated by semicolons.

- Remember that the TAB function can be used only to advance the print position. Therefore, each column number should be larger than the previous one.

- When using LOCATE, be careful to place the row number first and the column number second.

- It is good programming practice to clear the output screen before displaying new output. It may be necessary to clear the screen several times during a program.

- Using a spacing chart can simplify creating attractive, easy-to-read reports.

- When using the PRINT USING statement, remember to place the control characters in quotation marks.

- If you want a control character, such as a dollar sign, to float, be sure to use two symbols in the PRINT USING statement.

- Remember that when you use the Clear option in the Edit menu, whatever is removed is permanently deleted; it cannot be pasted into another location.

SUMMARY POINTS

- The INPUT statement allows the user to enter data while the program is running. Therefore, the values used can change each time the program is run.

- When an INPUT statement is encountered during program execution, the program stops running until the user types the needed data and presses $\boxed{\text{Enter} \leftarrow}$. Each data value entered is then assigned to the corresponding variable in the INPUT statement.

- When data must be entered by the user, the program should display a prompt telling exactly what data is to be entered and its type.

■ Unlike the assignment statement, the INPUT statement is ideally suited for programs in which the data changes often.

■ When more than one item is to be printed on a single output line, the spacing can be controlled by the use of commas and semicolons.

■ The semicolon causes the next item output to be placed in the next available print position, whereas the comma causes output to begin in the next print zone.

■ TAB instructs output to begin at a specified column number.

■ SPC causes the specified number of spaces to be left between output items.

■ LOCATE allows the programmer to specify the row and column at which screen output should begin.

■ LPRINT allows you to send program output to the printer so that it can be printed on paper.

■ The PRINT USING statement can be used to format output in a variety of ways, such as aligning numbers at the decimal point.

■ The Edit menu provides an easy way of moving or copying program statements from one location to another.

KEY TERMS

Inquiry-and-response mode – 95
Prompt – 94

REVIEW QUESTIONS

1. What does QBasic do when it encounters an INPUT statement?

2. What is a prompt used for? What two things should a prompt tell the user?

3. What will be the output of the following program segment?
```
X$ = "MOUNTAIN"
Y$ = "MOLEHILL"
PRINT X$; Y$
```

4. In which zone will the word *Returns* appear if the following statement is executed?
```
PRINT "Happy",, "Returns"
```

5. When using commas, what happens if there are more items listed in a PRINT statement than there are print zones?

6. What will be the output of the following program segment (be sure to indicate blank spaces)?

```
W1$ = "LET'S"
W2$ = "SURF"
W3$ = "THE"
W4$ = "WEB"
PRINT W1$,, W2$
PRINT W3$; " "; W4$"!"
```

7. What will be the output of the following statement (be sure to indicate any blank spaces)?

```
PRINT TAB(20); 10; TAB(35); "TIME"; TAB(45); 8
```

8. How is the SPC function different from the TAB function?

9. Name an advantage that the LOCATE statement has over the TAB function.

10. List some of the rules for creating well-formatted output.

11. What are the advantages of creating a format statement that uses a PRINT USING statement?

12. Explain the purpose of three format control characters that can be used with the PRINT USING statement.

13. Explain the difference between the Cut and Clear options in the Edit menu.

14. How can you use the keyboard to select a portion of a program? How can you use the mouse?

15. Explain the steps necessary to move a statement from one location in a program to a different location.

DEBUGGING EXERCISES

Locate any errors in the following programs or program segments and debug them.

1.
```
'*** Prompt the user to enter a job title and yearly salary. ***
'*** Then calculate and display the person's monthly salary. ***
INPUT "Enter your job title" Job$
INPUT "Enter your yearly salary"; Salary
PRINT "Your monthly salary is"; 12 / Salary
```

2.
```
'*** Prompt the user to enter a country. ***
PRINT "Input the name of a country"; Country$
```

3.
```
'*** Display three headings on the screen, starting at ***
'*** columns 20, 50, and 80.                          ***
Heading1$ = "First Score"
Heading2$ = "Second Score"
Heading3$ = "Final Exam"
PRINT TAB(20); Heading1$; TAB(50); Heading2$; Tab(80); Heading3$
```

4.
```
'*** Start printing the heading in the 30th column, 10 row ***
'*** of the screen. ***
LOCATE 30, 10
PRINT "Freemont Office Supplies ***
PRINT "Third Quarter Report ***
```

5.
```
'*** Print a list of employees and salaries. ***
F$ = \           \   $$###,###.##
PRINT USING F$; "J. Jones"; 35,400
PRINT USING F$; "P. Peters"; 48,200
PRINT USING F$; "M. Martin"; 32,800
```

PROGRAMMING PROBLEMS

Level 1

1. Write a program segment that asks for the name of an object and its weight in pounds. The program should then calculate the weight in kilograms (1 pound = 0.453592 kilograms) and display the name, weight in pounds, and weight in kilograms, each in a different print zone.

2. Write a program that uses the INPUT statement to enable the user to enter any two numbers. The program should then display the sum, difference, product, and quotient of these two numbers. Your output should be similar to the following:

```
Enter any two numbers.
(Separate the numbers with a comma) XXX,XXX
XXX + XXX = XXXX
XXX - XXX = XXX
XXX * XXX = XXXXX
XXX / XXX = XXX
```

3. The Persian Pots Company is running a sale of 10 percent off all plants for Arbor Day. Write a program that prompts the user to enter the given data. Use the TAB function to create a table containing the sale prices of the following plants:

Plant	Regular Price
Swedish ivy	1.50
Boston fern	2.00
Poinsettia	5.40
Cactus	1.70

The columns in the table should be 20 spaces apart.

4. Alter Problem 3 so that it uses the SPC function instead of the TAB function. Place 20 spaces between the longest item in the first column and the second column.

5. Martha's Dance School charges a flat hourly rate of $6.75. Martha would like a program to determine the total amount owed by a particular student. The program should prompt the user to enter the number of hours of instruction. The total amount owed should then be displayed.

6. Chopped wood is traditionally measured in units called *cords*. One cord is equal to 128 cubic feet. Write a program that prompts the user to enter a given number of cords and then calculates and displays the number of cubic feet required to store this amount of wood.

Level 2

1. Write a program segment using the PRINT USING statement to duplicate the following table:

COMPANY	ASSETS	SALES	MARKET VALUE
Magma	7,074,365	15,537,788	1,227,533
Webscape	86,716,989	32,815,582	38,570,218
Superline	2,539,319	1,879,845	3,707,422

2. Write a program that calculates a baseball player's batting average. Use INPUT statements to allow the necessary data to be entered. The program should prompt the user to enter the times at bat, the number of walks, and the number of hits. Subtract the number of walks from the times at bat, and then divide the number of hits by this value to calculate the batting average. Output this batting average with an appropriate label.

3. Write a program to compute an individual's typing speed. The program should prompt the user to enter the following data: person's name, number of words typed, number of minutes spent typing, and the number of errors. The formula to be used for calculating words typed per minute is

$$\text{WPM} = \frac{\text{Number of words typed} - (\text{Number of errors} \times 5)}{\text{Number of minutes spent typing}}$$

4. You have joined a commercial online service. The service provides you with five free hours of basic service every month. Every additional hour of basic service costs $2.00. In addition, certain services are classified as premium services. The charge for premium services is $5.50/hour (there is no free time for premium services). Write a program that prompts the user to enter the number of basic hours and the number of premium hours used. The total amount owed should then be displayed.

5. Write a program to list several activities and the number of calories expended during 15, 30, and 60 minutes of each activity. Use the following data:

Activity	Calories Burned per Minute
Sleeping	2.3
Jogging	15.0
Sitting	1.7

Use assignment statement to assign the following data to variables. Then use commas to space the output so that it looks similar to the following:

```
Activity        15 Minutes      30 Minutes      60 Minutes
Sleeping        xxx.xx          xxx.xx          xxx.xx
Jogging         xxx.xx          xxx.xx          xxx.xx
Sitting         xxx.xx          xxx.xx          xxx.xx
```

6. Baymont High School needs a program to calculate the percentage of students absent in each of the grades 9 through 12. The input is the current date, the total number of students in each class, and the number of students absent in each class. The output should be an attendance report listing all of these values plus the percentage of students absent from each class. The report should be printed on paper and should be formatted as follows:

```
               Baymont High School
           Attendance Report for: 10/25/98

           Total Number        Number        Percentage
Grade      of Students         Absent          Absent
- - - - - - - - - - - - - - - - - - - - - - - - - - - - - - - -
  9            110               7             6.4%
 10            143              12             8.4%
 11            118               5             4.2%
 12            167              14             8.4%
```

Challenge Problems

1. Dr. Henry teaches astronomy at Northern University and needs your help in developing a program to calculate the weighted average of three test scores. The weights for each test are 0.3, 0.25, and 0.45.

   Input:

   Prompt user to enter each of the 3 scores.

   Processing requirements:

   a. Multiply each score by its weight.

   b. Determine the average of the three weighted scores.

   Output:

   The output should be displayed on the monitor screen and include both the weighted score for each test and the weighted average. The results should be formatted as follows:

```
                     Weighted Scores


  Test 1          Test 2          Test 3          Average
  - - - - - - - - - - - - - - - - - - - - - - - - - - - - -
    82              83              87              84.5
```

2. The Acme Concrete Company has bought a new computer and would like a program to calculate the cost of a given amount of concrete and the cost of the labor to pour it.

   Input:

   Prompt the user to enter the length, width, and depth of the concrete to be poured.

   Processing Requirements:

   a. Determine the charge for the concrete, based on a cost of $32 per cubic yard.

      Hint: there are 27 cubic feet in a cubic yard.

   b. Determine the labor charge based on a cost of $20 per cubic yard.

   c. Determine the total cost of the job.

   Output:

   The output should be displayed on the monitor screen and look similar to the following:

```
CONCRETE COSTS

IN FEET:                  CUBIC      CONCRETE AT    LABOR AT     TOTAL
LENGTH    WIDTH   DEPTH    YARDS      $32/CU. YD.    $20/CU. YD.  COST
  20       15      2       22.2        $711.11        $444.44     $1,155.56
```

Introduction to Control Structures

Outline

Objectives

After studying this chapter, you will be able to:

▐ Define the term *control structure*.

▐ Use block IF statements to create decision structures.

▐ Explain the difference between single-alternative and double-alternative decision structures.

▐ Explain the meaning of the relational operators and use relational operators in expressions.

▐ Define the term *collating sequence*.

▐ Use the SELECT CASE statement in programs.

▐ Write programs using menus.

▐ Use the logical operators NOT, AND, and OR to check for specific conditions.

INTRODUCTION

This chapter introduces the control structure, a powerful programming tool that will be used in virtually all programs from this point forward. **Control structures** allow the programmer to determine whether or not specific statements are executed. The two types of control structures are decision structures and loops. This chapter discusses decision structures. Loops are presented in Chapter 7. As explained in Chapter 2, decision structures are used to make comparisons. Two types of decision structures are presented here: the block IF statement and the SELECT CASE statement.

Control structure *A structure that allows the programmer to determine whether or not specific statements are executed.*

THE BLOCK IF STATEMENT

In real life, people are constantly making decisions. Many decisions are based on a particular situation. Past experiences are often taken into account. You start making decisions when you awake in the morning. Is there time for a shower and breakfast? If it's raining outside, what coat should you wear? If you do not feel well, should you stay in bed?

Computer programs also need to handle decisions. In QBasic, the block IF statement is useful in this type of situation. For example,

```
IF Age = 18 THEN
    PRINT "Be sure to register to vote."
END IF
```

The statement between the keywords THEN and END IF— PRINT "Be sure to register to vote."—is executed only if Age equals 18. Otherwise, no action is taken. Execution then continues to the next statement. Any number of statements can be included in the body of the block IF; this group of statements is referred to as a *statement block*. The following block IF has two statements in its statement block; both are executed if "Age = 18" is true:

```
IF Age = 18 THEN
    PRINT "Happy 18th Birthday!"
    PRINT "Be sure to register to vote."
END IF
```

Notice that the statement block has been indented. QBasic does not require this indentation; however, it greatly improves readability.

Relational Operators

Boolean expression *An expression that evaluates as either true or false.*

Relational operator *An operator used to compare two expressions.*

The execution of the block IF is controlled by a **Boolean** (or **logical**) **expression**, which is an expression that is either true or false. The block IF uses a **relational operator** to compare two expressions, determining whether the first expression is greater than, equal to, or less than the second one. Table 5-1 shows the relational operators used in QBasic. The values of the expressions can be either numeric or character strings. However, both expressions must be of the same type. Therefore, the following statement comparing two character strings is valid:

```
IF "Jon" < "Jonathan" THEN
    PRINT "This is a nickname."
END IF
```

However, the next statement is *invalid* because it attempts to compare a character string to a number:

```
IF "Jon" < 5 THEN
    PRINT "Wrong name."
END IF
```

Collating sequence *The internal ordering that the computer assigns to the characters it can recognize. This ordering allows the computer to make comparisons between different character values.*

It is easy to understand how the computer can compare numbers, but you may be wondering how it compares character strings. All computers assign an internal ordering to the set of characters they are able to recognize. This ordering is referred to as the computer's **collating sequence**. Many different collating sequences are available, depending on the type of computer being used. Most computers use ASCII (American Standard Code for Information Interchange). Table 5-2 shows the most commonly used ASCII codes; Appendix C contains a complete listing. From examining this table, you can determine that *A* is less than *D* because 65 is less than 68. In addition, notice that uppercase letters are always less than lowercase letters.

TABLE 5-1 RELATIONAL OPERATORS

Operator	Meaning	Example
<	Less than	1 < 10
<=	Less than or equal to	"Y" <= "Z"
>	Greater than	1043.4 > 1043
>=	Greater than or equal to	"SAMUEL" >= "SAM"
=	Equal to	10 + 4 = 14
<>	Not equal to	"Jones" <> "James"

TABLE 5-2 ASCII TABLE (PARTIAL)

ASCII Value	Character Displayed	ASCII Value	Character Displayed	ASCII Value	Character Displayed
32	SPC	64	@	96	`
33	!	65	A	97	a
34	"	65	B	98	b
35	#	67	C	99	c
36	$	68	D	100	d
37	%	69	E	101	e
38	&	70	F	102	f
39	'	71	G	103	g
40	(	72	H	104	h
41	)	73	I	105	i
42	*	74	J	106	j
43	+	75	K	107	k
44	,	76	L	108	l
45	-	77	M	109	m
46	.	78	N	110	n
47	/	79	O	111	o
48	0	80	P	112	p
49	1	81	Q	113	q
50	2	82	Ṙ	114	r
51	3	83	R	115	s
52	4	84	T	116	t
53	5	85	U	117	u
54	6	86	V	118	v
55	7	87	W	119	w
56	8	88	X	120	x
57	9	89	Y	121	y
58	:	90	Z	122	z
59	;	91	[	123	{
60	<	92	\	124	|
61	=	93	]	125	}
62	>	94	^	126	~
63	?	95	_	127	DELETE

When the computer compares two character strings, it compares each character, from left to right. The first character of one string is compared to the first character of the other string, then the second character of each string is compared, and so on until a character of one string is found to be less than the corresponding character of the other string (or the end of one string is reached). For example, the expression

```
"Chase" < "Chaz"
```

is true because S is less than Z.

When two strings of unequal length are compared, and all the letters of the shorter string match the corresponding letters of the longer string, the shorter string is considered to be less than the longer string. Thus, the following expression is true:

```
"HOPE" < "HOPEFUL"
```

Be aware that leading and trailing blanks are significant. Because a blank has a smaller ASCII value (32) than any letter or digit, the following expressions are true:

```
" CAT" < "CAT"      (Blank < C)
"PAY" < "PAY  "     (Second string has 5 characters)
```

Let's develop a program using the block IF statement. The local music store is having a sale. All CDs are marked down to $10. If you buy six or more CDs, you get 10 percent off the total price. The complete program is shown in Figure 5-1. The number of CDs being purchased is entered during execution. Next, the program determines the regular price (Number * 10). The following block IF charges the customer only 90 percent of the regular price if more than five CDs are being purchased:

```
IF Number >= 6 THEN
    Cost = Cost * .9
END IF
```

This statement could also be written

```
IF Number > 5 THEN
    Cost = Cost * .9
END IF
```

The end result will be the same either way.

FIGURE 5-1

Program Demonstrating Single-Alternative Block IF
Statement

```
'***                    CD Cost Program 1               ***

'*** This program determines the cost of CDs at $10 each.  ***
'*** If 6 or more are purchased, a 10% discount is given.  ***
'*** Major variables:                                      ***
'***      Number       Number of CDs                       ***
'***      Cost         Cost of CDs                          ***

CLS
INPUT "Enter the number of CDs: ", Number
Cost = Number * 10

'*** If more than 6 purchased, subtract 10% discount. ***
IF Number >= 6 THEN
    Cost = Cost * .9
END IF

Format$ = "\                    \ $$##.##"
PRINT USING Format$; "The cost of the CDs is"; Cost

END
```

```
Enter the number of CDs: 6
The cost of the CDs is  $54.00
```

Learning Check 5-1

1. _____ structures alter the order in which statements are executed.

2. The end of the block IF statement is marked by _____.

3. Must the expression in the block IF statement always evaluate as either true or false?

4. True or false? If the body of the block IF statement is not indented, QBasic will not be able to execute the statement.

5. _____ operators are used to compare values.

6. Use Table 5-2 to determine the ASCII code for the letter *M*.

The Double-Alternative Decision Structure

Single-alternative decision structure *A decision structure in which an action is taken if the specified condition is true. Otherwise, control continues to the next statement.*

Double-alternative decision structure *A decision structure in which one action is taken if the specified condition is true and another action if it is false.*

The block IF statements discussed so far have been **single-alternative decision structures**. They can be flowcharted as shown in Figure 5-2. In a single-alternative decision structure, an action is taken only if the condition is true; otherwise, execution simply continues to the next statement. In this section, we will discuss **double-alternative decision structures**, in which one action is taken if the condition is true and another if it is false. Figure 5-3 shows how the double-alternative decision structure can be flowcharted. An example follows of how a block IF statement can be used to write a double-alternative decision structure:

```
IF Speed <= 65 THEN
    PRINT "You are going"; Speed; "miles an hour."
ELSE
    PRINT "Pull over!"
    Tickets = Tickets + 1
END IF
```

The statement following the THEN is executed if the condition is true; otherwise, the condition following the ELSE is executed. Notice that in this example the THEN statement block contains a single statement whereas the ELSE statement block consists of two statements. Any number of statements can be contained in either block.

Let's alter the program in Figure 5-1 by changing the pricing arrangement used in the music store sale:

1 to 5 CDs $10.00 each
6 or more CDs $9.75 each

FIGURE 5-2

Flowchart of Single-Alternative Decision Structure

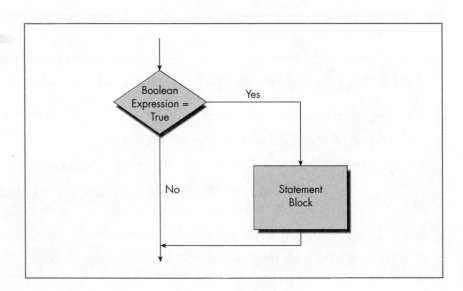

FIGURE 5-3

Flowchart of Double-
Alternative Decision
Structure

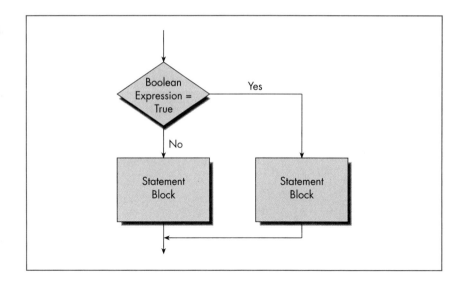

Figure 5-4 shows how this new program can be written. Examine the block IF statement:

```
IF Number >= 6 THEN
    Cost = Number * 9.75
ELSE
    Cost = Number * 10
END IF
```

If six or more CDs are purchased, the cost is $9.75 each; otherwise, the cost is $10 apiece.

The ELSEIF Clause

Inserting one or more ELSEIF clauses into a block IF statement allows the statement to check for one of several conditions. The following example shows how an appropriate message could be displayed depending on how many points a player earned on a video arcade game:

```
IF Score > 50000 THEN
    PRINT "Congratulations! You earned the rank of intergalactic warrior."
ELSEIF Score > 35000 THEN
    PRINT "You earned the rank of star fleet commander."
ELSEIF Score > 20000 THEN
    PRINT "You earned the rank of space ship captain."
ELSE
    PRINT "You earned the rank of space cadet."
END IF
```

Figure 5-4

Program Demonstrating Double-Alternative Block IF
Statement

```
'***                    CDs Cost Program 2                    ***

'*** This program determines the cost of CDs at $10 each      ***
'*** for 5 or fewer CDs. If 6 or more are purchased, they     ***
'*** are $9.75 each.                                          ***
'*** Major variables:                                         ***
'***      Number      Number of CDs                           ***
'***      Cost        Cost of CDs                             ***

CLS
INPUT "Enter the number of CDs: ", Number
IF Number >= 6 THEN
    Cost = Number * 9.75
ELSE
    Cost = Number * 10
END IF

Format$ = "\                       \ $$##.##"
PRINT USING Format$; "The cost of the CDs is"; Cost

END
```

```
Enter the number of CDs: 7
The cost of the CDs is  $68.25
```

The execution of the statement on the preceding page works as follows:

1. If Score is greater than 50000, "Congratulations! You earned the rank of intergalactic warrior." is displayed; otherwise, execution continues to the first ELSEIF.

2. If Score is greater than 35000, "You earned the rank of star fleet commander." is displayed; otherwise, execution continues to the second ELSEIF.

3. If Score is greater than 20000, "You earned the rank of space ship captain." is displayed; otherwise, execution continues to the ELSE clause.

4. If Score is equal to or less than 20000, "You earned the rank of space cadet." is displayed.

It is important to realize that when this program segment is executed, *something* will always happen. If none of the specified conditions is true, the ELSE clause will be executed.

Once again, let's alter the sale prices for the music store CDs:

1 to 5 CDs	$10.00
6 to 9 CDs	$9.75
10 or more CDs	$9.50

The following block IF statement is an efficient solution to this problem:

```
IF Number >= 10 THEN
    Cost = Number * 9.5
ELSEIF Number >= 6 THEN
    Cost = Number * 9.75
ELSE
    Cost = Number * 10
END IF
```

If Number is greater than or equal to 10, the statement following the THEN is executed, and if it is less than 10 but greater than or equal to 6, the statement in the ELSEIF clause is executed; otherwise, the statement in the ELSE clause is executed. Figure 5-5 contains the complete program.

The Block IF Statement

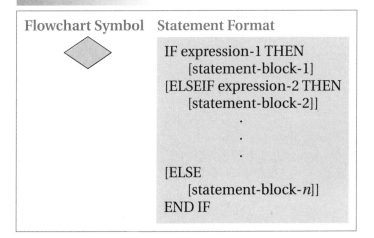

Flowchart Symbol	Statement Format

◇	IF expression-1 THEN
	    [statement-block-1]
	[ELSEIF expression-2 THEN
	    [statement-block-2]]
	.
	.
	.
	[ELSE
	    [statement-block-*n*]]
	END IF

Nesting Statements

It is possible to nest block IF statements by placing them inside one another. This allows the programmer to check for several conditions. Study the following example:

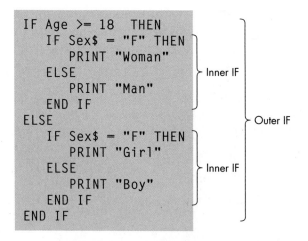

FIGURE 5-5

Program Demonstrating Nested Block IF

```
'***                    CDs Cost Program 3                    ***

'*** This program calculates the cost of CDs as follows:     ***
'***     5 or fewer     $10.00 each                          ***
'***     6 to 9         $9.75 each                           ***
'***     10 or more     $9.50 each                           ***
'*** Major variables:                                        ***
'***     Number        Number of CDs                         ***
'***     Cost          Cost of CDs                           ***

CLS
INPUT "Enter the number of CDs: ", Number
IF Number >= 10 THEN
   Cost = Number * 9.5
ELSEIF Number >= 6 THEN
   Cost = Number * 9.75
ELSE
   Cost = Number * 10
END IF

Format$ = "\                        \ $$##.##"
PRINT USING Format$; "The cost of the CDs is"; Cost

END


Enter the number of CDs: 9
The cost of the CDs is  $87.75
```

A number of actions are taken when these nested IF statements are executed. The first IF determines whether Age is greater than or equal to 18. If this condition is true, the first inner IF is executed and determines whether Sex$ equals F. If both conditions are true, *Woman* is displayed. If only the first one is true, *Man* is displayed. If the outer IF is false, we know that the person is under 18 and execution continues to the ELSE clause. The IF statement nested in the ELSE clause checks to see if Sex$ equals F; if true, *Girl* is output; otherwise, *Boy* is output. Nesting statements in this manner allows the program to check for several unrelated conditions, in this case age and sex.

Notice in the preceding nested IF statement that the two inner IFs are indented inside the outer IF. This indentation makes the logic easier to follow. Care must be taken when nesting decision structures. Each IF must have its own END IF.

INDENTING CONTROL STRUCTURES

Indenting block structures makes their logic easier to follow. An easy method is to use the tab key. Ordinarily, when [Tab↹] is pressed, the cursor will move eight spaces to the right; eight is the "default" value. However, programs are more readable if the indentation is smaller. Three or four spaces is common. Fortunately, the tab setting can be altered by following these steps:

1. Open the Options menu.

2. Choose Display.

3. Click on the number to the right of the Taps Stops option at the lower-right side of the screen.

4. Enter the new tab setting, for example, 3.

5. Click OK.

The new tab setting is now in effect. For example, if you entered 3, pressing [Tab↹] will now move the cursor three spaces to the right.

SINGLE-LINE IF STATEMENTS
QBasic also allows the programmer to use a single-line IF statement. For example:

```
IF X > 0 THEN PRINT "X is positive." ELSE IF X = 0
PRINT "X is zero." ELSE PRINT "X is negative."
```

If you have used older versions of BASIC, you are aware of this type of statement. The problem with the single-line IF statement is that it makes program logic difficult to follow. If a number of actions need to be taken, the statement becomes lengthy and each action must be separated from the next one by a colon. In addition, there is a maximum number of characters (usually 255) allowed in a statement, thereby limiting the number of actions. Because of the difficulties with the single-line IF statement, it is not used in this textbook. Using a block IF is preferable.

THE SELECT CASE STATEMENT

The SELECT CASE statement allows an action to be selected from a list of alternatives. For example:

```
INPUT "Enter your class (1 - 4)"; Class
SELECT CASE Class
    CASE 1
        PRINT "Freshman"
    CASE 2
        PRINT "Sophomore"
    CASE 3
        PRINT "Junior"
    CASE 4
        PRINT "Senior"
    CASE ELSE
        PRINT "Invalid class number."
END SELECT
```

Like the block IF, the SELECT CASE is a block structure; it begins with the keyword SELECT and ends with END SELECT. Each CASE clause includes a block of one or more statements that are to be executed if the stated variable equals the listed value. In this example, if Class equals 1, the statement following CASE 1 is executed; if Class equals 2, the statement following CASE 2 is executed; and so forth. If the value of Class is invalid (that is, outside the 1-4 range), the statement in the CASE ELSE clause is executed.

This CASE ELSE clause is optional, but is useful for checking for invalid input. Figure 5-6 shows a flowchart for the SELECT CASE statement.

The SELECT CASE Statement

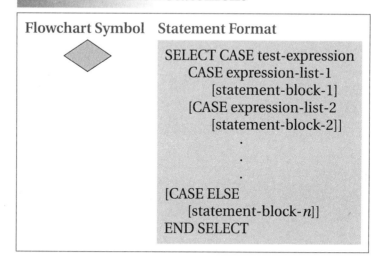

Flowchart Symbol	Statement Format

◇	SELECT CASE test-expression
	   CASE expression-list-1
	      [statement-block-1]
	     [CASE expression-list-2
	       [statement-block-2]]
	        .
	        .
	        .
	   [CASE ELSE
	     [statement-block-*n*]]
	END SELECT

FIGURE 5-6

Flowchart of SELECT CASE Statement

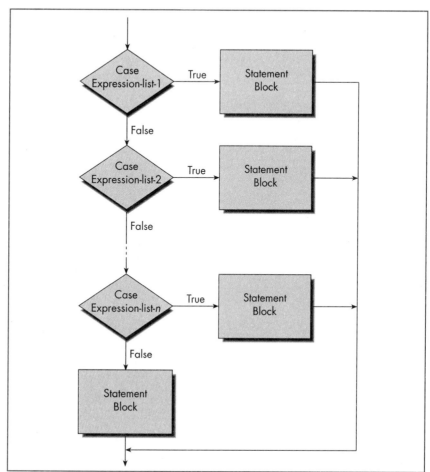

SELECT CASE may be used with character string data as shown in the following example:

```
SELECT CASE Language$
    CASE "Spanish"
        PRINT "Buenos dias."
    CASE "English"
        PRINT "Good day."
    CASE "French"
        PRINT "Bonjour."
    CASE "German"
        PRINT "Guten Tag."
    CASE ELSE
        PRINT "Invalid entry."
END SELECT
```

Several expressions can be listed in a single CASE clause. Figure 5-7 illustrates this option. This program determines the number of days in a particular month. Notice what happens if the user enters February. The user must indicate whether this is a leap year; a block IF statement then assigns the correct number of days.

The following program segment was previously written using a block IF statement. Notice how the SELECT CASE statement is used to check for a range of values:

```
SELECT CASE Score
    CASE IS > 50000
        PRINT "Congratulations! You earned the rank of intergalactic warrior."
    CASE 50000 TO 35001
        PRINT "You earned the rank of star fleet commander.
    CASE 35000 to 20001
        PRINT "You earned the rank of space ship captain."
    CASE IS <= 20000
        PRINT "You earned the rank of space cadet."
END SELECT
```

Examine the first expression:

```
CASE Score IS > 50000
```

If you do not insert IS when using a relational operator, QBasic will insert it automatically. When checking for ranges, the keyword TO is used:

```
CASE 50000 TO 35001
```

FIGURE 5-7

Program Demonstrating the SELECT CASE Statement

```
'***                    Days in Month                    ***

'*** This program prompts the user to enter the name of  ***
'*** a month and then displays the number of days        ***
'*** in that month.                                       ***
'*** Major variables:                                     ***
'***     Month$       Name of month                       ***
'***     Days         Number of days in month             ***
'***     LeapYear$    Leap year (Y/N)?                     ***

CLS
INPUT "Enter the month: ", Month$
PRINT

'*** Determine days in the month. ***
SELECT CASE Month$
   CASE "April", "June", "September", "November"
      Days = 30
   CASE "January", "March", "May", "July", "August", "October", "December"
      Days = 31
   CASE "February"
      '*** Check for leap year. ***
      INPUT "Is this a leap year (Y/N): ", LeapYear$
      IF LeapYear$ = "Y" THEN
         Days = 29
      ELSE
         Days = 28
      END IF
   CASE ELSE            'If invalid month,
      Days = 0          'assign zero to Days
END SELECT

'*** If valid month, display number of days; ***
'*** otherwise, display error message.       ***
PRINT
IF Days <> 0 THEN
   PRINT "There are"; Days; "days in "; Month$
ELSE
   PRINT "Invalid month."
END IF

END
```

Continued on next page

FIGURE 5-7

Continued

```
Enter the month: February

Is this a leap year (Y/N): N

There are 28 days in February
```

MENUS

Menu *A list of functions a program can perform; the user chooses the desired function from the list.*

A **menu** is a list of the functions that a program can perform. Just as a customer in a restaurant looks at the menu to choose a meal, so a program user looks at a menu displayed on the screen to choose a desired function. The user makes the selection by entering a code, usually a simple number or letter, at the keyboard, as in the following example:

```
Please enter one of the following numbers:
    1  -  Convert to Japanese Yen
    2  -  Convert to Egyptian Pounds
    3  -  Convert to Mexican Pesos
    4  -  Convert to German Marks
```

The SELECT CASE statement is often used in menu programs, such as the one shown in Figure 5-8 along with the menu it produces. After entering the number of dollars to be converted, the user enters a 1, 2, 3, or 4 to indicate the type of currency desired. SELECT CASE determines which calculation should be performed. If the user enters an invalid code, the CASE ELSE clause displays an error message.

FIGURE 5-8

Program Using a Menu to Perform Currency Conversion

```
'***                  Money Conversion Program             ***

'*** Converts U.S. dollars to a specific foreign currency.  ***

CLS
PRINT
INPUT "Enter number of dollars to be converted: ", Dollars
'*** Display the menu. ***
PRINT
PRINT "Please enter one of the following numbers:"
PRINT TAB(4); "1  -  Convert to Japanese Yen"
PRINT TAB(4); "2  -  Convert to Egyptian Pounds"
PRINT TAB(4); "3  -  Convert to Mexican Pesos"
PRINT TAB(4); "4  -  Convert to German Marks"
INPUT Code
PRINT


'*** Perform the conversion and display result. ***
SELECT CASE Code
   CASE 1
      Result = Dollars * 108
      PRINT "There are "; Result; "Japanese Yen in"; Dollars; "U.S. dollars."
   CASE 2
      Result = Dollars * 3.35
      PRINT "There are "; Result; "Egyptian Pounds in"; Dollars; "U.S. dollars."
   CASE 3
      Result = Dollars * 7.5
      PRINT "There are "; Result; "Mexican Pesos in"; Dollars; "U.S. dollars."
   CASE 4
      Result = Dollars * 1.5
      PRINT "There are "; Result; "German Marks in"; Dollars; "U.S. dollars."
      '*** If invalid code was entered, display error message. ***
   CASE ELSE
      PRINT
      PRINT "Invalid conversion number."
END SELECT


END
```

Continued on next page

FIGURE 5-8

Continued

```
Enter number of dollars to be converted: 100

Please enter one of the following numbers:
   1  -  Convert to Japanese Yen
   2  -  Convert to Egyptian Pounds
   3  -  Convert to Mexican Pesos
   4  -  Convert to German Marks
? 2

There are  335 Egyptian Pounds in 100 U.S. dollars
```

Learning Check 5-2

1. _____ allow the user to efficiently choose from a list of options.

2. In the SELECT CASE statement, the _____ will be executed if no value matches the expression in the SELECT clause.

3. The SELECT CASE statement ends with _____.

4. When one decision structure is placed inside another one, they are _____.

5. Given the following program segment, determine what the output will be for each of the values of *X* and *Y* in parts **a** through **c**.

```
IF X > Y THEN
   IF 10 * 2 = X THEN
      PRINT X
   ELSE
      PRINT Y
   END IF
ELSE
   PRINT X + Y
END IF
```

    a. X = 4, Y = 3

    b. X = 20, Y = 10

    c. X = 30, Y = 35

> ### No GOTOs
>
> If you have used other versions of BASIC, you may be wondering why we have not introduced the GOTO statement. This statement allows for program control to be transferred to a specified location. However, GOTOs (also called *unconditional branches*) make the logic of a program difficult to follow. A program that uses many GOTOs is referred to as *spaghetti code* because it is as hard to trace the program's execution as it is to follow the path of a single strand in a large plate full of spaghetti. GOTO statements also can lead to errors because it is easy to "GOTO" the wrong location. Because QBasic provides a wide variety of well-designed control statements, the GOTO is no longer needed. Therefore, it is not used in this textbook.

LOGICAL OPERATORS

Logical operator *An operator that acts on one or more conditions to produce a value of true or false.*

In addition to arithmetic operators (^, *, /, + , –) and relational operators (=, <>, <, >, <=, >=), there is a third group of operators, **logical** (or **Boolean**) **operators**. A logical operator acts on one or more expressions that evaluate as true or false to produce a statement with a true or false value. The three most commonly used logical operators are AND, OR, and NOT.

The operator AND combines two expressions and produces a value of true only when both of these conditions are true. For example, the combined logical expression

```
IF (Score > 75) AND (Time < 50) THEN
    PRINT Nme$
END IF
```

evaluates as true *only* if the expressions Score > 75 and Time < 50 are both true. If one or the other is false, the entire statement is false, and the THEN clause of the statement is ignored. The parentheses in the preceding statement are not necessary, but they improve the readability of the statement.

The logical operator OR also combines two expressions, but only one of the expressions needs to evaluate as true for the entire statement to be true. Thus, the statement

```
IF (Score > 75) OR (Time < 50) THEN
    PRINT Nme$
END IF
```

evaluates as true if either Score > 75 *or* Time < 50 is true, or if both are true. The entire condition is false only if the expressions Score > 75 and Time < 50 are both false.

The third logical operator, NOT, is a **unary operator** (an operator used with only one operand) and is used with a single expression. The effect of NOT is to reverse (negate) the logical value of the expression it precedes. For example, if the variable Pet$ has the value *Dog*, the condition of the following statement is false:

Unary operator *An operator, such as NOT, that is used with a single operand*

```
IF NOT (Pet$ = "Dog") THEN
     Felines = Felines + 1
END IF
```

Because the condition Pet$ = "Dog" evaluates as true, the NOT operator reverses this value to false, making the final result of the entire condition false. If Pet$ contained any other value, the condition Pet$ = "Dog" would evaluate as false, and the NOT would make the value of the entire condition true.

When a single statement contains more than one logical operator, the operators are evaluated in the following sequence:

1. NOT

2. AND

3. OR

Table 5-3 shows the hierarchy of operations for all operators used so far. For example, the following expression combines AND and OR:

```
IF (Pet$ = "Dog") OR (Age = 3) AND (Weight = 10)
```

Given the predefined order of evaluation, the following diagram shows how the preceding statement would be evaluated if Pet$ = "Do", Age = 3, and Weight = 9:

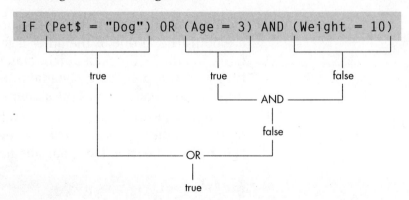

The AND portion of the expression is evaluated first. That result is then combined with the OR portion of the statement to deter-

TABLE 5-3 HIERARCHY OF OPERATIONS

1. Anything in parentheses
2. Exponentiation (^)
3. Unary plus or minus sign (a sign used alone in front of a number)
4. Multiplication and division (*, /)
5. Addition and subtraction (+, –)
6. Relational operators (=, <> , <, >, <=, >=)
7. NOT
8. AND
9. OR

mine the final value of the entire condition. In this case, the statement condition is true, so the THEN clause would be executed.

The precedence of logical operators (like that of arithmetic operators) can be altered by using parentheses. The previous example, using the same variable values as before, could be rewritten as

```
IF ((Pet$ = "Dog") OR (Age = 3)) AND (Weight = 10)
```

In this example, the OR portion of the expression is evaluated before the AND portion. Thus, the parentheses can change the final result of the evaluation, as shown in the following diagram. Compare the evaluation of this statement with the previous diagram.

```
IF ((Pet$ = "Dog") OR (Age = 3)) AND (Weight = 10)
```

Even if the desired order of evaluation is the same as the predefined order, it is good programming practice to use parentheses in order to make the logic clear.

NOT can also be combined with AND and OR in a single statement, as shown in the following diagram. Study the evaluation of the condition, making sure that you understand how the use of parentheses and the predefined order of operators have determined the final result of the evaluation. Assume that Pet$ = "Pig", Age = 6, and Weight = 1500.

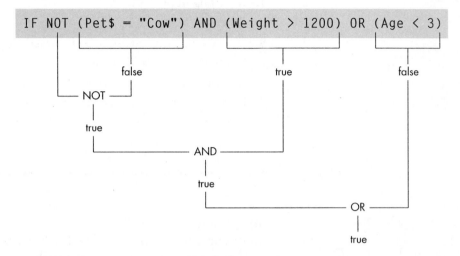

Table 5-4 shows additional examples of expressions using logical operators.

The program in Figure 5-9 demonstrates how logical operators can be used to determine if a triangle is scalene, isosceles, or equilateral. A triangle is scalene if it has no equal sides, isosceles if it has two equal sides, and equilateral if all three sides are equal. Notice that the first test uses the AND operator to determine if all three sides are equal:

```
IF (Side1 = Side2) AND (Side2 = Side3)
```

The test for an isosceles triangle is more complex and involves checking for three different conditions. Only one of these conditions needs to be true for the triangle to be isosceles; therefore, this test involves the OR operators. If none of these conditions is true, the triangle must be scalene. As shown by this program, logical operators allow for a variety of conditions to be checked efficiently and simultaneously.

TABLE 5-4 EXAMPLES OF CONDITIONS USING LOGICAL OPERATORS

Condition	Evaluates As
NOT (1 * 4 = 5)	True
(18 < 16) OR (7 + 2 = 9)	True
(18 < 16) AND (7 + 2 = 9)	False
((2 + 8) <= 11) AND (17 * 2 = 34)	True
NOT (12 > 8 - 2)	False

FIGURE 5-9

Program Demonstrating the Use of Logical Operators

```
'*** Determine the type of a triangle: scalene,    ***
'*** isosceles, or equilateral.                    ***
'*** Major variables:                              ***
'***     Side1 - Side3   Length of each side       ***

CLS
INPUT "Enter the three sides: ", Side1, Side2, Side3
PRINT "This triangle is ";
IF (Side1 = Side2) AND (Side2 = Side3) THEN
   PRINT "equilateral"
ELSEIF (Side1 = Side2) OR (Side2 = Side3) OR (Side1 = Side3) THEN
   PRINT "isosceles"
ELSE
   PRINT "scalene"
END IF

END
```

```
Enter the three sides: 8,6,8
This triangle is isosceles
```

Learning Check 5-3

1. The three logical operators, in their order of evaluation, are _____, _____, and _____.

2. The unary logical operator is _____.

3. With the _____ operator, only one of the conditions listed must evaluate as true for the entire expression to be true.

4. In the following condition, which of the logical operators is evaluated first?

```
(Letter <> "X") AND (NOT (Tree > 10))
```

5. Evaluate the following:

   a. ("Y" <> "X") AND (143.55 < 143.55)

   b. (0 = 14) OR (6 ^ 2 - 3 <= 4 / 2 + 8)

   c. NOT (6 = 7) AND (44 > 33)

MASTERING PROGRAM DEVELOPMENT

Problem Definition

The manager of Smiley's Pizza Parlor would like a program to calculate customers' bills. The program should be written so that the user enters the data at the keyboard and the total bill is then displayed. Pizza prices are based on the following:

Size:

6-inch personal	$4.00
10-inch small	$7.50
14-inch regular	$9.25
16-inch super	$12.90

Cost of toppings:

6-inch personal	50¢ each
10-inch small	60¢ each
14-inch regular	75¢ each
16-inch super	90¢ each

Extra cheese:

6- or 10-inch	$1.00 extra
14- or 16-inch	$2.00 extra

In addition, a 6 percent state sales tax must be added to the bill. Selections should be made from a menu similar to the following:

```
        Welcome to Smiley's

   1.   6-inch personal pizza
   2.   10-inch small pizza
   3.   14-inch regular pizza
   4.   16-inch super pizza

Enter the number (1 - 4) corresponding to the size pizza: 3
Enter the number of toppings: 2
Do you want extra cheese? Y


The total cost of your pizza is   $13.52
THANK YOU FOR COMING TO SMILEY'S
```

Solution Design

The needed input data is the size, number of toppings, and a variable indicating whether extra cheese is requested. The only output variable required is the bill.

Looking again at the problem, we see that the program must accomplish five basic jobs:

1. Display the menu.
2. Calculate the basic cost.
3. Add the cost of extra cheese, if requested.
4. Add 6 percent sales tax.
5. Display the total bill.

Step 2 consists of four substeps:

2.A. Prompt user to enter size.

2.B. Prompt user to enter number of toppings.

2.C. Calculate the basic cost, depending on size.

2.D. Add the cost of toppings.

The other steps are fairly straightforward and have not been sub-divided. The structure chart in Figure 5-10 shows the steps outlined above.

After the menu is displayed, INPUT statements can be used to obtain the size and number of toppings. Because both the cost and the topping price vary depending on the size, this is an ideal situation for the SELECT CASE statement. We can determine the basic cost and the price for the toppings in the SELECT CASE. Next the program must ask if extra cheese is desired. The user will need to enter yes or no (Y or N) at this prompt. Because there are only two different charges, a block IF is used here. Once the tax is added, we have the total bill. A PRINT USING statement will be

FIGURE 5-10

Structure Chart for Pizza Billing Problem

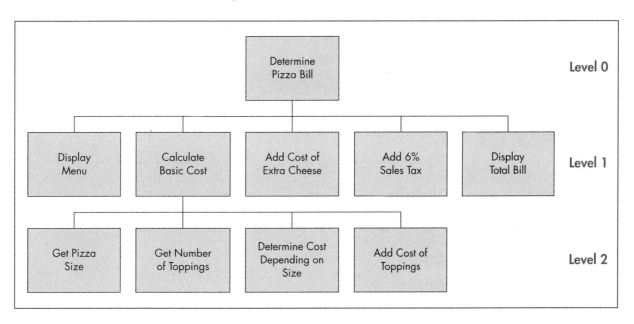

used to display this amount in monetary form. Figure 5-11 contains the flowchart and pseudocode for this solution.

The Program

Study the final program shown in Figure 5-12. First, the screen is cleared and the menu displayed. The user is prompted to enter the number (1–4) corresponding to the size of the pizza. Then, he or she is prompted to enter the number of toppings. Both the basic cost and the toppings cost are determined in the SELECT CASE. An INPUT statement prompts the user to enter Y or N for extra cheese. Examine the block IF statement that adds on the extra cheese cost. If the user enters any value other than a capital Y, the entire IF is skipped; otherwise, the inner IF determines the amount of the charge and adds it to Bill. The sales tax is added and a PRINT USING statement outputs the formatted value of Bill.

FIGURE 5-11

Flowchart and Pseudocode for Pizza Billing Program

```
Begin
    Display the pizza menu
    Prompt user to enter pizza size
    Prompt user to enter number of toppings
    Size = 6 inches, then bill = 4.00 + toppings x .50
    Size = 10 inches, then bill = 7.50 + toppings x .60
    Size = 14 inches, then bill = 9.25 + toppings x .75
    Size = 16 inches, then bill = 12.90 + toppings x .90
    Ask user if pizza should have extra cheese
    If extra cheese then
        IF size = 6 inches or size = 10 inches
            Add 1.00 to bill
        Else if size = 14 inches or size = 16 inches
            Add 2.00 to bill
        End if
    End if
Add 6% sales tax
Display total bill
Display thank-you message
End
```

FIGURE 5-11

Continued

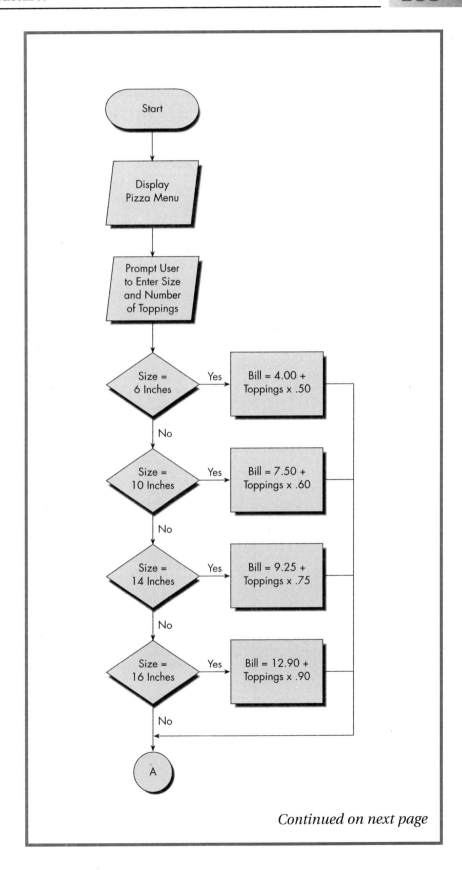

Continued on next page

FIGURE 5-11

Continued

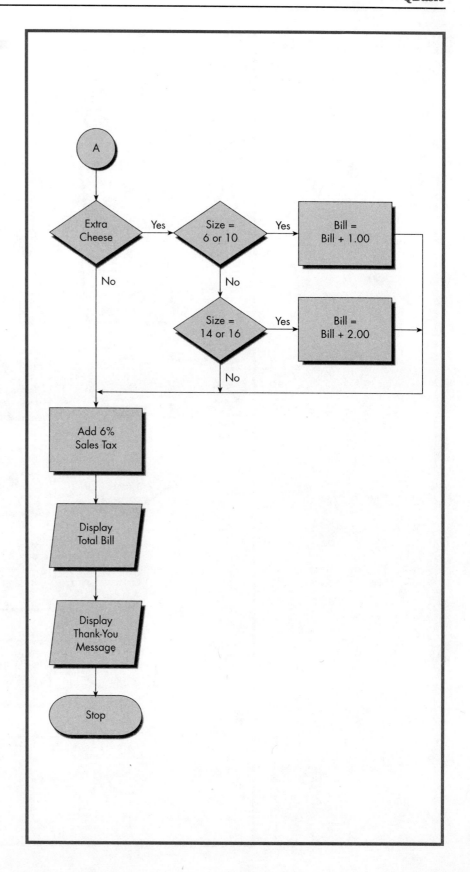

FIGURE 5-12

Program for Smiley's Pizza Parlor

```
'***              Smiley's Pizza Parlor              ***

'*** This program calculates the cost of a customer's ***
'*** pizza, based on the following:                  ***
'***     Sizes:                                      ***
'***          6 inch     $4.00                       ***
'***         10 inch     $7.50                       ***
'***         14 inch     $9.25                       ***
'***         16 inch     $12.90                      ***
'***     Toppings:                                   ***
'***          $.50/each for 6 inch                   ***
'***          $.60/each for 10 inch                  ***
'***          $.75/each for 14 inch                  ***
'***          $.90/each for 16 inch                  ***
'***     Extra cheese:                               ***
'***          $1.00 for 6 or 10 inch                 ***
'***          $2.00 for 14 or 16 inch                ***
'***     A 6% sales tax is added to the cost.  The   ***
'***     final bill is then displayed.               ***
'***     Major variables:                            ***
'***        Bill            Price of the pizza       ***
'***        Toppings        Number of toppings       ***
'***        Cheese$ (Y/N)   Extra cheese?            ***

'*** Display the menu. ***
CLS
PRINT
PRINT TAB(15); "Welcome to Smiley's"
PRINT
PRINT TAB(10); "1.    6-inch personal pizza"
PRINT TAB(10); "2.    10-inch small pizza"
PRINT TAB(10); "3.    14-inch regular pizza"
PRINT TAB(10); "4.    16-inch super pizza"
PRINT

'*** Prompt user to enter size and number of toppings. ***
INPUT "Enter the number (1 - 4) corresponding to the size pizza: ", Size
INPUT "Enter the number of toppings: ", Toppings

'*** Determine cost depending on size and number of toppings. ***
SELECT CASE Size
  CASE 1
    Bill = 4 + Toppings * .5
  CASE 2
    Bill = 7.5 + Toppings * .6
```

Continued on next page

FIGURE 5-12

Continued

```
   CASE 3
       Bill = 9.25 + Toppings * .75
   CASE 4
       Bill = 12.9 + Toppings * .9
END SELECT

'*** If extra cheese is desired, add cost. ***
INPUT "Do you want extra cheese"; Cheese$
IF Cheese$ = "Y" THEN
   IF Size = 1 OR Size = 2 THEN
       Bill = Bill + 1
   ELSEIF Size = 3 OR Size = 4 THEN
       Bill = Bill + 2
   END IF
END IF


'*** Add 6% tax. ***
Bill = Bill + Bill * .06

'*** Display total bill. ***
PRINT
PRINT
Format$ = "\                          \ $$##.##"
PRINT USING Format$; "The total cost of your pizza is"; Bill

PRINT "THANK YOU FOR COMING TO SMILEY'S"

END
```

FIGURE 5-12

Continued

```
                Welcome to Smiley's

        1.   6-inch personal pizza
        2.   10-inch small pizza
        3.   14-inch regular pizza
        4.   16-inch super pizza

Enter the number (1 - 4) corresponding to the size pizza: 4
Enter the number of toppings: 3
Do you want extra cheese? N


The total cost of your pizza is    $16.54
THANK YOU FOR COMING TO SMILEY'S
```

PROGRAMMING HINTS

- Remember that the first line of the block IF must end with the keyword THEN. The ELSE clause (and any ELSEIF clauses) must begin on separate lines.

- Check to make certain all block IF statements conclude with an END IF and all SELECT CASE statements conclude with an END SELECT. It is particularly easy to forget the ENDs when decision structures are nested.

- Always indent decision structures to improve readability.

- When using a block IF or a SELECT CASE statement to check for ranges of values, be very careful in specifying expressions. For example, the opposite of X > 10 is X <= 10, *not* X < 10.

- When using logical operators, it is best to insert parentheses, even when they are not required. Parentheses make the logic of the expression easier for humans to understand.

Summary Points

▌ Control structures allow the programmer to alter the normal flow of statement execution.

▌ Decision structures compare two values. What happens next depends on the result of the comparison. In QBasic the block IF can be used to implement a decision structure.

▌ In a single-alternative decision structure, an action is taken only if the expression is true, whereas in a double-alternative decision structure, one action is taken if it is true and a second action if it is false.

▌ Decision structures such as block IFs can be nested inside of one another. This allows for an action to be taken only if two or more expressions are true.

▌ The SELECT CASE statement allows for a program to select one action from a list of actions depending on the value of a stated expression.

▌ Menus display a list of program functions and allow the user to select from this list. A SELECT CASE statement can then be used to perform the selected function.

▌ The logical operators NOT, AND, and OR are used with Boolean expressions (expressions that always evaluate as true or false).

▌ NOT is a unary operator that negates a condition. An expression containing AND evaluates as true only when both conditions joined by the AND are true. A condition containing OR is true if at least one of the joined conditions is true.

Key Terms

Boolean expression – 128

Collating sequence – 128

Control structure – 127

Double-alternative decision structure – 132

Logical operator – 145

Menu – 142

Relational operator – 128

Single-alternative decision structure – 132

Unary operator – 146

REVIEW QUESTIONS

1. What is the purpose of control structures?

2. Create a flowchart for the following:

   If mid-term is tomorrow then
       Study until 2
   Else
       Go to movie

   What kind of decision structure is this?

3. Evaluate the following Boolean expressions:

   a. 6 * 3 <> 16
   b. 'b' < 'd'
   c. 102 − 77 = 77
   d. 476.32 <= 476.0

4. Refer to Figure 5-4. Write the block IF statement in this figure in an alternative way.

5. How is a single-alternative decision structure different from a double-alternative decision structure?

6. What is the purpose of indenting control structures such as the block IF?

7. What is a collating sequence?

8. Explain how the SELECT CASE statement works.

9. What is a nested IF? What is the advantage of using nested IFs?

10. Rewrite the following program segment so that it uses the SELECT CASE statement:

    ```
    IF Quantity > 1000 THEN
       Discount = 20
    ELSEIF Quantity > 800 THEN
       Discount = 17
    ELSEIF Quantity > 500 THEN
       Discount = 14
    ELSEIF Quantity > 300 THEN
       Discount = 10
    END IF
    ```

11. Given the following program segment, what will be printed for each of the values of Trout$ in parts **a** through **e**?

    ```
    SELECT CASE Trout$
        CASE "Brown"
            PRINT "The limit is 5."
        CASE "Rainbow"
    ```

```
      PRINT "The limit is 7."
   CASE "Lake", "Brook"
      PRINT "The limit is 10."
   CASE ELSE
      PRINT "Invalid type."
END SELECT
```

a. Brown

b. Lake

c. Native

d. Brook

e. Rainbow

12. Rewrite the program segment in Question 11 so that it uses a block IF instead of a SELECT CASE statement.

13. Rewrite the following block IF so that it uses a Boolean operator instead of nested IFs:

```
IF Rate = 8.00 THEN
   IF Time > 12 THEN
      Rate = 8 + 8 * .5
   END IF
END IF
```

14. Evaluate the following expressions, assuming that $X = 4$, $Y = 3$, and $Z = 12$:

a. `(Z - X ^ 3 > 12) AND (NOT (X > 3))`

b. `(X ^ Y * 2 < 20) OR ((X <= 12) AND (Z - Y <> 9))`

c. `NOT (Y - X > 0) AND (Y ^ Y >= 4)`

d. `NOT ((Z - 6 > X + Y) OR (Y + X < Z / 2))`

15. The Happy Hedonist Health Club has updated its requirements for membership. New members must be between the ages of 21 and 55, with an income of no less than $50,000 a year. The income requirement is waived if the prospective member has credit for at least $5,000 with a major credit agency. Write a condition expressing these requirements.

DEBUGGING EXERCISES

Locate any errors in the following programs or program segments and debug them.

```
1.
'*** If Number > 150, print Number. ***
INPUT "Enter number"; Number
IF Number THEN
   PRINT Number
END IF
```

```
2.
'*** Determine whether Number is positive, negative, ***
'*** or zero.                                         ***
INPUT "Enter number"; Number
IF Number > 0
   THEN PRINT "Number is positive."
ELSEIF Number = 0

   THEN PRINT "Number is zero."
ELSE
   PRINT "Number is negative."
END IF

3.
'*** Print an appropriate message, depending ***
'*** on distance of trip.                    ***
INPUT "How many miles is trip"; Miles
IF Miles < 250 THEN
   PRINT "Drive car."
ELSE
   PRINT "Take Piper Cub."
END

4.
'*** Determine the year a student will graduate. ***
INPUT "Enter your class: ", Class$
SELECT Class$
   CASE "Freshman"
      GraduationYear = 2000
   CASE "Sophomore"
      GraduationYear = 1990
   CASE "Junior"
      GraduationYear = 1998
   CASE "Senior"
      GraduationYear = 1997
   ELSE
      PRINT "Invalid class."
END SELECT
```

PROGRAMMING PROBLEMS

Level 1

1. Write a block IF statement that compares a variable Name$ to the character string "Norma Jean". If they are equal, the statement "The name is found." should be displayed.

2. Write a program to determine the cost of a movie ticket. The program should prompt the user to enter the customer's age.

If the age is 12 or less, the ticket is $2.50. If the age is 13 or more, the cost is $4.00. Display the cost of the ticket.

3. Write a program segment to determine whether a student is eligible for honors on graduation day. The student must be a senior with at least a 3.5 cumulative grade-point average out of a possible 4.0.

4. Write a program segment that displays the name of the teacher for a particular class when the name of that class is entered. Use a SELECT CASE statement and the following data:

American History	Ms. Mansfield
Calculus	Ms. Mueller
Spanish	Mr. Johnson
English	Mr. Ramirez
Algebra II	Mr. Ling

5. The local paint store wants a program that will conveniently list its best-selling shades of a given color. Use the SELECT CASE statement to display a menu listing the choices available. The data is as follows:

Color	Shade
Blue	Cote d'Azur, Periwinkle, Cornflower
Brown	Mocha, Sandalwood
Green	Kelly, Forest, Key Lime
Yellow	Mellow, Iced Lemon, True Saffron

The user should be prompted to enter one of the four colors; the corresponding shades then should be displayed.

Level 2

1. Write a program that uses logical operators to determine if an employee is eligible for a promotion. An employee is eligible if he or she has been with the company for more than four years and is employed as a salesperson. The program should prompt the user to enter the needed data and output an appropriate message.

2. Use a block IF statement to write a program segment that will read an outdoor temperature and output the sport appropriate for that temperature using the following guidelines:

Sport	Temperature
Swimming	Temp > 85
Tennis	70 < Temp <= 85
Golf	32 < Temp <= 70
Skiing	10 < Temp <= 32
Checkers	Temp <= 10

3. Mickey Koth likes to go on cross-country bike trips. She needs a way of calculating the amount of time a particular bike trip will take. The distance she can travel in an hour depends on the weather conditions. They are as follows:

   E — excellent conditions: 25 miles/hour
   G — good conditions: 20 miles/hour
   P — poor conditions: 13 miles/hour

   Write a program that will allow Mickey to enter the distance in miles and then enter a code (E, G, or P) for the weather conditions. The amount of time the trip will take her should then be output in hours.

4. The Wastenot Utility Company charges $20.00 a month for electricity. In addition, the customer is charged $0.03 for each kilowatt hour over 300. Write a program that prompts the user to enter the old and new electric meter readings. The number of kilowatt hours and the total bill should be displayed.

5. Patricia McGill's band charges its clients $78.00 an hour for every hour up to midnight and time-and-a-half for every hour after midnight. Write a program to allow Patricia to enter the client's name and the number of hours worked before and after midnight. The program should display the client's name and the amount owed.

Challenge Problems

1. The payroll manager of the Drake Encyclopedia Company is processing the monthly checks for its door-to-door sales agents. Write a program that will calculate the amount owed each agent.

   Input:

   a. Prompt user to enter each sales agent's name

   b. Prompt user to enter number of sets of encyclopedias sold

   Processing Requirements:

   a. Calculate the sales agent's basic commission based on the following:

   Encyclopedias sell for $200.00 a set.

   Agents receive a 35 percent commission on all sales.

   b. If an agent's commission is over $1,200.00, he or she receives a $50.00 bonus.

   c. If an agent's commission is under $500.00, a $25.00 processing fee is subtracted from the commission.

Output:

The agent's total sales and the amount of the commission should be displayed. The output should be formatted similar to the following:

```
            Drake Encyclopedia Company


        Name            Total Sales      Commission
    _____

        S. Petersen        $4,600.00       $1,660.00
```

2. Charlene's Car Rental Company needs a program to calculate customer bills.

Input:

The user should be prompted to enter the following:

Type of car (compact, full-size, minivan)

Number of days rented

Whether or not insurance is needed

Processing Requirements:

a. Calculate the cost per day based on the following:

   Compact—$25.00/day
   Full-size—$30.00/day
   Minivan—$40.00/day

b. Multiply the cost per day by the number of days.

c. Add on $6.00 a day if insurance is requested.

d. Add on a 6 percent sales tax.

Output:

The final bill should be formatted as follows and printed on paper:

```
        Charlene's Car Rental Company

        Daily Rate:        $40.00
        Insurance:         $30.00
        Subtotal:         $230.00


        Total:            $243.80
```

Modularizing Programs

Outline

Objectives

After studying this chapter, you will be able to:

- Write programs that use SUB procedures.
- Use structure charts to determine how programs should be modularized.
- Correctly pass arguments in CALL statements to their corresponding parameters in SUB procedures.
- Identify and explain the purpose of local variables.
- Pass arguments either by reference or by value.
- Use stubs in developing programs.
- List several advantages of modularizing programs.

INTRODUCTION

Chapter 2 explained that an important characteristic of structured programming is the division of programs into subprograms or modules. This modularization process, often referred to as the "divide and conquer" method, makes the job of writing a large program less formidable. If you think of tasks you have performed, you can readily see that this is true. For example, the job of cleaning a messy apartment might seem overwhelming if tackled all at once, but if it is divided into subtasks and these are dealt with one at a time, the job becomes more manageable. Your energy is focused on just one part rather than on the whole. This is definitely more efficient than randomly going around the apartment, haphazardly doing part of a job here and there. Also, by performing each subtask from start to finish in turn, the end result is likely to be more thorough.

This same analogy applies when using top-down design to develop programs. In cleaning an apartment, it is a good idea to make a list of the subtasks needed to complete the job. Everything necessary to complete the overall task should be included. Likewise, in top-down design, a structure chart is used to specify each subtask to be performed. It also indicates how each subtask is related to the others.

In QBasic, subprograms are referred to as *procedures*, of which there are two types: SUB procedures and FUNCTION procedures. SUB procedures are covered in this chapter and FUNCTION procedures are covered in Chapter 8. A **SUB procedure** is essentially a program within a program and is designed to perform a specific task needed by the program. An example might be a procedure that reads program data, or one that prints a table of results.

SUB procedure *A module that is essentially a program within a program. It starts with the keyword SUB and ends with END SUB.*

AN EXAMPLE OF A SIMPLE SUB PROCEDURE

The first line of a SUB procedure must contain the keyword SUB and the SUB procedure's name. The rules for naming procedures are the same as those for naming variables. For example,

```
SUB DividingLine
```

Next comes the SUB procedure's body, which can contain any number of statements. The keywords END SUB mark its end. Below is a short SUB procedure that prints a dividing line that can be used when displaying program output:

```
SUB DividingLine
   '*** This procedure prints blank lines and a row of      ***
   '*** hyphens to divide sections of the output.           ***

   PRINT
   PRINT "----------------------------------------------------"
   PRINT

END SUB
```

CALL statement *A statement that causes a SUB procedure to be executed.*

A **CALL statement** can be used to execute a SUB procedure. The programmer places it in the calling program at the point where the SUB procedure needs to be executed. Procedures can be called either from the main part of the program (called the *main module* or the *main body*) or from another procedure. The CALL statement contains the keyword CALL followed by the procedure's name. For example, when this statement is encountered,

```
CALL DividingLine
```

control is transferred to the SUB procedure DividingLine and the three statements contained in this procedure are executed. Finally, the END SUB statement returns control to the first statement following the CALL.

Figure 6-1 contains a complete program that uses SUB procedure DividingLine. This program determines a student's grade in a calculus class. The main module is listed first, followed by procedure DividingLine. When this program is executed, the scores on three tests are entered and assigned to variables, added, and then a SELECT CASE assigns the appropriate grade. Finally, the results are displayed. Notice that DividingLine is called two times: once to print a line before the results, and once afterward. Remember that an important advantage of using procedures is that they can be called any number of times, saving the programmer from having to rewrite the same code. In this example, the procedure is very short, but when procedures become lengthy, reusing them results in a distinct time savings.

The CALL Statement

Flowchart Symbol	Statement Format
	CALL name[(argument-list)]

Figure 6-1

Example of a Program That Uses a SUB Procedure

```
DECLARE SUB DividingLine ()

'***                     Calculus Grading Program          ***

'*** This program calculates a student's grade based on    ***
'*** 3 test scores.  Grades are assigned as follows:       ***
'***      A     > 88                                        ***
'***      B      77 - 88                                    ***
'***      C      68 - 76                                    ***
'***      D      55 - 67                                    ***
'***      F      < 55                                       ***
'*** Major variables:                                       ***
'***      Student$          Student's name                  ***
'***      Test1 - Test3     3 test scores                   ***
'***      Score             Total score on three tests      ***
'***      Grade$            Student's final grade           ***


'*** Prompt user to enter the needed data. ***
CLS
INPUT "Enter the student's name: ", Student$
INPUT "Enter the 3 test scores: ", Test1, Test2, Test3

'*** Find sum of 3 tests. ***
Score = Test1 + Test2 + Test3

'*** Determine the grade. ***
SELECT CASE Score
   CASE IS > 88
      Grade$ = "A"
   CASE 77 TO 88
      Grade$ = "B"
   CASE 68 TO 76
      Grade$ = "C"
   CASE 55 TO 67
      Grade$ = "D"
   CASE ELSE
      Grade$ = "F"
END SELECT

CLS
'*** Call procedure to display upper dividing line. ***
CALL DividingLine
```

Continued on next page

FIGURE 6-1

Continued

```
'*** Display results. ***
PRINT "Name"; TAB(20); "Test 1"; TAB(28); "Test 2"; TAB(36); "Test 3";
TAB(44); "Grade"
Format$ = "\               \      ##        ##        ##        &"
PRINT USING Format$; Student$; Test1; Test2; Test3; Grade$

'*** Call procedure to display lower dividing line. ***
CALL DividingLine

END

SUB DividingLine
    '*** This procedure prints blank lines and a row of      ***
    '*** hyphens to divide sections of the output.           ***

    PRINT
    PRINT "----------------------------------------------------"
    PRINT

END SUB
```

```
Enter the student's name: Peter LaSalle
Enter the 3 test scores: 23, 21, 47
```

```
----------------------------------------------------

Name                Test 1  Test 2  Test 3  Grade
Peter LaSalle          23      21      47      A

----------------------------------------------------
```

TYPING PROCEDURES

In QBasic, each module (including the main module) is entered in its own separate window. To begin entering a new procedure, simply enter its SUB statement anywhere in the calling module; a separate window immediately appears. For example, if you type in

```
SUB DividingLine
```

a new window opens, as shown in Figure 6-2. (Alternatively, choosing the New SUB option from the Edit menu causes QBasic to prompt you to enter the new procedure's name and then open a new window.)

Notice in Figure 6-2 that the name of this procedure is displayed in the title bar and that the SUB and END SUB statements are entered for you. All you need do is type in the procedure's body. If you wish to switch back to the window containing the main module, simply press F2. A dialog box similar to the one shown in Figure 6-3 appears. In this example, the program was named FIG61.BAS (if it has not yet been saved, the word *Untitled* appears here). Use the cursor movement arrows to highlight the module you want displayed, and press Enter←. The selected module appears. This feature of QBasic allows you to move quickly among program modules, a handy feature in longer programs with many procedures.

FIGURE 6-2

Each SUB procedure is entered in a separate window.

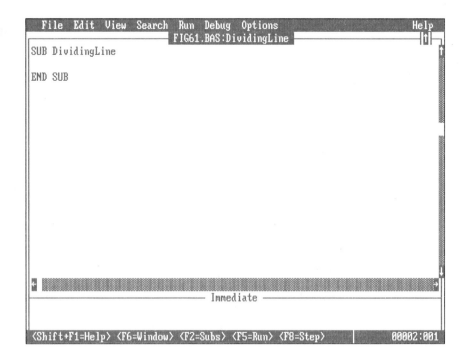

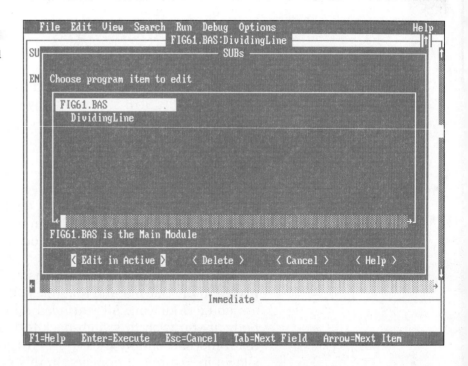

FIGURE 6-3

A dialog box allows you to switch from one program module to another.

If, after entering a procedure, you wish to delete it, press F2, highlight the name of the procedure, press Tab↹ until <Delete> is highlighted, and then press Enter↵ twice. The procedure will be removed.

To print a program, from the File menu, choose Print, make certain that Entire Program is chosen, and then press Enter↵. The program, plus all the procedures associated with it, will be sent to the printer.

Learning Check 6-1

1. The two types of QBasic procedures are _____ procedures and _____ procedures.

2. The _____ key is used to switch from one module of a program to another.

3. A(n) _____ statement can be used to cause a SUB procedure to be executed.

4. Each SUB procedure must end with _____.

5. To where does program control transfer after a procedure finishes executing?

PASSING ARGUMENTS TO SUB PROCEDURES

Let's alter the calculus grading program in Figure 6-1 so that the grade is assigned in a separate SUB procedure, which we name DetermineGrade. This procedure adds the three test scores and assigns the correct letter grade. Therefore, it needs to manipulate the following variables:

```
Test1, Test2, Test3
Grade$
Score
```

The main module needs to use the following variables:

```
Student$
Test1, Test2, Test3
Grade$
```

The variables used by both DetermineGrade and the main module must be transferred (or, as programmers say, *passed*) to the procedure. In this particular example, four variables (Test1, Test2, Test3, and Grade$) must be passed to DetermineGrade. This is done through the use of arguments and parameters. **Arguments** are expressions placed in parentheses in a CALL statement. For example:

> **Argument** *An expression placed in parentheses in a CALL statement. It allows values to be passed between a procedure and the calling module.*

```
CALL DetermineGrade(Test1, Test2, Test3, Grade$)
```

Parameters are "dummy" variables placed in parentheses after the SUB procedure's name:

> **Parameter** *A "dummy" variable placed in parentheses after a SUB procedure's name. When the procedure is called, the value of the corresponding argument is placed in the parameter.*

```
SUB DetermineGrade (Test1, Test2, Test3, Grade$)
```

When DetermineGrade is called, the value of each argument is assigned to its corresponding parameter. Because Grade$ does not yet have a value, the null (empty) string will be passed to the procedure; however, a value is assigned to it in the procedure and this value will be returned to the main module so that it can be printed at the end of the program. Figure 6-4 contains this complete program and Figure 6-5 (p. 177) shows how the values of the arguments are assigned to the parameters in the SUB statement.

There are two important rules to follow when passing arguments to a procedure:

1. The number of arguments and parameters must match.
2. The data type of each argument must match its corresponding parameter. For example, if the first argument is a string variable, the first parameter cannot be a numeric variable.

FIGURE 6-4

Example of Procedure That Uses Parameters

```
DECLARE SUB DetermineGrade (Test1!, Test2!, Test3!, Grade$)
DECLARE SUB DividingLine ()

'***                    Calculus Grading Program            ***

'*** This program calculates a student's grade based on    ***
'*** 3 test scores. Grades are assigned as follows:        ***
'***      A      > 88                                       ***
'***      B      77 - 88                                    ***
'***      C      68 - 76                                    ***
'***      D      55 - 67                                    ***
'***      F      < 55                                       ***
'*** Major variables:                                      ***
'***     Student$         Student's name                   ***
'***     Test1 - Test3    3 test scores                    ***
'***     Grade$           Student's final grade            ***

'*** Prompt user to enter the needed data. ***
CLS
INPUT "Enter the student's name: ", Student$
INPUT "Enter the 3 test scores: ", Test1, Test2, Test3

'*** Call procedure DetermineGrade to calculate student's grade. ***
CALL DetermineGrade(Test1, Test2, Test3, Grade$)


CLS
'*** Call procedure DividingLine to display upper dividing line. ***
CALL DividingLine


'*** Display results. ***
PRINT "Name"; TAB(20); "Test 1"; TAB(28); "Test 2"; TAB(36); "Test 3";
   TAB(44); "Grade"
Format$ = "\                \    ##       ##       ##       &"
PRINT USING Format$; Student$; Test1; Test2; Test3; Grade$

'*** Call procedure DividingLine to display lower dividing line. ***
CALL DividingLine


END
```

FIGURE 6-4

Continued

```
SUB DetermineGrade (Test1, Test2, Test3, Grade$)
    '*** This procedure determines the student's grade and ***
    '*** returns this value to the calling program.          ***


    '*** Find sum of 3 tests. ***
    Score = Test1 + Test2 + Test3


    '*** Determine the grade. ***
    SELECT CASE Score
        CASE IS > 88
            Grade$ = "A"
        CASE 77 TO 88
            Grade$ = "B"
        CASE 68 TO 76
            Grade$ = "C"
        CASE 55 TO 67
            Grade$ = "D"
        CASE ELSE
            Grade$ = "F"
    END SELECT

END SUB


SUB DividingLine
    '*** This procedure prints blank lines and a row of    ***
    '*** hyphens to divide sections of the output.         ***


    PRINT
    PRINT "-------------------------------------------------------"
    PRINT

END SUB
```

```
Enter the student's name: Peter LaSalle
Enter the 3 test scores: 23, 21, 47
```

Continued on next page

FIGURE 6-4

Continued

```
----------------------------------------------------

Name              Test 1  Test 2  Test 3  Grade
Peter LaSalle       23      21      47      A

----------------------------------------------------
```

It is important to realize, however, that the variable name of an argument need not match the name of the corresponding parameter. Therefore, the following statements could also be used to call procedure DetermineGrade:

```
CALL DetermineGrade(T1, T2, T3, G$)
CALL DetermineGrade(First, Second, Third, Letter$)
```

Each argument is substituted for the corresponding parameter on the basis of its position in the list, not on the basis of the variable name.

When you save a program on disk, QBasic automatically places DECLARE statements before the beginning of the main program. There is one DECLARE statement for each procedure. The next time you open the program, you will see them. For the program in Figure 6-4, these statements would look like this:

```
DECLARE SUB DetermineGrade (Test1!, Test2!, Test3!, Grade$)
DECLARE SUB DividingLine ()
```

These statements explain the SUB procedures and their parameters to the QBasic system. If you edit a parameter list by adding or deleting variables or changing ther order, you must also change the DECLARE statement so that it matches. Or, you can delete the DECLARE statement, forcing QBasic to create a new one. Note that QBasic has automatically inserted an exclamation point (!) at the end of each numeric variable name (for example, Test1!). The meanings of these symbols are explained in detail in Chapter 10. For now, you need not be concerned with them.

FIGURE 6-5

Substituting Arguments for Parameters

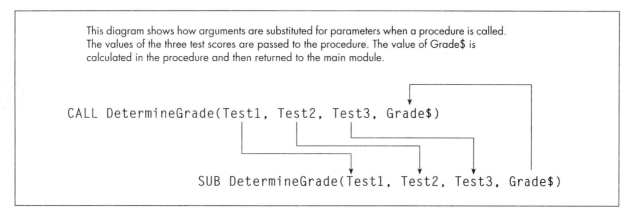

This diagram shows how arguments are substituted for parameters when a procedure is called. The values of the three test scores are passed to the procedure. The value of Grade$ is calculated in the procedure and then returned to the main module.

```
CALL DetermineGrade(Test1, Test2, Test3, Grade$)

      SUB DetermineGrade(Test1, Test2, Test3, Grade$)
```

LOCAL VARIABLES

Local variable *A variable that is used only in a specific procedure. A local variable exists only while the procedure is executing and its value is not known to the calling module.*

Refer back to Figure 6-4. There is one variable, Score, which is used in DetermineGrade but is not used elsewhere in the program. Score is referred to as a **local variable** because it is local to this procedure, it exists only while the procedure is executing, and its value is not known to the calling module, in this case, the main module. To prove this, let's assume we have inserted the following statement into the main module, immediately before the END statement:

```
PRINT Score
```

This statement will output a zero. Even though DetermineGrade assigned a value to Score, the main module does not "know" about this value. If we wanted to transfer this value back to the main module, we would have to alter the argument and parameter lists to include it:

```
CALL DetermineGrade(Test1, Test2, Test3, Grade$, Score)
SUB DetermineGrade (Test1, Test2, Test3, Grade$, Score)
```

However, in the example program in Figure 6-4, there is no need for the main module to use the variable Score; therefore, it is appropriate for it to be a local variable.

Local variables serve as a safeguard to protect a program from accidental changes to variable values. They are extremely useful in business programming where a team of programmers typically works on a single project. If two programmers use the same variable name in different procedures, any alterations to one variable

Side effect *An accidental change to a variable that is not local to the procedure.*

will not affect the other. Accidental changes to variables are referred to as **side effects** and can lead to errors that are very difficult to detect. The use of local variables goes a long way toward preventing side effects.

Using Structure Charts to Modularize Programs

So far in this textbook, we have been using structure charts to help analyze the steps necessary to solve programming problems. Structure charts enable us to visualize the specific tasks a program must perform to achieve the desired results. Because structure charts represent the subtasks involved in solving a problem, they are useful in developing modularized programs. Once the tasks of a program are identified, each task can be implemented in the program as a separate subroutine.

Consider again the Smiley's Pizza Parlor program that was developed at the end of Chapter 5 (Figure 5-12). Let's rewrite this program so that it is modularized. An easy way of doing this is to refer to the structure chart that was originally shown in Figure 5-10. A similar structure chart is shown in Figure 6-6. From this structure chart, we can see that the pizza program could be written using five procedures. However, the fourth module, which

FIGURE 6-6

Structure Chart for Pizza Program

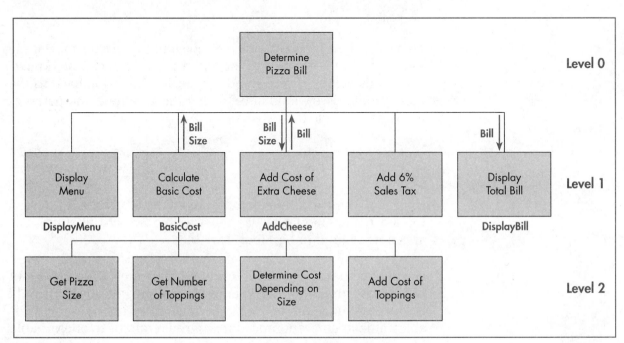

adds the sales tax, consists of only one statement. Therefore, we will place this statement in the main module, rather than in a procedure. Whether or not to leave small steps in the main module or write a separate procedure for them is up to the discretion of the programmer.

Refer again to the structure chart in Figure 6-6. Notice that below four of the modules is the name of the procedure that will correspond to that step. Also notice that each of these procedure's parameters are listed (DisplayMenu does not have any parameters). Pay particular attention to the arrows going to and from each module. An arrow going down to a module indicates the procedure will use the value of this parameter. An arrow pointing back to the calling module indicates that this parameter is used to return a value to the calling module. The final modularized program is shown in Figure 6-7 and has four procedures:

1. DisplayMenu displays the menu of pizza sizes.

2. BasicCost determines cost, depending on size and number of toppings.

3. AddCheese adds the cost of extra cheese, if requested.

4. DisplayBill displays the total amount owed.

Notice that when a program is printed, QBasic automatically places the program's procedures in alphabetical order, not in the order in which they are called.

One of the difficult tasks when modularizing programs is determining what arguments to pass between a procedure and the calling module. DisplayMenu requires no arguments: It simply displays a list of choices. However, both BasicCost and AddCheese calculate the bill; in both cases, the value of Bill must be returned to the main module. Procedure BasicCost must return the value of Size to the main module because its value is needed in procedure AddCheese. Notice that BasicCost has one local variable, Toppings, and AddCheese also has one local variable, Cheese$.

Figure 6-7 is an example of a **driver program** in which the main module consists primarily of calls to procedures that perform the actual processing. Driver programs simply "drive" the modules. When writing programs, attempt to place all but the simplest tasks in procedures, rather than in the driver program. This simplifies the program logic and makes later modification easier.

PASS BY REFERENCE VERSUS PASS BY VALUE

In the examples so far, we have been using **pass by reference**. In pass by reference, any changes made to variables in a procedure are returned to the calling program. For example, in Figure 6-4, the new value of Grade$ was returned to the main module so that

Driver program *A program whose primary purpose is to call procedures; the actual processing of the program is performed in the called procedures.*

Pass by reference *The process of passing an argument to a procedure parameter in which the address of the argument's storage location is passed to the parameter rather than the value itself.*

FIGURE 6-7

Modularized Pizza Program

```
DECLARE SUB DisplayMenu ()
DECLARE SUB BasicCost (Bill!, Size!)
DECLARE SUB AddCheese (Bill!, Size!)
DECLARE SUB DisplayBill (Bill!)

'***              Smiley's Pizza Parlor              ***

'*** This program calculates the cost of a customer's ***
'*** pizza, based on the following:                 ***
'***    Sizes:                                      ***
'***            6 inch      $4.00                    ***
'***           10 inch      $7.50                    ***
'***           14 inch      $9.25                    ***
'***           16 inch     $12.90                    ***
'***    Toppings:                                   ***
'***            $.50/each for 6 inch                ***
'***            $.60/each for 10 inch               ***
'***            $.75/each for 14 inch               ***
'***            $.90/each for 16 inch               ***
'***    Extra cheese:                               ***
'***            $1.00 for 6 or 10 inch              ***
'***            $2.00 for 14 or 16 inch             ***
'***    A 6% sales tax is added to the cost. The final ***
'***    bill is then displayed.                     ***
'***    Major variables:                            ***
'***       Bill            Price of the pizza       ***
'***       Size            Size of the pizza        ***

'*** Call procedure to display the menu. ***
CALL DisplayMenu

'*** Call procedure to calculate basic cost. ***
CALL BasicCost(Bill, Size)

'*** Call procedure to add cost of extra cheese. ***
CALL AddCheese(Bill, Size)

'*** Add 6% tax. ***
Bill = Bill + Bill * .06
```

FIGURE 6-7

Continued

```
'*** Call procedure to display total bill. ***
CALL DisplayBill(Bill)


END

SUB AddCheese (Bill, Size)
   '*** This procedure adds the cost of extra cheese, if ***
   '*** it is requested.                                ***

   INPUT "Do you want extra cheese"; Cheese$
   IF Cheese$ = "Y" THEN
      IF Size = 1 OR Size = 2 THEN
         Bill = Bill + 1
      ELSEIF Size = 3 OR Size = 4 THEN
         Bill = Bill + 2
      END IF
   END IF

END SUB


SUB BasicCost (Bill, Size)
   '*** This procedure calculates the basic cost of the pizza. ***

   '*** Prompt user to enter size and number of toppings. ***
   INPUT "Enter the number (1 - 4) corresponding to the size pizza: ", Size
   INPUT "Enter the number of toppings: ", Toppings

   '*** Determine cost depending on size and number of toppings. ***
   SELECT CASE Size
      CASE 1
         Bill = 4 + Toppings * .5
      CASE 2
         Bill = 7.5 + Toppings * .6
      CASE 3
         Bill = 9.25 + Toppings * .75
      CASE 4
         Bill = 12.9 + Toppings * .9
   END SELECT

END SUB
```

Continued on next page

FIGURE 6-7

Continued

```
SUB DisplayBill (Bill)
   '*** This procedure displays amount of the bill. ***

   PRINT
   PRINT
   Format$ = "\                                 \ $$##.##"
   PRINT USING Format$; "The total cost of your pizza is"; Bill
   PRINT "THANK YOU FOR COMING TO SMILEY'S"

END SUB
```

```
SUB DisplayMenu
   '*** This procedure displays Smiley's menu.    ***

   CLS
   PRINT
   PRINT TAB(15); "Welcome to Smiley's"
   PRINT
   PRINT TAB(10); "1.   6-inch personal pizza"
   PRINT TAB(10); "2.   10-inch small pizza"
   PRINT TAB(10); "3.   14-inch regular pizza"
   PRINT TAB(10); "4.   16-inch super pizza"
   PRINT

END SUB
```

```
            Welcome to Smiley's

     1.    6-inch personal pizza
     2.    10-inch small pizza
     3.    14-inch regular pizza
     4.    16-inch super pizza

Enter the number (1 - 4) corresponding to the size pizza: 4
Enter the number of toppings: 3
Do you want extra cheese? Y


The total cost of your pizza is    $18.66
THANK YOU FOR COMING TO SMILEY'S
```

it could be displayed (this process was illustrated in Figure 6-5). In pass by reference, the actual storage location of the argument is passed to the parameter. Any changes made to this storage location will be returned to the calling module.

Pass by value *The process of passing a copy of an argument's current value to a procedure parameter. Any changes to the parameter are not returned to the calling program.*

However, it is also possible to use **pass by value**, in which a copy of the argument's current value is passed to the procedure. Because only this copy is altered (assuming any changes are made), the value of the argument in the calling module remains unchanged. In our example programs so far, all arguments have been variable names. However, arguments can also be constants or expressions. For example,

```
CALL DetermineGrade(23, 22, 44, Grade$)
```

In this CALL statement, the actual test scores are sent to the procedure. Expressions can also be used as arguments:

```
CALL DetermineGrade(12 + 11, 11 * 2, 45 - 1, Grade$)
```

When constants or expressions are used as arguments, QBasic always uses pass by value because a value cannot be returned to a constant or an expression. Only a variable can be assigned a value. It is also possible to use variables when passing by value. An easy way of doing this is to place the variable names in parentheses, turning them into expressions rather than variables:

```
CALL DetermineGrade((Test1), (Test2), (Test3), Grade$)
```

Because procedure DetermineGrade does not alter the values of the three tests (their values were assigned in the main module), pass by value can be used here. Even if these values were altered in DetermineGrade, the new value would not be returned to the calling module. However, variable Grade$ must be passed by reference because the value assigned to Grade$ must be returned to the main module.

Figure 6-8 contains two programs. Notice the difference in the CALL statements and in the output. The first program passes Price1 by reference whereas the second program passes Price2 by value. Figure 6-9 illustrates what occurs in main memory when the arguments are passed to the procedures. Remember that even though constants and expressions can be used in CALL statements, the corresponding parameters in the SUB statement must be variables. This is because when the SUB procedure is called, values will be assigned to these variables.

FIGURE 6-8

Programs Demonstrating Pass by Reference and Pass by
Value

```
DECLARE SUB Discount1 (Price1!, Quantity1!)

'***                    Program Find Discount 1              ***

'*** This program subtracts 10% from the value of Price1 ***
'*** if Quantity1 is greater than 20. Because both          ***
'*** arguments are passed by reference, the new value of ***
'*** Price1 is passed back to the main module.              ***

CLS
Price1 = 14.95
Quantity1 = 22
CALL Discount1(Price1, Quantity1)
PRINT
PRINT
PRINT "The value of Price1 in the main module is"; Price1
PRINT "The value of Quantity1 in the main module is"; Quantity1

END

SUB Discount1 (Price1, Quantity1)

   '*** If quantity is greater than 20, give a 10% discount. ***

   IF Quantity1 > 20 THEN
       Price1 = (Price1 * Quantity1) - ((Price1 * Quantity1) * .1)
   END IF

   PRINT
   PRINT "The value of Price1 in procedure Discount1 is"; Price1
   PRINT "The value of Quantity1 in procedure Discount1 is"; Quantity1

END SUB
```

```
The value of Price1 in procedure Discount1 is 296.01
The value of Quantity1 in procedure Discount1 is 22


The value of Price1 in the main module is 296.01
The value of Quantity1 in the main module is 22
```

FIGURE 6-8

Continued

```
DECLARE SUB Discount2 (Price2!, Quantity2!)

'***                    Program Find Discount 2           ***

'*** This program subtracts 10% from the value of Price2 ***
'*** if Quantity2 is greater than 20.  Because Price2    ***
'*** is passed by value, the value assigned to it in     ***
'*** procedure Discount2 is not returned to the calling  ***
'*** program.                                            ***

CLS
Price2 = 14.95
Quantity2 = 22
CALL Discount2((Price2), Quantity2)

PRINT
PRINT
PRINT "The value of Price2 in the main module is"; Price2
PRINT "The value of Quantity2 in the main module is"; Quantity2

END

SUB Discount2 (Price2, Quantity2)

   '*** If quantity is greater than 20, give a 10% discount. ***

   IF Quantity2 > 20 THEN
      Price2 = (Price2 * Quantity2) - ((Price2 * Quantity2) * .1)
   END IF

   PRINT
   PRINT "The value of Price2 in procedure Discount2 is"; Price2
   PRINT "The value of Quantity2 in procedure Discount2 is"; Quantity2

END SUB
```

```
The value of Price2 in procedure Discount2 is 296.01
The value of Quantity2 in procedure Discount2 is 22


The value of Price2 in the main module is 14.95
The value of Quantity2 in the main module is 22
```

FIGURE 6-9

Comparison of Pass by Reference and Pass by Value

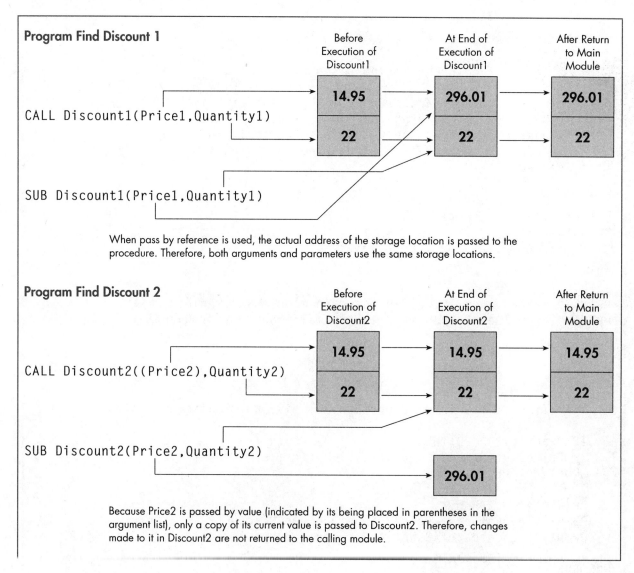

When pass by reference is used, the actual address of the storage location is passed to the procedure. Therefore, both arguments and parameters use the same storage locations.

Because Price2 is passed by value (indicated by its being placed in parentheses in the argument list), only a copy of its current value is passed to Discount2. Therefore, changes made to it in Discount2 are not returned to the calling module.

Many people find it useful to use a structured method of determining the value of variables at different points in a program. Figure 6-10 contains two tables that show the values of the different variables at different points during program execution. Creating these types of tables can be very helpful when tracing through a program.

FIGURE 6-10

Tracing the Values of Variables

Program Find Discount 1

Variable	Value Before Procedure Discount1 Is Called	Value at End of Procedure Discount1	Value at End of Main Program
Price1	14.95	296.01	296.01
Quantity1	22	22	22

Program Find Discount 2

Variable	Value Before Procedure Discount2 Is Called	Value at End of Procedure Discount2	Value at End of Main Program
Price2	14.95	296.01	14.95
Quantity2	22	22	22

Learning Check 6-2

1. When a SUB procedure is called, the _____ in the CALL statement are substituted for the _____ in the SUB statement.

2. True or False? The arguments in a CALL statement are always placed in double quotation marks.

3. When using pass by _____, any changes in a parameter are not returned to the calling module.

4. If you want a procedure to alter the value of a variable and return this new value to the calling module, you must use _____.

5. A variable used only in a procedure and whose value is unknown outside that procedure is a(n) _____ variable.

6. A(n) _____ is an accidental change to a variable.

ADVANTAGES OF USING PROCEDURES

We have previously mentioned several advantages associated with modularizing programs. These advantages are reviewed here to pull together a number of the concepts introduced in this chapter:

1. Each procedure may be called any number of times. If the same operation needs to be performed more than once, use of a procedure will shorten the program. In addition, procedures can be easily transferred to other programs where similar tasks are required.

2. Procedures help to break down a large, complex program into more manageable modules. This technique greatly simplifies the writing of the program. In addition, the logic of the final program is easier to follow.

3. Modularized programs are easier to debug than unmodularized programs. For example, if the program output is incorrectly formatted, the programmer need only modify the procedure performing this task. The rest of the program is left alone.

4. Because procedures use parameters to alter the values of variables, side effects can be prevented. This advantage is particularly important in programs written by a group of programmers. Two programmers can use an identical variable name in two different modules without interfering with one another.

5. It is easier to modify a modularized program. If a program needs to be altered at a later date, the programmer need modify only the procedure or procedures affected by the change.

USING STUBS TO IMPLEMENT PROGRAMS

So far, considerable attention has been given to top-down development of programming solutions. It is also possible to use a top-down method when entering a program into the computer. Indeed, when writing a large program that contains many modules, it is poor programming practice to enter the entire program at once. A far wiser approach is to start by entering the main module (the driver) and one or two procedures.

Procedures that are not yet implemented are called, but each of these nonimplemented procedures consists merely of a **stub**. A stub contains a SUB statement, an END SUB statement, and a PRINT statement indicating that the procedure was called but is not yet implemented. The idea is to enter the program in manageable segments, which can then be executed and tested for errors in an orderly way. As segments of the program are debugged and eventually work properly, more procedures can be added and tested gradually.

Let's see how the program in Figure 6-7 could have been developed using stubs. First, the main module must be entered. At this

Stub *A procedure that has yet to be written and consists only of SUB and END SUB statements and a PRINT statement indicating that the procedure was called. Stubs are used to test the calling program.*

point, we need to decide which subroutine to implement now and which ones to add later. A good decision would be to implement DisplayMenu first because it merely displays a listing. At this point, the program would appear similar to the one shown in Figure 6-11. We would then execute the program to determine whether the menu was properly formatted. Next, DisplayBill could be entered. Once again, the program should be run to make certain the output is properly displayed. Because no values have yet been assigned to the variables, numeric variables will output zeros and string variables will output the null string. The last step is to add the modules that prompt the user to enter data and calculate the bill. After these modules are entered, the program must be run and the output must be checked for accuracy. The use of stubs allows the programmer to enter and test programs in a structured manner.

As you are working on a program, you may wish to move statements from one module to another. You can use the options in the Edit menu to perform this task. For example, to move a group of statements, select the statements, choose Cut from the Edit menu, switch to the module where you want to move the statements, and choose Paste from the Edit menu. The statements will appear in the new location.

Learning Check 6-3

1. The options in the _____ menu allow you to efficiently move or copy portions of a program, such as moving several statements from one SUB procedure to another.

2. True or False? It is more difficult to modify a modularized program than one that has not been modularized.

3. _____ are used to indicate that a procedure has been called but is not yet implemented.

4. What is the maximum number of times a SUB procedure can be called in a program?

FIGURE 6-11

Program with Stubs

```
DECLARE SUB DisplayMenu ()
DECLARE SUB BasicCost (Bill!, Size!)
DECLARE SUB AddCheese (Bill!, Size!)
DECLARE SUB DisplayBill (Bill!)

'***              Smiley's Pizza Parlor              ***

'*** This program calculates the cost of a customer's ***
'*** pizza, based on the following:                   ***
'***     Sizes:                                       ***
'***            6 inch    $4.00                        ***
'***           10 inch    $7.50                        ***
'***           14 inch    $9.25                        ***
'***           16 inch    $12.90                       ***
'***     Toppings:                                    ***
'***            $.50/each for 6 inch                   ***
'***            $.60/each for 10 inch                  ***
'***            $.75/each for 14 inch                  ***
'***            $.90/each for 16 inch                  ***
'***     Extra cheese:                                ***
'***            $1.00 for 6 or 10 inch                 ***
'***            $2.00 for 14 or 16 inch                ***
'***     A 6% sales tax is added to the cost. The     ***
'***     final bill is then displayed.               ***
'***     Major variables:                             ***
'***        Bill              Price of the pizza       ***
'***        Size              Size of the pizza        ***

'*** Call procedure to display the menu. ***
CALL DisplayMenu


'*** Call procedure to calculate basic cost. ***
CALL BasicCost(Bill, Size)


'*** Call procedure to add cost of extra cheese. ***
CALL AddCheese(Bill, Size)


'*** Add 6% tax. ***
Bill = Bill + Bill * .06
```

FIGURE 6-11

Continued

```
'*** Call procedure to display total bill. ***
CALL DisplayBill(Bill)

END

SUB AddCheese (Bill, Size)

    PRINT "Procedure AddCheese called but not yet implemented."

END SUB


SUB BasicCost (Bill, Size)

    PRINT "Procedure BasicCost called but not yet implemented."

END SUB


SUB DisplayBill (Bill)

    PRINT "Procedure Displaybill call but not yet implemented."

END SUB


SUB DisplayMenu
    '*** This procedure displays Smiley's menu.    ***

    CLS
    PRINT
    PRINT TAB(15); "Welcome to Smiley's"
    PRINT
    PRINT TAB(10); "1.    6-inch personal pizza"
    PRINT TAB(10); "2.    10-inch small pizza"
    PRINT TAB(10); "3.    14-inch regular pizza"
    PRINT TAB(10); "4.    16-inch super pizza"
    PRINT

END SUB
```

MASTERING PROGRAM DEVELOPMENT

Problem Definition

The Bowsher Public Library would like a program to calculate patron fines for overdue books. Fines are determined as follows:

Paperbacks

Regular	$0.20/day with a maximum of $5.00
Best-sellers	$0.50/day with a maximum of $10.00
Magazines	$0.25/day with a maximum of $4.00
Hardcover books	$0.30/day with a maximum of $20.00

The program should prompt the user to enter the following information at the keyboard:

Patron's library card number (a four-digit number)

Patron's name

Patron's address

Type of book

Number of days overdue

A sample interactive session is shown below:

```
Enter the patron's card number: 2089
Enter the patron's name: Erica Robinson
Enter the patron's address: 204 Seaman
Enter the book's title: Digital Systems


1.  Paperback - Regular
2.  Paperback - Bestseller
3.  Magazine
4.  Hardcover book
Enter number corresponding to type of book (1-4): 4


Enter the number of days overdue: 11
```

The fine information should then be displayed:

```
                    Bowsher Library


Library Card Number:        2089
Patron's Name:              Erica Robinson
Address:                    204 Seaman
Item's title:               Digital Systems
Amount of fine:             $ 3.30
```

Solution Design

The tasks to be performed are as follows:

1. Get the data.

2. Calculate the fine.

3. Display the fine information.

The first step can be further divided:

1.A. Prompt user for card number.

1.B. Prompt user for patron's name.

1.C. Prompt user for patron's address.

1.D. Prompt user for item's title.

1.E. Display menu of book type categories and prompt user to enter category.

1.F. Prompt user for days overdue.

Step 2 can also be further divided:

2.A. Calculate fine for paperbacks.

2.B. Calculate fine for magazines.

2.C. Calculate fine for hardcover books.

Step 3 contains basic two substeps:

3.A. Display patron information.

3.B. Display title and fine.

Figure 6-12 contains the structure chart for this problem. Notice that the parameters have been listed for each module. Step 1 involves displaying a simple menu and prompting the user for input. These tasks can easily be performed in a SUB procedure. All of the data entered will need to be returned to the main module. Step 2 is somewhat more complex. A SUB procedure will be used to calculate the fine. It can then use a SELECT CASE to determine the amount of the fine, which must then be returned to the calling module. The last module is straightforward and can use PRINT USING statements to display the fine information.

The flowchart and pseudocode are contained in Figure 6-13. Take a moment to notice how flowcharts for modularized programs are written. Each module is represented by a separate flowchart. In addition, the ▢ symbol is used to represent a call to a module. The pseudocode is also divided by module.

FIGURE 6-12

Structure Chart for Library Fine Problem

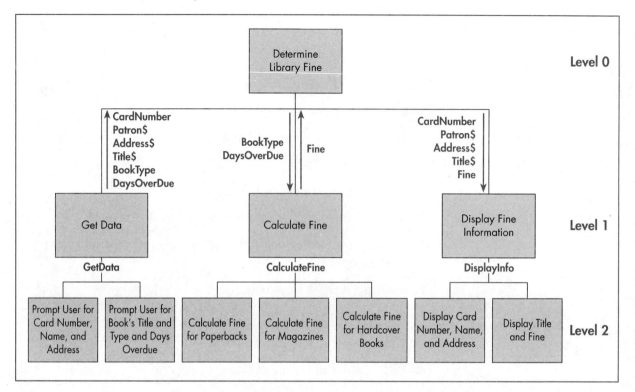

The Program

The program, with its three SUB procedures, is shown in Figure 6-14. This is an example of a driver program: The main module consists only of calls to procedures.

The SUB procedure GetData clears the screen, prompts the user to enter the needed values, and returns this data to the main module. CalculateFine is called next to determine the actual fine. Notice that four assignment statements are used to assign the fine rates to variables Rate1 through Rate4. This makes the program easier to modify: If the fine rates should change at a later date, only these four assignment statements will need to be altered. Remember that each category has a maximum fine. Block IF statements are used within the SELECT CASE statement to check for these maximums. Last, DisplayInfo clears the screen and outputs the results. Three different formats are used with PRINT USING: Format1$ through Format3$. Format1$ is used for string output, Format2$ for numeric output formatted as an integer (it is used for the card number), and Format3$ for monetary output (it is used to display the amount of the fine).

FIGURE 6-13

Flowchart and
Pseudocode for Library
Fine Problem

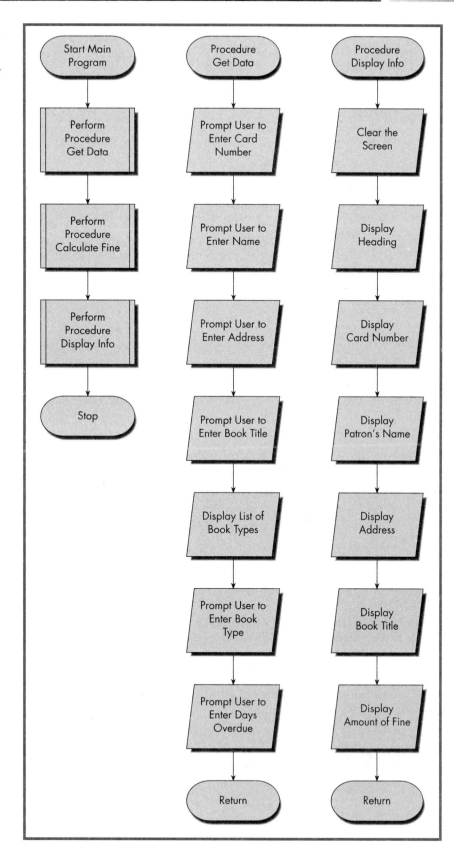

Continued on next page

Figure 6-13

Continued

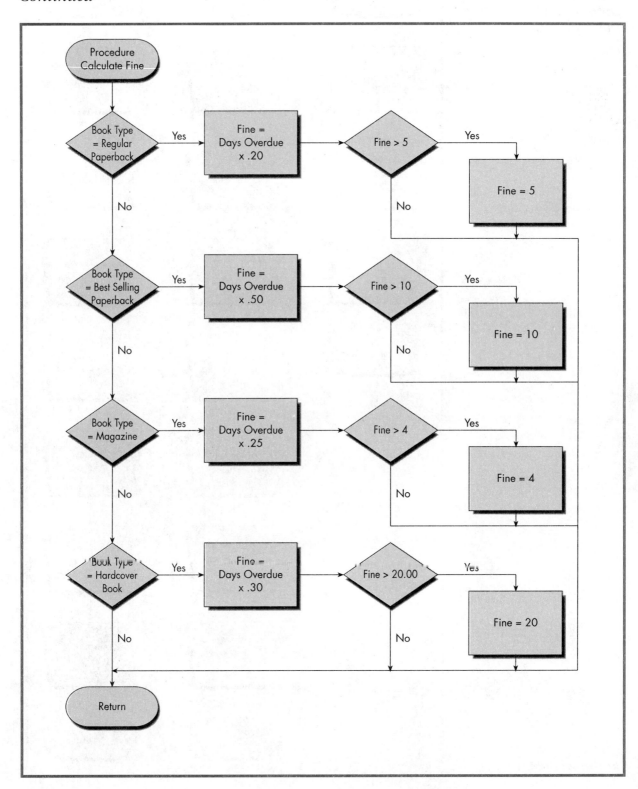

Figure 6-13

Continued

```
Begin main program
    Call GetData
    Call CalculateFine
    Call DisplayInfo
End main program

Begin GetData
    Prompt user to enter card number
    Prompt user to enter patron's name and address
    Display book type categories
    Prompt user to enter book type category
    Prompt user to enter days overdue
End GetData

Begin CalculateFine
    Select book type of:
        Regular paperback
            Fine = .20 × days overdue
            If fine > $5 then
                Fine = $5
            End if
        Best selling paperback
            Fine = .50 × days overdue
            If fine > $10 then
                Fine = $10
            End If
        Magazine
            Fine = .25 × days overdue
            If fine > $4 then
                Fine = $4
            End if
        Hardcover book
            Fine = .30 × days overdue
            If fine > $20 then
                Fine = $20
            End if
End CalculateFine

Begin DisplayInfo
    Display heading
    Display card number
    Display patron's name and address
    Display item's title
    Display amount of fine
End DisplayInfo
```

FIGURE 6-14

Library Fine Program

```
DECLARE SUB CalculateFine (BookType!, DaysOverDue!, Fine!)
DECLARE SUB GetData (CardNumber!, Patron$, Address$, Title$, BookType!,
   DaysOverDue!)
DECLARE SUB DisplayInfo (CardNumber!, Patron$, Address$, Title$, Fine!)

'***                Library Overdue Book Fines              ***

'*** This program calculates the amount of the fine owed ***
'*** on an overdue library book.  Fines are determined   ***
'*** as follows:                                         ***
'***      Paperbacks                                     ***
'***          Regular      $.20 / day with maximum of $5  ***
'***          Best-sellers $.50 / day with maximum of $10 ***
'***      Magazines        $.25 / day with maximum of $4  ***
'***      Hardcover books  $.30 / day with maximum of $20 ***
'*** Major variables:                                    ***
'***      CardNumber       Patron's library card number   ***
'***      Patron$          Patron's name                  ***
'***      Address$         Patron's address               ***
'***      Title$           Book's title                   ***
'***      BookType         Type of book                   ***
'***      DaysOverDue      Number of days book is overdue  ***
'***      Fine             Amount of fine owed             ***

'*** Call GetData to prompt user to enter needed data. ***
CALL GetData(CardNumber, Patron$, Address$, Title$, BookType, DaysOverDue)

'*** Call CalculateFine to determine amount of fine. ***
 CALL CalculateFine(BookType, DaysOverDue, Fine)

'*** Call DisplayInfo to Display the fine information. ***
CALL DisplayInfo(CardNumber, Patron$, Address$, Title$, Fine)

END
```

FIGURE 6-14

Continued

```
SUB CalculateFine (BookType, DaysOverDue, Fine)
   '*** This procedure calculates the amount of the fine ***
   '*** based on the type of book and days overdue.      ***

   '*** Assign fine rates. ***
   Rate1 = .2                'Regular paperback rate
   Rate2 = .5                'Bestselling paperback rate
   Rate3 = .25               'Magazine rate
   Rate4 = .3                'Hardcover book rate

   SELECT CASE BookType
      CASE 1                 'Calculate fine for regular paperback
         Fine = DaysOverDue * Rate1
         IF Fine > 5 THEN
            Fine = 5
         END IF
      CASE 2                 'Calculate fine for bestselling paperback
         Fine = DaysOverDue * Rate2
         IF Fine > 10 THEN
            Fine = 10
         END IF
      CASE 3                 'Calculate fine for magazine
         Fine = DaysOverDue * Rate3
         IF Fine > 4 THEN
            Fine = 4
         END IF
      CASE 4                 'Calculate fine for hardcover book
         Fine = DaysOverDue * Rate4
         IF Fine > 20 THEN
            Fine = 20
         END IF
   END SELECT

END SUB
```

Continued on next page

FIGURE 6-14

Continued

```
SUB DisplayInfo (CardNumber, Patron$, Address$, Title$, Fine)
    '*** This procedure displays information on the fine owed,    ***
    '*** including the amount.                                    ***

    CLS
    PRINT
    PRINT TAB(20); "Bowsher Library"
    PRINT
    Format1$ = "\                              \    \                \"
    Format2$ = "\                              \  ####"
    Format3$ = "\                              \  $##.##"
    PRINT USING Format2$; "Library Card Number:"; CardNumber
    PRINT USING Format1$; "Patron's Name:"; Patron$
    PRINT USING Format1$; "Address:"; Address$
    PRINT USING Format1$; "Item's title:"; Title$
    PRINT USING Format3$; "Amount of fine:"; Fine

END SUB


SUB GetData (CardNumber, Patron$, Address$, Title$, BookType,
    DaysOverDue)
    '*** This procedure prompts the user to enter the needed data. ***

    CLS
    PRINT
    INPUT "Enter the patron's card number: ", CardNumber
    INPUT "Enter the patron's name: ", Patron$
    INPUT "Enter the patron's address: ", Address$
    INPUT "Enter the book's title: ", Title$
    PRINT
    PRINT "1.   Paperback - Regular"
    PRINT "2.   Paperback - Bestseller"
    PRINT "3.   Magazine"
    PRINT "4.   Hardcover book"
    INPUT "Enter number corresponding to type of book (1-4): ", BookType
    PRINT
    INPUT "Enter the number of days overdue: ", DaysOverDue

END SUB
```

FIGURE 6-14

Continued

```
Enter the patron's card number: 2089
Enter the patron's name: Erica Robinson
Enter the patron's address: 204 Seaman
Enter the book's title: Digital Systems

1.   Paperback - Regular
2.   Paperback - Bestseller
3.   Magazine
4.   Hardcover book
Enter number corresponding to type of book (1-4): 4

Enter the number of days overdue: 11
```

```
                    Bowsher Library

Library Card Number:        2089
Patron's Name:              Erica Robinson
Address:                    204 Seaman
Item's title:               Digital Systems
Amount of fine:             $ 3.30
```

PROGRAMMING HINTS

- Developing a structure chart greatly helps in determining how to modularize a program.

- Remember that if you want a procedure to access a variable in the calling module, you must pass it to the procedure.

- Double-check the positioning of the arguments in the CALL statement to make certain they correspond to the parameters in the SUB statement.

- Constants and expressions can be used as arguments; however, they will always be passed by value. If you wish a value to be returned to the calling program, you must use a variable as the argument.

- Parameters must always be variables.

- From this point on, use stubs when developing programs of any significant length. You will discover that your debugging time will be greatly decreased and you will enjoy programming more.

SUMMARY POINTS

- QBasic has two types of procedures: SUB procedures and FUNCTION procedures. This chapter presents SUB procedures.

- Each SUB procedure should be designed to perform a distinct task. It begins with a SUB statement and concludes with END SUB. The statements in between are the body.

- The CALL statement causes a SUB procedure to be executed. Control is transferred from the call to the first line of the procedure. After the entire procedure is executed, control returns to the first line after the CALL statement.

- Each SUB procedure is entered in its own window. The F2 key is used to switch between windows.

- Values can be passed between the calling program and a procedure by placing arguments in the CALL statement. Corresponding parameters must be listed in the SUB statement. When the procedure is called, the arguments are assigned to the parameters. The numbers and types of arguments must correspond to the parameters.

- Variables used only in a particular procedure are local variables. Values assigned to them are not returned to the calling module.

▮ Structure charts are useful in determining how to divide a program into modules.

▮ When arguments are passed by reference, the actual storage location is passed to the procedure. Any changes are returned to the calling program. When they are passed by value, only a copy of the argument's current value is passed to the procedure. Any changes are not returned to the calling program. Constants and expressions are always passed by value. Ordinarily, variables are passed by reference. However, you can pass variables by value by placing them in parentheses in the argument list.

▮ Stubs allow a program to be developed in a methodical fashion. Rather than entering a program into the computer all at once, the programmer can add and test modules gradually. Once those parts already entered work properly, more modules can be entered.

▮ Modularizing programs offers significant advantages because the same procedure can be used many times, the program's logic is easier to follow, and modularized programs are easier to debug, implement, and modify.

KEY TERMS

Argument – 173
CALL statement – 168
Driver program – 179
Local variable – 177
Parameter – 173
Pass by reference – 179
Pass by value – 183
Side effect – 178
Stub – 188
SUB procedure – 167

REVIEW QUESTIONS

1. State at least three advantages of modularizing programs.

2. What statements are used to indicate the beginning and end of a SUB procedure?

3. What symbol is used in a flowchart for a CALL statement?

4. How are arguments related to parameters?

5. What is the advantage of using local variables? Are there any local variables in Figure 6-14? If yes, list them.

6. What is a driver program?

7. How can a structure chart help when modularizing a program?

8. How are stubs used to simplify implementing programs?

9. What happens when the following program is executed? Why?

```
'*** Determine the average of three numbers. ***
INPUT "Enter the three sizes"; Size1, Size2, Size3
CALL DetermineAverage(Average)
PRINT "The average is"; Average
END
SUB DetermineAverage (Average)
    Average = (Size1 + Size2 + Size3) / 3
END SUB
```

10. Explain the difference between passing by reference and passing by value.

11. Why are constants and expressions always passed by value?

12. Write at least two valid CALL statements for the following SUB statement.

```
SUB Lesson (Teacher$, Time$, Day$, Number)
```

13. Parameters are often described as serving as templates. If you do not know what this word means, look it up in a dictionary. Then write an explanation of why parameters can be thought of as templates.

14. What is the purpose of the New SUB option in the Edit menu?

15. Assume that you want to move four statements that are currently in the main program to a SUB procedure. How could you use the Cut and Paste options in the Edit menu to perform this task?

DEBUGGING EXERCISES

Locate any errors in the following programs or program segments, and debug them.

1.
```
'*** Determine the sum of three numbers. ***
CALL DetermineAverage((Sum))
PRINT "The average is"; Average
END
```

```
SUB DetermineAverage (96)
    INPUT "Enter the three numbers"; Num1, Num2, Num3
    Sum = Num1 + Num2 + Num3
END SUB
```

2.
```
'*** If Price is under $100,000, call procedure ***
'*** to increment variable Moderate.            ***
IF Price < 100000 THEN
    CALL IncrementModerate
END IF
    .
    .
    .

END


SUB IncrementModerate
    Moderate = Moderate + 1
    PRINT "This house is in the moderate price range."
END
```

3.
```
'*** Call SUB Procedure Promotion if ***
'*** employee's age is over 40 and   ***
'*** salary is over 29000.           ***
IF Age > 40 AND Salary > 29000 THEN
    CALL Promotion (Age, Salary)
END IF
    .
    .
    .

SUB Promotion Salary, Age
    .
    .
    .
```

4.
```
'*** Call procedure to prompt user to ***
'*** enter charge account bills and   ***
'*** add on 2% interest.  The new     ***
'*** account balance should be re-    ***
'*** turned to the calling program.   ***
INPUT "Enter old balance"; Balance
CALL UpdateBalance(Balance)
PRINT "The new balance is"; Balance
    .
    .
    .
```

```
UpdateBalance (AmountOwed)
    INPUT "Enter amount of purchases this month"; NewCharges
    Balance = Balance + NewCharges
    Balance = Balance * .02
END SUB
```

PROGRAMMING PROBLEMS

Level 1

1. Write a SUB procedure that calculates the new balance of a checking account. The user should be prompted to enter the old balance, total deposits, and total amount of checks written.

2. Write a SUB procedure that has a specific number of minutes passed to it. The procedure should convert the minutes to the corresponding number of hours. For example, assume that the variable Minutes contains 135 when the procedure is called. The procedure should assign the value 2.25 to the variable Hours. This value should then be returned to the calling program.

3. Think of a song you know that contains a refrain. Write a program that will display the words to this song. Use a different procedure for each of the verses and a procedure for the refrain. Then, after each verse is displayed, call the refrain procedure to display the refrain.

4. Urbank's Well Drilling Company drills water and oil wells for businesses and individuals. A water well costs $15 a foot to drill. An oil well costs $20 a foot to drill for the first 10,000 feet; below that, it costs $35 a foot. Write a SUB procedure that calculates the cost of drilling a given well and returns this value to the calling program.

5. Write a SUB procedure to determine the area of a right triangle. The base and height of the triangle should be passed to the SUB procedure, which should then calculate and return the area. Use the following formula: area = ½ × base × height.

6. Write a SUB procedure that will receive a specific number of quarters, dimes, nickels, and pennies, and then translate these coins into a dollar amount. The dollar amount should be returned to the calling program. For example, for the following values, the dollar amount returned to the calling program would be 2.02: quarters: 5; dimes: 3; nickels: 8; and pennies: 7.

Level 2

1. Fran's Frame Station specializes in framing custom artwork. Fran would like a program that will calculate the cost for framing a particular piece of art. The program should prompt the user for the length and the width of the item. First the amount of glass needed (in square inches) and the cost of the glass should be determined. Assume the glass costs 2 cents per square inch. Next the cost of the framing material should be determined. The wood used for framing costs $1.45 per foot. Use SUB procedures as appropriate.

2. Write a program to compute how much a person would weigh on the moon and on the planets listed in the following table:

Planet	Percentage of Earth Weight
Moon	16
Jupiter	264
Venus	85
Mars	38

    Use the percentages in the right column to perform the conversions. Modularize the program, as appropriate.

3. Fun-for-All Rental provides clowns for parties, seasonal celebrations, and other special occasions. The basic fee is $45 for the first hour and $25.99 for every additional hour. The company needs a program to help calculate its clients' bills. The program should call a SUB procedure to perform the actual calculations.

4. Write a program that acts as a computerized address book. When the user enters a number corresponding to a person's name, the program should print that person's address, phone number, and birthdate. The name should be chosen from a menu of 5 to 10 names. The program should then branch to a SUB procedure to print the address, phone number, and birthdate. Develop your own data for the program.

5. Shangri-La Realty needs a program to assist its agents in keeping track of the various apartments available for rent. Write a program using SUB procedures that will give the user a choice of a studio, one-bedroom, or two-bedroom apartment. The monthly rent depends on the size of the apartment and whether it is to be furnished or unfurnished (this data should also be entered by the user). Use the following data:

Type	Deposit	Rent (Furnished)	Rent (Unfurnished)
Studio	$400	$450	$425
One-bedroom	500	500	550
Two-bedroom	600	725	665

The program should print the apartment description, required deposit, and monthly rent according to the choices entered, using the following format:

Description : Two-bedroom furnished
Deposit : $600
Rent : $725

6. At one time, telephone exchanges were alphabetic, and most telephones still have letters of the alphabet on the dial. Write a program that uses a SUB procedure to convert an alphabetic telephone number to an all-digit telephone number. At the end of the program, both the alphabetic and the numeric telephone numbers, should be displayed. The following diagram will help you:

Challenge Problems

1. Stan's Cable TV Corporation needs a program to help with the billing of its customers.

   Input:

   The user should be prompted to enter the following:

   a. Customer's name

   b. Customer's address

   c. Whether or not the bill is overdue

d. The types of premium service the customer receives. The premium services are:

Cable Plus
Home Cinema Channel
Continual Cartoon Channel
Arts and History Channel

Processing Requirements:

a. All customers receive the basic cable service. Add the cost of any premium services to this basic amount. Use the following table to determine the costs:

Basic cable service	$12.00
Cable Plus	4.00
Home Cinema Channel	5.00
Continual Cartoon Channel	5.00
Arts and History Channel	4.00

b. If the bill is overdue, add a 5 percent penalty for late payment.

Output:

Send the final bill to the printer. It should look similar to the following:

```
        Stan's Cable TV Corporation

Name:           Margie Parr              Due Date:   10/15/99
Address:        1045 Prairie Rd.

Services:
Basic Cable        $12.00
Cable Plus          $4.00
Arts and History    $4.00

Total Amount Due:   $20.00
After Due Date:     $21.00
```

2. Ms. Bergman, City High's art teacher, would like a program to determine the quantity of supplies she needs for an art class. Each student is required to make one of three projects:

Ceramic vase
Water color
Charcoal sketches

Input:

Prompt the user to enter the name of each project and the number of students making that project.

Processing:

a. Calculate the amount of each type of material needed based on the following table:

Project	Supplies
Ceramic vase	0.5 pounds of clay
	5 ounces of glaze
	1 brush
Water color	1 box water colors
	1 canvas
	1 brush
Charcoal sketches	4 pieces of charcoal
	8 pieces of newsprint

Output:

The quantity of each type of supply should then be displayed in a table similar to the following:

```
              Art Supplies

Clay:                 4 pounds
Glaze:                40 ounces
Brushes:              25
Canvases:             17
Water Colors:         17 boxes
Charcoal:             48 pieces
Newsprint:            96 sheets
```

Loop Structures

Outline

Objectives

After studying this chapter, you will be able to:

▌ Explain the importance of loop structures.

▌ List the elements of a loop.

▌ Write programs using the DO WHILE...LOOP and the DO UNTIL...LOOP.

▌ Use trailer values to control loops.

▌ Write counting loops.

▌ Use the FOR...NEXT loop appropriately in programs.

▌ Create nested loops.

▌ Determine which type of loop is appropriate in a particular programming situation.

INTRODUCTION

As discussed in Chapter 2, structured programs have easy-to-understand logic, partly because the programs are modularized. In addition, these programs should attempt to use only the three basic logic structures: the sequence, the decision structure, and the loop structure. So far, you have learned to write programs that use sequences and decision structures. This chapter introduces the loop structure, which allows a specified group of statements to be executed as many times as needed. This chapter discusses two types of looping statements: the DO...LOOP and the FOR...NEXT loop.

ADVANTAGES OF LOOPS

Often a situation arises where a task must be performed repeatedly. For example, an instructor may need a program to find the average test score for each of the students in a course. The job of processing one student's data is simple enough, as shown in Figure 7-1. However, consider the problem of repeating these steps for 30 students, as shown in Figure 7-2. The same three statements used to process one student's data would have to be written 30 times—a tedious and error-prone task. To simplify the job, the statements could be written once, then executed as many

FIGURE 7-1

Flowchart for Finding One Student's Average Score

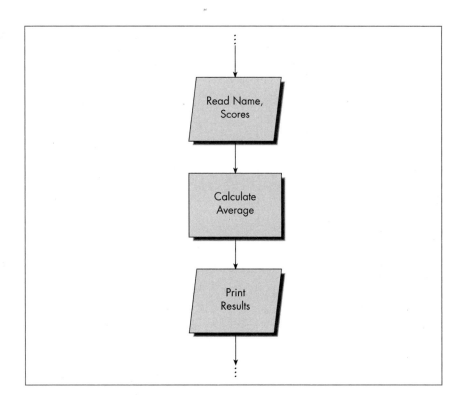

FIGURE 7-2

Flowchart for Finding Average Scores for 30 Students

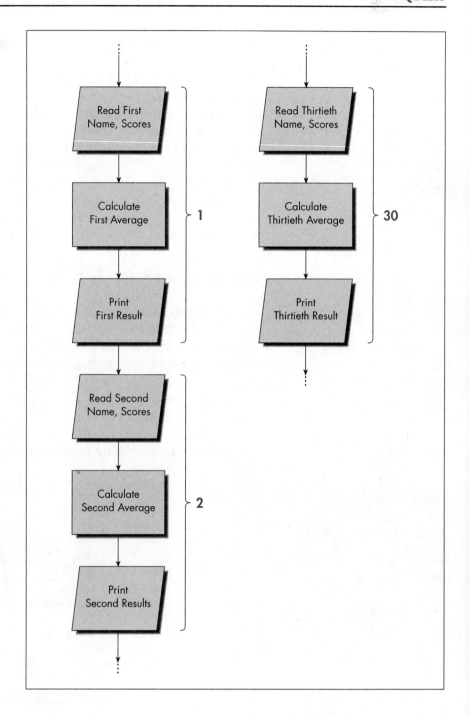

times as necessary. This process, called **looping** (or **iteration**), is illustrated in Figure 7-3.

A variety of loop structures exists among the many programming languages used today, but all share some basic components. They all use a **loop control variable**, whose value determines whether a loop will be repeated. In the example of the student test scores, the loop control variable could contain the current num-

FIGURE 7-3

FIGURE 7-3

Flowchart for Finding
Average Scores for Any
Number of Students
Using a Loop

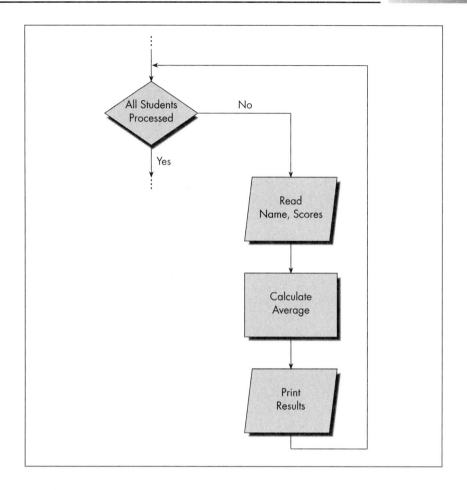

Loop body *The statement(s)
that are executed each time a
loop repeats.*

ber of students processed. All loops contain some action to be
performed repeatedly; the statements that perform such an
action make up the **loop body**. In the student test score example,
the loop body consists of three steps: (1) prompt the user to enter
the name and scores, (2) calculate the average, and (3) print the
result.

Execution of the basic loop structure consists of five steps:

1. The loop control variable is initialized to a particular value
   before loop execution begins.

2. The program tests the loop control variable to determine
   whether to execute the loop body or exit from the loop.

3. The loop body, consisting of any number of statements, is
   executed.

4. At some point during loop execution, the value of the loop
   control variable is modified to allow an exit from the loop.

5. The loop is exited when the decision of Step 2 determines
   that the right number of loop repetitions has been made.
   Execution continues with the next statement following the
   loop.

FIGURE 7-4

Flowchart of Loop
Elements

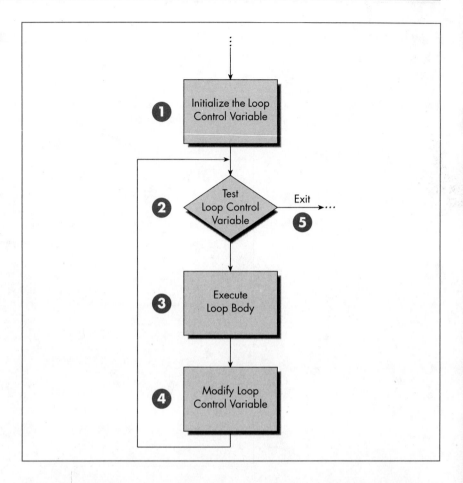

Figure 7-4 pictures the elements of a loop in the form of a flow-chart. Keep the five loop elements in mind as the next section presents one way to form a loop in QBasic, using the DO...LOOP.

THE DO...LOOP

The DO...LOOP is controlled by a Boolean expression (remember that Boolean expressions always evaluate as either true or false). We discuss two variations of this loop: the DO WHILE...LOOP and the DO UNTIL...LOOP.

The DO WHILE...LOOP

A DO WHILE...LOOP is executed as long as the expression at the top of the loop is true. If it is false, control transfers to the first statement after LOOP, which marks the loop's end. The flowchart in Figure 7-5 illustrates the structure of the DO WHILE...LOOP. Figure 7-6 contains a program that totals a list of positive integers. Notice that the parts of the loop are labeled. The execution of the loop proceeds as follows:

1. The expression in the DO WHILE is evaluated as true or false. In Figure 7-6, as long as the expression "Number <> -1" is true, the body of the loop is executed.

2. If the expression is true, the statements in the loop's body are executed until LOOP is encountered; if the expression is false, control passes to the first statement after LOOP. As with the block IF and the SELECT CASE, the body of a DO...LOOP consists of a statement block. Its boundaries are clearly marked by the keywords DO and LOOP. The body of the loop in Figure 7-6 contains two statements:

```
Sum = Sum + Number
INPUT "Enter the next number (-1 to quit): ", Number
```

3. When LOOP is encountered, control passes back to the DO WHILE, and the expression is checked again.

4. If the expression is still true, the loop body is executed again; if false, the loop is exited.

You may be wondering why this program contains two INPUT statements. The first INPUT gets the first number before the loop is entered:

```
INPUT "Enter the first number (-1 to quit): ", Number
```

Priming read *A statement used to initialize a loop control variable before the loop is entered for the first time.*

This is referred to as a **priming read** and initializes Number to a starting value before the condition in the DO WHILE is evaluated for the first time. The second INPUT is at the bottom of the loop and reads the subsequent numbers. It is important that this second INPUT be the last statement in the loop body because if it occurred before Number was added to Sum, the first value of Number would be lost before it was added.

FIGURE 7-5

Flowchart of the
DO WHILE...LOOP

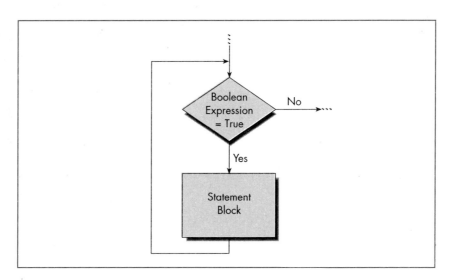

FIGURE 7-6

Program Demonstrating the DO WHILE...LOOP

```
'***   This program adds a list of positive integers. ***

'***   Major variables:                               ***
'***      Number  Current number being added to Sum   ***
'***      Sum     Sum of the numbers                  ***
CLS
Sum = 0
INPUT "Enter the first number (-1 to quit): ", Number
DO WHILE Number <> -1
   Sum = Sum + Number
   INPUT "Enter the next number (-1 to quit): ", Number
LOOP
PRINT "The sum is"; Sum

END
```

```
Enter the first number (-1 to quit): 24
Enter the next number (-1 to quit): 18
Enter the next number (-1 to quit): 91
Enter the next number (-1 to quit): -1
The sum is 133
```

Notice that Sum is set to zero immediately before the loop is entered. This is because we want Sum to start at zero and then add numbers to it. Technically, however, this statement setting Sum to zero is not needed. Before a program is executed, QBasic automatically sets the values of numeric variables to zero. In addition, string variables are automatically set to the null (empty) string. However, it is good programming practice to initialize variables yourself, rather than depending on "default" initializations.

The DO WHILE ... LOOP Statement

Statement Format

```
DO WHILE expression
   [statement block]
LOOP
```

Learning Check 7-1

1. Another name for looping is _____.

2. Name the five elements of the loop structure.

3. The execution of a DO...LOOP is controlled by a(n) _____ expression.

4. How many times will the following loop execute? What is the output?

```
Result = 14
DO WHILE Result > 4
   Print Result;
   Result = Result - 3
LOOP
```

5. An INPUT statement that occurs before a loop is entered for the first time is referred to as a(n) _____ read.

Controlling Loops

One of the most difficult aspects of using loops is making them stop executing at the proper time. In this section, we discuss two methods of controlling loop repetition: the use of trailer values and counting loops.

Trailer value *A data value indicating that a loop should stop executing. It must be a value that would not ordinarily occur in the input data.*

Trailer Values. A **trailer value** is a "dummy" value that follows, or trails, the data items being processed. It is sometimes referred to as a **sentinel value**. The trailer value signals to the program that all data has been entered. The loop in Figure 7-6 uses a trailer value of –1. When the user enters that value, the loop stops, and Sum is displayed. The trailer value can be either a numeric value or a character string, depending on the type of data being input, but it should always be a value outside the range of the actual data. For example, if a program prompts the user to enter people's ages, a good trailer value might be –1. If names are being input, an example of a good trailer value would be "Finished."

As previously mentioned, a priming read should be used to assign a value to the loop control variable before loop repetition begins. Subsequent values are assigned to the loop control variable at the bottom of the loop. If the loop control variable's value does not equal the trailer value, the loop is repeated. The program in Figure 7-7 shows another loop using a trailer value. Figure 7-8 contains the corresponding flowchart with the loop elements identified. This program calculates the wages of employees of the Village Hotel. After each employee's data is entered, the following statement tests for the trailer value:

```
DO WHILE Nme$ <> "Finished"
```

FIGURE 7-7

Loop Controlled by a Trailer Value

```
'***                    The Village Payroll              ***

'***   This program calculates employee salaries.       ***
'***   Major variables:                                 ***
'***       Nme$        Employee's name                  ***
'***       Rate        Hourly pay rate                  ***
'***       Hours       Number of hours worked in this pay period ***
'***       Wage        Gross pay                        ***

CLS
Rate = 8
INPUT "Enter name and number of hours: ", Nme$, Hours
DO WHILE Nme$ <> "Finished"
   Wage = Rate * Hours
   PRINT "Name", "Wage"
   PRINT Nme$, Wage
   PRINT
   INPUT "Enter next name and number of hours: ", Nme$, Hours
   PRINT
LOOP
PRINT "Finished"

END
```

```
Enter name and number of hours: Fetterman, 78
Name            Wage
Fetterman        624

Enter next name and number of hours: Hossler, 32

Name            Wage
Hossler          256

Enter next name and number of hours: Maderas, 41

Name            Wage
Maderas          328

Enter next name and number of hours: Finished, 0

Finished
```

FIGURE 7-8

Flowchart of a Loop Using a Trailer Value

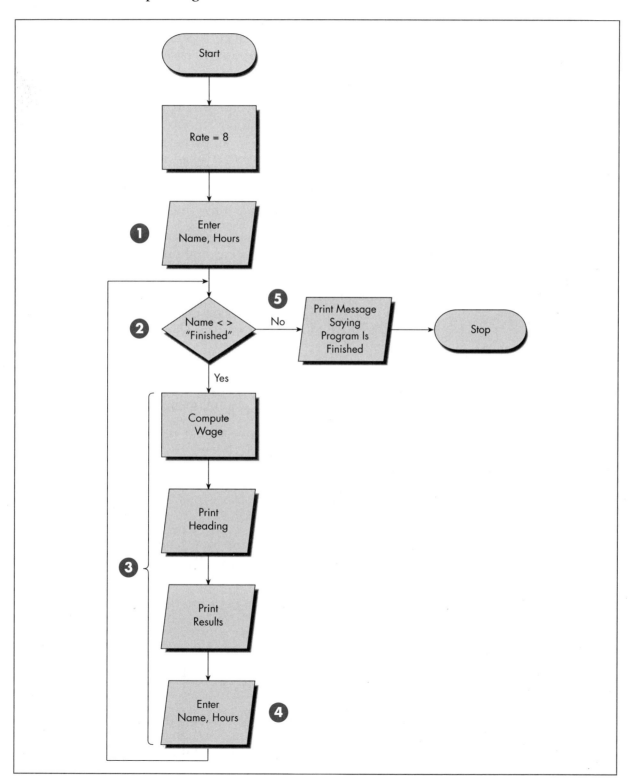

If the condition is true, the loop's body is executed; otherwise, execution passes to the first statement following the loop.

Counting Loop. A second method of controlling a loop is to create a loop control variable, called a **counter**, that keeps track of the number of times the loop has been executed. In a **counting loop**, the counter is incremented or decremented during each repetition. When it reaches a specified value, loop execution stops. A counting loop is useful when the programmer knows before the loop is first entered how many times it should execute. The following steps are used to set up a counting loop:

1. Initialize the counter by setting it to a beginning value before entering the loop.

2. Increment the counter each time the loop is executed.

3. Test the counter each time the loop is executed to see if the loop has been repeated the needed number of times.

The program in Figure 7-7 has been rewritten in Figure 7-9 to use a counter rather than a trailer value. The corresponding flowchart is shown in Figure 7-10. Data on three employees must be entered, so the loop is executed three times.

Always be careful to initialize the loop control variable to the starting value before entering the loop. In addition, make certain that at some point the loop control variable reaches the value needed to stop the loop. In the following loop, the loop control variable is never modified:

```
Count = 1
DO WHILE Count < 50
    PRINT Count
LOOP
```

> **Counter** *A numeric variable used to control a loop. It is incremented (or decremented) and tested each time the loop is executed.*
>
> **Counting loop** *A loop executed a specific number of times. The number of repetitions must be determined before the loop is first entered.*

This is an example of an **infinite loop**. The loop will execute infinitely (or at least until the computer's resources are used up). This loop can be correctly written as follows:

```
Count = 1
DO WHILE Count < 50
    PRINT Count
    Count = Count + 1
LOOP
```

> **Infinite loop** *A loop that executes indefinitely. This occurs because the condition controlling loop execution never reaches the value needed for the loop to stop executing.*

If your program becomes caught in an infinite loop, stop the execution by pressing Ctrl Break. You can then correct the problem and choose the Continue option from the Run menu to continue execution.

FIGURE 7-9

Program Demonstrating a Counting Loop

```
'***                      The Village Payroll              ***

'***   This program calculates employee salaries.         ***
'***   Major variables:                                   ***
'***       Nme$        Employee's name                    ***
'***       Rate        Hourly pay rate                    ***
'***       Hours       Number of hours worked in this pay period ***
'***       Wage        Gross pay                          ***
'***       Counter     Loop control variable              ***

CLS
Rate = 8
Counter = 1
DO WHILE Counter <= 3
    INPUT "Enter next name and number of hours: ", Nme$, Hours
    Wage = Rate * Hours
    PRINT "Name", "Wage"
    PRINT Nme$, Wage
    PRINT
    Counter = Counter + 1
LOOP
PRINT "Finished"

END
```

```
Enter next name and number of hours: Fetterman, 78
Name           Wage
Fetterman      624

Enter next name and number of hours: Hossler, 32
Name           Wage
Hossler        256

Enter next name and number of hours: Maderas, 41
Name           Wage
Maderas        328

Finished
```

FIGURE 7-10

Flowchart Showing Elements of a Counting Loop

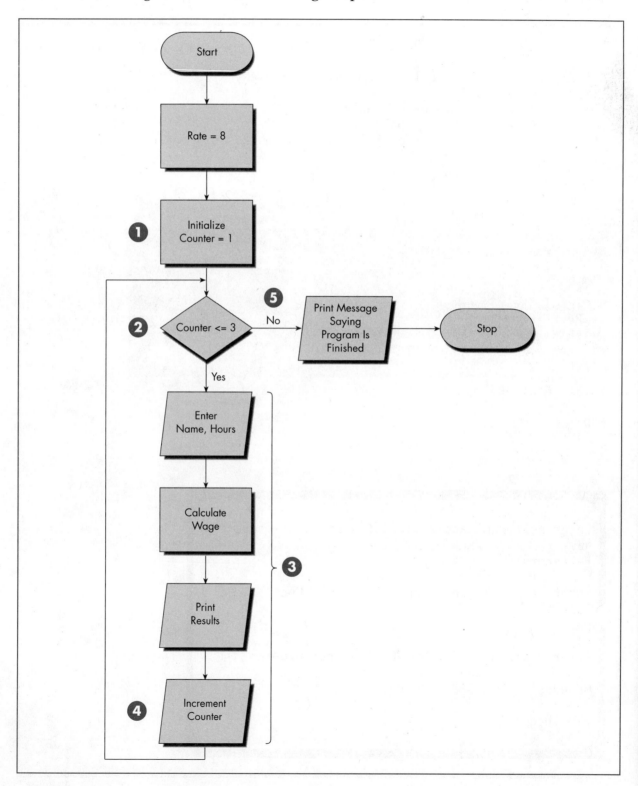

The DO UNTIL...LOOP

The second type of DO...LOOP, the DO UNTIL...LOOP, is very similar to the DO WHILE...LOOP. The only difference is that the loop is executed *until* the Boolean expression becomes true rather than *while* it is true. Therefore, the controlling condition at the top of the loop in Figure 7-6 would be rewritten as follows:

```
DO UNTIL Number = -1
```

Other than this change, the program would remain exactly the same. Rather than executing while Number does not equal –1, the loop executes until Number equals –1. Because the end result is the same, any DO WHILE...LOOP can be rewritten as a DO UNTIL...LOOP. The basic flowchart of a DO UNTIL...LOOP is shown in Figure 7-11. Figure 7-12 shows how the program in Figure 7-7 could be rewritten using a DO UNTIL...LOOP.

The DO UNTIL ... LOOP Statement

Statement Format

DO UNTIL expression
    [statement block]
LOOP

FIGURE 7-11

Flowchart of the
DO UNTIL...LOOP

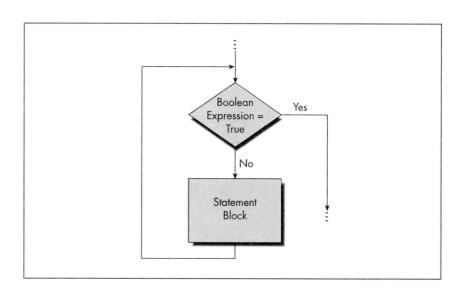

FIGURE 7-12

Program Demonstrating the DO UNTIL...LOOP

```
'***                    The Village Payroll                    ***

'***   This program calculates employee salaries.             ***
'***   Major variables:                                       ***
'***        Nme$        Employee's name                       ***
'***        Rate        Hourly pay rate                       ***
'***        Hours       Number of hours worked in this pay period ***
'***        Wage        Gross pay                             ***

CLS
Rate = 8
INPUT "Enter name and number of hours: ", Nme$, Hours
DO UNTIL Nme$ = "Finished"
    Wage = Rate * Hours
    PRINT "Name", "Wage"
    PRINT Nme$, Wage
    PRINT
    INPUT "Enter next name and number of hours: ", Nme$, Hours
    PRINT
LOOP
PRINT "Finished"

END
```

```
Enter name and number of hours: Fetterman, 78
Name            Wage
Fetterman        624

Enter next name and number of hours: Hossler, 32

Name            Wage
Hossler          256

Enter next name and number of hours: Maderas, 41

Name            Wage
Maderas          328

Enter next name and number of hours: Finished, 0

Finished
```

THE EXIT STATEMENT

Occasionally, it may be necessary to exit a loop prematurely. Most commonly, this occurs if an error condition is encountered, for example, if invalid data has been entered. The EXIT statement can be placed anywhere in a DO...LOOP and causes execution to be immediately transferred to the first statement after LOOP. For example, the following program segment is supposed to prompt the user to enter the names of 12 voters. However, if a value of less than 18 is read for Age, an error message is displayed and the loop terminates.

```
'*** Prompt user to enter names of 12 voters. ***
Count = 1
INPUT "Enter person's name: ", Voter$
INPUT "Enter person's age: ", Age
DO WHILE Count <= 12
    '*** If underage, display error message and stop loop. ***
    IF Age < 18 THEN
        PRINT
        PRINT Voter$; " is not eligible to vote."
        EXIT DO
    END IF
    Count = Count + 1
    INPUT "Enter person's name: ", Voter$
    INPUT "Enter person's age: ", Age
LOOP
```

If the EXIT DO statement is executed, control transfers to the first statement after LOOP. However, this statement is executed only if a value less than 18 is entered for Age. The EXIT statement can be used with other structures, such as SUB procedures. The statement EXIT SUB allows control to be transferred immediately back to the calling program. However, a word of warning: The EXIT statement can lead to program errors. It also makes program logic more difficult to follow. Therefore, it is best to avoid its use.

Learning Check 7-2

1. The _____ executes as long as the controlling expression is false.

2. A trailer value is also referred to as a(n) _____ value.

3. The _____ statement can be used to leave a loop immediately if an error condition is encountered.

4. True or False? Any DO WHILE...LOOP can also be written as a DO UNTIL...LOOP

5. The _____ statement marks the end of a DO UNTIL...LOOP.

The FOR...NEXT Loop

The FOR...NEXT loop is used to create a counting loop. For example, this loop

```
FOR Counter = 1 TO 8 STEP 1
    PRINT Counter;
NEXT Counter
```

executes eight times and outputs the following:

```
1   2   3   4   5   6   7   8
```

The loop control variable starts at 1 and is incremented by 1 at the end of each repetition until its value is greater than 8. The FOR marks the beginning of the loop, and the NEXT marks its end; a statement block makes up the loop's body. Figure 7-13 shows a sample loop with its components labeled. The step value determines the amount by which the loop control variable is incremented. If the step value is changed to 2

```
FOR Counter = 1 TO 8 STEP 2
    PRINT Counter;
NEXT Counter
```

the following is displayed:

```
1   3   5   7
```

If no step value is specified, QBasic assumes a value of 1. Therefore, the following two statements are equivalent:

```
FOR Counter = 1 TO 8 STEP 1
FOR Counter = 1 TO 8
```

The loop control variable must be a numeric variable. The initial and terminal values and the optional step value, taken together, determine the number of times the loop body is executed. These values must be numeric. They can consist of constants, variables, or expressions. Figure 7-14 shows how the DO WHILE...LOOP in Figure 7-9 can be rewritten using a FOR...NEXT loop.

A number of actions occur when a FOR statement is first encountered:

1. The initial, terminal, and (if given) step value expressions are evaluated.

2. The loop control variable is assigned the initial value.

3. The value of the loop control variable is tested against the terminal value.

FIGURE 7-13

Labeled Parts of a
FOR...NEXT Loop

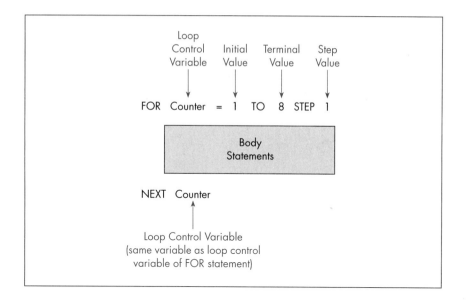

4. If the loop control variable is less than or equal to the terminal value, the loop body is executed.

5. If the loop control variable is greater than the terminal value, the loop body is skipped, and control passes to the first statement following the NEXT. This means that the loop will not be executed at all.

Here is what happens when the NEXT is encountered:

1. The step value indicated in the FOR statement is added to the loop control variable. If the step value is omitted, +1 is added.

2. A check is performed to determine if the value of the loop control variable exceeds the terminal value.

3. If the loop control variable is less than or equal to the terminal value, control transfers back to the statement after the FOR statement, and the loop is repeated. Otherwise, the loop is exited, and execution continues with the statement following the NEXT.

It is possible to use a negative, rather than a positive, step value. In this case, the loop control variable is decremented, rather than incremented, after each loop execution. Therefore, the following statement is valid:

```
FOR Count = 8 TO 4 STEP -2
```

When a negative step value is used, the loop body is executed if the loop control variable is greater than or equal to the terminal value. When the NEXT is encountered, the step value is added to the loop control variable as usual; and because this value is nega-

FIGURE 7-14

Payroll Program Using a FOR...NEXT Loop

```
'***                     The Village Payroll                    ***

'***   This program calculates employee salaries.              ***
'***   Major variables:                                         ***
'***       Nme$       Employee's name                           ***
'***       Rate       Hourly pay rate                           ***
'***       Hours      Number of hours worked in this pay period ***
'***       Wage       Gross pay                                 ***
'***       Counter    Loop control variable                     ***

CLS
Rate = 8
FOR Counter = 1 TO 3
   INPUT "Enter next name and number of hours: ", Nme$, Hours
   Wage = Rate * Hours
   PRINT "Name", "Wage"
   PRINT Nme$, Wage
   PRINT
NEXT Counter

PRINT "Finished"

END
```

```
Enter next name and number of hours: Fetterman, 78
Name            Wage
Fetterman        624

Enter next name and number of hours: Hossler, 32
Name            Wage
Hossler          256

Enter next name and number of hours: Maderas, 41
Name            Wage
Maderas          328


Finished
```

tive, the loop control variable is decremented. For example, this program segment

```
FOR Count = 10 TO 1 STEP -1
    PRINT Count;
NEXT Count
PRINT "*** IGNITION! ***"
```

displays the following:

10   9   8   7   6   5   4   3   2   1 *** IGNITION! ***

The FOR ... NEXT Statement

Statement Format

FOR loop-control-variable = initial TO terminal [STEP step-value]
    [statement-block]
NEXT loop-control-variable

Rules for Using FOR...NEXT Loops

The following rules apply to FOR...NEXT loops:

- The initial, terminal, and step values cannot be modified in the loop body.

- It is possible to modify the loop control variable in the loop body, *but this should never be done.* Note how unpredictable the execution of the following loop would be. The value of Count is dependent on the integer entered by the user.

```
FOR Count = 1 TO 10
    INPUT "Enter an integer"; X
    Count = X
NEXT Count
```

If the step value is zero, an infinite loop is created, as in the following example:

```
FOR X = 10 TO 20 STEP 0
```

This loop could be written correctly so that it would execute 11 times as follows:

```
FOR X = 10 TO 20 STEP 1
```

- Each FOR statement should be associated with a corresponding NEXT statement.

NESTED LOOPS

Chapter 5 showed how block IF statements could be nested in one another. Similar nesting can be done with all types of loops. A pair of nested FOR...NEXT loops looks like this:

```
FOR Outer = 1 TO 4
    FOR Inner = 1 TO 2
        .
        .
        .
    NEXT Inner
NEXT Outer
```

Nested loops should be indented as shown to improve readability. In this example, each time the outer loop is executed once, the inner loop is executed twice, since Inner varies from 1 to 2. When the inner loop has terminated, control passes to the first statement after the NEXT Inner statement, which in this case is NEXT Outer. This statement causes Outer to be incremented by 1 and tested against the terminal value of 4. If Outer is still less than or equal to 4, the body of loop Outer is executed again. Loop Inner is again encountered, the value of Inner is reset to 1, and the inner loop again is executed until Inner is greater than 2. Altogether, the outer loop is executed four times and the inner loop is executed eight (4×2) times. Figure 7-15 graphically illustrates the execution of another nested FOR...NEXT loop.

Nesting loops can easily lead to errors. Be sure to follow these rules:

- Each loop must have a unique loop control variable.

- The NEXT statement for an inner loop must appear within the body of the outer loop, so that one loop is entirely contained within another.

Incorrect	Correct
```FOR I = 1 TO 5```	```FOR I = 1 TO 5```
``` FOR J = 1 TO 10```	``` FOR J = 1 TO 10```
``` .```	``` .```
``` .```	``` .```
``` .```	``` .```
``` NEXT I```	``` NEXT J```
```NEXT J```	```NEXT I```

In the invalid example, the J loop is not entirely inside the I loop but extends beyond the NEXT I statement.

FIGURE 7-15

Tracing Nested
FOR...NEXT Loops

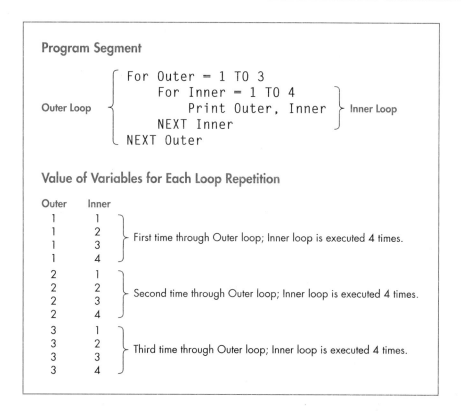

Program Segment

```
         ┌ For Outer = 1 TO 3
         │     For Inner = 1 TO 4
Outer Loop │         Print Outer, Inner    Inner Loop
         │     NEXT Inner
         └ NEXT Outer
```

Value of Variables for Each Loop Repetition

Outer	Inner
1	1
1	2	First time through Outer loop; Inner loop is executed 4 times.
1	3
1	4
2	1
2	2	Second time through Outer loop; Inner loop is executed 4 times.
2	3
2	4
3	1
3	2	Third time through Outer loop; Inner loop is executed 4 times.
3	3
3	4

Figure 7-16 uses nested loops to print the multiplication tables for the numbers 1, 2, and 3, with each table in a separate column. The inner loop controls the printing in each of the three columns, while the outer loop controls the printing of the rows. Check the output of the program by following the execution from beginning to end, performing each statement by hand. (This is referred to as *desk checking* the program.)

COMPARING LOOP STRUCTURES

Either type of DO...LOOP can always be used in place of the FOR...NEXT loop, but the reverse is not true. The FOR...NEXT loop is used for counting loops that execute a prespecified number of times, as stated by the initial and terminal values of the loop control variable. The DO...LOOP can also execute a given number of times, if the programmer initializes the loop control variable before the loop begins and tests for the given value at the top of the loop. However, the DO...LOOP can also be used when the final number of loop executions is not known, such as when a trailer value is used. In such a situation, a FOR...NEXT loop would be inappropriate.

When creating counting loops, there are several advantages to using the FOR...NEXT loop. The loop control variable is automatically initialized and incremented. In addition, it is compared to the terminal value. When using a DO...LOOP, the programmer must write statements to perform these tasks. Because the FOR...NEXT loop does them automatically, it is easier to use and less error prone.

FIGURE 7-16

Multiplication Program Using Nested Loops

```
'***   Display three multiplication tables.          ***

'***   Major variables:                              ***
'***       Outer       Outer loop control variable   ***
'***       Inner       Inner loop control variable   ***

CLS
FOR Outer = 1 TO 10
   FOR Inner = 1 TO 3
      PRINT Inner; "*"; Outer; "="; Inner * Outer,
   NEXT Inner
   PRINT
NEXT Outer


END
```

```
1 * 1 = 1       2 * 1 = 2       3 * 1 = 3
1 * 2 = 2       2 * 2 = 4       3 * 2 = 6
1 * 3 = 3       2 * 3 = 6       3 * 3 = 9
1 * 4 = 4       2 * 4 = 8       3 * 4 = 12
1 * 5 = 5       2 * 5 = 10      3 * 5 = 15
1 * 6 = 6       2 * 6 = 12      3 * 6 = 18
1 * 7 = 7       2 * 7 = 14      3 * 7 = 21
1 * 8 = 8       2 * 8 = 16      3 * 8 = 24
1 * 9 = 9       2 * 9 = 18      3 * 9 = 27
1 * 10 = 10     2 * 10 = 20     3 * 10 = 30
```

Learning Check 7-3

1. The FOR statement _____.

   a. initializes the loop control variable

   b. increments the loop control variable by the step value

   c. passes control to the NEXT statement

2. How many times would a loop containing the following statement be executed?

```
FOR Count = 30 TO 12 STEP -5
```

3. When no step value is specified in a FOR statement, it is assumed to be _____.

4. When the terminal value is exceeded in a FOR...NEXT loop (using a positive step value), control passes to what statement?

5. True or False? Two or more nested loops can have the same loop control variable.

MASTERING PROGRAM DEVELOPMENT

Problem Definition

The salespeople at Joe's Appliance Store are trying to encourage customers to purchase energy-efficient appliances. Although these models are more expensive to purchase than regular models, the consumer ends up saving money in the long run because of savings on electricity bills. The owner would like a program that allows the user to enter the prices of two models (one regular, one energy-efficient) and each model's monthly operating costs. The program should determine how many months it will take until the consumer begins saving money by purchasing the energy-efficient model. The user should be able to enter as many appliances as desired. The output should be printed on paper and appear as shown below:

```
                  Joe's Appliances
     Estimated Savings on Energy-Efficient Appliances
     _____


     Appliance:    Refrigerator

     Model                 Purchase Price    Monthly Cost
     Regular                  $950.00           $12.50
     Energy-Efficient        $1070.00            $9.00

     You will begin saving money after 35 months.

     _____
```

Solution Design

This program's tasks can be divided as follows:

1. Print the headings.
2. Get the data for each appliance.
3. Determine the number of months until the savings begin.
4. Print the report.

The first step is fairly simple, involving printing the store's name and a report title. The second step can be subdivided as follows:

2.A. Get the type of appliance.

2.B. Get the regular model's purchase price.

2.C. Get the regular model's monthly operating cost.

2.D. Get the energy-efficient model's purchase price.

2.E. Get the energy-efficient model's monthly operating cost.

The third step needs to use a loop. This structure will require a little thought to develop correctly. We will need to begin by assigning the purchase price of each model to a variable. We can then add the monthly operating cost to this variable each time the loop executes. The loop should stop executing when the total cost for the energy-efficient model becomes less than the total cost for the regular model. By counting the number of loop repetitions, we will know how many months it takes for the energy-efficient model to begin saving the consumer money.

The fourth step prints the report and contains the following substeps:

4.A. Print the type of appliance.

4.B. Print each model's purchase price.

4.C. Print each model's monthly operating costs.

4.D. Print the number of months until savings begin.

Figure 7-17 contains the structure chart for this solution.

Another item must be dealt with when developing this program. The user must be allowed to enter as many appliances as desired. This requires a loop. The loop will always be executed at least once. However, before it is repeated, the user must be asked whether or not there is another appliance to be entered. If the user wants to continue, the loop should be repeated; otherwise, program execution should terminate. The flowchart and pseudocode for this problem are shown in Figure 7-18.

The Program

The final program is shown in Figure 7-19 and contains two loops: one to allow the user to enter more than one appliance, a second

FIGURE 7-17

Structure Chart for Energy-Efficiency Program

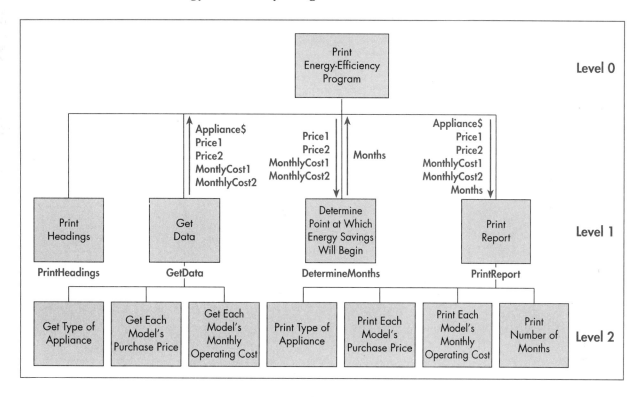

one to calculate the months until the consumer starts seeing savings. Note that the headings are printed before the outer loop is executed the first time. This is necessary because we only want the headings to be printed one time. If these LPRINT statements were placed inside the loop, they would appear before each appliance. The loop control variable More$ is initially set to "Y" so that the loop will always execute once; the user is prompted to enter a "Y" or an "N" at the bottom of the loop to determine whether it will be repeated.

The heart of the program is contained in SUB procedure DetermineMonths. Notice that the variable Months is set to 0 before the loop is entered. It is then incremented by 1 each time the loop is repeated. In addition, Cost1 and Cost2 are initially set to the purchase prices of the appliances. These variables are then incremented by the monthly costs (MonthlyCost1 and MonthlyCost2) each time the loop is repeated. This allows the program to keep a running tab of the total costs. The expression controlling loop repetition:

```
DO WHILE Cost1 < Cost2
```

FIGURE 7-18

Flowchart and Pseudocode for Energy-Efficiency Program

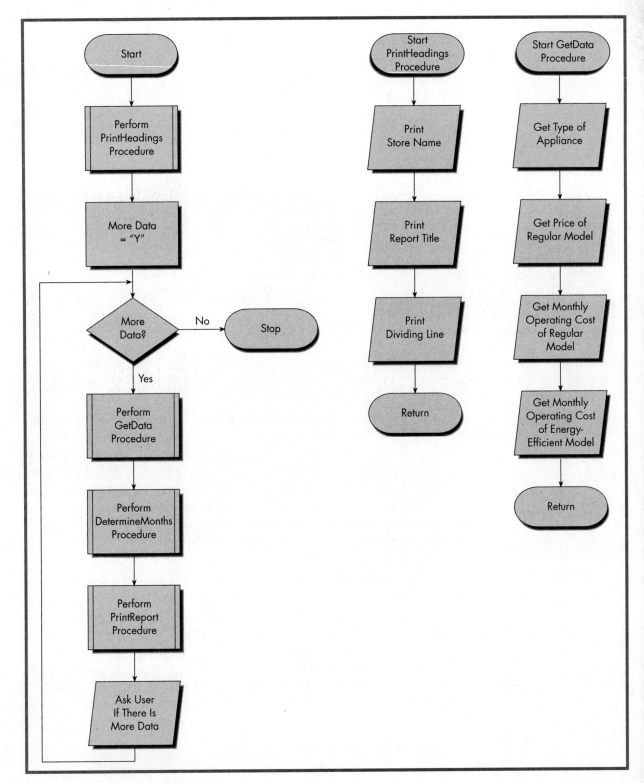

FIGURE 7-18

Continued

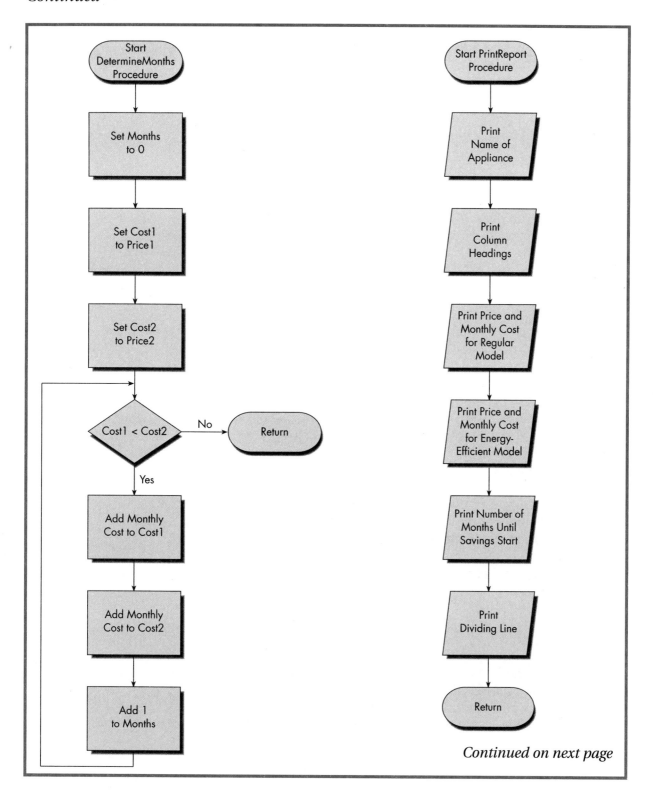

Continued on next page

FIGURE 7-18

Continued

```
Begin main program
    Call PrintHeadings
    Do while more data to enter
        Call GetData
        Call DetermineMonths
        Call PrintReport
        Ask user if there is more data to enter
    End loop
End main program

Begin PrintHeadings
    Print name of appliance store
    Print report title
    Print dividing line
End PrintHeadings

Begin GetData
    Prompt user to enter type of appliance
    Prompt user to enter price of regular model
    Prompt user to enter monthly operating cost of regular model
    Prompt user to enter price of energy-efficient model
    Prompt user to enter monthly operating cost of energy-efficient model
End GetData

Begin DetermineMonths
    Set months to 0
    Set regular model's cost to its price
    Set energy-efficient model's cost to its price
    Do while regular model's cost is less than energy-efficient model's cost
        Add monthly electricity cost to regular model's cost
        Add monthly electricity cost to energy-efficient model's cost
        Add 1 to months
    End Loop
End DetermineMonths

Begin PrintReport
    Print name of appliance
    Print column headings
    Print price and monthly cost for regular model
    Print price and monthly cost for energy-efficient model
    Print number of months until savings start for energy-efficient model
    Print dividing line
End PrintReport
```

becomes true only at the point when the energy-efficient appliance becomes cost effective. The loop is not repeated, and the value of Months is returned to the calling program. This variable tells consumers how long it will take before they save money on the energy-efficient appliance.

FIGURE 7-19

Energy Efficiency Program

```
DECLARE SUB PrintHeadings ()
DECLARE SUB GetData (Appliance$, Price1!, Price2!, MonthlyCost1!,
   MonthlyCost2!)
DECLARE SUB DetermineMonths (Price1!, Price2!, MonthlyCost1!,
   MonthlyCost2!, Months!)
DECLARE SUB PrintReport (Appliance$, Price1!, Price2!, MonthlyCost1!,
   MonthlyCost2!, Months!)

'***              Appliance Energy-Efficiency Program           ***

'*** This program allows the user to compare the total costs of     ***
'*** energy-efficient appliances, including initial purchase prices ***
'*** and estimated monthly electricity costs, with those of regular ***
'*** appliances. The resulting table is printed on paper.           ***
'*** Major variables:                                               ***
'***      More$          More data to be entered? (Y/N)             ***
'***      Appliance$     Name of the appliance                      ***
'***      Price1         Price of regular model                     ***
'***      Price2         Price of energy-efficient model            ***
'***      MonthlyCost1   Monthly operating cost of regular model    ***
'***      MonthlyCost2   Monthly operating cost of energy-efficient ***
'***                         model                                  ***
'***      Months         Number of months until owner begins saving ***
'***                         money by purchasing energy-efficient model ***


'*** Call PrintHeadings to print the report headings. ***
CALL PrintHeadings

CLS
More$ = "Y"


DO WHILE More$ = "Y"

   '*** Call GetData to get the information on appliances. ***
   CALL GetData(Appliance$, Price1, Price2, MonthlyCost1, MonthlyCost2)
```

Continued on next page

FIGURE 7-19

Continued

```
      '*** Call DetermineMonths to determine how many months are ***
      '*** required until savings begin. ***
      CALL DetermineMonths(Price1, Price2, MonthlyCost1, MonthlyCost2,
         Months)

      '*** Call PrintReport to print the information on savings. ***
      CALL PrintReport(Appliance$, Price1, Price2, MonthlyCost1,
         MonthlyCost2, Months)

      '*** Ask user if there is more data to be entered. ***
      INPUT "Do you wish to enter data on another appliance (Y/N)"; More$
      PRINT
   LOOP

END

SUB DetermineMonths (Price1, Price2, MonthlyCost1, MonthlyCost2, Months)
   '*** This procedure determines point at which appliance owner      ***
   '*** begins saving money by purchasing an energy-efficient model. ***

   Months = 0
   Cost1 = Price1
   Cost2 = Price2

   '*** Perform loop until total cost of regular model exceeds the ***
   '*** total cost of the energy-efficient model. ***
   DO WHILE Cost1 < Cost2
      Cost1 = Cost1 + MonthlyCost1
      Cost2 = Cost2 + MonthlyCost2
      Months = Months + 1
   LOOP

END SUB

SUB GetData (Appliance$, Price1, Price2, MonthlyCost1, MonthlyCost2)
   '*** This procedure prompts the user to enter prices of the       ***
   '*** regular model and the energy-efficient model along with      ***
   '*** estimated monthly electricity cost for each model.           ***

   '*** Get name of the appliance. ***
   INPUT "Enter the name of the appliance: ", Appliance$
```

FIGURE 7-19

Continued

```
    '*** Get data for regular model. ***
    INPUT "Enter price of the regular appliance: ", Price1
    INPUT "Enter monthly operating cost for regular appliance: ",
      MonthlyCost1

    '*** Get data for energy-efficient model. ***
    INPUT "Enter price of the energy-efficient appliance: ", Price2
    INPUT "Enter monthly operating cost for energy-efficient appliance: ",
      MonthlyCost2
    PRINT

END SUB

SUB PrintHeadings
    '*** This procedure prints, on paper, the name of the appliance ***
    '*** store and the report heading.                              ***

    LPRINT
    LPRINT TAB(20); "Joe's Appliances"
    LPRINT "Estimated Savings on Energy-Efficient Appliances"
    LPRINT "_____"

END SUB

SUB PrintReport (Appliance$, Price1, Price2, MonthlyCost1, MonthlyCost2,
    Months)
    '*** This procedure prints the appliance's name and purchase price ***
    '*** of regular and energy-efficient models. It then prints        ***
    '*** number of months it will require for the consumer to begin    ***
    '*** saving money by purchasing the energy-efficient model.        ***

    LPRINT
    LPRINT
    LPRINT "Appliance:   "; Appliance$
    LPRINT
    LPRINT "Model"; TAB(20); "Purchase Price"; TAB(37); "Monthly Cost"
    Format$ = "\              \   $$#####.##          $$###.##"
    LPRINT USING Format$; "Regular"; Price1; MonthlyCost1
    LPRINT USING Format$; "Energy-Efficient"; Price2; MonthlyCost2
    LPRINT
    LPRINT "You will begin saving money after"; Months; "months."
    LPRINT
    LPRINT "_____"

END SUB
```

Continued on next page

FIGURE 7-19

Continued

```
Enter the name of the appliance: Refrigerator
Enter price of the regular appliance: 950.00
Enter monthly operating cost for regular appliance: 12.50
Enter price of the energy-efficient appliance: 1070.00
Enter monthly operating cost for energy-efficient appliance: 9.00

Do you wish to enter data on another appliance (Y/N)? Y

Enter the name of the appliance: Dishwasher
Enter price of the regular appliance: 379.00
Enter monthly operating cost for regular appliance: 8.40
Enter price of the energy-efficient appliance: 440.00
Enter monthly operating cost for energy-efficient appliance: 6.10

Do you wish to enter data on another appliance (Y/N)? N
```

```
                       Joe's Appliances
         Estimated Savings on Energy-Efficient Appliances
         _____


Appliance:    Refrigerator

Model                 Purchase Price    Monthly Cost
Regular                   $950.00          $12.50
Energy-Efficient        $1070.00           $9.00

You will begin saving money after 35 months.

         _____




Appliance:    Dishwasher

Model                 Purchase Price    Monthly Cost
Regular                   $379.00          $8.40
Energy-Efficient          $440.00          $6.10

You will begin saving money after 27 months.

         _____
```

PROGRAMMING HINTS

- Remember that the DO WHILE...LOOP executes *while* the Boolean expression is true whereas the DO UNTIL...LOOP executes *until* the expression is true. Take care when creating the Boolean expression that controls execution to make certain the loop will stop at the correct point.

- Be careful to initialize the loop control variable of a DO...LOOP before entering the loop for the first time.

- If the loop control variable of a DO...LOOP is not modified in the loop body, an infinite loop is created.

- The DO WHILE...LOOP executes until the expression of the DO WHILE is tested and found to be false. It does not stop executing the moment the loop control variable is modified in the loop body, making the expression false.

- Make sure the initial, terminal, and step values of a FOR...NEXT statement are all numeric, and that the proper values have been specified to produce the desired number of loop repetitions.

- A loop control variable should never be modified within a FOR...NEXT loop.

- Special care should be given to nested FOR...NEXT loops; overlapping loops or missing FOR or NEXT statements can result in errors.

SUMMARY POINTS

▎ The basic elements of the loop structure are as follows:
  1. The loop control variable is initialized to a particular value before loop execution begins.
  2. The loop control variable is tested to determine whether the loop body should be executed or the loop exited.
  3. The loop body, consisting of any number of statements, is executed.
  4. At some point during loop execution, the value of the loop control variable must be modified to allow an exit from the loop.
  5. The loop is exited when the stated condition determines that the right number of loop repetitions has been performed.

▎ There are two types of DO...LOOP statements: the DO WHILE...LOOP, which executes while the Boolean expression is true, and the DO UNTIL...LOOP, which executes until the expression becomes true.

- Trailer values and counters can be used to control loop execution. A trailer value is a dummy value indicating the end of input data. When the trailer value is encountered, the loop stops executing. A counter can be used to control a loop if the number of desired loop repetitions is known in advance.

- The DO...LOOP can be used to create any type of loop whereas the FOR...NEXT should be used only to create counting loops.

- The FOR...NEXT loop executes the number of times specified in the FOR statement. The NEXT statement increments the loop control variable, tests it against the terminal value, and returns control to the statement immediately following the FOR statement if another loop execution is required.

- Loops may be nested inside one another.

KEY TERMS

Counter – 222
Counting loop – 222
Infinite loop – 222
Loop body – 215
Loop control variable – 214
Looping (iteration) – 214
Priming read – 217
Trailer (sentinel) value – 219

REVIEW QUESTIONS

1. When should a loop structure be used in a program?

2. What is the output from the following program segment?
```
X = 7
DO WHILE X <= 1
   PRINT X,
   X = X - 1
LOOP
```

3. Explain how trailer values can be used to control loops.

4. What is a counting loop? Which loop statements can be used to write counting loops?

5. How is the DO WHILE...LOOP different from the DO UNTIL...LOOP?

6. Can the DO WHILE...LOOP in Figure 7-7 be rewritten using a FOR...NEXT loop? Why or why not?

7. Rewrite the following program, using a loop controlled by a trailer value:

```
PRINT "GRAFFITI"
INPUT "Enter two names: ", Nme1$, Nme2$
PRINT Nme1$; " LOVES "; Nme2$
INPUT "Enter two names: ", Nme1$, Nme2$
PRINT Nme1$; " LOVES "; Nme2$
INPUT "Enter two names: ", Nme1$, Nme2$
PRINT Nme1$; " LOVES "; Nme2$
END
```

8. What is the purpose of the EXIT statement?

9. What happens when the step value of a FOR statement is zero?

10. What happens when no step value is specified in a FOR statement?

11. Which of the following FOR statements will cause a loop to be executed at least once?

    a. `FOR I = 8 TO 7`

    b. `FOR K = 15 TO 20 STEP 6`

    c. `FOR N = 3 TO 5 STEP 1`

    d. `FOR X = -2 TO -1 STEP -1`

    e. `FOR I = 1 TO 100 STEP 20`

12. How many times is the following inner loop executed? How many times is the outer loop executed?

```
Q = 10
W = 5
L1 = 4
FOR L1 = (Q - W) TO 1 STEP -1
    FOR L2 = 1 TO W STEP 1
        PRINT L1, L2
    NEXT L2
NEXT L1
```

13. When is a DO...LOOP a more appropriate choice than a FOR...NEXT loop?

14. When the step value of a FOR...NEXT loop is negative, will a loop terminate when the loop control variable is greater or less than the terminal value?

15. How many times are each of the following nested loops executed?

```
FOR Outer = 50 TO 5 STEP - 10
    FOR Middle = 1 TO 6 STEP 2
        FOR Inner = 5 TO 5
            Print Outer; Middle; Inner
```

```
      NEXT Inner
     NEXT Middle
   NEXT Outer
```

DEBUGGING EXERCISES

Locate any errors in the following programs or program segments, and debug them.

1.
```
'*** Get names and populations of 5 cities and keep track ***
'*** of largest one. ***
Count = 1
Population = 0
DO WHILE Count <= 5
    Count = Count + 1
    INPUT "Enter city: ", City$
    INPUT "Enter city's population: ", Population
    IF LargestPop < Population THEN
        LargestCity$ = City$
        LargestPop = Population
    END IF
LOOP
```

2.
```
'*** Get names and amounts owed on 20 charge accounts. ***
'*** If the amount owed is $20 or more, print the      ***
'*** customer's name and amount.                       ***
Count = 1
DO UNTIL Count <= 20
    INPUT Customer$, Amount
    IF Amount >= 20 THEN
        PRINT Customer$, Amount
        Count = Count + 1
LOOP
```

3.
```
'*** Cube numbers between 10 and 20. ***
FOR X = 10 TO 20
    Cubed = X ^ 3
    PRINT Cubed
NEXT Cubed
```

4.
```
'*** Count backwards by 5 from 100. ***
FOR Count = 1 TO 100 STEP -5
    PRINT Count;
NEXT Count
```

PROGRAMMING PROBLEMS

Level 1

1. Write a DO WHILE...LOOP that counts by fives until a given value (which should be called Limit) is reached. For example, if the value of Limit is 49, the output should be similar to the following:

    5   10   15   20   25   30   35   40   45

2. Rewrite Problem 1 using a DO UNTIL...LOOP instead of a DO WHILE...LOOP.

3. Rewrite Problem 1 using a FOR...NEXT loop instead of a DO WHILE...LOOP.

4. Write a program that uses nested FOR...NEXT loops to output the following pattern:

    ```
            *
          * * *
        * * * * *
      * * * * * * *
        * * * * *
          * * *
            *
    ```

5. Mr. Williams came up with a way of saving money to donate to his favorite charity. He wants to start with a penny on the first day and double the amount he gives for each subsequent day. Write a program to determine how much he will have donated after 15 days.

6. Write a loop that will display a motivational message for your school's football team. A FOR...NEXT loop should be used to display the message 100 times. For example, if your school's team is named the Tigers, you might display "Go Tigers!" 100 times.

Level 2

1. Write a program that will determine whether students are eligible for honors on graduation day. The student must be a senior with at least a 3.5 cumulative grade-point average out of a possible 4.0. The program should use a DO WHILE...LOOP to prompt the user to enter each student's name, class, and grade-point average. A message should then be displayed stating whether the student will graduate with honors. Use the following data to test your program:

    Sue Bartell   Senior   3.42

Tom Bix	Junior	3.60
Jenny Gomez	Senior	3.63
XXXXXXXXXXX	XXXXXX	0

Notice that the last line of data contains a trailer value for which the DO WHILE...LOOP can check.

2. Write a program to calculate the gas mileage for a car for each of four weeks. Prompt the user to enter the needed data for each week and then calculate and display the miles per gallon of gasoline. Use the following data to test your program:

Week of	Gallons	Miles
Jan. 1	5.0	173
Jan. 8	4.5	121
Jan. 15	6.0	201
Jan. 22	4.5	142

3. The mathematics department needs a program that prints, in a horizontal bar graph, the number of students enrolled in each class section 300 through 309. The user should be prompted to enter each section number and the number of students enrolled in that section. The resulting chart should be printed on paper. Use asterisks to create the chart. Each asterisk represents one student; for example:

```
Section
300       ***************************
301       **********************************
302       *****************************
 .
 .
 .
```

Use the following data to test your program:

Section	Students
300	20
301	15
302	32
303	17
304	28
305	35
306	26
307	29
308	19
309	27

4. Maria Maderas is thinking about starting a business selling pet rabbits. She currently has one pair of rabbits and would like to know approximately how many rabbits will be born

during a given period of time. Assume that each female rabbit will reproduce every four months and that the litters will have an average of eight rabbits. Also assume that half of the rabbits are female. The program should allow Maria to enter a given number of months and then output the number of rabbits she should have by the end of that time period.

5. Write a program that determines whether employees are eligible for a Christmas bonus. The user should be prompted to enter each employee's name, number of years of experience, position code, and weekly pay. The program should allow the user to calculate as many bonuses as necessary. Each employee is assigned a Christmas bonus based on the following rules:

Position Code	Bonus
1	1 week's pay
2	2 weeks' pay; maximum $700
3	1 week's pay

Employees with more than 10 years of experience receive an additional $100. Employees with fewer than 2 years of experience receive half the usual bonus. Write a program to compute each employee's bonus.

6. Your biology project is to determine the rate of growth of a particular type of bacteria. You suspect that the bacteria population increases at the same rate as the Fibonacci numbers. In this sequence of numbers, each number is equal to the sum of its two immediate predecessors. Therefore, the first few Fibonacci numbers are

```
0  1  1  2  3  5  8  13  21...
```

Assume that your bacteria reproduce asexually once every minute. You will be starting with a single bacterium. The program should allow you to enter a given number of minutes. Then the number of bacteria at the end of this time should be output. Use a FOR...NEXT loop.

Challenge Problems

1. The book reviewer for the local newspaper would like a program that prints a chart showing how many stars she has given each book she has reviewed. The chart should be printed on paper and each bar on the chart should have from one to five stars, depending on the rating that book received.

Input:

The user should be prompted to enter the following for each book:

a. The book's title

b. The book's author

c. The book's rating (a number from 1 to 5)

Processing Requirements:

a. Print each book's title and author.

b. Print the appropriate number of stars.

c. Ask the user if data on another book needs to be entered.

d. Continue this process until the user is done entering data.

Output:

The report should be printed on paper. Its format should be as follows:

```
                    Book Review Ratings

Title                                      Author      Rating

Learning to Love C                         P. Lord     *****
The Survivor                               I. Bulas    ***
Don't Look Now                             H. Poirot   *
You Too Can Become a Programmer            J. Hacker   ***
Neon Sun                                   A. Ranier   ****
```

Use the following data to test your program:

Title	Author	Rating
Learning to Love C	P. Lord	5
The Survivor	I. Bulas	3
Don't Look Now	H. Poirot	1
You Too Can Become a Programmer	J. Hacker	3
Neon Sun	A. Ranier	4

2. Stewart and Sons Jewelers needs a program that prompts the user to enter data on each salesperson's sales for each of four months. The program should then print, on paper, the total sales and average sales for each person, and the total sales for all salespeople for the four-month period.

Input:

The program should prompt the user to enter the following data on each salesperson:

a. Name

b. Total sales for each of the four months

Processing Requirements:

a. Calculate total sales for each salesperson.

b. Calculate average sales for each salesperson

c. Calculate total sales for all salespeople.

d. Allow the user to enter data on as many salespeople as needed.

Output:

The results should be printed on paper and appear similar to the following:

```
Salesperson          Total              Average
XXXXX                $XXXXX.XX          $XXXX.XX
  .                    .                  .
  .                    .                  .
  .                    .                  .
Total Sales          $XXXXXX.XX
```

Use the following data to test your program:

Stewart Birsch	7457.00	5071.63	4921.16	5717.05
Monica Bulas	1125.16	927.19	1674.84	1970.15
Carolyn Lieh	2257.08	3716.84	2116.93	1877.45
David Toth	871.69	1199.72	1299.60	941.38
Irene Kumata	4412.77	2128.91	3008.97	2365.33
Anne Swetlick	2740.08	3165.75	2981.39	1886.40

CHAPTER 8

Functions and Debugging and Testing

Outline

Objectives

After studying this chapter, you will be able to:

▌ Use the standard numeric functions INT, SQR, SGN, ABS, and RND.

▌ Use the standard string functions LEN, STRING$, LEFT$, RIGHT$, MID$, LCASE$, UCASE$, ASC, CHR$, VAL, STR$, and DATE$.

▌ Use FUNCTION procedures to meet specific needs.

▌ Define the term *user friendly*.

▌ Write user-friendly programs.

▌ Protect programs from invalid user input.

▌ Use desk checking and program tracing to locate program errors.

▌ Use QBasic's integrated debugger.

▌ Test programs using correctly selected data.

INTRODUCTION

Function *A subprogram designed to return a single value to the calling program. The two types are standard functions and user-defined functions.*

Standard function *A function that is built into QBasic.*

User-defined function *A function written by a programmer to meet a specific need.*

A useful feature of QBasic is the **function**, a subprogram designed to perform a specific task and return a single value. QBasic contains a number of **standard**, or **library**, **functions**, which perform common operations, such as finding the square root of a number or converting a letter from uppercase to lowercase. Standard functions spare the programmer the necessity of writing the statements otherwise needed to perform these operations. In some cases, however, it is useful for the programmer to write a function to meet a particular need. These functions written by the programmer are called **user-defined functions**. This chapter discusses both standard and user-defined functions.

Despite the many advantages of structured programming, programs rarely work correctly the first time they are executed. Fortunately, QBasic has several features that allow you to debug your programs efficiently. We discuss some techniques for testing your program to determine whether it obtains correct results with a wide variety of data.

STANDARD FUNCTIONS

Standard functions are part of the QBasic system and can be easily referenced by the user. To use a standard function, it must be called. A function call can be used in place of a constant, a variable, or an expression. For example, the SQR function determines the square root of a positive number. The following statement calls SQR and assigns the square root of 125 to variable Square-Root:

```
SquareRoot = SQR(125)
```

The argument (which is placed in parentheses) can be a constant, a variable, an expression, or another function. Some more statements using SQR follow:

```
SquareRoot = SQR(Number)
PRINT SQR(14 + 15)
SquareRoot = SQR(SQR (16))
```

The last statement contains nested function calls that result in the number 2 being assigned to SquareRoot.

Function calls are always evaluated before other operations in the statement are performed. Therefore, a function call has a higher priority than arithmetic, relational, and logical operators.

Numeric Functions

Table 8-1 summarizes the numeric functions discussed here. These functions allow the programmer to manipulate numbers in a variety of ways.

INT. The integer, or INT, function computes the largest integer less than or equal to the argument. For example:

X	INT (X)
8	8
5.34	5
16.9	16
–2.75	–3
–0.5	–1

If the argument is a positive value with a fractional part, the digits to the right of the decimal point are truncated (cut off). Notice from the preceding examples that truncation does not occur when the argument is negative. For instance, when the argument equals –2.75, the INT function returns –3, the largest integer less than or equal to that value. This fact can be seen on the number line, where the farther to the left a number lies, the less value it has:

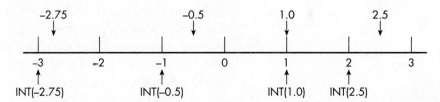

Although the INT function alone does not round its argument, it can be used in an expression that rounds to the nearest integer, nearest tenth, nearest hundredth, or any other degree of accuracy

TABLE 8-1 COMMON NUMERIC FUNCTIONS

Function	Operation	Example
ABS(number)	Returns the absolute value of number.	ABS(–12.5) is 12.5
INT(number)	Returns the largest integer less than or equal to number.	INT(85.67) is 85
RND	Returns a random number between 0 and 1.	RND returns a random number
SGN(number)	Returns +1 if number is positive, 0 if number is zero, and –1 if number is negative.	SGN(–15) is –1
SQR(number)	Returns the square root of number (number must be positive).	SQR(16) is 4

desired. For example, a number can be rounded to the nearest integer by adding 0.5 to it before using the INT function:

```
I = INT(Number + 0.5)
```

The program in Figure 8-1 rounds a number to the nearest integer, nearest tenth, and nearest hundredth.

SQR. The square root, or SQR, function determines the positive square root of its argument. The argument must be a positive number. Square roots are used often in mathematical formulas, for example, to calculate the length of the hypotenuse of a right triangle. The Pythagorean theorem is used to determine the length of the hypotenuse:

$$\text{Hypotenuse} = \sqrt{(\text{side 1})^2 + (\text{side 2})^2}$$

FIGURE 8-1

Rounding with the INT Function

```
'***   This program rounds a number to the nearest        ***
'***   integer, tenth, and hundredth.                     ***

CLS
INPUT "Please enter a number: ", Number

PRINT
PRINT "Nearest"; TAB(12); "Nearest"; TAB(24); "Nearest"
PRINT "Integer"; TAB(13); "Tenth"; TAB(23); "Hundredth"
PRINT R1; TAB(13); R2; TAB(24); R3
R1 = INT(Number + .5)
R2 = INT((Number + .05) * 10) / 10
R3 = INT((Number + .005) * 100) / 100

END
```

```
Please enter a number: 11.427

Nearest      Nearest      Nearest
Integer       Tenth      Hundredth
  11          11.4         11.43
```

This formula can be translated into QBasic as follows:

```
Hypotenuse = SQR ((Side1 ^ 2) + (Side2 ^ 2))
```

Figure 8-2 contains the complete program.

SGN. The sign, or SGN, function determines the sign of a number. If $X > 0$, then $SGN(X) = 1$; if $X = 0$, then $SGN(X) = 0$; and if $X < 0$, then $SGN(X) = -1$. For example:

X	SGN (X)
8.5	1
0	0
−1005	−1

The following program segment shows how the SGN function could display a message stating whether a number is positive, negative, or zero:

```
IF SGN(Number) = 1 THEN
   PRINT "This number is positive."
ELSEIF SGN(Number) = 0 THEN
    PRINT "This number is zero."
ELSEIF SGN(Number) = -1 THEN
    PRINT "This number is negative."
END IF
```

ABS. The absolute value, or ABS, function returns the absolute value of its argument. If the argument has a negative value, the ABS function serves to remove the negative sign. For example:

X	ABS (X)
−2	2
0	0
3.54	3.54

This function is often used to identify significant differences between given values. Suppose the Internal Revenue Service wants to know which individuals owe a substantial sum or are owed a substantial sum by the government. Figure 8-3 shows how the ABS function could be used to identify such individuals.

RND. The random number, or RND, function produces a random number from 0 to 1. Zero is included in this range, but 1 is not. The term **random** indicates that any value in a given set of values is equally likely to occur. The function is useful for any situation requiring an input quantity of which the exact value is unpre-

Random *A term describing a group of values, such as numbers, in which each value has an equal chance of occurring.*

FIGURE 8-2

Program Demonstrating the SQR Function

```
'*** This program uses the Pythagorean theorem to deter- ***
'*** mine the length of the hypotenuse of a right         ***
'*** triangle:                                            ***

CLS
'*** Get data. ***
INPUT "Enter the base: ", Bse
INPUT "Enter the height: ", Height

'*** Calculate hypotenuse. ***
Hypotenuse = SQR((Bse ^ 2) + (Height ^ 2))

'*** Display result. ***
PRINT "The length of the hypotenuse is"; Hypotenuse

END
```

```
Enter the base: 12
Enter the height: 17
The length of the hypotenuse is 20.80865
```

dictable. It is particularly useful in applications involving statistics, computer simulations, and games.

At first it might not seem hard to produce random values. The task is difficult for computers, however, because of their precise structure and logic. The numbers produced by a computer are not truly random, such as those resulting from a throw of dice, but are more accurately described as pseudorandom. To produce a sequence of seemingly unrelated numbers, the RND function uses a special algorithm. The particular sequence of numbers generated by this algorithm depends on a value known as a *seed*. When a new seed value is supplied to the algorithm, a new sequence of numbers is produced. If the seed is never changed, however, a program containing the RND function produces the same series of "random" numbers each time it is run. For example, each time the following program segment is executed,

```
X = RND
PRINT X
```

FIGURE **8-3**

Program Demonstrating the ABS Function

```
'*** This program identifies IRS audit candidates.        ***

CLS
PRINT
INPUT "Enter the taxpayer's name (XXX to stop): ", Nme$
DO WHILE Nme$ <> "XXX"
    INPUT "Enter the amount of taxes: ", Tax
    IF ABS(Tax) >= 1000 THEN
        PRINT Nme$; " is to be audited."
    END IF
    PRINT
    INPUT "Enter the taxpayer's name (XXX to stop): ", Nme$
LOOP

END
```

```
Enter the taxpayer's name (XXX to stop): M. Couch
Enter the amount of taxes: 999

Enter the taxpayer's name (XXX to stop): S. Mandez
Enter the amount of taxes: 1020
S. Mandez is to be audited.

Enter the taxpayer's name (XXX to stop): C. Lininger
Enter the amount of taxes: -1430
C. Lininger is to be audited.

Enter the taxpayer's name (XXX to stop): XXX
```

the same number is displayed. The RANDOMIZE statement is needed to provide a new random number seed, resulting in a truly random result. Its format is

```
RANDOMIZE [integer]
```

or

```
RANDOMIZE TIMER
```

The integer, if used, must be changed each time the program runs to produce new numbers. If the integer is omitted, the prompt message asks the user to enter a number within the indicated range.

If TIMER is specified, a new number seed determined by the computer's clock is generated for each program run, and no prompt appears. For example, the following statements

```
RANDOMIZE TIMER
PRINT RND
```

cause the computer to display a different number each time they are executed. You need only place the RANDOMIZE statement into a program once, before the first random number is generated.

Random numbers greater than 1 can be produced by combining the RND function with other mathematical operations. The following formula generates a random number R between Low (the low limit) and High (the high limit):

```
R = RND * (High - Low) + Low
```

The value of Low will be contained within the range of random numbers, but High will not. Use the INT function if you wish to generate only integer values:

```
I = INT(RND * (High - Low) + Low)
```

If you want the range of the random integers to include High, the value 1 is added to High – Low as follows:

```
I  = INT(RND * (High - Low + 1) + Low)
```

For example, the following statement generates a random number between 7 and 12:

```
Number = INT(RND * 6) + 7
```

Figure 8-4 contains a guessing game that uses the RND function to generate an integer between 1 and 100.

FIGURE 8-4

Using the RND Function to Play a Guessing Game

```
'***                    Guessing Game                    ***

'*** This program prompts the player to guess an integer ***
'*** value from 1 to 100.  When the player enters the    ***
'*** correct value, the game stops.                      ***

RANDOMIZE TIMER
'*** Add 1 to upper number so that 100 will be included in range. ***
High = 100 + 1
Low = 1
'*** Generate the answer. ***
Answer = INT(RND * (High - Low) + Low)
CLS
PRINT "This is a guessing game."
PRINT
PRINT "Try to guess the number between 1 and 100."
'*** Set Guess to number outside possible range so that loop will ***
'*** always execute as least once. ***
Guess = -1

DO UNTIL Guess = Answer
    INPUT "Enter your guess: ", Guess
    IF Guess = Answer THEN
        PRINT "CORRECT!! You are a winner!"
    ELSEIF Guess > Answer THEN
        PRINT "Wrong answer -- too high."
    ELSE
        PRINT "Wrong answer -- too low."
    END IF
LOOP

END
```

FIGURE 8-4

Continued

```
This is a guessing game.

Try to guess the number between 1 and 100.
Enter your guess: 50
Wrong answer -- too high.
Enter your guess: 25
Wrong answer -- too low.
Enter your guess: 37
Wrong answer -- too high.
Enter your guess: 30
Wrong answer -- too low.
Enter your guess: 33
Wrong answer -- too low.
Enter your guess: 34
Wrong answer -- too low.
Enter your guess: 35
CORRECT!! You are a winner!
```

Learning Check 8-1

1. Another name for standard functions is _____ functions.

2. True or False? The argument for a numeric function must always be a variable.

3. The _____ function returns the largest integer less than or equal to the value specified as the argument.

4. The _____ function is used to generate unpredictable numbers that are useful in statistics and when developing games.

5. What are the values of the following expressions?

    a. INT((2 - 4) / 4)

    b. SQR(4 * 3 + 4)

    c. ABS(INT (4 / 5) - 1)

    d. SGN(ABS (4 ^ 2 - 20))

String Functions

Up to this point, we have manipulated numbers but have done little with strings except to print them or compare them with one another. Many programming applications require more sophisticated manipulation of strings.

Concatenate *To join together two or more data items, such as character strings, to form a single item.*

String functions allow programmers to modify, **concatenate** (join together), compare, and analyze the composition of strings. These functions are useful for sorting lists of names, determining subject matter in text, printing mailing lists, and so forth. For example, the use of string functions can enable a program to determine that John J. Simmons is the same as Simmons, John J. The string functions discussed here are summarized in Table 8-2.

TABLE 8-2 COMMON STRING FUNCTIONS

Function	Operation	Example
string1 + string2	Concatenation; joins two strings.	"KUNG " + "FU" is "KUNG FU"
ASC(string)	Returns the ASCII code for the first character in the string.	If A$ = "DOG", then ASC(A$) is 68
CHR$(expression)	Returns the string representation of the ASCII code of the expression.	CHR$(68) is "D"
DATE$	Returns the current date.	"05-19-1998"
LCASE$(string)	Converts any uppercase letters in string to lowercase.	IF N$ = "George III", then LCASE$(N$) is "george iii"
LEFT$(string, expression)	Returns the specified number of leftmost characters of a string specified by the expression.	LEFT$("ABCD", 2) is "AB"
LEN(string)	Returns the length of a string.	If N$ = "HI THERE", then LEN(N$) is 8
MID$(string, expression1 [,expression2])	Starting with the character at expression1, returns the number of characters specified by expression2.	MID$("MARIE", 2, 3) is "ARI"
RIGHT$(string, expression)	Returns the number of rightmost characters specified by the expression.	RIGHT$("ABCDE", 2) is "DE"
STR$ (expression)	Converts a number to its string equivalent.	STR$(123) is "123"
STRING$(expression, character)	Generates a single character a specified number of times.	STRING$(30, "#") generates 30 # symbols
UCASE$(string)	Converts any lowercase letters in string to uppercase.	IF N$ = "Yes", then UCASE$(N$) is "YES"
VAL (string)	Returns the numeric value of a number string.	If N$ = "35263" then VAL(N$) is 35263

Concatenation. Concatenation serves to join two strings end to end, forming a new string. Technically, it is not a function, as are the other string functions discussed here; instead, it is an operation performed on two string operands, just as the arithmetic operators +, −, *, and / act on two numeric values. The plus sign (+) serves as the concatenation operator. For example, the statement

```
A$ = "NIGHT" + "MARE"
```

assigns the string *NIGHTMARE* to the variable A$. Similarly, the following segment results in X$ containing the value *SAN FRAN-CISCO*:

```
A$ = "SAN "
B$ = "FRAN"
C$ = "CISCO"
X$ = A$ + B$ + C$
```

The program in Figure 8-5 demonstrates the use of concatenation.

LEN. The length, or LEN, function returns the number of characters in the single string that is its argument. (Remember that blanks in quoted strings are counted as characters.) LEN is useful when centering a heading. For example, the following program segment centers "R. W. Horton Advertising" on an 80-column line:

```
Start = (80 - LEN("R. W. Horton Advertising")) / 2
PRINT TAB(Start); "R. W. Horton Advertising"
```

The steps in centering a heading are as follows:

1. Find the length of the heading.

2. Subtract this length from the entire length of the line (in this example, 80).

3. Divide this value by 2 to determine the starting column.

4. Tab to the starting column and print the heading.

STRING$. The simplest way to repeat a character a specific number of times is to use the STRING$ function. For example, the following statement prints a row of 40 asterisks:

```
PRINT STRING$(40, "*")
```

FIGURE 8-5

Program Demonstrating Concatenation

```
'***  This program generates a form letter. ***

CLS
INPUT "Enter last name: ", LastName$
INPUT "Enter a 1 for male, 2 for female: ", Code

'*** Determine form of address. ***
IF Code = 1 THEN
   Title$ = "Mr. "
ELSE
   Title$ = "Ms. "
END IF
'*** Print the letter on paper. ***
LPRINT
LPRINT
LPRINT "Dear " + Title$ + LastName$ + ","

LPRINT TAB(7); "We are sorry, but your work does"
LPRINT "not coincide with our needs at this time."
LPRINT
LPRINT TAB(20); "The Hack Publishing House"

END
```

```
Enter last name: Csongas
Enter a 1 for male, 2 for female: 2
```

```
Dear Ms. Csongas,
     We are sorry, but your work does
not coincide with our needs at this time.

                    The Hack Publishing House
```

This can be very useful when creating dividing lines among portions of output. For example, the following program segment places an underline below a centered heading:

```
Start = (80 - LEN("R. W. Horton Advertising")) / 2
PRINT TAB(Start); "R. W. Horton Advertising"
PRINT TAB(Start); STRING$(LEN("R. W. Horton Advertising"), "-")
```

LEFT$ and RIGHT$. The LEFT$ function returns a string that consists of the leftmost portion of the string argument, from the first character to the character position specified by the expression. For instance, the following statement assigns to ByeNow$ the value SEE YA LATE:

```
ByeNow$ = LEFT$("SEE YA LATER ALLIGATOR!", 11)
```

The LEFT$ function is often useful when comparing character strings. Suppose a program asks the user to answer a yes or no question but does not specify whether the question should be answered by typing the entire word *YES* or *NO* or just the first letter, *Y* or *N*. The LEFT$ function can compare just the first character of the user's responses, allowing the user to type either YES/NO or Y/N. The program in Figure 8-6 illustrates this.

The format of the RIGHT$ function is similar to that of the LEFT$ function. It returns the number of characters specified by the expression from the right end of the string. The following statement assigns *GATOR!* to ByeNow$:

```
ByeNow$ = RIGHT$("SEE YA LATER ALLIGATOR!", 6)
```

MID$. The MID$ function has the following format where the two expressions are integers:

```
MID$(string, expression1[, expression2])
```

This function returns the portion of the string beginning at the character position defined by *expression1* and extending for the number of characters given by *expression2*. If *expression2* is omitted, the characters from the starting position of *expression1* to the end of the string are returned. The following statement assigns to ByeNow$ a string four characters long, starting at the fourteenth character, *ALLI*:

```
ByeNow$ = MID$("SEE YA LATER ALLIGATOR!", 14, 4)
```

FIGURE 8-6

Program Demonstrating the LEFT$ Function

```
'*** This program uses the LEFT$ function to examine    ***
'*** only the first character of a user response.       ***

CLS
INPUT "Are you allergic to any medications (Y/N)"; Answer$
Answer$ = LEFT$(Answer$, 1)

IF Answer$ = "Y" THEN
   PRINT "Allergies"
ELSE
   PRINT "No allergies"
END IF

END
```

```
Are you allergic to any medications (Y/N)? Yes
Allergies
```

LCASE$ and UCASE$. LCASE$ converts all the letters in a string to lowercase letters. When the following statement is executed, *computer* is assigned to Small$:

```
Small$ = LCASE$("COMPUTER")
```

Alternatively, UCASE$ converts letters to uppercase. For example,

```
PRINT UCASE$("Halt!")
```

displays *HALT!* Note that the letter *H* remains uppercase.

These commands are useful in programs requiring the user to enter a single letter as a response. Consider the following program segment:

```
INPUT "Do you wish to continue (Y/N)"; Answer$
Answer$ = UCASE$(Answer$)
IF Answer$ = "Y" THEN
   CALL ProcessData
END IF
```

The UCASE$ function is used to convert the value of Answer$ to uppercase. Therefore, it no longer matters whether the user enters a lowercase or uppercase response.

ASC and CHR$. The ASC function returns the ASCII value of the first character of its string argument. For example, the following statement assigns the value 67 to Cvalue:

```
Cvalue = ASC("C")
```

If the argument has more than one character, only the first one is examined. The following statement assigns 82 (the value of R) to Rvalue:

```
Rvalue = ASC("Return a value")
```

The CHR$ function performs the reverse operation of the ASC function: It returns the single character that corresponds to a given ASCII value. The argument must be an integer in the range 0 through 255. The following statement assigns the value *HI!* to Message$:

```
Message$ = CHR$(72) + CHR$(73) + CHR$(33)
```

The ASC and CHR$ functions are demonstrated in the program in Figure 8-7, which prints a listing of the alphabet with its corresponding ASCII values.

VAL and STR$. The VAL function converts a numeric string expression (such as "12.34") to its equivalent numeric value. The following statement assigns *40.12* to Number:

```
X$ = "40.12"
Number = VAL(X$)
```

The characters can include the digits 0 through 9, the plus and minus signs, and the decimal point. Any leading blanks in the string are ignored. If the first nonblank character of the string is nonnumeric, the function returns a value of zero. For example, the following statement would output 0:

```
PRINT VAL("BG, OH 43402")
```

Otherwise, the function examines the string one character at a time until an unacceptable character is encountered. A blank is

FIGURE 8-7

Program to Display Letters and Corresponding ASCII Codes

```
'***   This program displays each letter of the alphabet   ***
'***   along with its corresponding ASCII code.            ***

CLS
PRINT "CHARACTER", "ASCII CODE"
PRINT

FOR Count = ASC("A") TO ASC("Z")
   PRINT CHR$(Count), Count
NEXT Count

END
```

```
CHARACTER     ASCII CODE

A             65
B             66
C             67
D             68
E             69
F             70
G             71
H             72
I             73
J             74
K             75
L             76
M             77
N             78
O             79
P             00
Q             81
R             82
S             83
T             84
U             85
V             86
W             87
X             88
Y             89
Z             90
```

acceptable within a numeric string; it is simply ignored. The following statement assigns N1 the value *1084*:

```
N1 = VAL(" 1084 Welsh View Dr.")
```

By using the VAL function, it is possible to change a number in a character string to a number that can be used in mathematical computations. The program in Figure 8-8 assigns an integer value to a string variable and uses the VAL function to compute the sum of its digits.

The STR$ function performs the reverse of the VAL function operation: It converts a number to a string. For example, when the statement

```
S1$ = STR$ (104)
```

is executed, S1$ will be assigned the character string "104".

FIGURE 8-8

Program Demonstrating the VAL Function

```
'*** This program calculates the sum of the digits of    ***
'*** an integer.                                          ***

CLS
Sum = 0
INPUT "Enter a nonnegative integer: ", Number$
Length = LEN(Number$)
FOR Position = 1 TO Length
   Digit$ = MID$(Number$, Position, 1)
   NDigit = VAL(Digit$)

   Sum = Sum + NDigit
NEXT Position
PRINT "Sum of digits = "; Sum

END


Enter a nonnegative integer: 469
Sum of digits =  19
```

DATE$. The DATE$ function returns the current date. If today's date is May 19, 1998, and the statement

```
PRINT DATE$
```

is executed, the following is output:

05-19-1998

The DATE$ function is useful when creating reports or letters in which you want the current date to appear in the heading.

Learning Check 8-2

1. _____ is the joining of strings.

2. The _____ function returns the number of characters in a string.

3. What value is assigned to T$ by the following statement?

T$ = MID$("419-358-4448", 5, 3)

4. What does the ASC function do? What function performs the reverse operation of the ASC function?

5. True or False? The VAL function converts a random number into a numeric string.

FUNCTION PROCEDURES

FUNCTION procedure *A subprogram designed to return a single value to the calling program.*

Standard functions can be very useful. However, there will be times when you wish to create your own customized functions. These custom functions are generally referred to as user-defined functions. In QBasic the **FUNCTION procedure** allows you to create user-defined functions. The FUNCTION procedure is similar to the SUB procedure, except that it returns a single value. This value is returned in the function itself, not as an argument. The following FUNCTION procedure returns the area of a right triangle using the formula ½ * height * base:

```
FUNCTION Area (Bse, Height)
    '*** This function calculates area of a right triangle. ***
    Area = .5 * (Bse * Height)
END FUNCTION
```

Notice that the result is assigned to the function itself. FUNCTION procedures are not called in the same manner as SUB procedures.

A function is called by using its name in an expression. For example, the following statement could be placed in the main module to call Area:

```
TriangleArea = Area (Height, Bse)
```

More examples follow of statements that can be used to call Area:

```
PRINT Area (Height, Bse)
Answer = Area (10, 12)
Result = Area (2 * 20, 30)
```

The complete program using FUNCTION procedure Area is shown in Figure 8-9.

As with SUB procedures, each FUNCTION procedure must be entered in a separate View window from the main program. As usual, use the [F2] key to switch between the main modules and the procedures.

The arguments of a FUNCTION procedure should not be altered in the function body. If a procedure needs to return more than one value, a SUB procedure should be used instead.

FUNCTION procedures can also be used to determine and return character strings. Examine Figure 8-10. It contains a modified version of Figure 6-4, which calculates a student's grade. Notice that DetermineGrade$ has been changed from a SUB procedure to a FUNCTION procedure (a dollar sign has been added to the name because it will be assigned a character value). FUNCTION procedures, like SUB procedures, can have local variables. In DetermineGrade$, Score is a local variable. The value of this local variable is not known to the calling program.

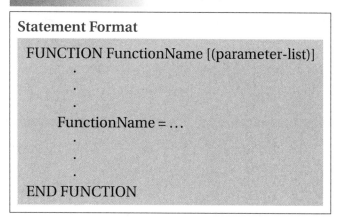

The FUNCTION Statement

Statement Format

FUNCTION FunctionName [(parameter-list)]
         .
         .
         .
         FunctionName = ...
         .
         .
         .
END FUNCTION

FIGURE 8-9

Program Using a FUNCTION Procedure to Perform a
Mathematical Calculation

```
DECLARE FUNCTION Area! (Bse!, Height!)

'***                     Triangle Area                    ***

'*** This program calculates the area of a right tri-     ***
'*** angle using the formula:  1/2 * (Base * Height).     ***
'*** Major variables:                                     ***
'***      Bse            Length of base of triangle       ***
'***      Height         Height of the triangle           ***
'***      TriangleArea   Area of the triangle             ***

CLS
'*** Get data. ***
INPUT "Enter the length of the triangle's base: ", Bse
INPUT "Enter the triangle's height: ", Height

'*** Call function to calculate area. ***
TriangleArea = Area(Bse, Height)

'*** Display result. ***
PRINT "The area of this triangle is"; TriangleArea

END

FUNCTION Area (Bse, Height)
   '*** This function calculates the area of a right triangle. ***

   Area = .5 * (Bse * Height)

END FUNCTION
```

```
Enter the length of the triangle's base: 6
Enter the triangle's height: 11
The area of this triangle is 33
```

FIGURE 8-10

Program Using a FUNCTION Procedure to Determine a
Grade

```
DECLARE FUNCTION DetermineGrade$ (Test1!, Test2!, Test3!)
DECLARE SUB DividingLine ()
DECLARE SUB DividingLine ()

'***                      Calculus Grading Program          ***

'*** This program calculates a student's grade based on  ***
'*** 3 test scores.  Grades are assigned as follows:     ***
'***      A      > 88                                    ***
'***      B      77 - 88                                 ***
'***      C      68 - 76                                 ***
'***      D      55 - 67                                 ***
'***      F      < 55                                    ***
'*** Major variables:                                    ***
'***      Student$        Student's name                 ***
'***      Test1 - Test3   3 test scores                  ***
'***      Grade$          Student's final grade          ***

CLS
'*** Call procedure to display upper dividing line. ***
CALL DividingLine

'*** Get the needed data. ***
INPUT "Enter student's name: ", Student$
PRINT
INPUT "Enter student's 3 test scores: ", Test1, Test2, Test3

'*** Call function DetermineGrade$ to calculate student's grade. ***
Grade$ = DetermineGrade$(Test1, Test2, Test3)

PRINT
'*** Display grade. ***
PRINT "Grade: "; Grade$

'*** Call procedure to display lower dividing line. ***
CALL DividingLine

END

FUNCTION DetermineGrade$ (Test1, Test2, Test3)
    '*** This FUNCTION procedure determines the student's   ***
    '*** grade and returns this value to the calling program. ***
```

Continued on next page

FIGURE 8-10

Continued

```
    '*** Find sum of 3 tests. ***
    Score = Test1 + Test2 + Test3

    '*** Determine the grade. ***
    SELECT CASE Score
        CASE IS > 88
            DetermineGrade$ = "A"
        CASE 77 TO 88
            DetermineGrade$ = "B"
        CASE 68 TO 76
            DetermineGrade$ = "C"
        CASE 55 TO 67
            DetermineGrade$ = "D"
        CASE ELSE
            DetermineGrade$ = "F"
    END SELECT

END FUNCTION

SUB DividingLine
    '*** This procedure prints blank lines and a row of      ***
    '*** hyphens to divide sections of the output.           ***

    PRINT
    PRINT STRING$(50, "-")
    PRINT

END SUB
```

```
--------------------------------------------------

Enter student's name: Sam Sung

Enter student's 3 test scores: 24, 23, 45

Grade: A

--------------------------------------------------
```

WRITING USER-FRIENDLY PROGRAMS

User friendly *A term used to describe a program that is written to be as easy and enjoyable as possible for people to use.*

User friendly is a term often heard in the world of programming. A program is user friendly when it is written to be as easy and enjoyable as possible for people to use. Some characteristics of user-friendly programs are as follows:

- The prompts are easy to understand, and the program is written to make it as easy as possible for the user to enter responses. For example, if the user is directed to respond to a prompt with a *y* (for *yes*), a well-written program might also accept the following responses as the equivalent: *Y, Yes, yeah,* and *YES.*

- If the user has a number of options to choose from, a clearly stated menu should list all of these options and the codes necessary for choosing them.

- The program should be able to handle invalid input and display a clear and polite error message. If the program is interactive, the user should be prompted to reenter the necessary input.

- If the data to be entered must be within a given range, the program should make certain it meets the specified requirements before continuing. If it does not meet those requirements, an error message should be displayed, and the user should be prompted to reenter the data.

A program segment follows in which the user is supposed to enter a digit from 1 through 7 representing a day of the week:

```
INPUT "Enter an integer representing the day (1-7)"; Day
DO WHILE (Day < 1) OR (Day > 7)
    PRINT "The number must be between 1 and 7."
    INPUT "Please reenter the day"; Day
LOOP
```

If the user enters a number outside the allowable range, he or she is prompted to reenter the number. However, if the user enters a nonnumeric character, QBasic displays an error message. To protect this program segment from nonnumeric input, it can be rewritten like this:

```
INPUT "Enter an integer representing the day (1-7)"; Day$
DO WHILE (ASC(Day$) < 49) OR (ASC(Day$) > 55)
    PRINT "The number must be between 1 and 7."
    INPUT "Please reenter the day"; Day$
LOOP
```

The value that the user enters should be an integer. However, the value is assigned to the string variable Day$, so that the program can prompt the user to reenter the data if nonnumeric data is entered. The ASCII value of the character is checked to make certain that it falls within the 1 through 7 range. Programs that are user friendly should be able to handle any type of invalid data. This is often referred to as "defensive programming"—the program is defended against any kind of data that the user could possible enter.

The program discussed at the end of this chapter (in the "Mastering Program Development" section) illustrates the characteristics of a user-friendly program.

Learning Check 8-3

1. _____ procedures are subprograms designed to return a single value.

2. What must *always* happen in the body of a FUNCTION procedure?

3. A(n) _____ program politely prompts the user to reenter invalid input.

4. The last statement of a FUNCTION procedure is _____.

DEBUGGING AND TESTING

As discussed in Chapter 2, program errors can be divided into three broad categories: syntax, run time, and logic. Each of these types is discussed here, along with techniques for avoiding and correcting them.

The most common type of error for beginning programmers is the syntax error. Fortunately, it is also the easiest type of error to locate and correct. Syntax errors are violations of the grammatical rules of a programming language. Mistyping a word is the most frequent cause. Depending on the type of syntax error you make, QBasic may or may not display an error message. For example, if you type in

```
IF X >= 8
```

and press Enter ⏎, QBasic informs you that you forgot the THEN which must be on the same line as the IF. This error message is shown in Figure 8-11. All you need to do is press Enter ⏎ and then correct the syntax by inserting the THEN.

However, if you misspell PRINT as follows:

```
PIRNT X, Y
```

FIGURE 8-11

An Example of an Error
Message

no error message appears when [Enter ←] is pressed, but you will get
a message when you attempt to execute the program. Most syntax
errors can be caught by careful proofreading. Syntax errors must
be corrected before a program can be executed.

Run-time errors cause a program to stop executing before it
should. For example, if the program attempts to divide a number
by zero as follows:

```
Amount = 887 / 0
```

QBasic will stop program execution and display an error message
stating that division by zero was attempted. You can then press
[Enter ←] (or use the mouse to click OK in the error message box)
and correct this error. In this example, the error may seem obvious, but suppose this program segment were rewritten to look like
this:

```
INPUT "Enter the divisor"; Divisor
Amount = 887 / Divisor
```

The program is dependent on the user to enter a number that can
be used as a divisor. The programmer should rewrite it so that if
the user enters an unusable value such as zero, he or she will be
asked to reenter the divisor. It could be done like this:

```
INPUT "Enter the divisor"; Divisor
DO WHILE Divisor = 0
    PRINT "Division by zero is not allowed."
    INPUT "Please enter a divisor other than zero"; Divisor
LOOP
Amount = 887 / Divisor
```

Error trapping *The technique of writing a program
in such a way that it "traps"
or catches input errors, such
as invalid data.*

This DO WHILE...LOOP will be executed only if the user enters a
zero; the user then will be asked to reenter the number. This new
number will be checked to make certain it is not also a zero. This
technique is referred to as **error trapping**. The program has been
written so that the error (which in this case is caused by invalid
input) is trapped. Program execution cannot continue until the
user enters a value for Divisor that can be used by the program.

A major difficulty with run-time errors is that, like logic errors, they often do not show up every time a program is executed. In the preceding example, the program will continue to execute correctly as long as a zero is not entered for the value of Divisor.

As previously discussed, logic errors are caused by flaws in the algorithm that was developed to solve a programming problem. At least some of the time, program output will be incorrect. The integrated debugger, which is discussed in the next section, can be very helpful in locating this type of error.

The Integrated Debugger

Debugging programs can be very time consuming, especially as programs become larger and more complex. Fortunately, QBasic contains an integrated debugger. This debugger allows you to trace (or "step") through program execution, a line at a time. You can then print the values of variables at different points in the program. This process is helpful in pinpointing the location of logic errors.

Look at the program at the top of Figure 8-12, which is supposed to calculate the following:

$$N + (N-1) + (N-2) + ...$$

When the value 3 is entered into this program, the value printed for Sum is 3. We can calculate the correct output by hand and determine that it should be 6. One way of determining what is happening is to use the Debug menu's Step command (see Figure 8-13). This command allows you to see the order in which program statements are being executed. Each time you open the Debug menu and choose Step, a single statement is executed. (Alternatively, you can use the shortcut key F8 to execute each statement in turn.) Theoretically, we know that the value of Sum should be equal to N at the end of the first loop execution. We can check this value by stepping through the program until the LOOP statement is highlighted and then using F6 to switch to the Immediate window. Typing in the following causes the current value of Sum to be displayed:

```
PRINT Sum  Enter ⏎
```

The value displayed will be 2. However, we know that after the first loop execution, Sum should actually be 3. By examining the loop body, we can now determine the problem: The value of N should be added to Sum *before* N is decremented by 1. Therefore, the two statements in the loop body must be switched. The program should be altered as shown at the bottom of Figure 8-12. Using the integrated debugger to step through the program simplified locat-

FIGURE 8-12

Off-by-One Error

```
'***    Add the numbers 1 through N for a given   ***
'***    number N.                                 ***

CLS
Sum = 0
INPUT "Enter the number: ", N
DO WHILE N > 0
    N = N - 1
    Sum = Sum + N
LOOP

PRINT "The sum is"; Sum

END
```

```
Enter the number: 3
The sum is 3
```

```
'***    Add the numbers 1 through N for a given   ***
'***    number N.                                 ***

CLS
Sum = 0
INPUT "Enter the number: ", N
DO WHILE N > 0
    Sum = Sum + N
    N = N - 1
LOOP

PRINT "The sum is"; Sum

END
```

```
Enter the number: 3
The sum is 6
```

FIGURE 8-13

The Debug Menu

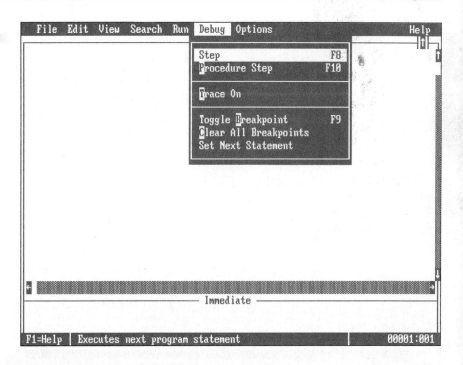

integrated debugger to step through the program simplified locating this error.

A second debugging method involves using the Toggle Breakpoint option in the Debug menu. Toggle Breakpoint allows you to place markers at specific program locations. When QBasic encounters one of these markers, it stops executing. You can then use the Immediate window to display the values of critical variables. To set a breakpoint, highlight the desired line and choose Toggle Breakpoint from the Debug menu. You also can use the shortcut key F9. After you are done debugging your program and wish to remove any breakpoints, choose the Clear All Breakpoints option in the Debug menu.

Testing Methods

It has been estimated that about 80 percent of professional programmers' time is spent testing and modifying programs that have already been written. Even after the programmer thinks that a program is working correctly, it is virtually impossible to determine if it will always work properly with all types of data. The ability of a program to work properly regardless of the data entered to it is referred to as its **reliability**.

Once a program appears to be working, it must be tested. Program testing falls into two basic categories: complete program testing and selective program testing. **Complete program testing** involves testing all possible paths of program execution. This approach is possible only with very small programs. The number

Reliability *The ability of a program to work properly regardless of the data entered to it.*

Complete program testing *Testing all possible paths of program execution.*

of possible paths in moderate to large programs is so great that the complete testing approach is not practical. **Selective program testing**, which involves testing the program using data with specific characteristics, is therefore normally used. One common method of selective testing is to make certain that a program works properly for boundary cases. Boundary cases are values that fall at the very extremes of the legal range of allowable data. Consider the following block IF statement:

```
IF Age > 21 THEN
    PRINT "This person is an adult."
END IF
```

The purpose of this segment is to print the "adult" message if the person is 21 years of age or over. If we tested this segment by assigning a value of 21 to Age (21 is at the boundary of the adult range), however, we would find that no message was displayed. The problem is that the condition has been improperly stated. It is correctly written like this:

```
IF Age >= 21 THEN
    PRINT "This person is an adult."
END IF
```

This statement should also be run with Age equal to 20 to make certain that nothing is displayed. Checking the boundary cases helps us to determine that the controlling condition is expressed properly. This procedure is more involved, however, for a more complex program segment such as the following:

```
IF Ounces >= 12 THEN
    IF Ounces >= 20 THEN
        SIZE$ = "A"
    ELSE
        SIZE$ = "B"
    END IF
ELSE
    SIZE$ = "C"
END IF
```

Drawing a flowchart, such as that in Figure 8-14, to visualize all possible paths of program execution can be helpful. From this flowchart, we can determine that the following boundary values should be assigned to variable Ounces for testing purposes: 12, 11, 19, and 20. If the program assigns the correct value to SIZE$ for each of these cases, we can be fairly certain that this statement is working properly.

FIGURE 8-14

Using a Flowchart to
Determine Boundary
Values

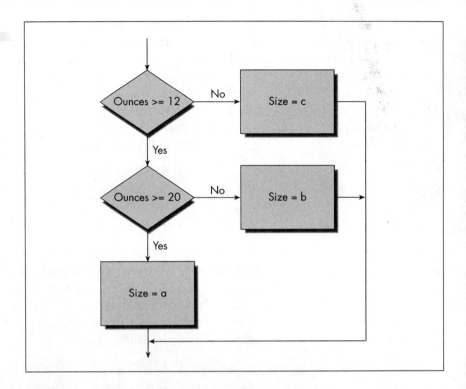

MORE ON DOCUMENTATION

As your programs become more complex and lengthy, documentation becomes increasingly important. It is important to include an overall explanation of each SUB procedure or FUNCTION procedure so that the reader knows its purpose. In addition, remarks should be placed before control structures and other statements whose purpose is not immediately evident. As previously mentioned, in the business world, most of a programmer's time is spent modifying existing code; typically, this is code written by someone else. Therefore, it is imperative that these programs be well documented.

Remarks contained within a program are referred to as *internal documentation*. In addition to internal document, software typically comes with *external documentation*, that is, documentation not contained in the program itself. This type of documentation often consists of user's manuals. However, more and more often, user instructions are provided in the form of online help, such as the online help contained in QBasic. This form of documentation allows users to obtain the answers they need without leaving the computer.

Learning Check 8-4

1. Errors caused by not following the rules of a language are _____ errors.

2. _____ errors occur when there is a flaw in a program's algorithm.

3. What command allows you to step through the execution of a program one statement at a time?

4. _____ program testing involves testing all possible paths of execution in a program.

MASTERING PROGRAM DEVELOPMENT

Problem Definition

This "Problem Definition" section is somewhat different from the ones in previous chapters. Rather than developing a new program, we discuss how the program developed at the end of Chapter 5 can be modified to handle invalid user input.

Solution Design

This program requires that the user enter the following data:

1. The number corresponding to the desired pizza size (1–4).

2. The number of toppings.

3. Whether or not extra cheese is desired (this requires a response of Y or N).

The first two values can be placed in string variables. The VAL function can then determine whether they are valid integers (remember, VAL returns a value of zero if they are invalid). In addition, the program will need to make certain that the size is in the 1 through 4 range.

When asking whether the customer wants extra cheese, the program should obtain only the first letter of the response and convert it to uppercase using the UCASE$ function. This process allows the user to enter an uppercase or lowercase letter. In addition, the program should work properly if the user enters a word, such as YES, rather than a single letter. The LEFT$ function will be used to obtain the first character of the user's response.

The Program

The modified program is shown in Figure 8-15. Notice that it is modularized in the same way as the original program. Only the AddCheese and BasicCost procedures have been altered.

Let's study AddCheese first. After the user enters a response, the LEFT$ function obtains the first character of Cheese$. Next, UCASE$ converts this value to uppercase (if it is already uppercase, nothing will happen). Notice the condition controlling execution of the loop. This loop will execute until Cheese$ equals "Y" or "N".

BasicCost validates both the size and the number of toppings. In both cases, the user's response is placed in a character string variable. The VAL function determines whether the response is a valid integer. If it is, processing continues; otherwise, loops are used to prompt the user to reenter the data. The program also determines whether Size is in the 1 through 4 range.

PROGRAMMING HINTS

- The argument of a function must always be placed in parentheses.

- A function is immediately evaluated as a single value; it has a higher priority than arithmetic, relational, and logical operators.

- Remember that the INT function does not round to the nearest integer; instead, it returns the largest integer less than or equal to its argument.

- The RANDOMIZE statement must be used with the RND function to generate a new series of random numbers each time the program is run. (Otherwise, the same series of numbers will be generated each time.)

- When using FUNCTION procedures, remember that the body of the function must contain a statement that assigns a value to the function's name.

- Double-check any conditions controlling execution of loops or decision structures to make certain they are properly stated.

FIGURE 8-15

Pizza Program Protected from Invalid User Input

```
DECLARE SUB DisplayMenu ()
DECLARE SUB BasicCost (Bill!, Size!)
DECLARE SUB AddCheese (Bill!, Size!)
DECLARE SUB DisplayBill (Bill!)

'***            Smiley's Pizza Parlor              ***

'*** This program calculates the cost of a customer's  ***
'*** pizza, based on the following:                 ***
'***     Sizes:                                     ***
'***          6 inch      $4.00                     ***
'***         10 inch      $7.50                     ***
'***         14 inch      $9.25                     ***
'***         16 inch      $12.90                    ***
'***     Toppings:                                  ***
'***          $.50/each for 6 inch                  ***
'***          $.60/each for 10 inch                 ***
'***          $.75/each for 14 inch                 ***
'***          $.90/each for 16 inch                 ***
'***     Extra cheese:                              ***
'***          $1.00 for 6 or 10 inch                ***
'***          $2.00 for 14 or 16 inch               ***
'***     A 6% sales tax is added to the cost.  The  ***
'***     final bill is then displayed.              ***
'***     Major variables:                           ***
'***        Bill            Price of the pizza      ***
'***        Size            Size of the pizza       ***

'*** Call procedure to display the menu. ***
CALL DisplayMenu

'*** Call procedure to calculate basic cost. ***
CALL BasicCost(Bill, Size)

'*** Call procedure to add cost of extra cheese. ***
CALL AddCheese(Bill, Size)

'*** Add 6% tax. ***
Bill = Bill + Bill * .06

'*** Call procedure to display total bill. ***
CALL DisplayBill(Bill)

END
```

Continued on next page

FIGURE 8-15

Continued

```
SUB AddCheese (Bill, Size)
    '*** This procedure adds the cost of extra cheese, if ***
    '*** it is requested.                                  ***

    INPUT "Do you want extra cheese"; Cheese$
    '*** Examine only the first letter entered. ***
    Cheese$ = LEFT$(Cheese$, 1)
    '*** If lowercase letter is entered, convert to uppercase. ***
    Cheese$ = UCASE$(Cheese$)

    '*** If invalid response, prompt user to reenter it. ***
    DO WHILE (Cheese$ <> "Y") AND (Cheese$ <> "N")
        PRINT
        INPUT "Invalid response. Enter Y or N: ", Cheese$
        Cheese$ = LEFT$(Cheese$, 1)
        Cheese$ = UCASE$(Cheese$)
    LOOP


    '*** Add cost of extra cheese.***
    IF Cheese$ = "Y" THEN
        IF Size = 1 OR Size = 2 THEN
            Bill = Bill + 1
        ELSEIF Size = 3 OR Size = 4 THEN
            Bill = Bill + 2
        END IF
    END IF

END SUB

SUB BasicCost (Bill, Size)
    '*** This procedure calculates the basic cost of the pizza. ***

    '*** Prompt user to enter size. ***
    INPUT "Enter the number (1 - 4) corresponding to the size pizza: ",
        Size$

    '*** If invalid size is entered, prompt user to reenter it. ***
    Size = VAL(Size$)
    DO WHILE (Size < 1) OR (Size > 4)
        PRINT
        PRINT "Invalid size."
        INPUT "Please enter a number from 1 - 4: ", Size$
        Size = VAL(Size$)
    LOOP
```

FIGURE 8-15

Continued

```
'*** Prompt user to enter number of toppings. ***
PRINT
INPUT "Enter the number of toppings: ", Toppings$

'*** If invalid number, prompt user to reenter it. ***
Toppings = VAL(Toppings$)
DO WHILE Toppings = 0
    PRINT
    PRINT "Invalid number of toppings."
    INPUT "Please reenter the number of toppings: ", Toppings$
    Toppings = VAL(Toppings$)
LOOP

'*** Determine cost depending on size and number of toppings. ***
SELECT CASE Size
    CASE 1
        Bill = 4 + Toppings * .5
    CASE 2
        Bill = 7.5 + Toppings * .6
    CASE 3
        Bill = 9.25 + Toppings * .75
    CASE 4
        Bill = 12.9 + Toppings * .9
END SELECT

END SUB

SUB DisplayBill (Bill)
    '*** This procedure displays amount of the bill. ***

    PRINT
    PRINT
    Format$ = "\                              \ $$##.##"
    PRINT USING Format$; "The total cost of your pizza is"; Bill
    PRINT "THANK YOU FOR COMING TO SMILEY'S"

END SUB
```

Continued on next page

FIGURE 8-15

Continued

```
SUB DisplayMenu
    '*** This procedure displays Smiley's menu.    ***

    CLS
    PRINT
    PRINT TAB(15); "Welcome to Smiley's"
    PRINT
    PRINT TAB(10); "1.    6-inch personal pizza"
    PRINT TAB(10); "2.    10-inch small pizza"
    PRINT TAB(10); "3.    14-inch regular pizza"
    PRINT TAB(10); "4.    16-inch super pizza"
    PRINT

END SUB
```

```
                Welcome to Smiley's

        1.    6-inch personal pizza
        2.    10-inch small pizza
        3.    14-inch regular pizza
        4.    16-inch super pizza

Enter the number (1 - 4) corresponding to the size pizza: 5

Invalid size.
Please enter a number from 1 - 4: 3

Enter the number of toppings: 3
Do you want extra cheese? m

Invalid response. Enter Y or N: n


The total cost of your pizza is    $12.19
THANK YOU FOR COMING TO SMILEY'S
```

SUMMARY POINTS

▌ A function always returns a value. Library (or standard) functions are part of the QBasic system. They can be divided into numeric and string functions.

▌ The INT function computes the greatest integer less than or equal to the value of its argument.

▌ The SGN function produces a 1, 0, or –1, depending on whether the argument is positive, zero, or negative, respectively.

▌ The ABS function returns the absolute value of its argument.

▌ QBasic string functions permit modification, concatenation, comparison, and analysis of the composition of strings.

▌ Concatenation (+) joins two strings together.

▌ LEN is used to find the number of characters in a string.

▌ STRING$ provides an easy way to print a single character repeatedly.

▌ LEFT$ returns the specified number of leftmost characters of a string, whereas RIGHT$ returns the specified number of rightmost characters.

▌ MID$ enables the programmer to gain access to characters in the middle of a string.

▌ ASC returns the ASCII code for the first character in a string.

▌ CHR$ returns the string representation of the ASCII code of the expression.

▌ VAL is used to find the numeric equivalent of a string expression.

▌ STR$ acts as the reverse of the VAL function by converting a number to its string equivalent.

▌ DATE$ returns the current date.

▌ The programmer can write user-defined functions by using FUNCTION procedures. A value is returned in the function itself.

▌ User-friendly programs are pleasant to use and handle invalid input properly.

▌ Syntax, run-time, and logic errors are the three basic types of program errors.

▌ Syntax errors can often be avoided by careful typing and proofreading of the program before it is executed.

▌ Run-time errors cause program execution to stop prematurely.

▌ The QBasic integrated debugger is helpful in locating logic errors. It allows you to examine the values of variables at critical execution points.

▌ Program testing is the process of systematically checking a program to determine its reliability, that is, its ability to work properly at all times.

KEY TERMS

Complete program testing – 284
Concatenate – 266
Error trapping – 281
Function – 257
FUNCTION procedure – 274
Random – 260
Reliability – 284
Selective program testing – 285
Standard function – 257
User-defined function – 257
User friendly – 279

REVIEW QUESTIONS

1. What are the two types of standard functions discussed in this chapter?

2. What is the result of INT(–14.24)? Why?

3. The ABS function always returns _____.

   a. a number greater than or equal to 0

   b. a number less than or equal to 0

   c. a whole number

   d. an even number

4. What is the purpose of the RND function? Give examples of some situations in which it would be useful.

5. What are the values of the following expressions?

   a. SGN (340.4)

   b. ABS (–1.7)

   c. SQR (144)

   d. INT (ABS (17))

6. The argument *X* in SQR (X) can be _____.

   a. any number
   b. any nonnegative number
   c. only a positive integer
   d. any negative number

7. How can the LCASE$ and UCASE$ functions be used when evaluating user responses to prompts?

8. Explain the use of the LEFT$, RIGHT$, and MID$ functions.

9. What is the purpose of the RANDOMIZE statement?

10. Give an example of a situation in which the STRING$ function would be useful.

11. What statement indicates the beginning of a FUNCTION procedure? What statement indicates the end?

12. How is a FUNCTION procedure different from a SUB procedure?

13. List several characteristics of user-friendly programs.

14. How can the Toggle Breakpoint command help when debugging a program?

15. Explain the difference between internal and external documentation.

DEBUGGING EXERCISES

Locate any errors in the following programs or program segments, and debug them.

1.
```
'*** Print the square root of A. ***
LET A = -22
B = SQR(A)
PRINT B
```

2.
```
'*** Print address if it is on an avenue (Ave.) ***
INPUT "Enter address"; Street$
IF LEFT$(ST$, 4) = "Ave." THEN
    PRINT Street$
END IF
```

3.
```
'*** Display a row of 45 plus signs. The row should be centered on a 60
'*** character line.
Start = ((60 - 45))
PRINT TAB(Start); STRING$("+", 45)
```

4.
```
FUNCTION ComputeInterest (Principal, MonthlyRate)
'***  This function computes the amount  ***
'***  of interest on a savings account.  ***
Interest = Principal * MonthlyRate * 12
END FUNCTION
```

PROGRAMMING PROBLEMS

Level 1

1. Write a program segment that prompts the user to enter a checking account balance. Use a library function to display a message stating whether the account is overdrawn.

2. Write a program to simulate the tossing of a coin 10 times. After the 10 tosses, the program should display the total number of heads and tails. Generate random numbers to represent the tosses, where 1 = heads and 2 = tails.

3. Write a program that prompts the user to enter a social security number and then determines whether the fourth and fifth digits are 64. Allow the user to check as many social security numbers as desired. Use the following numbers to test your program: 316642789, 341426743, and 480848902.

4. The residents of Morton Avenue want to add 100 to their street addresses. They need a program to change their current addresses to their new addresses. Write a program that prompts the user to enter a current address and then calculates the new address. The new address should be assigned to a variable named Address$. Allow the user to enter as many addresses as necessary. Use the following data to test your program:

   35 Morton Avenue
   41 Morton Avenue
   67 Morton Avenue

   The output should look like this:

   135 Morton Avenue
   141 Morton Avenue
   167 Morton Avenue

5. Write a program that prompts the user to enter a sentence and then switches all lowercase letters to capitals and all uppercase letters to lowercase. Use the ASC function to know which letters to switch. Test your prompt with the following data:

   Baah, Ram, Ewe

Miss B. was seen Saturday at Serendipity with a British musician.

6. Write a program that calculates the cost of a season pass to Fancher High School athletic events. The cost is as follows:

Children under 5   Free
Senior citizens and students $24.00
Other adults $32.00

Write the program so that it is protected from invalid user input. Prompt the user to enter the category of ticket and then display its price.

Level 2

1. Rewrite the last program in Chapter 7 (Figure 7-19) so that it is protected from invalid data.

2. Conduct a survey in which you give at least 20 people a list of six professional basketball teams and ask them to pick their favorite team from this list. Then write a program that prompts the user to enter the number of votes each team received. The program should use a function to calculate each team's percentage of the votes. The function should round the percentage to the nearest whole number. At the end of the program, each team's percentage should be displayed.

3. You have been hired to write a program to evaluate teachers. You have come up with a formula that will evaluate a teacher according to the following scale:

negative number   bad teacher
zero   average teacher
positive number   good teacher

The formula operates on four variables—A, B, C, and X—which are evaluations of the teacher's performance. The rating is calculated as follows:

Rating = 5 + Z * 0.85

where $Z = X + A - (X * B) + (C / X)$. Write a program that will prompt the user to enter a teacher's name and rating variables X, A, B, and C, and calculate the rating. Define a function to calculate the rating. Use the following data to test your program:

Teacher	X	A	B	C
Dixon	5	10	7	4
Meronk	10	1	1	6
Hastings	2	10	3	1
Mishler	10	9	3	7

Display each teacher's name and rating with appropriate headings.

4. Write a user-defined function that will receive a positive integer as a character string and display it with commas inserted where appropriate if the number has four or more digits. (*Hint:* Concatenate digits with commas starting from the right end of the number.) Use the following data to test your program:

45
1345623
100000
0
999
3900

5. Write a program that prompts the user to enter four names and prints each name's initials. The approximate value of *e* is 2.7183. Use the following data:

Merlin Michael Mueller
Kara Lee Martin
Mary Lynn Deep
Pamela Ann Kim

The initials should be in caps and printed in the following format:

X.X.X.

A procedure should be called to concatenate the initials.

6. Your deadly bacteria culture experiment for biology is out of control. Write a program to calculate the population of the culture after 30, 60, 90, and 120 minutes if you started with 500 bacteria. Use the formula

$$P = P_o * e^{kt}$$

where P_o is the initial population size, t is the elapsed time in minutes, and k is the constant 0.032. The approximate value of *e* is 2.7183. Use a loop to read the time values and display the population for each time.

Challenge Problems

1. The All-American Automobile Association needs a program that will help car owners in the state of Ohio determine the month in which their license plates should be renewed and the cost of the license. The renewal month is based on the first letter of the driver's last name, according to the following schedule:

A-F	January
G-L	February
M-Q	March
R-Z	April

The fee is:

Membership in the Automobile Association:	$19.00
Nonmembership	$22.00

Input:

Prompt user to enter driver's last name.

Prompt user to enter whether driver is a member of the Automobile Association.

Required Processing:

a. Determine the renewal month.

b. Determine the cost of the license.

c. Allow user to enter as many drivers as desired.

d. Protect the program from invalid user input.

Output:

The last name, month of renewal, and license cost should be displayed on the screen. Interactive sessions should look similar to the following:

```
Enter the driver's last name: Maderas
Are you a member of the Automobile Association (Y/N)? Y

Name                Renewal Month         Fee
Maderas               March             $19.00



More drivers to process? Enter 'Y' or 'N': Y

Enter the driver's last name: Dawkins
Are you a member of the Automobile Association (Y/N)? N

Name                Renewal Month         Fee
Dawkins              January            $22.00



More drivers to process? Enter 'Y' or 'N': N
```

2. A shoe store has devised a system to help detect errors in recording inventory. The last two digits of every stock number must be the sum of the preceding three digits. For example, the stock number QB412.07 is valid because 07 is the sum of the 4 + 1 + 2. The shoe store would like a program that allows an employee to enter a series of stock numbers and then determines whether each one is valid. You can assume

that the stock number is always eight characters long and that the sixth character is always a decimal point.

Input:

Prompt user to enter the stock number.

Processing Requirements:

a. Call a FUNCTION procedure to determine whether the number is valid.

b. Allow the user to enter as many stock numbers as desired.

c. Use the following stock numbers to test your program:
    AB458.17
    MM314.08
    JP977.23

Output:

Interactive sessions should look similar to the following:

```
Enter the stock number: QB458.17
QB458.17 is a valid stock number.

Do you want to check another stock number (Y/N)? Y

Enter the stock number: MM214.08
MM314.08 is an invalid stock number.

Do you want to check another stock number (Y/N)? Y

Enter the stock number: JP977.23
JP977.23 is a valid stock number.

Do you want to check another stock number (Y/N)? N
```

Arrays and Searching and Sorting

Outline

Objectives

After studying this chapter, you will be able to:

- Explain the purpose of subscripts.
- Use the DIM statement to dimension arrays.
- Store data in, print, and manipulate one- and two-dimensional arrays.
- Total values stored in array columns and rows.
- Sort arrays using the bubble sort.
- Sort arrays using a Shell sort.
- Search for data items in an array using both the sequential and binary searches.

INTRODUCTION

All of our programs thus far have used simple variables such as Pounds, Title$, or Hours to represent single values. If a program was required to handle many single values of the same type (such as 100 student scores), a loop was used to allow one variable to represent these values one at a time. Now consider the problem of a television network poll. A program is needed that prompts users to enter how much time 10 randomly selected people spend viewing television, calculates the average viewing time, and displays the difference between each person's viewing time and the average in the following format:

Name	Hours	Difference from Average
P. Busch	1	–3
C. Carstens	5	1
J. Drake	0	–4
H. Poirot	2	–2
M. Bulas	7	3
D. Zongas	3	–1
C. Ramirez	4	0
T. Zekly	11	7
S. McKinnis	3	–1
G. Balducci	4	0

One method for calculating averages is to set up a loop to prompt the user to enter each value and store the value in a single variable. Each time a new value is entered, however, the previous value stored in the variable is lost. Thus, in the problem involving the television poll, we would not be able to compare each person's viewing time with the calculated average viewing time. To make the comparison, we must store each person's viewing time in a separate memory location. It is possible to use 10 different variables to hold these values, but this is a cumbersome solution that would be even more impractical when dealing with a larger number of values.

There is an easier way: QBasic permits us to deal with many related data items as a group by means of a structure known as an **array**. This chapter explains how arrays can be used in a situation such as the television poll problem, in which groups of data items must be stored and manipulated efficiently. Several methods of sorting and searching arrays are also discussed.

Array *An ordered group of related data items having a common variable name, all of the same data type.*

SUBSCRIPTS

Element *An individual data item within an array.*

The individual data items within an array are called **elements**. An array consists of a group of consecutive storage locations, each location containing a single element. The entire array is given one name, and the programmer indicates an individual element within the array by referring to its position in the array. To illustrate, suppose that there are five test scores to be stored: 97, 85, 89, 95, and 100. The scores could be put in an array called Tests, which we might visualize like this:

97	85	89	95	100
Tests(1)	Tests(2)	Tests(3)	Tests(4)	Tests(5)

The array name Tests now refers to all five storage locations containing the test scores. To gain access to a single test score within the array, an array **subscript** (or **index**) is used. A subscript is a value enclosed in parentheses that identifies the position of a given element in the array. For example, the first element of array Tests (containing the value 97) is referred to as Tests(1). The second test score is in Tests(2), the third test score is in Tests(3), and so on. Therefore, the following statements are true:

Subscript *A value used to identify the position of a particular array element; it is enclosed in parentheses after the array name.*

```
Tests(1) = 97
Tests(2) = 85
Tests(3) = 89
Tests(4) = 95
Tests(5) = 100
```

The subscript enclosed in parentheses does not have to be an integer constant; it can consist of any valid numeric expression. When an array element subscript is indicated by an expression, QBasic carries out the following steps:

- It evaluates the expression within the parentheses.
- If the result is a real number, it rounds it to an integer.
- It accesses the indicated element in the array.

Keep in mind that the subscript value of an array element is entirely different from the contents of that element. In the previous example, the value of Tests(4) is 95; the subscript 4 indicates where in the array the value 95 is located.

Subscripted variable *A variable that refers to a specific element within an array.*

Unsubscripted variable *A variable that refers to a single, independent storage location.*

Variables that refer to specific elements of arrays [such as Tests(4)] are called **subscripted variables**. In contrast, simple variables, such as we have used in previous chapters, are called **unsubscripted variables**. Both kinds of variables can store a single numeric or string value, and both can be used in statements in the same manner. The important difference between the two is that a subscripted variable refers to one value in a group; it is possible to access a different value in the group simply by changing the subscript. An unsubscripted variable, on the other hand, does not necessarily have any special relationship to the values stored before or after it in memory.

The same rules that apply to naming simple variables also apply to naming arrays. Remember that only numeric values can be stored in arrays with numeric variable names, and that character string arrays can contain only string values. It is possible to use the same name for both a simple variable and an array in the same program, but this is not good programming practice because it makes the logic of the program difficult to follow.

Assume that the array Digits and the variables A and B have the following values:

```
Digits(1) = 2      A = 3
Digits(2) = 15     B = 5
Digits(3) = 16
Digits(4) = 17
Digits(5) = 32
```

The following examples show how the various forms of subscripts are used:

Example	Reference
Digits(3)	Third element of Digits, or 16
Digits(B)	B = 5; thus the fifth element of Digits, or 32
Digits(A + 1)	A = 3; 3 + 1 = 4; thus the fourth element of Digits, or 17
Digits(Digits(1))	Digits(1) = 2; thus the second element of Digits, or 15

DIMENSIONING AN ARRAY

When a subscripted variable is found in a program, QBasic recognizes it as part of an array and automatically reserves storage locations for 11 array elements, with subscripts from 0 through 10. The programmer does not have to fill all of the reserved array storage spaces with values; it is illegal, however, to refer to array elements for which space has not been reserved.

The DIM, or dimension, statement allows the programmer to override this standard array space reservation and reserve space for an array of any desired size. The following statement dimensions a numeric array with subscripts 1 through 20, which can contain a maximum of 20 elements:

```
DIM Scores(1 TO 20)
```

The subscript range need not start at 1; the following DIM statement specifies that array Scores can have up to 10 elements with subscripts 21 through 30:

```
DIM Scores(21 TO 30)
```

A DIM statement is not required for arrays of 11 or fewer elements, but it is good programming practice to specify DIM statements for all arrays to document array usage.

The DIM Statement

Flowchart Symbol	Statement Format
	DIM array-name(lower-subscript TO upper-subscript)

More than one array can be declared in a DIM statement. For example, the following statement dimensions Account, Nam$, and Overdrawn:

```
DIM Account(1 TO 30), Nam$(10 TO 50), Overdrawn(100 TO 200)
```

A DIM statement must appear in a program before the first reference to the array it dimensions; a good practice is to place any DIM statements at the beginning of the program.

ONE-DIMENSIONAL ARRAYS

Storing Data in an Array

A major advantage of using arrays is the ability to use a variable rather than a constant as a subscript. Because a single expression such as Tests(Count) can refer to any element in the array Tests, depending on the value of Count, this subscripted variable name can be used in a loop that varies the value of the subscript Count. A FOR...NEXT loop can provide an efficient method of placing data into an array if the exact number of items to be entered is known in advance. The following program segment prompts the user to enter five scores and then stores them in the array Tests:

```
FOR Count = 1 TO 5
   INPUT "Enter test score: ", Tests(Count)
NEXT Count
```

The first time this loop is executed, the loop control variable Count equals 1. The first value entered is assigned to Tests(1). The second time through the loop, Count equals 2; therefore the second score is assigned to Tests(2). The loop processing continues until all five numbers have been entered and stored. Assuming that the user enters the scores 85, 71, 63, 51, and 99, the following table shows how the data will be stored at the end of each loop repetition:

For Count =	Action	Array Tests				
1	INPUT Tests(1)	85	?	?	?	?
2	INPUT Tests(2)	85	71	?	?	?
3	INPUT Tests(3)	85	71	63	?	?
4	INPUT Tests(4)	85	71	63	51	?
5	INPUT Tests(5)	85	71	63	51	99

It is often possible to enter data into several arrays within a single loop. In the following segment, the user enters three values, each of which is assigned to a different array:

```
DIM Nam$(1 TO 5), Age(1 TO 5), SSN$(1 TO 5)
FOR Count = 1 TO 5
    Input "Enter student's name: ", Nam$(Count)
    Input "Enter student's age: ", Age(Count)
    Input "Enter student's ID number: ", SSN$(Count)
NEXT Count
```

Parallel arrays *Arrays in which the values in corresponding elements are related to one another.*

Nam$, Age, and SSN$ are referred to as **parallel arrays** because the values in each corresponding name, age, and social security number are in the same array positions. For example, the social security number in SSN$(4) belongs to the person in Nam$(4).

When the exact number of items to be entered into an array is unknown, a DO WHILE...LOOP and a trailer value can be used. This method is demonstrated in the following segment, where entering a value of –1 will cause the loop to stop executing. Care must be taken, however, that the number of items entered does not exceed the size of the array.

```
'*** Calculate the total weight of items to be shipped. ***
DIM Weight(1 TO 50)
Count = 1
INPUT "Enter weight of item (-1 to quit): ", Temp
DO WHILE (Count < 50) AND (Temp <> -1)
    Weight(Count) = Temp
    TotalWeight = TotalWeight + Weight(Count)
    Count = Count + 1
    INPUT "Enter weight of item (-1 to quit): ", Temp
LOOP
Count = Count - 1
```

Notice that the weight the user enters is temporarily assigned to the variable Temp. Before the weight is placed into the array, we want to make certain that the value entered was not the sentinel value. We do not want the sentinel value to be stored in the array. Notice that after the loop is completed, the value of Count is decreased by one. If this was not done, Count would end up being one more than the number of items entered.

Printing the Contents of an Array

A FOR...NEXT loop can be used to print the contents of array Tests, as shown in the following segment:

```
FOR Count = 1 TO 5
    PRINT Tests(Count)
NEXT Count
```

```
85
71
63
51
99
```

Because there is no punctuation at the end of the PRINT statement, each value will be printed on a separate line. The values could be displayed on the same line by placing a semicolon at the end of the line:

```
FOR Count = 1 TO 5
    PRINT Tests(Count);
NEXT Count
```

```
85   71   63   51   99
```

As the loop control variable Count varies from 1 to 5, so does the value of the array subscript, and the computer prints elements 1 through 5 of array Tests.

Performing Calculations on Array Elements

Now consider again the problem of the television viewing poll presented earlier in this chapter. The output format required that each line contain the viewer's name, number of viewing hours, and the difference between those hours and the average hours of all the viewers. This problem is solved in the program shown in Figure 9-1. The solution can be broken into the following steps:

1. Prompt the user to enter the data and store it in two arrays: a character string array for the names and a numeric array for the hours.

2. Calculate the average viewing hours.

3. Calculate for each viewer the difference between his or her hours and the average; these differences can be stored in a third array.

4. Display the required information stored in the three arrays.

FIGURE 9-1

TV Viewing Poll Program

```
'***                Network Viewing Time Survey          ***

'*** This program calculates average television viewing  ***
'*** time, based on the viewing habits of ten individual ***
'*** viewers. Each viewer's difference from the average  ***
'*** is calculated. The results are then displayed.      ***
'*** Major variables:                                    ***
'***      Viewer$         Array of viewers               ***
'***      Hours           Array of viewing hours         ***
'***      Difference      Array of differences from average ***
'***                          viewing hours              ***
'***      Average         Average viewing hours          ***
'***      TotalHours      Total viewing hours for all viewers ***

'*** Dimension the array sizes. ***
DIM Viewer$(1 TO 10), Hours(1 TO 10), Difference(1 TO 10)

TotalHours = 0

'*** Get data and calculate total hours. ***
CLS
PRINT
FOR Count = 1 TO 10
   INPUT "Enter person's name: ", Viewer$(Count)
   INPUT "Enter person's total viewing hours: ", Hours(Count)
   TotalHours = TotalHours + Hours(Count)
NEXT Count

'*** Calculate average number of hours for all viewers. ***
Average = TotalHours / 10

'*** Calculate each viewer's difference from the average. ***
FOR Count = 1 TO 10
   Difference(Count) = Hours(Count) - Average
NEXT Count

'*** Display the results. ***
CLS
PRINT "Name", "Hours"; TAB(22); "Difference from Average"
FOR Count = 1 TO 10
   PRINT Viewer$(Count), Hours(Count), Difference(Count)
NEXT Count
```

Continued on next page

FIGURE 9-1

Continued

```
PRINT
PRINT "Average Viewing Time = "; Average

END
```

```
Enter person's name: P. Busch
Enter person's total viewing hours: 1
Enter person's name: C. Carsten
Enter person's total viewing hours: 5
Enter person's name: J. Drake
Enter person's total viewing hours: 0
Enter person's name: H. Poirot
Enter person's total viewing hours: 2
Enter person's name: M. Bulas
Enter person's total viewing hours: 7
Enter person's name: D. Zongas
Enter person's total viewing hours: 3
Enter person's name: C. Ramirez
Enter person's total viewing hours: 4
Enter person's name: T. Zekly
Enter person's total viewing hours: 11
Enter person's name: S. McKinnis
Enter person's total viewing hours: 3
Enter person's name: G. Balducci
Enter person's total viewing hours: 4
```

```
Name          Hours   Difference from Average
P. Busch       1              -3
C. Carsten     5               1
J. Drake       0              -4
H. Poirot      2              -2
M. Bulas       7               3
D. Zongas      3              -1
C. Ramirez     4               0
T. Zekly      11               7
S. McKinnis    3              -1
G. Balducci    4               0

Average Viewing Time =  4
```

This program contains three parallel arrays: Viewer$, Hours, and Difference. The viewers' names and hours are placed in their appropriate arrays in the first FOR...NEXT loop. In addition, the elements of Hours are added to TotalHours, accumulating the total viewing hours. When this loop is exited, the arrays Viewer$ and Hours are filled with values, and the unsubscripted variable TotalHours contains the sum of all the values contained in array Hours. TotalHours is divided by 10 to obtain the average viewing time. The second FOR...NEXT loop then calculates the difference from the average viewing time for each viewer and stores the results in array Difference. All of the information is output in the last FOR...NEXT loop.

Sometimes not every element of an array needs to be manipulated in the same way. If we wanted to find the product of only the odd-numbered entries in an array Odd that contains 25 numbers, we could use the following statements:

```
DIM Odd(1 TO 25)
Product = 1
FOR Count = 1 TO 25 STEP 2
    Product = Product * Odd(Count)
NEXT Count
```

Learning Check 9-1

1. A(n) _____ is used to indicate the position of an element in an array.

2. The _____ statement reserves storage space for the elements in an array.

3. True or False? An array subscript can consist of any legal numeric or character expression.

4. True or False? If an array is dimensioned as follows, it must contain 20 elements:

```
DIM Table(1 TO 20)
```

5. Write a DIM statement for an array that will hold the names of up to 90 inventory items. The array name should be Inventory$.

TWO-DIMENSIONAL ARRAYS

One-dimensional array *An array that contains a single list of elements.*

Two-dimensional array *An array in which elements are arranged in both columns and rows.*

The arrays shown so far in this chapter have all been **one-dimensional arrays**; that is, arrays that store values in the form of a single list. **Two-dimensional arrays** enable a programmer to represent more complex groupings of data. For example, suppose that a fast-food restaurant chain is running a four-day promotional T-shirt sale at its three store locations. It might keep the following table of data concerning the number of shirts sold by each of the three restaurants.

		Store 1	Store 2	Store 3
		1	**2**	**3**
	1	12	14	15
Day	**2**	10	16	12
	3	11	18	13
	4	9	9	10

Each row of the data refers to a specific day of the sale, and each column contains the sales data for one store. Thus, the number of shirts sold by the second store on the third day of the sale (18) can be found in the third row, second column. Data items that can be grouped into rows and columns such as this can be stored easily in a two-dimensional array. A two-dimensional array named TShirts that contains the preceding data can be pictured like this:

Array TShirts

12	14	15
10	16	12
11	18	13
9	9	10

Array TShirts consists of 12 elements arranged as four rows and three columns. To reference a single element of a two-dimensional array such as this, two subscripts are needed: one to indicate the row and a second to indicate the column. For instance, the subscripted variable TShirts(4,1) contains the number of shirts sold on the fourth day by the first store (9). The first subscript gives the row number and the second subscript gives the column number.

The rules regarding one-dimensional arrays also apply to two-dimensional arrays. Two-dimensional arrays are named in the same way as other variables and cannot use the same name as another array (of any dimensions) in the same program. A two-dimensional array can contain only one type of data; numeric and character string values cannot be mixed. As with one-dimensional arrays, subscripts of two-dimensional arrays can be indicated by any legal numeric expression:

```
TShirts(3,3)
TShirts(1,2)
TShirts(I,J)
TShirts(1,Count+6)
```

Assume that I = 4 and J = 2, and that the array Numbers contains the following 16 elements:

Array Numbers

10	15	20	25
50	55	60	65
90	95	100	105
130	135	140	145

The following examples show how the various forms of subscripts are used:

Example	Refers To
Numbers(4,I)	Numbers(4,4)—the element in the fourth row, fourth column of Numbers, which is 145
Numbers(J,I)	Numbers(2,4)—the element in the second row, fourth column of Numbers, which is 65
Numbers(3,J+1)	Numbers(3,3)—the element in the third row, third column which is 100
Numbers(I-1,J-1)	Numbers(3,1)—the element in the third row, first column, which is 90

As with one-dimensional arrays, the dimensions of two-dimensional arrays can be set with a DIM statement. For example, the following statement dimensions a two-dimensional character array with up to 15 rows and five columns:

```
DIM Student$(1 TO 15,1 TO 5)
```

This array can hold a maximum of 75 (15 × 5) elements.

Storing Data in and Printing Two-Dimensional Arrays

Recall from previous sections of this chapter that a FOR...NEXT loop is a convenient means of accessing all the elements of a one-dimensional array. FOR...NEXT loops can also be used to place data into a two-dimensional array. It may be helpful to think of a two-dimensional array as a group of one-dimensional arrays, with each row making up a single one-dimensional array. A single FOR...NEXT loop can be used to store values in one row. This process is repeated for as many rows as the array contains; therefore, the FOR...NEXT loop that stores data in a single row is nested within a second FOR...NEXT loop controlling the number of rows being accessed.

The array TShirts of the previous example can be filled from the sales data table one row at a time, moving from left to right across the columns. The following program segment shows the nested FOR...NEXT loops that do this:

```
FOR Row = 1 TO 4
   FOR Column = 1 TO 3
      PRINT "Enter sales for store"; Column; "on day"; Row; ": "
      INPUT TShirts(Row, Column)
   NEXT Column
NEXT Row
```

Each time the INPUT statement is executed, one value is placed in a single element of the array; the element is determined by the current values of Row and Column. This statement is executed $4 \times 3 = 12$ times, which is the number of elements in the array.

The outer loop (with the loop control variable Row) controls the rows, and the loop control variable Column controls the columns. Each time the outer loop is executed once, the inner loop is executed three times. While Row = 1, Column becomes 1, 2, and finally 3 as the inner loop is executed. Therefore, if the user enters 12, 14, and 15 for the first three sales, these values are stored in TShirts(1,1), TShirts(1,2), and TShirts(1,3), and the first row is filled:

	Column =		
	1	**2**	**3**
Row = 1	12	14	15

While Row equals 2, Column again varies from 1 to 3, and values entered are placed into TShirts(2,1), TShirts(2,2), and TShirts(2,3) to fill the second row. Assuming the next three values entered are 10, 16, and 12, the array would now look like this:

	Column =		
	1	**2**	**3**
	12	14	15
Row = 2	10	16	12

Row is incremented to 3 and then to 4, and the third and fourth rows are filled in the same manner.

To print the contents of the entire array, the programmer can substitute a PRINT statement for the INPUT statement in the nested FOR...NEXT loops. The following segment prints the contents of the array TShirts, one row at a time:

```
Blank = 10
FOR Row = 1 TO 4
    FOR Column = 1 TO 3
        PRINT TAB(Blank*Column); TShirts(Row,Column);
    NEXT Column
    PRINT
NEXT Row
```

The semicolon at the end of the PRINT statement tells QBasic to print the three values on the same line. After the inner loop is executed, a blank PRINT statement causes a carriage return so that the next row is printed on the next line.

The program in Figure 9-2 shows how sales data can be entered into this array, totaled, and then printed, on paper, in table form with appropriate headings. Notice that as the sales data is entered, the following statement keeps track of the total sales:

```
TotalShirts = TotalShirts + TShirts(Row, Column)
```

The value of TotalShirts is then printed at the bottom of the report.

Adding Rows

Once data has been stored in an array, it is often necessary to manipulate certain array elements. For instance, the sales manager in charge of the T-shirt promotional sale might want to know how many shirts were sold on the last day of the sale.

Because the data for each day is contained in a row of the array, it is necessary to total the elements in one row of the array (the fourth row) to find the number of shirts sold on the fourth day. The fourth row can be thought of by itself as a one-dimensional array. One loop is therefore required to access all the elements of this row:

```
Day4Sales = 0
FOR Column = 1 TO 3
    Day4Sales = Day4Sales + TShirts(4,Column)
NEXT Column
```

Notice that the first subscript of TShirts(4,Column) restricts the computations to the elements in row 4, while Column varies from 1 to 3. The process is pictured in the following diagram:

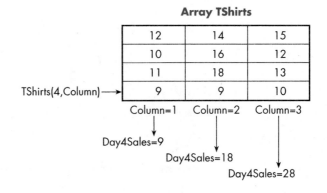

Array TShirts

12	14	15
10	16	12
11	18	13
9	9	10

TShirts(4,Column) →

Column=1   Column=2   Column=3

Day4Sales=9

Day4Sales=18

Day4Sales=28

FIGURE 9-2

T-Shirt Sales Report Program

```
'***              T-Shirt Sales Report              ***

'*** This program calculates the total T-shirt sales  ***
'*** for three stores in a fast-food chain for a four- ***
'*** day period. At the end of the program, a sales    ***
'*** report is printed on paper.                       ***
'*** Major variables:                                  ***
'***     TShirts (4,3)      Sales for the 4-day period ***
'***                        for each of the 3 stores   ***
'***     TotalShirts    Total shirts sold in all stores ***

DIM TShirts(1 TO 4, 1 TO 3)
TotalShirts = 0

CLS

'*** Prompt user to enter T-shirt sales and place in array. ***
FOR Row = 1 TO 4
   PRINT
   FOR Column = 1 TO 3
      PRINT "Enter sales for store"; Column; "on day"; Row;
      INPUT TShirts(Row, Column)
      '*** Keep a running total of all sales. ***
      TotalShirts = TotalShirts + TShirts(Row, Column)
   NEXT Column
NEXT Row

'*** Print table showing the number of T-shirts sold. ***
LPRINT
LPRINT TAB(8); "T-Shirt Sales Report"
LPRINT
LPRINT "Day #"; TAB(10); "Store 1"; TAB(20); "Store 2"; TAB(30); "Store 3"
```

FIGURE 9-2

Continued

```
FOR Row = 1 TO 4
    LPRINT Row;
    FOR Column = 1 TO 3
        LPRINT TAB(Column * 10); TShirts(Row, Column);
    NEXT Column
    LPRINT
NEXT Row


'*** Print total number of T-shirts sold. ***
LPRINT
LPRINT "Total T-shirt sales for all stores: "; TotalShirts

END
```

```
Enter sales for store 1 on day 1 ? 12
Enter sales for store 2 on day 1 ? 14
Enter sales for store 3 on day 1 ? 15

Enter sales for store 1 on day 2 ? 10
Enter sales for store 2 on day 2 ? 16
Enter sales for store 3 on day 2 ? 12

Enter sales for store 1 on day 3 ? 11
Enter sales for store 2 on day 3 ? 18
Enter sales for store 3 on day 3 ? 13

Enter sales for store 1 on day 4 ? 9
Enter sales for store 2 on day 4 ? 9
Enter sales for store 3 on day 4 ? 10
```

```
        T-Shirt Sales Report

Day #      Store 1     Store 2     Store 3
  1          12          14          15
  2          10          16          12
  3          11          18          13
  4           9           9          10

Total T-shirt sales for all stores:  149
```

Adding Columns

To find the total number of T-shirts sold by the third store, it is necessary to total the elements in the third column of the array. This time we can think of the column by itself as a one-dimensional array of four elements. This operation calls for a FOR...NEXT loop, as shown here:

```
Store3 = 0
FOR Row = 1 TO 4
    Store3 = Store3 + TShirts(Row,3)
NEXT Row
```

The third statement restricts the value of the column subscript to 3 while the row subscript varies from 1 to 4. This process is pictured in the following diagram:

Array TShirts   TShirts(Column3)

| 12 | 14 | 15 | Row = 1 → Store3 = 15
| 10 | 16 | 12 | Row = 2 → Store3 = 27
| 11 | 18 | 13 | Row = 3 → Store3 = 40
| 9 | 9 | 10 | Row = 4 → Store3 = 50

Learning Check 9-2

1. A(n) _____ array stores values as a table of rows and columns.

2. The first subscript of a two-dimensional array refers to the _____ of the element, and the second subscript refers to the _____.

3. Write a DIM statement for a two-dimensional array Schedule containing 30 rows and eight columns.

4. Write a program segment that totals the columns of array Numbers, whose DIM statement follows, putting the sums of the columns in a one-dimensional array named ColumnTotals:

```
DIM Numbers(1 TO 10,1 TO 15)
```

SORTING AN ARRAY

Many programming applications require data items stored in arrays to be sorted or ordered in some way. For example, names must be alphabetized, social security numbers must be arranged from lowest to highest, sports statistics must be arranged by numeric value, and so on. Lists can be sorted in **ascending order**

Ascending order *Items arranged so that they go from smallest to largest (in the case of numbers) or from a to z (in the case of letters).*

Descending order *Items arranged so that they go from largest to smallest (in the case of numbers) or from z to a (in the case of letters).*

(from smallest to largest) or in **descending order** (from largest to smallest).

Of course, when dealing with short lists of data, it is no problem to arrange the items mentally in their proper order. In the following example, it is a simple matter to arrange these test scores in ascending order:

Array 1 (Unsorted)	Array 2 (Sorted)
75	55
92	66
66	75
100	92
55	100

If there were 100 test scores to sort, however, the operation would be quite tedious and time consuming. Fortunately, the computer is well suited to this task. The programmer can use various methods to sort data items, some more efficient than others. Two methods are presented here: the bubble sort and the Shell sort.

Bubble Sort

Bubble sort *A type of sort in which adjacent list items are compared and, if they are out of order, switched. This process is repeated until the entire list is in order.*

The basic idea behind the **bubble sort** is to arrange the elements of an array progressively in ascending or descending order by making a series of comparisons of the adjacent values in the array. If the adjacent values are out of sequence, they are exchanged.

When arranging an array in ascending order, the bubble sort "bubbles" the largest values to the end. The values of adjacent array elements are compared and switched if the value of the first element is larger than the value of the second. Then the next pair of adjacent elements is compared and switched if necessary.

This sequence of comparisons (called a *pass*) is then repeated, starting from the beginning. After each complete pass through the array, however, the element moved to the end of the array need not be included in the comparisons of the next pass, because it is now in its proper position. Successive passes are continued through the array until no elements are switched, indicating that the entire array is sorted.

To illustrate this bubbling procedure, an array consisting of five integers is sorted into ascending order in Figure 9-3. Notice that after each pass is completed, the largest of the numbers compared in that pass is moved to the end of those numbers. After one pass through the array, some of the numbers are closer to their proper positions, but the array is not yet completely ordered. The largest value, 7, has been successfully positioned at the end of the array and is therefore not included in the comparisons of the following passes. The process starts over at the beginning of the array, comparing each set of adjacent integers up to the number 1. At the end of this second pass, the number 5 is positioned correctly. After a fourth pass through, the array is completely arranged in ascending order. From this illustration, we get an idea of the steady "bubbling" process involved in this sorting routine.

Now let's take a look at the actual code for a bubble sort, as illustrated in Figure 9-4.

This program sorts ten astronaut names in alphabetical order. Because the computer automatically assigns a collating sequence (or ASCII) value to each character it is capable of representing, it compares the ASCII values for each letter to determine that the letter A is less than the letter B, B is less than C, and so on. Procedure GetNames simply prompts the user to enter the astronaut's

FIGURE 9-3

Bubble Sort Process

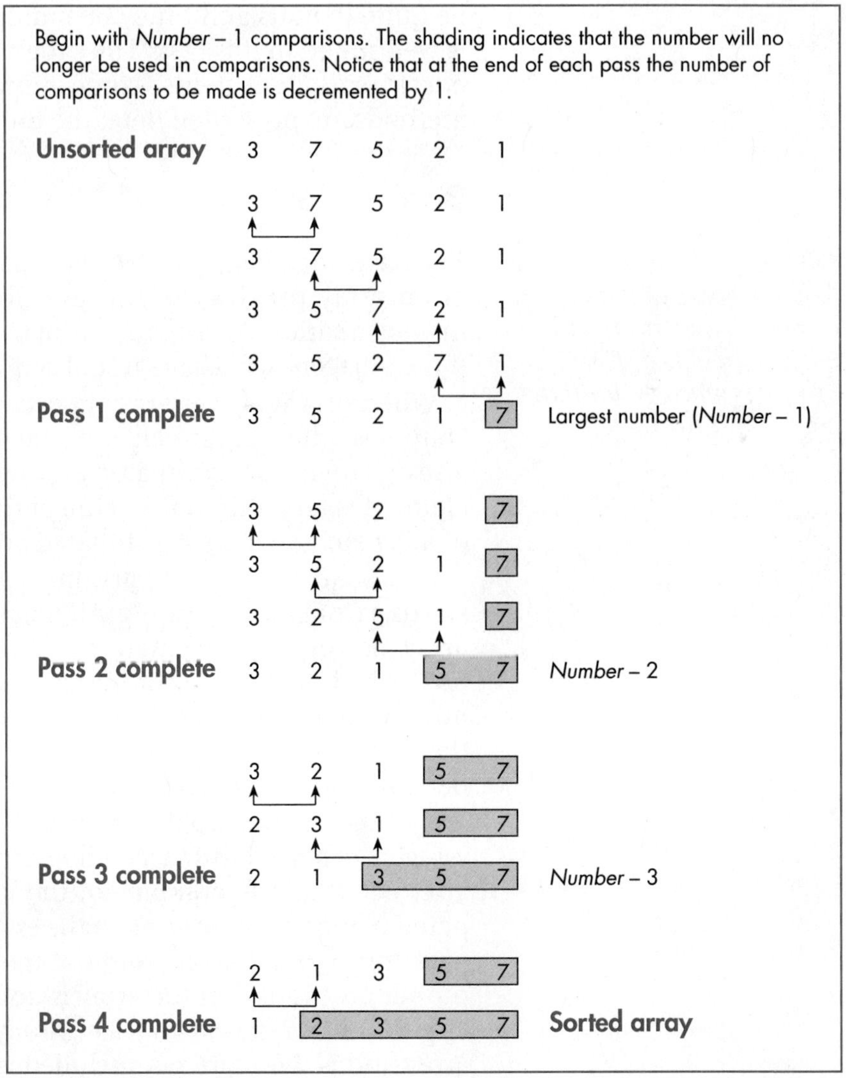

Begin with *Number* − 1 comparisons. The shading indicates that the number will no longer be used in comparisons. Notice that at the end of each pass the number of comparisons to be made is decremented by 1.

FIGURE 9-4

Bubble Sort Program

```
DECLARE SUB GetNames (Astro$())
DECLARE SUB SortNames (Astro$())
DECLARE SUB DisplayList (Astro$())

'***                     Astronaut's Mix-up             ***

'*** This program uses a bubble sort to sort the astro-  ***
'*** nauts of the Astro Air Station into alphabetical    ***
'*** order.                                              ***
'*** Major variables:                                    ***
'***      Astro$          Names of the astronauts        ***

'*** Set up name array size. ***
DIM Astro$(1 TO 10)

'*** Place unsorted names into an array. ***
CALL GetNames(Astro$())

'*** Sort names in alphabetical order. ***
CALL SortNames(Astro$())

'*** Display sorted list. ***
CALL DisplayList(Astro$())

END

SUB DisplayList (Astro$())
   '*** This procedure displays the alphabetically sorted  ***
   '*** list.                                              ***

   CLS
   PRINT
   PRINT "Astro Air Station -- Sorted"
   PRINT
   FOR Count = 1 TO 10
      PRINT Astro$(Count)
   NEXT Count

END SUB
```

Continued on next page

FIGURE 9-4

Continued

```
SUB GetNames (Astro$())
    '*** This procedure prompts the user to enter each name. ***
    '*** The names are stored in array Astro$. The array is   ***
    '*** returned to the calling program.                     ***

    CLS
    PRINT
    FOR Count = 1 TO 10
        INPUT "Enter astronaut's name: ", Astro$(Count)
    NEXT Count

END SUB

SUB SortNames (Astro$())
    '*** This procedure uses the bubble sort to alphabetically  ***
    '*** sort the array Astro$. The sorted array is returned to ***
    '*** the calling program.                                   ***

    Final = 9
    Flag = 1

    '*** Execute loop until no exchanges are made. ***
    DO WHILE Flag = 1
        Flag = 0
        FOR Count = 1 TO Final
            '*** If names are out of order, switch them. ***
            IF Astro$(Count) > Astro$(Count + 1) THEN
                SWAP Astro$(Count), Astro$(Count + 1)
                Flag = 1            '***Reset Flag, indicating a switch
            END IF
        NEXT Count
        Final = Final - 1
    LOOP

END SUB
```

FIGURE 9-4

Continued

```
Enter astronaut's name: Jetson
Enter astronaut's name: Solong
Enter astronaut's name: Quirk
Enter astronaut's name: Skywaltzer
Enter astronaut's name: Mader
Enter astronaut's name: McSoy
Enter astronaut's name: Kanobi
Enter astronaut's name: Speck
Enter astronaut's name: OHorror
Enter astronaut's name: Checkup
```

```
Astro Air Station -- Sorted

Checkup
Jetson
Kanobi
Mader
McSoy
OHorror
Quirk
Skywaltzer
Solong
Speck
```

names and stores them in array Astro$. SortNames performs the bubble sort. Let us examine it carefully to see what happens.

Notice that Flag is set to 1 before the loop is entered. Its value is later checked to determine if the entire array is in order. Final is set to one less than the number of items to be sorted. This is because two items at a time are compared. Count varies from 1 to 9, which means that eventually item 9 will be compared with item 9 + 1. If Final were set to 10 (the number of names), QBasic would try to compare item 10 with item 11, which does not exist in the array.

Examine the block IF statement in the FOR...NEXT loop. This statement determines whether two adjacent values should be exchanged. For example, when Count = 1, Jetson is compared with Solong. Because J is less than S, there is no need to switch these two items. Then Count is incremented to 2, and Solong is compared with Quirk. Because Quirk comes before Solong, these two names must be exchanged. QBasic has a special statement, called the SWAP statement, that allows the values in two variables to be exchanged. The following program segment demonstrates SWAP; after it is executed, X will equal 10 and Y will equal 20:

```
X = 20
Y = 10
SWAP X, Y
```

As the bubble sort is performed, the SWAP statement switches any out-of-order elements. In addition, Flag is set to 1, indicating that a switch has taken place.

The FOR...NEXT loop continues until each pair of adjacent elements has been compared. After one pass through the FOR...NEXT loop, Astro$ looks like this:

```
Jetson
Quirk
Skywaltzer
Mader
McSoy
Kanobi
Solong
OHorror
Checkup
Speck
```

Although several switches have been made, the list is not completely sorted. That is why we need the DO WHILE...LOOP. As long as Flag equals 1, QBasic knows that switches have been made, and the sorting process must continue. When the loop is completed without setting Flag equal to 1—that is, when no switches are made—the program finds Flag equal to 0 and knows that the list is in order. Numbers can also be sorted by this same method.

Refer back to the procedure calls and parameter lists in Figure 9-4. Notice that the array names are followed by a set of empty parentheses, for example, Astro$(). These empty parentheses tell QBasic that these variables are arrays.

Shell Sort

The bubble sort is relatively easy to understand and code. It is not very efficient, however, because it can exchange only adjacent elements of the list being sorted. If an element is far from its proper position, many exchanges are necessary to move it to the correct spot. The **Shell sort**, named after its creator, Donald Shell, avoids this difficulty.

A comparison of the sequence of an array after one pass through using a bubble sort and after one pass through using the Shell sort shows how much more efficient the Shell sort is:

Original list:	75	35	48	55	12	5	63	42
Bubble sort pass 1:	35	48	55	12	5	63	42	75
Shell sort pass 1:	12	5	48	42	75	35	63	55

Notice that, after only one pass with the Shell sort, numbers far from their proper positions have made much greater progress toward their final places than with the bubble sort.

When using the Shell sort, the programmer chooses a gap that is equal to one-half the size of the list. In the example in Figure 9-5, the gap is equal to 4 because the list has eight elements. The elements of the list are separated by the chosen gap and grouped into sublists. The first sublist begins with the first element of the

FIGURE 9-5

Shell Sort Process

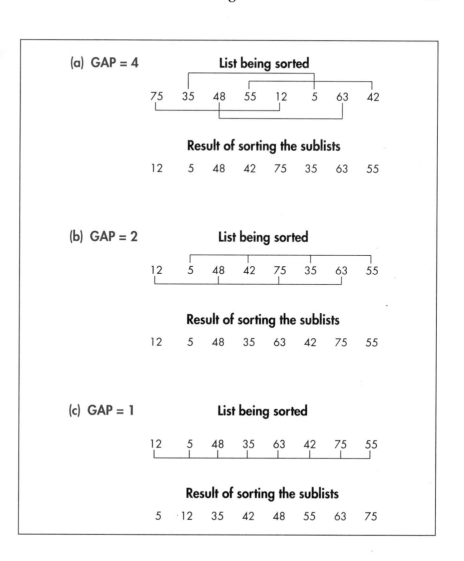

list. The next member of the first sublist is the fifth element, four positions away. The next member would be the ninth element, if the lists contained that many elements, and so forth. The second sublist begins with the second list element and also contains the sixth element, which is four positions away. This grouping process continues until each element belongs to a sublist. Our example has four sublists, each containing two elements (see Figure 9-5a).

Each sublist is sorted independently of the others; the results of this first sort are shown in the second list in Figure 9-5a. Notice that the elements within each sublist are in their proper order. The sorting proceeds rapidly because the sublists are short. Because the gap between the elements in each sublist is large, elements far out of place make large movements toward their final positions.

Next, the gap is divided in half, and the previously described process is repeated with a gap of 2. This gives two sublists, one consisting of all the elements in odd-numbered positions and another made up of elements in even-numbered positions. Each sublist is sorted; the results are shown in Figure 9-5b.

The final step involves dividing the gap in half again, giving a gap of 1. This leaves us with a single sublist, as shown in Figure 9-5c.

At first glance, the Shell sort may appear less efficient than the bubble sort. In fact, however, the entire sequence of sorts called for by the Shell sort takes less time than a single bubble sort, particularly for longer lists. Generally speaking, the Shell sort is more efficient than the bubble sort when sorting lists of 100 or more elements.

There are a number of different versions of the Shell sort, each using a different method to sort the sublists. Figure 9-6 contains one version. Notice that the DO WHILE...LOOP continues to execute as long as the size of the gap is not 0. The FOR...NEXT loop goes through each sublist, switching any out-of-order elements.

The Shell sort is a good compromise between speed and simplicity. Other sorting algorithms are faster, but they are generally more complex to use.

SEARCHING

Sequential Search

Now, assume that we want to find a specific value in an array. One way of searching an array is to examine each array element in turn, starting with the first one, until the desired value or values are found. For example, you might want to know the number of

FIGURE 9-6

Shell Sort Procedure

```
SUB SortNames (Astro$())
    '*** This procedure uses the Shell sort to alphabetically   ***
    '*** sort the array Astro$. The sorted array is returned to ***
    '*** the calling program.                                   ***

    Final = 10
    '*** Make initial gap half the length of list. ***
    Gap = INT(Final / 2)
    '*** Continue decreasing size of gap until it is zero. ***
    DO WHILE Gap <> 0
        Flag = 1
        '*** Make one pass of comparisons. ***
        FOR Count = 1 TO (Final - Gap)
            '*** If elements are out-of-order, switch them. ***
            IF Astro$(Count) > Astro$(Count + Gap) THEN
                SWAP Astro$(Count), Astro$(Count + Gap)
                Flag = 0   '** Reset flag, indicating switches were made.
            END IF
        NEXT Count
        '*** If no switches were made, decrease size of the gap. ***
        IF Flag = 1 THEN
            Gap = INT(Gap / 2)
        END IF
    LOOP

END SUB
```

scores greater than 89 in an array Quiz containing 40 test scores.
The following segment performs this task:

```
Count = 0
FOR Position = 1 TO 40
    IF Quiz(Position) > 89 THEN
        Count = Count + 1
    END IF
NEXT Position
```

The variable Count keeps track of the number of scores greater
than 89. The loop is set up to check the value of each array element in numeric order, and Count is incremented only if the score
being checked is greater than 89.

Another type of search might involve locating a single value.
Suppose you wanted information regarding the August 19 concert
at the local concert hall. The computer might prompt you to enter

the date of the concert in which you are interested. It then would search an array of concert dates until it located the given date. Finally, the computer would access the corresponding values from the arrays containing the rest of the concert information and display those values on the screen, as depicted in Figure 9-7.

Both the searches just described are **sequential searches**. This type of search examines the first element, then the second element, then the third, and so on in numeric sequence until the desired element is found or the end of the array is reached. This type of search is adequate for a relatively small number of items (fewer than 100, generally speaking) but becomes slow with larger arrays. If the elements in an array can first be arranged in an ascending or descending order, the binary search is much faster and more efficient.

> **Sequential search** *A search that examines array elements, from the first to the last, until the specified value is found or the end of the array is reached.*

Binary Search

> **Binary search** *A search that repeatedly divides a sorted array into halves, comparing the target to the middle element and eliminating the portion that does not contain the target.*

A **binary search** divides a sorted array into portions, eliminating the portions that do not contain the desired value. It first finds the middle value of a list and checks to see if the desired value is greater. Because the list is in order, half the list can thus be immediately eliminated. The portion of the list containing the desired value is then divided again according to a new middle value and is checked to see which half contains the desired value. This process continues until the middle value equals the desired value.

Consider the example of the concert dates array. The dates are listed in ascending order. (The numbers are coded to reflect the month and date as MMDD.) The array Day can be pictured like this, with pointers at the first and last elements to be considered:

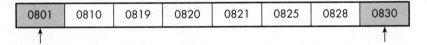

| 0801 | 0810 | 0819 | 0820 | 0821 | 0825 | 0828 | 0830 |

FIGURE 9-7

Performing a Sequential Search

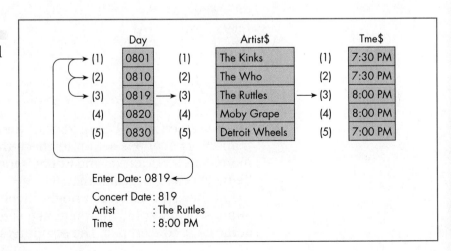

The desired date is 0819. To determine the middle, the subscripts of the first and last array elements are added and divided by 2:

$$\frac{1+8}{2} = \frac{9}{2} = 4.5$$

The result is 4.5, so the number is truncated to 4. The value of the fourth element is 0820. Because 0819 is less than 0820, elements 4 through 8 are ignored. Just one comparison has already eliminated half the array. The first and last elements to be considered are elements 1 and 3, and now a new middle value is calculated in the same manner as before:

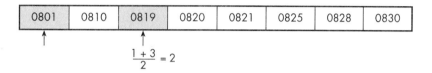

| 0801 | 0810 | 0819 | 0820 | 0821 | 0825 | 0828 | 0830 |

$$\frac{1+3}{2} = 2$$

The second element is now the middle value used to compare with the desired date 0819. Since 0810 is less than 0819, Day(1) and Day(2) can be ignored, and a new middle value is calculated:

| 0801 | 0810 | 0819 | 0820 | 0821 | 0825 | 0828 | 0830 |

$$\frac{3+3}{2} = 3$$

When Day(3) is checked against 0819, the two values are found to be equal, and the search is over.

Figure 9-8 shows a procedure that performs a binary search for a given date and then prints the needed information. The DO WHILE...LOOP performs the search as long as (1) the desired value does not match the value of the middle element (i.e., the desired value has not been found) and (2) the lower limit of the search is less than or equal to the upper limit. If the search has examined the first or last element of the array and still has not found the value, the lower limit will move past the upper limit. This condition indicates that the desired value is not located in the array. When the loop has terminated, the expression "IF Lower > Upper" checks this condition and a message is printed if necessary. Otherwise, the appropriate concert information is printed.

A binary search is more efficient than a sequential search because it can find a given value with far fewer comparisons. For example, with an array of 1,000 elements, the maximum number of comparisons a binary search requires to find a specified value is 11. If the desired value is the last one in the array, a sequential search requires 1,000 comparisons.

FIGURE 9-8

Binary Search Procedure

```
SUB BinarySearch (Target, Day(), Tme$(), Artist$())
    '*** This procedure uses a binary search to locate a      ***
    '*** target value in array Day.                           ***

    Upper = 8
    Lower = 1
    Middle = INT((Upper + Lower) / 2)

    '*** Loop until value is found or entire list has been searched. ***
    DO WHILE (Lower <= Upper) AND (Target) <> Day(Middle)
        IF Target < Day(Middle) THEN
            Upper = Middle - 1
        ELSE
            Lower = Middle + 1
        END IF
        Middle = INT((Upper + Lower) / 2)
    LOOP

    '*** Display appropriate message. ***
    IF Lower > Upper THEN
        PRINT "No concert scheduled."
    ELSE
        PRINT "Concert date: "; TAB(16); Target
        PRINT "Time: "; TAB(16); Tme$(Middle)
        PRINT "Artist: "; TAB(16); Artist$(Middle)
    END IF


END SUB
```

Learning Check 9-3

1. What is indicated when a bubble sort makes an entire pass without making an exchange?

2. A(n) _____ consists of examining the elements of an array, from beginning to end, until the desired value or values are found.

3. In a sequential search of this list, how many values will have been examined by the time 236 is located?

12   44   103   177   236   582   978   1235

4. If a binary search is made of the list in Question 3, how many values will be examined by the time 236 is located?

5. True or False? A sequential search is faster than a binary search when searching large arrays.

6. Must a list be in order to do a sequential search? Must a list be in order to do a binary search?

MASTERING PROGRAM DEVELOPMENT

Problem Definition

The scorekeepers of the Centrovian Open Ice Skating Championships need a program to determine the winner of the final round. Each competitor is given six scores, of which the highest and lowest are discarded. The remaining four scores are then averaged to obtain the final score. The maximum score for each event is 6.0. Write a program that prompts the user to enter the names and scores of 10 finalists and produces a listing of the skaters' names and final scores in order of finish. The user should be prompted to enter the needed data as follows:

```
Enter skater's name: Balducci
Enter the skater's 6 scores, separated by commas:
? 5.7, 5.3, 5.1, 5.0, 4.7, 4.8

Enter skater's name: Creed
Enter the skater's 6 scores, separated by commas:
? 3.1, 4.9, 4.1, 3.7, 4.6, 3.9

Enter skater's name: Williams
Enter the skater's 6 scores, separated by commas:
? 4.1, 5.3, 4.9, 4.4, 3.9, 5.4
```

```
Enter skater's name: Hamilton
Enter the skater's 6 scores, separated by commas:
? 5.1, 5.7, 5.6, 5.5, 4.4, 5.4

Enter skater's name: Hernandez
Enter the skater's 6 scores, separated by commas:
? 5.9, 4.8, 5.5, 5.0, 5.7, 5.7

Enter skater's name: Stravinski
Enter the skater's 6 scores, separated by commas:
? 5.1, 4.7, 4.1, 4.2, 4.6, 5.0

Enter skater's name: Montalban
Enter the skater's 6 scores, separated by commas:
? 5.1, 5.1, 4.9, 4.4, 5.5, 5.3

Enter skater's name: Schell
Enter the skater's 6 scores, separated by commas:
? 4.9, 4.3, 5.2, 4.5, 4.6, 4.9

Enter skater's name: Cranston
Enter the skater's 6 scores, separated by commas:
? 6.0, 6.0, 5.7, 5.8, 5.9, 5.9

Enter skater's name: Valdez
Enter the skater's 6 scores, separated by commas:
? 4.3, 5.2, 5.9, 5.3, 5.3, 6.0
```

Results should then be displayed:

```
    SKATING COMPETITION RESULTS

PLACE    NAME             SCORE
--------------------------------

  1      Cranston         5.900
  2      Hernandez        5.475
  3      Valdez           5.425
  4      Hamilton         5.400
  5      Montalban        5.100
  6      Balducci         5.050
  7      Schell           4.725
  8      Williams         4.675
  9      Stravinski       4.625
 10      Creed            4.075
```

Solution Design

This problem provides us with seven items of data for each skater—a name and six scores—and asks for a list of names and averages, sorted by average. Once the data items have been entered (the first step), two basic operations must be performed in order to produce the listing: The averages must be calculated and these averages with their associated names must be sorted. Thus, the program can be broken into four major tasks:

1. Enter the data.
2. Calculate the averages.
3. Sort the names and averages.
4. Display the sorted information.

The structure chart is shown in Figure 9-9.

The input for this problem consists of two types of data, alphabetic and numeric, so two arrays must be used to store them. The numeric array must have two dimensions, one dimension for each skater and a second dimension for each of the six scores. A third array must be created to store the averages calculated in the program. Variables also will be needed to keep track of the high and low scores, which will not be included in the average. Therefore, the main variables needed can be summarized as follows:

Input Variables

One-dimensional array of names	Skaters$
Two-dimensional array of scores	Scores

Program Variables

High score for current competitor	High
Low score for current competitor	Low

Output Variables

Array of averages	Averages

FIGURE 9-9

Structure Chart for Skating Scores Problem

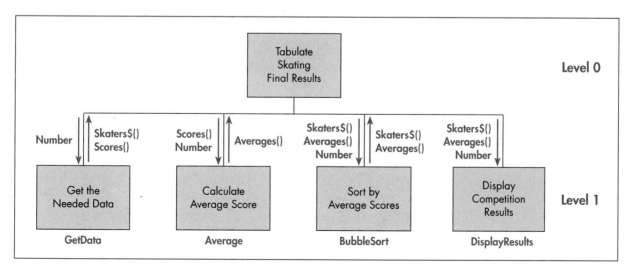

To calculate the averages, a search must be done on the six scores of each skater to find the high and low scores.

A sort is required in the third step of our algorithm. A descending-order bubble sort will be used. A crucial point is that as the averages are rearranged, the corresponding skater's name must be carried with each average. This means, for example, that the average for the fourth skater [Skaters$(4)] must be stored in Averages(4).

The flowchart and pseudocode shown in Figure 9-10 illustrate the logic of the solution.

The Program

The program in Figure 9-11 contains the solution to the problem. The DIM statement reserves space for a one-dimensional character array for the names (Skaters$), a two-dimensional numeric array for each skater's scores (Scores), and a one-dimensional array of average scores (Averages). Each row of array Scores contains the scores for one skater, so 10 rows of six columns each are dimensioned.

Procedure GetData simply prompts the user to enter each skater's name and six scores and stores them in the appropriate array location. Procedure Average is more complex. First, it performs a sequential search on each row of Scores to locate each skater's high and low score. Next, all six scores are totaled. Finally, Low and High are subtracted from Total and this result is divided by 4, the number of scores actually being averaged. This process is repeated for each of the 10 skaters.

The sorting of the final averages is performed in procedure BubbleSort. The condition Averages(Count) < Averages(Count+1) causes the averages to be sorted from highest to lowest. Every time a pair of averages is switched, the corresponding elements in array Skaters$ must also be switched. The sorted results are displayed by the procedure DisplayResults.

FIGURE 9-10

Flowchart and Pseudocode for Skating Scores Problem

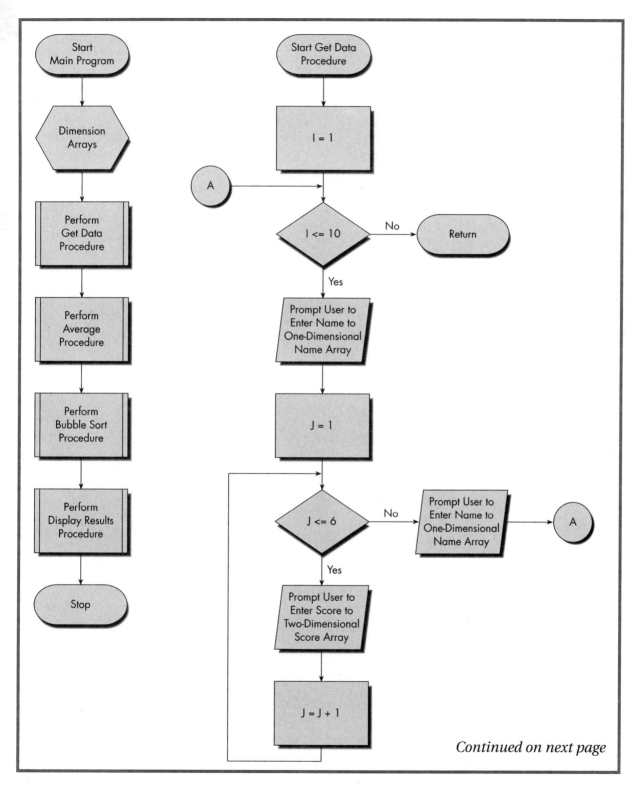

Continued on next page

FIGURE 9-10

Continued

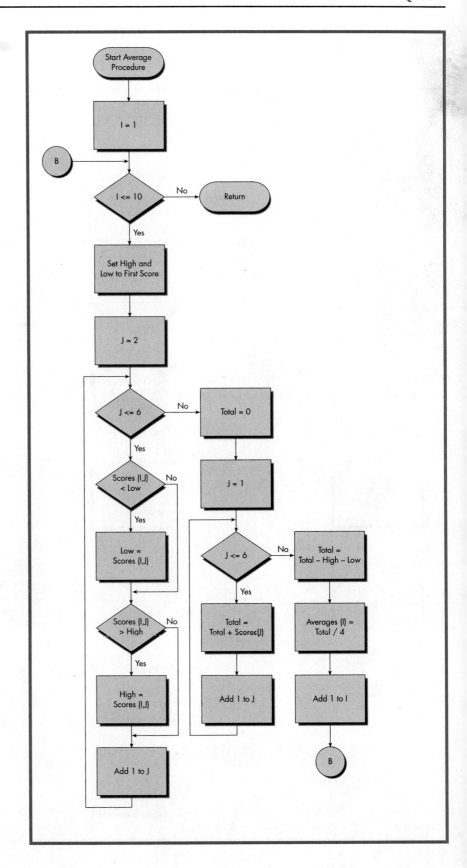

FIGURE 9-10

Continued

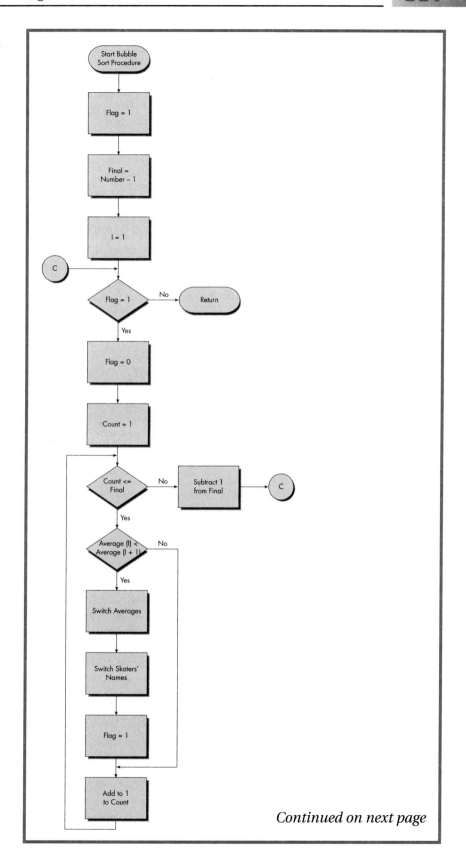

Continued on next page

FIGURE 9-10

Continued

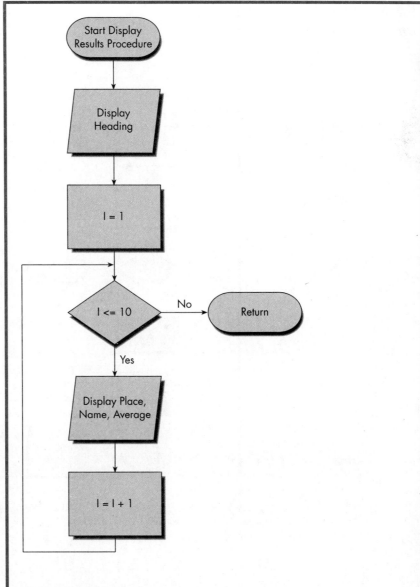

Begin main program
    Dimension arrays
    Perform procedure to get data
    Perform procedure to calculate averages
    Perform procedure to sort information
    Perform procedure to display results
End main program

Begin get data procedure
    Begin outer loop, do 10 times
        Prompt user to enter skater's name
        Begin inner loop, do 6 times

FIGURE 9-10

Continued

```
                    Prompt user to enter each score
                End inner loop
            End outer loop
        End get data procedure
        Begin average procedure
            Begin outer loop, do 10 times
                Set low and high scores to first score
                Begin inner loop, do 5 times
                    If current score < low score then
                        Set low score to current score
                    End if
                    If current score > high score then
                        Set high score to current score
                    End if
                End inner loop
                Set total of scores to 0
                Begin inner loop, do 6 times
                        Add current score to total score
                End inner loop
                Subtract high and low score from total score
                Calculate average
            End outer loop
        End average procedure

        Begin bubble sort procedure
            Initialize flag to indicate switch has taken place
            Begin outer loop; do until no switches
                Initialize flag to indicate no switches
                Begin inner loop; do until end of array
                    If adjacent scores are out-of-order then
                        Switch scores
                        Switch corresponding names
                        Set flag to indicate switch
                    End if
                    Go to next pair of array elements
                End inner loop
            End outer loop
        End bubble sort procedure

        Begin display results procedure
            Display headings
            Begin loop, do 10 times
                Display place, name, average
            End loop
        End display results procedure
```

FIGURE 9-11

Skating Scores Program

```
DECLARE SUB GetData (Skaters$(), Scores!(), Number!)
DECLARE SUB Average (Scores!(), Averages!(), Number!)
DECLARE SUB DisplayResults (Skaters$(), Averages!(), Number!)
DECLARE SUB BubbleSort (Skaters$(), Averages!(), Number!)

'***                 Skating Final Results               ***

'*** This program computes skaters' average scores. Each  ***
'*** skater receives 6 scores; the high and low scores are ***
'*** dropped and the average of the remaining 4 scores is  ***
'*** determined. The program then sorts the players'      ***
'*** average scores in descending order.                  ***
'*** Major variables:                                     ***
'***      Skaters$      Array of skaters' names           ***
'***      Scores        Array of scores                   ***
'***      Averages      Array of average scores           ***
'***      High, Low     Highest / lowest scores           ***

Number = 10        '*** Number of skaters

'*** Dimension the arrays. ***
DIM Skaters$(1 TO Number), Scores(1 TO Number, 1 TO 6),
    Averages(1 TO Number)


'*** Call procedure to prompt user to enter names and scores. ***
CALL GetData(Skaters$(), Scores(), Number)

'*** Call procedure to determine average scores. ***
CALL Average(Scores(), Averages(), Number)

'*** Call procedure to sort arrays. ***
CALL BubbleSort(Skaters$(), Averages(), Number)

'*** Call procedure to display results. ***
CALL DisplayResults(Skaters$(), Averages(), Number)

END

SUB Average (Scores(), Averages(), Number)
    '*** This procedures drops the high and low scores and   ***
    '*** then averages the remaining 4 scores.               ***
```

FIGURE 9-11

Continued

```
'*** Determine high and low scores.
FOR I = 1 TO Number
   High = Scores(I, 1)
   Low = Scores(I, 1)
   FOR J = 2 TO 6
      IF Scores(I, J) < Low THEN
         Low = Scores(I, J)
      END IF
      IF Scores(I, J) > High THEN
         High = Scores(I, J)
      END IF
   NEXT J

   '*** Total all 6 scores. ***
   Total = 0
   FOR J = 1 TO 6
      Total = Total + Scores(I, J)
   NEXT J

   '*** Subtract high and low score from total. ***
   Total = Total - Low - High
   '*** Divide remaining total by 4. ***
   Averages(I) = Total / 4
NEXT I

END SUB

SUB BubbleSort (Skaters$(), Averages(), Number)
   '*** This procedure sorts the arrays in descending order ***
   '*** by average score.                                   ***

   Flag = 1
   Final = Number - 1
   DO WHILE Flag = 1
      Flag = 0
      FOR Count = 1 TO Final
         IF Averages(Count) < Averages(Count + 1) THEN
            SWAP Averages(Count), Averages(Count + 1)
            SWAP Skaters$(Count), Skaters$(Count + 1)
            Flag = 1
         END IF
```

Continued on next page

FIGURE 9-11

Continued

```
      NEXT Count
      Final = Final - 1
   LOOP


END SUB

SUB DisplayResults (Skaters$(), Averages(), Number)
   '*** This procedure displays the sorted list of skaters   ***
   '*** in descending order by average score.                ***

   CLS
   PRINT
   Format$ = " ##         \                    \   ##.###"
   PRINT TAB(4); "SKATING COMPETITION RESULTS"
   PRINT
   PRINT "PLACE"; TAB(10); "NAME"; TAB(28); "SCORE"
   PRINT STRING$(32, "-")
   PRINT
   FOR Count = 1 TO Number
      PRINT USING Format$; Count; Skaters$(Count); Averages(Count)
   NEXT Count


END SUB

SUB GetData (Skaters$(), Scores(), Number)
   '*** This procedure prompts the user to enter each skater's   ***
   '*** name and 6 scores. The names are placed in array Skaters$ ***
   '*** and the corresponding scores are placed in array Scores.  ***
   '*** Both arrays are returned to the calling program.          ***

   CLS
   FOR I = 1 TO 10
      PRINT
      INPUT "Enter skater's name: ", Skaters$(I)
      PRINT "Enter the skater's 6 scores, separated by commas: "
      INPUT Scores(I, 1), Scores(I, 2), Scores(I, 3), Scores(I, 4),
         Scores(I, 5), Scores(I, 6)
   NEXT I


END SUB
```

FIGURE 9-11

Continued

```
Enter skater's name: Balducci
Enter the skater's 6 scores, separated by commas:
? 5.7, 5.3, 5.1, 5.0, 4.7, 4.8

Enter skater's name: Creed
Enter the skater's 6 scores, separated by commas:
? 3.1, 4.9, 4.1, 3.7, 4.6, 3.9

Enter skater's name: Williams
Enter the skater's 6 scores, separated by commas:
? 4.1, 5.3, 4.9, 4.4, 3.9, 5.4

Enter skater's name: Hamilton
Enter the skater's 6 scores, separated by commas:
? 5.1, 5.7, 5.6, 5.5, 4.4, 5.4

Enter skater's name: Hernandez
Enter the skater's 6 scores, separated by commas:
? 5.9, 4.8, 5.5, 5.0, 5.7, 5.7

Enter skater's name: Stravinski
Enter the skater's 6 scores, separated by commas:
? 5.1, 4.7, 4.1, 4.2, 4.6, 5.0

Enter skater's name: Montalban
Enter the skater's 6 scores, separated by commas:
? 5.1, 5.1, 4.9, 4.4, 5.5, 5.3

Enter skater's name: Schell
Enter the skater's 6 scores, separated by commas:
? 4.9, 4.3, 5.2, 4.5, 4.6, 4.9

Enter skater's name: Cranston
Enter the skater's 6 scores, separated by commas:
? 6.0, 6.0, 5.7, 5.8, 5.9, 5.9

Enter skater's name: Valdez
Enter the skater's 6 scores, separated by commas:
? 4.3, 5.2, 5.9, 5.3, 5.3, 6.0
```

Continued on next page

FIGURE 9-11

Continued

```
     SKATING COMPETITION RESULTS

 PLACE    NAME             SCORE
 ------------------------------------

    1     Cranston         5.900
    2     Hernandez        5.475
    3     Valdez           5.425
    4     Hamilton         5.400
    5     Montalban        5.100
    6     Balducci         5.050
    7     Schell           4.725
    8     Williams         4.675
    9     Stravinski       4.625
   10     Creed            4.075
```

PROGRAMMING HINTS

- Remember that only numbers can be stored in numeric variable arrays and only character strings can be stored in string variable arrays.

- QBasic automatically reserves room for only 11 elements if a one-dimensional array is not declared in a DIM statement, and 11 rows and columns for a two-dimensional array. It is good programming practice to dimension all arrays, regardless of their sizes.

- A DIM statement must appear before the array that it dimensions is used in the program.

- Remember, when using two-dimensional arrays, that the first subscript refers to the rows and the second subscript refers to its columns.

- Array subscripts may not fall outside the range established in the DIM statement.

- A name used for a two-dimensional array cannot be used for a one-dimensional array in the same program.

- When passing an array to a procedure, always place empty parentheses after the array name. For example, Score ().
- To use a binary search, the data in the array must be arranged in ascending or descending order.

SUMMARY POINTS

▌ An array is an ordered collection of related values stored under a single variable name.

▌ Individual array elements can be accessed by using subscripts.

▌ A subscript of an array element can be any legal numeric expression.

▌ The DIM statement sets up storage for arrays and must appear before the first reference to the array it describes.

▌ Array manipulation is carried out through the use of loops.

▌ A two-dimensional array stores values as a table, grouped into rows and columns.

▌ The first subscript of a two-dimensional array refers to the element's row and the second subscript to the column.

▌ The bubble sort places elements of an array in ascending or descending order by comparing adjacent elements.

▌ The Shell sort works by establishing a gap and then using the size of this gap to separate the list in sublists. Each sublist is sorted independently. The chosen gap is progressively diminished until the entire list is sorted.

▌ A sequential search of an array consists of examining each element in the array, from beginning to end, until the desired value is located.

▌ In a binary search, an ordered array is repeatedly divided in half. The half not containing the target value is ignored.

KEY TERMS

Array – 303
Ascending order – 319
Binary search – 328
Bubble sort – 319
Descending order – 319
Element – 303
One-dimensional array – 311
Parallel arrays – 307
Sequential search – 328

REVIEW QUESTIONS

1. What is an array?

2. Give two advantages of using arrays.

3. What is a subscript?

4. Where must the DIM statement appear in a program?

5. When an array is not dimensioned, its subscripts can vary in value from 0 to _____.

6. Given the following program segment, create a diagram showing how array Amount will appear in storage:

```
DIM Amount(1 TO 6)
X = 4
Amount(X-1) = 14.35
Amount(2^2) = 80.42
Amount (14-13) = 19.8
Amount(2*3) = 45.79
```

7. Assume X = 1, Y = 2, and Z = 3. What are the values of the variables A(X), A(Y–X), and A(X*Z) if array A contains the following values?

   Array A

1	11
2	42
3	37
4	90
5	17

8. Explain the difference between a two-dimensional and a one-dimensional array.

9. What is the maximum number of elements that can be contained in each of the following two-dimensional arrays?

   a. `DIM Position (1 TO 35, 1 TO 17)`

   b. `DIM Class (1 TO 6, 10 TO 20)`

   c. `DIM TAX (51 TO 100, 1 TO 85)`

10. Using the following program segment, create a diagram like the one below and show how array GrossPay will appear in storage:

```
DIM GrossPay(1 TO 3, 1 TO 5)
X = 7
Y = 3
GrossPay(Y-1, 4) = 1715.75
GrossPay(Y/3, 3) = 1203.01
GrossPay(X-4, 2*2) = 1593.09
GrossPay(3, 10-9) = 2080.52
```

	1	2	3	4	5
1					
2					
3					

11. How can nested loop statements be used to display the contents of a two-dimensional array?

12. Explain how the bubble sort works.

13. Explain how the Shell sort works.

14. Explain how you would use a sequential search to look up a telephone number. How would you use a binary search to look up the number?

15. How does sequentially searching a two-dimensional array differ from searching a one-dimensional array?

DEBUGGING EXERCISES

Locate any errors in the following programs or program segments, and debug them.

1.
```
'*** Prompt user to enter 20 numbers and store in array A.
Number = 20
FOR Count = 1 TO Number
    INPUT "Enter value"; A(Number)
NEXT Count
END
```

2.
```
'*** Total elements of array X. ***
DIM X(1 TO 10)
Total = 0
FOR Count = 1 TO 10
    Total = Total + X(1)
NEXT Count
```

3.
```
DIM Values(1 TO 26)
        .
        .
        .
'*** Bubble sort numbers in ascending order. ***
Flag = 1
Final = 26
DO WHILE Flag = 1
    Flag = 0
    FOR Count = 1 TO Final
        IF Values(Count) > Values(Count + 1) THEN
            SWAP Values(Count), Values(Count + 1)
            Flag = 1
        END IF
    NEXT Count
    Final = Final - 1
LOOP
```

4.
```
'*** Use Shell sort to sort 20 course names alphabetically. ***
Number = 20
    Gap = INT(Number / 2) '***Make initial gap half the length of list
    '*** Continue decreasing size of gap until it is zero. ***
    DO WHILE Gap = 0
        Flag = 1
        '*** Make one pass of comparisons. ***
        FOR Count = 1 TO (Number - Gap)
            '*** If elements are out-of-order, switch them. ***
            IF Course$(Count) > Course$(Count + Gap) THEN
                SWAP Course$(Count), Course$(Count + Gap)
                Flag = 0 '** Reset flag, indicating switches were made. ***
            END IF
        NEXT Count
LOOP
```

5.
```
'*** Locate Social Security Number 268-66-9843 in a list. ***
DIM S$(1 TO 50)
SSN$ = "268-66-9843"
Upper = 50
Lower = 1
Middle = INT((Upper + Lower) / 2)
DO WHILE (Lower <= Upper) AND (SSN$ <> S$(Middle))
    IF SSN$ < S$(Middle) THEN
        Lower = Middle - 1
        Middle = INT((Upper + Lower) / 2)
    END IF
LOOP
IF Lower > Upper THEN
    PRINT "Invalid number."
```

```
ELSE
    PRINT "Social security number found."
END IF
END
```

PROGRAMMING PROBLEMS

Level 1

1. Write a FOR...NEXT loop that prompts you to enter 30 numbers. The loop should store every other number (that is, those numbers with subscripts 2, 4, 6, etc.) in an array named List.

2. Assume that an array named Scores contains 50 numbers. Write a FOR...NEXT loop that will display all the numbers in Scores that are greater than 20 and less than 40. Use a sequential search to locate the numbers in this range.

3. Write a program that prompts the user to enter 12 numbers to array A and 12 numbers to array B. The program should compute the product of the corresponding elements of the two arrays, and place the results in array C. The program should display a table similar to the following:

   ```
   A   B   C
   2   3   6
   7   2   14
   .   .   .
   .   .   .
   .   .   .
   ```

4. Ask 50 students to name their favorite NFL team. Write a program that reads the names of each chosen team and the number of students voting for that team. Use a bubble sort to sort the teams so that the most popular is first and the least popular is last. Print the sorted list on paper.

5. Write a program that assigns all the even numbers between 1 and 20 to an array named Even and all the odd numbers between 1 and 20 to an array named Odd. Total the values in each array. Your output should look something like this:

   ```
   Even Numbers    Odd Numbers
          X              X
          X              X
          X              X
        -----          -----
         XXX            XXX
   ```

6. The Subterranean Art Gallery is preparing for its annual auction held in Washington Square. The Village Voice is preparing a circular containing information concerning the paintings to be auctioned:

Painting	Artist	Value in Millions
Starry Night	Van Gogh	5.5
Last Words	Picasso	3.8
Why?	Monika	.0005
Self Portrait	Dylan	1.2
Prodigal Son	Rembrandt	4.9
Call Me Abbie	Hoffman	3.6
Yippie Sandwich	Reubens	.08

The gallery has hired you to write a program that will prompt the user to enter the data and sort it into alphabetical order by the artists' names. The results should be printed on paper. Each artist's name should be printed first, followed by the artwork's title and the price.

Level 2

1. Write a program that prompts the user to enter a character string. Each character, except for any blanks, should be assigned to an array element. Then display the character string. For example, if the string entered is:

I was so much older then, I'm younger than that now.

The output should be:

Iwassomucholderthen,I'myoungerthanthatnow.

You can assume that a phrase will never be longer than 80 characters. (*Hint:* You may want to use the LEN and the MID$ functions when assigning the characters to the array.)

2. A department store is having a closeout sale on all its merchandise. Write a program that will prompt the user to enter each item's regular price and the percentage of the discount that should be given to that item. Store all the prices and discount percentages in one array. Then calculate the corresponding sale prices and store them in a second array. Display the original prices, the discount rates, and the corresponding sale prices. The output should be formatted similar to the following:

Price	Discount	Sale Price
3.50	.25	x.xx
4.00	.50	x.xx
5.25	.25	x.xx
6.00	.30	x.xx

3. The Klingons have captured Spock, science officer of the U.S.S. *Enterprise.* Captain Kirk has broken into their prison colony to free him. He has reached the computer that possesses information concerning all of the prisoners, including their cell numbers. Write a program to prompt the user to enter the following data into the program. The data should be stored in three parallel arrays:

Prisoner	Ship	Cell #
Kanobi	Falcon	328
Spock	Enterprise	562
Yoda	None	122
Mudd	Pleasure Dome	222
Khan	Botany Bay	009
Jetson	Astrofly	468
Rogers	Galaxy 2	727
Koenig	Alpher	999
Adama	Galactic	987
Who	Tardis	585

Alphabetize the data by name, and display information regarding a prisoner when his or her name is entered. Use a binary search routine in your program to speed Captain Kirk's search for Spock.

4. Write a program that will randomly generate 10 numbers between 1 and 10 and assign them to an array. Print the array with an asterisk beside each 5. Use a sequential search to locate all of the 5s. The output should have this format:

10 Random Numbers

```
        X
        X
        —
        —
        5*
        —
        —
        —
        5*
        X
```

5. Connor Video, Inc., operates three video games in four different arcades. Mr. Connor has received the following table of data concerning the number of games played at each of the four arcades:

Arcade	Krystal Kastles	Off Road	Copter Race
Video Madness	100	250	200
Sappy Sam's	500	600	700
Krazy Katie's	200	225	230
City Arcade	120	520	440

Mr. Connor would like to know how many games were played at each arcade, how many games per video were played, and the total number of games played altogether. The output should be displayed on the screen and include the preceding table.

6. As you know, QBasic contains a number of built-in functions. A useful one is the MID$ function, which allows you to locate a specified number of characters within a character string. Write your own procedure that performs this same task. The string's characters should be assigned to an array. Place each character (including any blanks and punctuation marks) in a separate array element. The array should be passed to the procedure, which should obtain the specified substring, place it in a second array, and return it to the calling program. The substring should then be displayed.

Challenge Problems

1. Write a program that determines whether a phrase is a palindrome. A palindrome is a phrase that is spelled the same backward or forward. For example, *madam* is a palindrome.

Input:

Prompt the user to enter the phrase to be tested.

Processing Requirements:

a. Store the phrase in an array, making certain to ignore any blank spaces in the phrase.

b. Compare each character in the array to the corresponding character at the other end of the array. For example, if the phrase is 15 characters long, you would compare the first element to the fifteenth, the second element to the fourteenth, and so forth.

c. Stop the comparison process as soon as you do not get a match.

d. You can assume that the user will not enter any punctuation. However, if you wish, you can write your program so that it ignores punctuation.

Output:

The output should be displayed on the monitor screen and look similar to the following:

Not a palindrome: mad dog

Palindrome: a man a plan a canal panama

2. This chapter explained two sorting algorithms: the bubble sort and the Shell sort. Another common sorting algorithm is the selection sort. It starts at the beginning of the array, examines each value in turn, and determines the smallest value in the entire array. This value is then placed in the first array element. It then examines every element from the second one on, until it finds the second smallest element, which is placed in the second position. This process continues until the entire array is sorted. Write a program that allows you to enter a list of 20 numbers and then calls a SUB procedure, which uses a selection sort to arrange the numbers in ascending order.

Input:

Prompt the user to enter 20 numbers.

Processing Requirements:

a. Send the unsorted array to a SUB procedure.

b. Use a selection sort to arrange the numbers in ascending order.

c. Return the sorted array to the calling program.

Output:

Display the sorted array.

Records and Files

Outline

Objectives

After studying this chapter, you will be able to:

▌ Use the DIM statement to specify the data types of variables.

▌ Define records and explain how records are different from arrays.

▌ Use records in programs.

▌ List several advantages of using data files.

▌ Discuss the relationship between files, records, and fields.

▌ Create a sequential file.

▌ Read from and write to a sequential file.

▌ Append data to the end of an existing sequential file.

▌ Create random-access files and define records to be used in them.

Introduction

As you learned in Chapter 9, array elements must all be of the same data type. An array cannot have some elements that contain numeric data and others that contain string data. Fortunately, QBasic provides another structure, called the *record*, as an alternative method of storing related data under a single variable name. The first portion of this chapter discusses using records.

Data files, presented in the second half of this chapter, provide an alternative means of organizing and storing related data. Data files allow us to store virtually limitless quantities of data.

Data Types

QBasic assigns a data type to each variable in a program. This data type determines what kind of data can be stored in that variable. So far, we have used string variables and single-precision numeric variables. String variables are used to store character strings and are recognized by the dollar sign ($) at the end of their name. Single-precision numeric variables can store real numbers. The "default" data type is single-precision numeric. This means that if a variable does not have a symbol at the end of its name, it is assumed to be single-precision numeric. However, you can specify that a variable is of this type by adding an exclamation point to its name. Therefore, to QBasic, the variable names NetProfit and NetProfit! are the same.

There is another type of real number data type: double-precision numeric. Double-precision numeric is used to store numbers with many digits. A single-precision variable is accurate to about seven decimal places. Double-precision variable names conclude with a number sign (#) and are accurate to about 15 decimal places. Examples are Infinitesmal# and BacteriaSize#. These variables are used when a high degree of accuracy is needed. The problems in this text do not require this high degree of accuracy; therefore, we are not using double-precision variables. Double-precision variables require more storage space than single-precision ones.

As you already know, integer values can be stored in single-precision numeric variables (we have been doing this all along in this book). QBasic simply converts the integer to a real number by adding a decimal point and a zero. However, it is also possible to specify that a variable be of data type *integer* by placing a percent sign (%) at the end of its name; for example, Age%. Age% can only store an integer value. If you attempted to assign the value 17.6 to this variable, the number would be *truncated* (cut off) and the integer 17 would be assigned to Age%. Integers can range from –32,768 to +32,767. If an integer outside of this range needs to be stored, a long-integer variable should be used. A long-integer variable has an ampersand (&) as its last character; for example, Factorial&, StarsInSky&, and BigNumber&. Long integers can range from –2,147,483,648 to +2,147,483,647.

A second way is available for specifying a variable's data type. In Chapter 9, you learned to use the DIM statement to declare an array and establish the range of its subscripts. The DIM statement can also be used to declare the type of a variable. For example, the following DIM statement declares Country as a string variable:

```
DIM Country AS STRING
```

When using a DIM statement, it is no longer necessary to include a $ as the last character of the string variable name; in fact QBasic will not allow you to include the dollar sign in the variable's name.

A variable named Population could be declared as an integer as follows:

```
DIM Population AS INTEGER
```

Now only whole numbers can be stored in Population. A single-precision real number variable named SquareMiles could be declared like this:

```
DIM SquareMiles AS SINGLE
```

Table 10-1 provides an overview of QBasic data types. The last column in this table indicates the amount of storage space required for each variable type. Storage space is commonly measured in bytes; as discussed in Chapter 1, a single byte is the amount of space required to store a single character. Integers generally require 2 bytes and single-precision variables require 4 bytes.

So far, we have been using *variable-length* strings. The length of these strings depends on the number of characters currently stored in them. However, QBasic has a second type of string, the *fixed-length string*. When using fixed-length strings, the string will always be of the same size, regardless of the number of characters assigned to that string. Consider the following DIM statement:

```
DIM Flower AS STRING * 12
```

TABLE 10-1 VARIABLE TYPES

Type	Symbol	Data Type	Storage Required (in bytes)
Single-precision	! (or none)	SINGLE	4
Double-precision	#	DOUBLE	8
Integer	%	INTEGER	2
Long integer	&	LONG	4

If *Violet* is assigned to the variable Flower, QBasic will add blanks to make the field the correct length:

| V | i | o | l | e | t | | | | | | |

If *Oriental Lilac* is assigned, QBasic truncates the name to fit the string:

| O | r | i | e | n | t | a | l | | L | i | l |

The following program segment illustrates this principle:

```
DIM Flower AS STRING * 12

Flower = "Daisy"
PRINT Flower;"*"
Flower = "African Violet"
PRINT Flower;"*"
```

```
Daisy        *
African Viol*
```

Notice that in both instances, the asterisk (*) is printed in the thirteenth position—immediately after the entire string is output.

RECORDS

Defining a Record

Record *A group of related data items, not necessarily of the same data type.*

Field *An individual data item in a record.*

A **record** is a group of related data items, not necessarily of the same type. Each data item is referred to as a **field**. For example, think of the information a school might have on a student:

Name

Birth date

Identification number

Grade-point average

Number of credits

A record would be ideal for storing this information. QBasic uses the TYPE statement to define a record. Each field in the record type definition must be assigned a data type. When a field is of type STRING, a fixed-length string must be used. The student record definition could look like this:

```
TYPE StudentRecord        ' declare the record type
    Nme AS STRING * 25
    IDNumber AS STRING * 11
    BirthDate AS STRING * 8
    GPA AS SINGLE
    Credits AS INTEGER
END TYPE
```

In this example, Nme can have up to 25 characters, IDNumber up to 11 characters (its format will be xxx-xx-xxxx), and BirthDate up to 8 characters (its format will be xx/xx/xx). GPA is a single-precision number because grade-point averages commonly have two decimal places. Because the number of credits is always an integer, the variable Credits is defined as data type INTEGER. TYPE definitions must be placed in the main program. DIM statements can appear either in the main program or in procedures. However, they must appear before the variable is used in the program.

To use StudentRecord in a program, a DIM statement must be used to declare a variable of this type:

```
DIM Student AS StudentRecord
```

Now the variable Student is a record of type StudentRecord.

When declaring a string field, be careful to make the field large enough to hold the maximum number of characters that will be assigned to it. Otherwise, the string will be truncated to fit in the field. For example, if Nme was declared in the format

```
Nme AS STRING * 10
```

and the program contained the assignment statement

```
Student.Nme = "Samuel Morris"
```

the string "Samuel Mor" would be assigned to Nme.

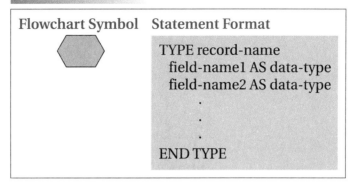

Storing Data in a Record

Values are assigned to the individual record fields by using the record variable name and field name, separated by a period. The following program segment shows how values could be assigned to each field of the Student record:

```
Student.Nme = "Jon Baumann"
Student.IDNumber = "479-50-5233"
Student.BirthDate = "08/06/78"
Student.GPA = 3.45
Student.Credits = 124
```

Figure 10-1 illustrates how this record could be represented in storage. INPUT statements can also be used to place values in fields. The program in Figure 10-2 shows how the user could be prompted to enter record data during program execution. PRINT statements then display the field's contents.

Arrays of Records

Generally speaking, records are used in groups. One way of storing a group of records in the computer is by using an array. Each array element will contain a single record. Assuming that Student-Record has already been defined, the following DIM statement sets up an array of 10 records:

```
DIM StudentList(1 TO 10) AS StudentRecord
```

You can refer to a specific record field within the array by using an array subscript and then the field's name. For example, the following statement assigns a number to the IDNumber field of the fourth record in array StudentList:

```
StudentList(4).IDNumber = "385-40-5560"
```

FIGURE 10-1

A Student Record

Jon Baumann	479-50-5233	08/06/78	3.45	124
Name	ID Number	Birth Date	GPA	Credits

Student Record

As you know from previous experience, the best way to access all of the elements within an array is to use a loop. The following program segment prompts the user to enter the data for 10 records. All of the records will be stored in array StudentList:

```
FOR I = 1 TO 10
    INPUT "Enter student's name: ", StudentList(I).Nme
    INPUT "Enter student's ID Number: ", StudentList(I).IDNumber
    INPUT "Enter student's birthdate: ", StudentList(I).BirthDate
    INPUT "Enter student's grade point average: ", StudentList(I).GPA
    INPUT "Enter student's total credits: ", StudentList(I).Credits
NEXT I
```

You also can use the same method to print the contents of the array.

FIGURE 10-2

Program to Insert Data into Student Record

```
'*** This program prompts the user to enter data to the ***
'*** student record and then displays the contents of   ***
'*** the record.                                         ***

TYPE StudentRecord        ' Declare the record type
    Nme AS STRING * 25
    IDNumber AS STRING * 11
    BirthDate AS STRING * 8
    GPA AS SINGLE
    Credits AS INTEGER
END TYPE

DIM Student AS StudentRecord

'*** Prompt user to enter data to the fields. ***
CLS
```

FIGURE 10-2

Continued

```
INPUT "Enter student's name"; Student.Nme
INPUT "Enter student's identification number"; Student.IDNumber
INPUT "Enter student's birth date"; Student.BirthDate
INPUT "Enter student's grade point average"; Student.GPA
INPUT "Enter number of credits"; Student.Credits


'*** Display the record fields. ***
CLS
PRINT "Name"; TAB(28); "ID Number"; TAB(41); "Birth Date"; TAB(53); "GPA";
   TAB(59); "Number of Credits"
PRINT Student.Nme; TAB(27); Student.IDNumber; TAB(42); Student.BirthDate;
   TAB(52); Student.GPA; TAB(65); Student.Credits


END
```

```
Enter student's name? Jon Baumann
Enter student's identification number? 479-50-5233
Enter student's birth date? 08/06/78
Enter student's grade point average? 3.45
Enter number of credits? 124
```

```
Name                      ID Number    Birth Date   GPA    Number of Credits
Jon Baumann               479-50-5233   08/06/78    3.45          124
```

Learning Check 10-1

1. Identify the type of each of the following variables:

   a. PineTrees%

   b. Biggie#

   c. Street$

   d. Subtotal

   e. TopDollar!

2. True or False? Each field in a record must be assigned a data type.

3. The last statement in a record declaration is _____.

4. How do you refer to a specific field in a record?

FILES

File *A collection of related data kept in secondary storage.*

A **file** is a collection of related data kept in secondary storage. As you may know, you have been creating files all along in this course. Your programs are stored in files. The name under which you save a program is a file name. Files containing programs are referred to as *program files*, whereas the files you will be creating in this chapter are *data files*; they store data to be processed by programs.

A major advantage of data files is that they are kept in secondary storage, such as diskettes (floppy disks) or hard disks. As previously mentioned, data kept in secondary storage, unlike that kept in the computer's main memory, is not lost when the system is turned off. Another advantage of using data files is that many users can access the same data file, and the file can be created and then accessed by another program at a later time. Files make it easy to update data.

Files are usually made up of a group of records (see Figure 10-3). As you already know, the individual data items within these records are called fields. A computer file can be compared to a filing cabinet. A particular filing cabinet often contains information on one general topic, such as the records of students. Each student record is kept in a separate folder. The individual pieces of information in each folder are similar to record fields.

Secondary Storage

The most commonly used types of secondary storage for microcomputer systems are diskettes (also called floppy disks) and hard

FIGURE 10-3

A File Containing Student Records

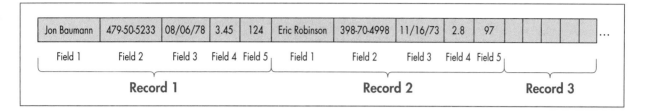

| Jon Baumann | 479-50-5233 | 08/06/78 | 3.45 | 124 | Eric Robinson | 398-70-4998 | 11/16/73 | 2.8 | 97 | | | | | | … |

Field 1 · Field 2 · Field 3 · Field 4 · Field 5 | Field 1 · Field 2 · Field 3 · Field 4 · Field 5

Record 1 · Record 2 · Record 3

disks. Although diskettes have relatively small storage capacities and are slower to access than hard disks, they make it easy to transfer data from one computer to another. In addition, they are cheap and you can easily buy more as needed. However, because of their speed, size, and reasonable cost, hard disks are the most popular storage media for microcomputers.

A hard disk consists of a group of disks that looks like a stack of record albums with a spindle passing through the middle (see Figure 10-4). Data is stored on each disk in *tracks*, which are series of concentric circles on the surface of the disk. A collection of concentric disk tracks with the same radius is called a *cylinder*. Both cylinders and tracks are numbered. Read/write heads retrieve and store data on the disks. The read/write arm, which holds the read/write heads, can move backward and forward, and the disks

FIGURE 10-4

Inside a Hard Disk

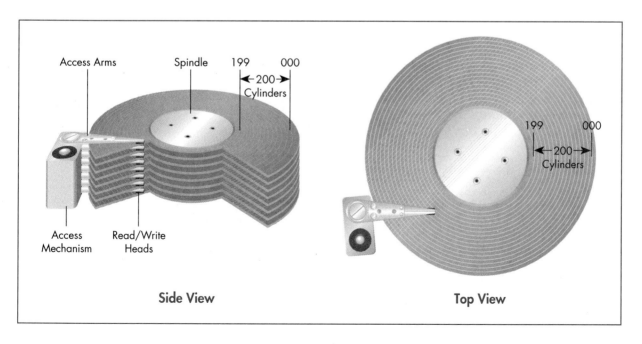

Side View · Top View

can rotate on the spindle as well. By using the numbered tracks and cylinders and the movement of the disks, records can be accessed either randomly or sequentially.

The most popular size of floppy disk is the 3½-inch size, which is contained in a hard plastic cover. As with hard disks, floppy disks contain tracks. As shown in Figure 10-5, each track is divided into sectors. The disk contains an index hole, which the computer uses to calculate the location of a particular sector by timing the disk's rotation. The read/write head then accesses the needed data.

File Access Methods

Access method *The way in which the computer transmits data between secondary storage and the primary storage unit.*

Sequential access *A method of file access in which data is accessed in the order in which it is physically stored in the file.*

Random access *A method of file access in which records are accessed directly, often by using their numbered locations in the file.*

An **access method** is the way in which the computer transmits data between secondary storage and primary storage. Because of the way in which disks are structured, two different access methods can be used with them: sequential and random.

When using **sequential access**, the data within the file is accessed in the order in which it is physically stored within the file. This means that if you want to access a particular data item, all the data that precedes the needed item must be accessed first. You can think of sequential access as being similar to a one-way street. If you visit the tenth house on the block and then wish to go back to the second house, you must drive around the block to the first house and then go on to the second house. **Random access** allows a record to be accessed directly, usually by using its numbered location in the file. The disk drive's read/write head allows it to move quickly to a specific disk location. Random

FIGURE 10-5

When diskettes are formatted, they are divided into tracks and sectors, which make accessing data easier.

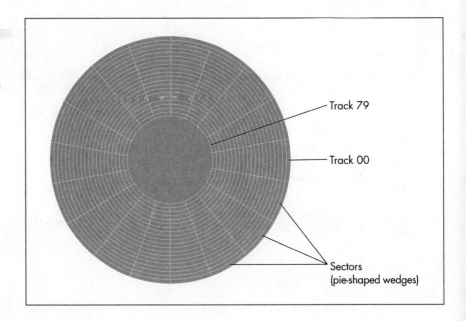

Track 79

Track 00

Sectors
(pie-shaped wedges)

access can be compared to dialing a telephone number. The number allows the system to connect you with a single telephone line out of many thousands of lines.

QBasic allows you to create two different types of files: sequential and random access. When you create a sequential file you must access the data within it sequentially. The records in random-access files, however, can be accessed directly. We first discuss creating and accessing sequential files, then move on to the discussion of random-access files.

Learning Check 10-2

1. Files are divided into _____, which are further subdivided into _____.

2. When using _____ access, you must access file data in the order in which it is stored.

3. True or False? Another name for a data file is a program file.

4. A(n) _____ is a collection of concentric disk tracks with the same radius.

USING SEQUENTIAL FILES

File Position Pointers

Before discussing the different statements used with sequential files, it is important to understand the concept of the file position pointer. Associated with each file is an imaginary **file position pointer** that "points to" the next record to be processed. This imaginary pointer can be thought of as a window that "looks ahead" to the next record. The computer adjusts this pointer when a file statement is executed in a program. For instance, when you first access a file to read its records, the pointer is set to the beginning of the file so that the first record in the file is available for processing. After the program reads this first record, the file pointer automatically advances to the next record. In the following diagram of a file called Names, the file pointer is set at the location of the record Mike when the file is first accessed:

> **File position pointer** *An imaginary pointer that indicates the next record to be processed.*

Mike	Linda	Justin	Carol

After the first record is read, the pointer advances to the next record, Linda:

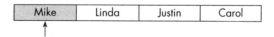

Mike	Linda	Justin	Carol

The file position pointer has no effect on the data contained in the file; it simply indicates the position of the next record to be processed.

Creating and Accessing a Sequential File

To use data files, you must be able to create new files and access existing ones. Both operations are performed by the OPEN statement, which provides QBasic with the following information:

1. *The name of the file.* The same rules apply to naming data files that apply to naming program files: The name may have from one to eight characters and an optional extension of one to three characters. You may wish to assign the same name to both the program file and its data file and use extensions to differentiate them. For example, if INVEN.BAS is an inventory program, the file storing the inventory data might be named INVEN.DAT.

2. *The mode, or way, in which the file is to be used.* The mode can be OUTPUT, INPUT, or APPEND. OUTPUT indicates that data is written to the file from the program. In INPUT mode, the contents of the file are being read into the program. APPEND mode allows new records to be added (appended) to an existing file.

3. *The number of the buffer to be associated with the file.* A **buffer** is a reserved part of the primary storage unit used as a temporary storage area for data that is being written to or read from a file. When data is being written to a file, it is first copied from the variable to the buffer and then copied from the buffer into the correct location in the file. Each file is assigned a numbered buffer.

> **Buffer** *A reserved part of the primary storage unit used to temporarily store data that is being written to or read from a file.*

The following statement creates a file named TICKETS.DAT:

```
OPEN "TICKETS.DAT" FOR OUTPUT AS #1
```

This statement instructs the system to do the following:

1. Create a new file named TICKETS.DAT. If a file with this name already exists, it is destroyed, and a new, empty file is created.

2. Prepare the file to receive data (the word OUTPUT indicates that this file will have data written to it).

3. Associate the file TICKETS.DAT with buffer #1 as long as this file is open. Buffer #1 will be used to temporarily hold data before it is written to the file on disk. Other statements in the program use this number to identify the file.

The OPEN Statement for Sequential Files

Flowchart Symbol   Statement Format

    OPEN "file-name" FOR mode AS [#]file-number

Note: The modes are OUTPUT (to be written to), INPUT (to be read), or APPEND (to have new records added to the end).

Closing a File

When a program is through using a file, the CLOSE statement closes the file. Closing the file causes its contents to be stored permanently on disk. If the file is opened for output, the CLOSE statement moves any data remaining in the buffer to the file (this is often referred to as *dumping the buffer*). No input or output can be performed on a closed file. The following statement closes the file that was previously opened:

```
CLOSE #1
```

Notice that the CLOSE statement does not use the name of the file (which is TICKETS.DAT), but rather its buffer number (#1). Any number of files can be closed in a single statement:

```
CLOSE #1, #3
```

If you use the CLOSE statement alone, it closes all files that have been opened in a program:

```
CLOSE
```

If you wish to change the mode of an open file, you must first close that file and then reopen it in another mode. The file can be reopened with the same or a different file number.

The CLOSE Statement

Flowchart Symbol   Statement Format

    CLOSE [#file-number1, #file-number2]...

Note: If no file-number is listed, all opened files are closed.

Learning Check 10-3

1. Write an OPEN statement that creates a new file CUSTLIST.DAT with a file number of 3. The file should be prepared to have records written to it.

2. Write an OPEN statement that creates a new file named ADDRESS.DAT that will have records written to it.

3. The file position _____ indicates which record in a file will be the next one accessed.

4. The _____ statement causes a file's contents to be permanently saved on disk.

Writing to a Sequential File

When a file will have new data written to it, it must be opened for output. The new file is created, but it is empty. To store data in a new file, perform the following steps:

1. Open the file for output.
2. Write data to the file.
3. Close the file to protect its contents.

The WRITE# statement places records in the file. It operates much like the PRINT statement, except that it sends values to a file in secondary storage rather than displaying them on the monitor screen. For example, the following statement sends the values of the variables Artist$, NumTickets, TicketCost, and Percent to file number 1:

```
WRITE #1, Artist$, NumTickets, TicketCost, Percent
```

The QBasic system places the values of Artist$, NumTickets, TicketCost, and Percent in the file at the storage location indicated by the file position pointer and advances the pointer to the next record position. The file now contains the data for one record.

The program in Figure 10-6 creates a sequential file TICKETS.DAT and allows the user to write records to it. The purpose of this file is to keep track of artist's total ticket sales at concerts. Each record contains the artist's name, the number of tickets sold at a single concert, the cost of each ticket, and the percentage of total sales to be given to the artist.

The WRITE Statement for Sequential Files

Flowchart Symbol	Statement Format
	WRITE #file-number, expression1, [expression2,]...

Figure 10-6

Program to Create a Sequential File

```
'***                    Create Ticket Sales File              ***

'*** This program creates a sequential file, TICKETS.DAT.     ***
'*** The user is prompted to enter the data which is then     ***
'*** written to the file.                                     ***
'*** File used:                                               ***
'***     TICKETS.DAT       Sequential file containing ticket  ***
'***                           sales information              ***
'*** Major variables used:                                    ***
'***     Artist$           Name of individual or group        ***
'***     NumTickets        Number of tickets sold             ***
'***     TicketCost        Cost of each ticket                ***
'***     Percent           Percentage of ticket sales that    ***
'***                           the artist receives            ***

OPEN "TICKETS.DAT" FOR OUTPUT AS #1

CLS

INPUT "Do you want to enter information on an artist (Y/N)"; Answer$
DO WHILE UCASE$(LEFT$(Answer$, 1)) = "Y"
   INPUT "Enter the artist's name: ", Artist$
   INPUT "Enter total number of tickets sold: ", NumTickets
   INPUT "Enter cost per ticket: ", TicketCost
   INPUT "Enter percentage artist is to receive: ", Percent
   WRITE #1, Artist$, NumTickets, TicketCost, Percent
   INPUT "Do you want to enter information on another artist (Y/N)";
      Answer$
LOOP
CLOSE #1


END
```

Continued on next page

FIGURE 10-6

Continued

```
Do you want to enter information on an artist (Y/N)? y
Enter the artist's name: Pete and the Piranhas
Enter total number of tickets sold: 850
Enter cost per ticket: 25.00
Enter percentage artist is to receive: 10
Do you want to enter information on another artist (Y/N)? Y
Enter the artist's name: Working Stiff
Enter total number of tickets sold: 384
Enter cost per ticket: 32.50
Enter percentage artist is to receive: 8
Do you want to enter information on another artist (Y/N)? Y
Enter the artist's name: Working Stiff
Enter total number of tickets sold: 458
Enter cost per ticket: 25.00
Enter percentage artist is to receive: 8
Do you want to enter information on another artist (Y/N)? Y
Enter the artist's name: Astrofly
Enter total number of tickets sold: 592
Enter cost per ticket: 24.00
Enter percentage artist is to receive: 8
Do you want to enter information on another artist (Y/N)? N
```

Appending Records to a Sequential File

If it is necessary to add records to an existing file, the OPEN statement must contain the APPEND clause. For example:

```
OPEN "TICKETS.DAT" FOR APPEND AS #1
```

When a file is opened for input or output, the file position pointer is placed at the first record in the file; however, new records can be written only at the *end* of a sequential file. The APPEND clause sets the file position pointer to the end of the specified file and thus permits the user to add new records without losing any of the old ones. The three basic steps for appending data to an existing sequential file are as follows:

1. Open the file for APPEND.
2. Write the new data to the end of the file.
3. Close the file.

Figure 10-7 shows a program that adds records to the TICKETS.DAT file created by the program in Figure 10-7. The only change is in the OPEN statement. When adding records to an existing file, be careful to open the file for APPEND rather than OUTPUT. The OUTPUT clause destroys the contents of an existing file.

The file TICKETS.DAT contains the following values after the program in Figure 10-7 is executed:

```
Pete and the Piranhas, 850, 25.00, 10
Working Stiff, 384, 32.50, 8
Working Stiff, 458, 25.00, 8
Astrofly, 592, 24.00, 8
Astrofly, 634, 30.00, 10
Next Time, 743, 36.50, 10
Next Time, 875, 40.00, 8
Next Time, 657 36.50, 10
```

Reading from a Sequential File

Writing data to a file is useful only if you are able to use that data at a later time. The transfer of data from a file to the computer's main memory is referred to as *reading a file*. The three steps involved in reading from a sequential file are as follows:

1. Open the file for input.
2. Read the data from the file.
3. Close the file.

The INPUT# statement reads data from a file and is similar to the INPUT statement. Whereas the INPUT statement accepts data from the keyboard, the INPUT# statement takes values from a file and assigns them to the listed variables on a one-to-one basis. The following example reads four data items (the first record) from the TICKETS.DAT file and assigns them to the variables Artist$, NumTickets, TicketCost, and Percent:

```
OPEN "TICKETS.DAT" FOR INPUT AS #2
INPUT #2, Artist$, NumTickets, TicketCost, Percent
```

These statements would cause variables Artist$, NumTickets, TicketCost, and Percent to be assigned the values *Pete and the Piranhas*, 850, 25.00, 10, respectively.

The INPUT# statement reads the record to which the file position pointer is currently pointing, and places its contents in the variables listed. After the INPUT# statement is executed, the file position pointer advances automatically to the next record. In a sequential file, an INPUT# operation begins with the first record

374

Figure 10-7

Program to Append Records to a Sequential File

```
'***                    Append Ticket Sales Program              ***

'*** This program appends new data to the end of an exist-       ***
'*** ing sequential file, TICKETS.DAT. The user enters           ***
'*** the new data, which is then appended to the file.           ***
'*** File used:                                                  ***
'***     TICKETS.DAT          Sequential file containing ticket  ***
'***                              sales information              ***
'*** Major variables used:                                       ***
'***     Artist$              Name of individual or group        ***
'***     NumTickets           Number of tickets sold             ***
'***     TicketCost           Cost of each ticket               ***
'***     Percent              Percentage of ticket sales that    ***
'***                              the artist receives            ***

OPEN "TICKETS.DAT" FOR APPEND AS #1

CLS
INPUT "Do you want to enter a new artist to the file (Y/N)"; Answer$
DO WHILE UCASE$(LEFT$(Answer$, 1)) = "Y"
   INPUT "Enter the artist's name: ", Artist$
   INPUT "Enter total number of tickets sold: ", NumTickets
   INPUT "Enter cost per ticket: ", TicketCost
   INPUT "Enter percentage artist is to receive: ", Percent
   WRITE #1, Artist$, NumTickets, TicketCost, Percent
   INPUT "Do you want to enter information on another artist (Y/N)";
      Answer$
LOOP
CLOSE #1

END
```

FIGURE 10-7

Continued

```
Do you want to enter a new artist to the file (Y/N)? Y
Enter the artist's name: Astrofly
Enter total number of tickets sold: 634
Enter cost per ticket: 30.00
Enter percentage artist is to receive: 10
Do you want to enter information on another artist (Y/N)? Y
Enter the artist's name: Next Time
Enter total number of tickets sold: 743
Enter cost per ticket: 36.50
Enter percentage artist is to receive: 10
Do you want to enter information on another artist (Y/N)? Y
Enter the artist's name: Next Time
Enter total number of tickets sold: 875
Enter cost per ticket: 40.00
Enter percentage artist is to receive: 8
Do you want to enter information on another artist (Y/N)? Y
Enter the artist's name: Next Time
Enter total number of tickets sold: 657
Enter cost per ticket: 36.50
Enter percentage artist is to receive: 10
Do you want to enter information on another artist (Y/N)? N
```

in the file (where the OPEN statement sets the pointer). Each successive INPUT# statement retrieves the next values in the file and places them in the listed variables.

The computer places a special character, called an *end-of-file marker*, after the last data item in a file. An attempt to read past this marker results in an error message and termination of program execution.

The end-of-file marker acts as a trailer value that is useful when reading the contents of a file. A special function, called the EOF (end-of-file) function, is used to check for the end-of-file marker. For example, the following expression determines whether the end-of-file marker for file number 1 has been reached:

```
EOF(1)
```

If there are more records to be read, EOF is false; when the end-of-file marker is reached, EOF becomes true.

Because the EOF function results in a value of true or false, it can be used to control the execution of a loop. The following loop reads and prints all of the data in TICKETS.DAT:

```
DO WHILE NOT EOF(1)
    INPUT #1, Artist$, NumTickets, TicketCost, Percent
    PRINT TAB(10); Artist$, TAB(30); NumTickets; TAB(45); TicketCost;
        TAB(60); Percent
LOOP
```

In this loop, every record in the file TICKETS.DAT is accessed. Consider a situation, however, where just one record from a file is needed. Suppose you want to display the fiftieth record of the file TICKETS.DAT. The rules of sequential access dictate that all preceding records must be accessed first, starting at the beginning of the file. You do this by reading, but not printing, the first 49 records of the file TICKETS.DAT. Remember that an INPUT# statement automatically advances the file position pointer to the next record in the file. After the second record is read, the pointer is set to the third record, and so forth, until the fiftieth record is reached. Later in this chapter we discuss random-access files, which offer a solution to this time-consuming process.

The INPUT# Statement for Sequential Files

Flowchart Symbol	Statement Format
	INPUT #file-number variable1[, variable2]…

CREATING A SUMMARY REPORT

Let's assume that we want to generate a ticket sales report based on the contents of the TICKETS.DAT file. The report should contain each artist's name, the number of tickets sold for that artist for all concerts, and the total earnings that artist should receive. In addition, at the end of the report, the total earnings for all artists should be displayed. This type of report is referred to as a *summary report* because it summarizes the input data. It does not contain all of the data, just the totals for each group of data. This type of report allows the reader to analyze the totals quickly without being distracted by unnecessary information.

Creating a report spacing chart will help you to determine how the report should appear. Figure 10-8 shows the report with its components labeled. As you know, there can be more than one record for each artist; however, all of the records for a single artist will be grouped together in the file. Therefore, we can determine

FIGURE 10-8

Report Spacing Chart for Ticket Sales Report

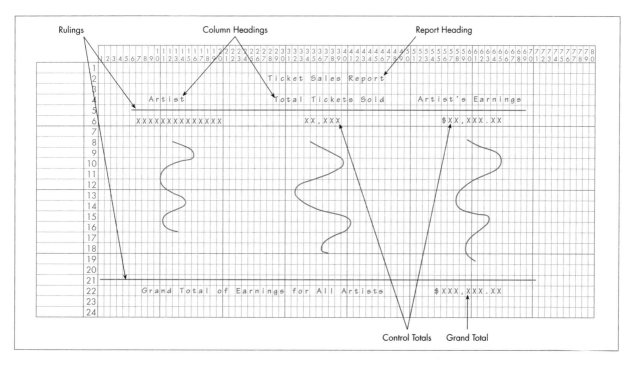

the amount of money owed to a single artist by reading the data for each concert, calculating the amount owed for that concert, and adding it to that artist's total. As soon as we encounter a record that contains a new artist's name, we must print the current artist's totals and start over with the new artist.

Locate the subtotals for each artist in the report spacing chart in Figure 10-8. This type of subtotal is referred to as a **control total**, a subtotal that is printed when the value of a specified variable (in this case Artist$) changes. When this program is written, special variables will be used to keep track of total ticket sales and total earnings for each artist. When a new artist is encountered, a **control break** occurs, signaling the program that a control total should be printed. The control breaks are indicated in the following list of data:

Control total *A subtotal that is output when the value of a specified variable changes.*

Control break *The situation that occurs when there is a change in the value of a specified variable.*

```
Pete and the Piranhas, 850, 25.00, 10
Working Stiff, 384, 32.50, 8        First control break occurs here
Working Stiff, 458, 25.00, 8
Astrofly, 592, 24.00, 8             Second control break occurs here
Astrofly, 634, 30.00, 10
Next Time, 743, 36.50, 10           Third control break occurs here
Next Time, 875, 40.00, 8
Next Time, 657 36.50, 10
```

The program in Figure 10-9 reads and displays the data stored in the file TICKETS.DAT, which was created in Figure 10-6 and appended in Figure 10-7. Notice the condition controlling the loop in procedure ProcessFile:

```
DO WHILE NOT EOF(1)
```

As long as the end of TICKETS.DAT is not reached, each record will be read from the file and displayed on the screen. The following IF statement checks to make certain that a control break has not occurred:

```
IF Previous$ = Artist$ THEN
```

If the artist for the last record is different from that in the record just read, the ELSE portion is executed and the program prints the control totals. In addition, Previous$ must be set to the current artist. If this value is not changed, a control break would automatically occur when the next record was read, regardless of the artist's name. Another important consideration is what happens when the last record in the file is read. Because the loop will not be executed when end-of-file is encountered, the values for this record will not be processed in the usual way. Therefore, it must be processed separately. This step happens immediately after the EOF loop is exited.

Learning Check 10-4

1. The _____ statement allows you to read the contents of a sequential file.

2. If you need to add new data to the end of an existing sequential file, you must open the file for _____.

3. The file BILLING.DAT consists of records containing two character string fields—a name and an address. Write a segment that will add one record to the file, which is associated with file #3.

4. Write a program segment that will read and display the first record of the file BILLING.DAT in Question 3.

5. A subtotal that is output when the value of a specified variable changes is called a(n) _____ total.

FIGURE 10-9

Program to Generate a Report from a Sequential File

```
DECLARE SUB PrintArtist (Previous$, Artist$, NumTickets!, TicketCost!, Percent!,
    TotalTickets!, Amount!)
DECLARE SUB InitialTasks ()
DECLARE SUB ProcessFile ()

'***              Artist Payment Report Program          ***

'*** This program reads a sequential file named TICKETS.DAT.  ***
'*** A loop is used to read each artist's data in turn.       ***
'*** The file can contain any number of records for a part-   ***
'*** icular artist. The program keeps track and prints the    ***
'*** total number of tickets and total earnings for each      ***
'*** artist. The artist's name, total number of tickets sold, ***
'*** and total earnings are then printed on paper.            ***
'*** File used:                                               ***
'***      TICKETS.DAT      Sequential file containing ticket  ***
'***                          sales information               ***
'*** Major variables used:                                    ***
'***      Artist$          Name of artist or group            ***
'***      NumTickets       Number of tickets sold for a       ***
'***                          particular performance          ***
'***      TicketCost       Cost of each ticket                ***
'***      Percent          Percentage of ticket sales that    ***
'***                          the artist receives             ***
'***      TotalTickets     Total number of tickets sold by a  ***
'***                          particular artist               ***
'***      Amount           Total earnings for a particular    ***
'***                          artist                          ***

CALL InitialTasks

'*** Call procedure to process each artist's data in turn  ***
'*** until the entire file has been read.                  ***
CALL ProcessFile

CLOSE #1

END
```

Continued on next page

FIGURE 10-9

Continued

```
SUB InitialTasks
   '*** This procedure performs several tasks that must be completed ***
   '*** before the file is read, including opening the file and       ***
   '*** printing the report title and headings.                       ***

   OPEN "TICKETS.DAT" FOR INPUT AS #1
   LPRINT
   Start = (70 - LEN("Ticket Sales Report")) / 2
   LPRINT TAB(Start + 5); "Ticket Sales Report"
   LPRINT

   '*** Print the report headings. ***
   Format1$ = "           \                   \ \              \ \              \"
   LPRINT USING Format1$; "Artist"; "Total Tickets Sold"; "Artist's Earnings"
   LPRINT TAB(6); STRING$(66, "-")

END SUB

SUB ProcessFile
   '*** This procedures reads each record and calculates earnings ***
   '*** based on ticket sales, cost per ticket, and artist's      ***
   '*** percentage. When a new artist is encountered, the         ***
   '*** previous artist's totals are printed. In addition, the    ***
   '*** total earnings for all artists is calculated and printed  ***
   '*** after the entire file is processed.                       ***

   Format2$ = "         \                 \       ###,###                $$###,###.##"
   Format3$ = "         \                                       \       $$###,###.##"

   TotalTickets = 0
   Amount = 0
   GrandTotal = 0
   First$ = "Yes"
```

FIGURE 10-9

Continued

```basic
DO WHILE (NOT EOF(1))
   '*** Read each record in the file. ***
   INPUT #1, Artist$, NumTickets, TicketCost, Percent

   '*** If this is the first record, make Previous$ equal to  ***
   '*** Artist$ so that a control break will not occur.       ***
   IF First$ = "Yes" THEN
      Previous$ = Artist$
      First$ = "No"
   END IF

   IF Previous$ = Artist$ THEN
      '*** Artist is the same as previous one; therefore, add  ***
      '*** new values to ticket sales and earnings totals.     ***
      TotalTickets = TotalTickets + NumTickets
      Amount = Amount + NumTickets * TicketCost * (Percent / 100)
   ELSE
      '*** A control break has occurred; update the grand total ***
      '*** and print the totals for the artist.                 ***
      GrandTotal = GrandTotal + Amount

      LPRINT USING Format2$; Previous$; TotalTickets; Amount
      Previous$ = Artist$
      TotalTickets = NumTickets
      Amount = NumTickets * TicketCost * (Percent / 100)
   END IF

LOOP


'*** Print the totals for last artist. ***
LPRINT USING Format2$; Artist$; TotalTickets; Amount

'*** Add last artist's total to grand total and print it. ***
GrandTotal = GrandTotal + Amount
LPRINT
LPRINT
LPRINT TAB(6); STRING$(64, "-")
LPRINT USING Format3$; "Grand Total of Earnings for All Artists: "; GrandTotal


END SUB
```

Continued on next page

FIGURE 10-9

Continued

```
                        Ticket Sales Report

        Artist              Total Tickets Sold    Artist's Earnings
    - - - - - - - - - - - - - - - - - - - - - - - - - - - - - - - - - - - - -
    Pete and the Piranhas          850               $2,125.00
    Working Stiff                  842               $1,914.40
    Astrofly                     1,226               $3,038.64
    Next Time                    2,275               $7,910.00


    - - - - - - - - - - - - - - - - - - - - - - - - - - - - - - - - - - - - -

    Grand Total of Earnings for All Artists          $14,988.04
```

USING RANDOM-ACCESS FILES

Random files have a distinct advantage over sequential files in that records can be accessed directly. It is no longer necessary to access the first 49 records in a file in order to update the fiftieth record. However, as you will see later in this section, random-access files can also be accessed sequentially.

Creating a Random-Access File

Random-access files consist of records. These records are declared using the TYPE statement. As an example, we will create a random-access file containing the Student records from Figure 10-2:

```
TYPE StudentRecord        'Declare the record type
    Nme AS STRING * 25
    IDNumber AS STRING * 11
    BirthDate AS STRING * 8
    GPA AS SINGLE
    Credits AS INTEGER
END TYPE
```

A DIM statement must be used to create a record:

```
DIM Student AS StudentRecord
```

Before a random-access file can be used, it must be opened. The OPEN statement for a file named STUDENT.DAT containing Student records might look like this:

```
OPEN "STUDENT.DAT" FOR RANDOM AS #3 LEN = LEN(Student)
```

Notice that the LEN function is used to determine the size of each record. QBasic must know how much space to allot for each record so that it can properly store the records.

After you are done accessing a random-access file, it must be closed in the same way as a sequential file.

The OPEN Statement for Random-Access Files

Flowchart Symbol	Statement Format
	OPEN "file-name" FOR RANDOM AS [#]file-number LEN = LEN (record-variable)

Storing Records in a Random-Access File

Data is assigned to each record by placing a period between the record name and the field name. For example, the following statement assigns 2.8 to the GPA field of the Student record:

```
Student.GPA = 2.8
```

After data has been assigned to each field, the PUT statement writes the data to the specified record location. For example, the following statement writes the current contents of Student to record number 4:

```
PUT #3, 4, Student
```

Notice that the file number must be the same as the one in the OPEN statement; this is how QBasic knows the record should be written to file STUDENT.DAT.

You can also use PUT to overwrite an existing record. If record fields must be updated, simply place the new values in the fields and write them to the old record location.

The PUT Statement for Random-Access Files

Flowchart Symbol	Statement Format
	PUT [#]file-number[, record-number] [, record-variable]

Reading Records in a Random-Access File

The GET statement performs the reverse process of the PUT, allowing you to assign the contents of a record to a record variable. Any record can be accessed directly by using its record number. For example, the following statement accesses record number 6 of this file:

```
GET #3, 6, Student
```

The values stored in this record are placed into the fields of the Student record.

Examine the program in Figure 10-10. It performs two tasks:

1. It allows the user to add a new record to a file.
2. It allows the user to display the contents of an existing record.

The PUT statement is used to write each new record to the file and the GET statement accesses the specified record.

If you want to read the entire contents of a random-access file, you can start with the first record and use the GET statement to read each record in turn. The LOF (length-of-file) function can be used to determine the number of bytes in the entire file. As we already know, the LEN function can determine the number of bytes per record. Therefore, by dividing the size of the file by the number of bytes per record, the number of records can be determined. A FOR...NEXT loop can then be used to read the entire file. For example, the following statement will cause a loop to be executed one time for each record in a file containing Student records:

```
FOR Count = 1 TO LOF(3) / LEN (Student)
```

The GET Statement

Flowchart Symbol	Statement Format
▱	GET [#]file-number[, record-number] [, record-variable]

FIGURE 10-10

Program Using a Random-Access File

```
DECLARE SUB AddRecord (Student AS ANY)
DECLARE SUB DisplayRecord (Student AS ANY)

'***                    Create Student File            ***

'*** This program creates a random file of student    ***
'*** records. Each record contains the following      ***
'*** fields:                                           ***
'***     Name                                          ***
'***     Identification number                         ***
'***     Birth date                                    ***
'***     Grade point average                           ***
'***     Number of credits student has earned          ***
'*** The user can add a new record or display an       ***
'*** existing record.                                  ***
'     File used:                                        ***
'        STUDENT.DAT                                    ***
'*** Major variables:                                  ***
'***     Student    Student record                     ***
'***     RecNum     Number of the current record       ***

TYPE StudentRecord          ' declare the record type
   Nme AS STRING * 25
   IDNumber AS STRING * 11
   BirthDate AS STRING * 8
   GPA AS SINGLE
   Credits AS INTEGER
END TYPE


DIM Student AS StudentRecord

OPEN "STUDENT.DAT" FOR RANDOM AS #3 LEN = LEN(Student)

DO UNTIL (Choice = 3)
   CLS
   LOCATE 6, 1
   PRINT "1. Add a new record"
   PRINT "2. Display an existing record"
   PRINT "3. Stop"
   PRINT
   INPUT "Enter number of operation you wish to perform: ", Choice
```

Continued on next page

FIGURE 10-10

Continued

```
    SELECT CASE Choice
        CASE 1
            CALL AddRecord(Student)
        CASE 2
            CALL DisplayRecord(Student)
        CASE 3
            PRINT "Goodbye."
        CASE ELSE
            PRINT "Invalid choice."
    END SELECT
LOOP

CLOSE #3


END

SUB AddRecord (Student AS StudentRecord)
    '*** This SUB procedure prompts the user to enter the data    ***
    '*** to a Student record and then writes the record to the    ***
    '*** specified record location.                               ***

    CLS
    '*** Determine the record number to which data should be written. ***
    INPUT "Enter student's record number: ", RecNum

    '*** Get the needed record data. ***
    INPUT "Enter student's name: ", Student.Nme
    INPUT "Enter student's identification number: ", Student.IDNumber
    INPUT "Enter student's birth date: ", Student.BirthDate
    INPUT "Enter student's grade point average: ", Student.GPA
    INPUT "Enter number of credits: ", Student.Credits

    '*** Write the record. ***
    PUT #3, RecNum, Student

END SUB

SUB DisplayRecord (Student AS StudentRecord)
    '*** This procedure prompts the user to enter a record number ***
    '*** and then displays this record's fields.                  ***
```

FIGURE 10-10

Continued

```
    CLS
    INPUT "Enter the student's number: ", RecNum
    GET #3, RecNum, Student


    '*** Display the fields. ***
    PRINT
    PRINT "Name"; TAB(28); "ID Number"; TAB(41); "Birth Date"; TAB(53);
        "GPA"; TAB(59); "Number of Credits"
    PRINT Student.Nme; TAB(27); Student.IDNumber; TAB(42);
        Student.BirthDate; TAB(52); Student.GPA; TAB(65); Student.Credits

    INPUT "Press <Enter> to return to main menu.", Go$

END SUB
```

```
1. Add a new record
2. Display an existing record
3. Stop

Enter number of operation you wish to perform: 1
```

```
Enter student's record number: 2
Enter student's name: Sam Patterson
Enter student's identification number: 379-60-7822
Enter student's birth date: 08/27/79
Enter student's grade point average: 3.2
Enter number of credits: 38
```

```
1. Add a new record
2. Display an existing record
3. Stop

Enter number of operation you wish to perform: 1
```

Continued on next page

FIGURE 10-10

Continued

```
Enter student's record number: 1
Enter student's name: Paula Linn
Enter student's identification number: 422-10-4033
Enter student's birth date: 12/01/78
Enter student's grade point average: 2.1
Enter number of credits: 108
```

```
1. Add a new record
2. Display an existing record
3. Stop

Enter number of operation you wish to perform: 2
```

```
Enter the student's number: 2

Name                     ID Number     Birth Date  GPA   Number of Credits
Sam Patterson            379-60-7822   08/27/79    3.2          38
Press <Enter> to return to main menu.
```

```
1. Add a new record
2. Display an existing record
3. Stop

Enter number of operation you wish to perform: 3
Goodbye.
```

COMPARISON OF RANDOM-ACCESS AND SEQUENTIAL FILES

The following points compare sequential files and random-access files:

- Data items in sequential files are written to the disk one after the other, starting at the beginning, whereas records in random-access files may be written in any order desired.

- Data in sequential files is read from the disk in the same order in which it was written, whereas random-access file records may be read in any order desired.

- Records in sequential files can be different lengths, whereas records in random-access files must all be the same length.

- Both sequential and random-access files must be opened before they can be accessed and closed when processing is completed.

Learning Check 10-5

1. Define a record type named VendorRecord with the following fields:

Name
Address
City
State
Zip

Write an OPEN statement to create a file named VENDOR.DAT that contains Vendor records.

2. Write a statement that will get the third record in the file VENDOR.DAT from Question 1.

3. The _____ statement is used to write an entire record to a random-access file.

4. The _____ function is useful in determining the size of a random-access file.

MASTERING PROGRAM DEVELOPMENT

Problem Definition

The manager of Gateway Concert Hall needs a program to help keep track of upcoming concerts. Because information on a particular concert must be accessed directly, a random-access file will be used to store the concert records. Each record must contain the following fields:

Artist's name

Date of concert

Time of concert

Cost per ticket

Number of tickets available

The program should allow the user to choose from three tasks: adding a record at a specified record location, purchasing tickets, or obtaining a printout of all upcoming concerts. The user will make a selection from a menu similar to the following:

```
Welcome to Gateway Concert Hall Computerized Ticket Service

1   Add a new concert
2   Purchase tickets
3   Obtain a printout of all upcoming concerts
4   Stop

Enter the number of your choice: 1
```

If the user chooses to purchase tickets, the program should prompt him or her to enter the number desired, subtract this number from the tickets available for this concert, and display the ticket's cost.

Solution Design

This program will create a random-access file, which we will call CONCERT.DAT. Each record in the file will contain the previously listed fields. The menu must be displayed in a loop so that the user can perform as many tasks as needed. Therefore, this loop will be placed in the main body of the program. The loop's body will consist mainly of calls to SUB procedures.

We can divide the tasks to be performed by this program as follows:

1. Allow the user to enter a new record.

2. Allow the user to purchase tickets.

3. Allow the user to obtain a printout of all upcoming concerts.

Step 1 can be further divided:

1.A. Prompt user to enter the concert's number.

1.B. Prompt user to enter artist's name.

1.C. Prompt user to enter concert's date.

1.D. Prompt user to enter concert's time.

1.E. Prompt user to enter cost per ticket.

1.F. Prompt user to enter total number of tickets available.

1.G. Write the record to the file.

Step 2 can be divided like this:

2.A. Prompt user to enter concert number.

2.B. Display the concert information.

2.C. Ask user how many tickets need to be purchased.

2.D. Check to see if this many tickets are available.

2.E. If they are, display total ticket cost and update number of tickets available.

2.F. If they are not, display a "sorry" message.

Step 3 involves sending the output to the printer:

3.A. Print headings.

3.B. Print all of the records in the CONCERT.DAT file.

Figure 10-11 shows this structure chart. Step 1 simply uses INPUT statements to get the needed data and place it in the record. A PUT statement then writes the record to the specified location. Step 2 needs to use a block IF to determine whether enough tickets are available. After the cost is determined, the field storing the number of available tickets must be updated and this modified

FIGURE 10-11

Structure Chart for Concert Information Program

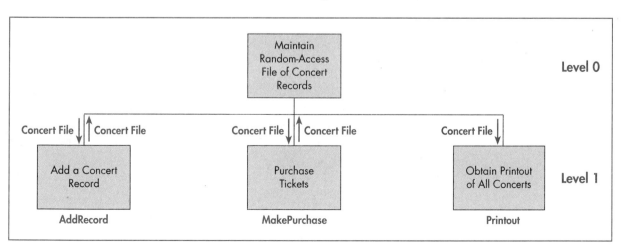

value must be written to the record. Step 3 requires the LPRINT statement to direct output to the printer. Also, the LOF function will be used to control a loop so that the entire file can be printed.

The flowchart and pseudocode containing the logic of the solution are shown in Figure 10-12.

The Program

The program (Figure 10-13) is modularized according to level 1 of the structure chart in Figure 10-11. The main program begins by defining the record type ConcertRecord and then using a DIM statement to declare Concert to be a record of this type. The file CONCERT.DAT is then opened. The DO WHILE...LOOP allows the user to perform as many tasks as desired.

SUB procedure AddRecord is called when the user enters a 1. It prompts the user to enter the data, including the record location where this data should be written. A PUT statement then writes the record to CONCERT.DAT.

When a 2 is entered, SUB procedure MakePurchase is executed, and the user is prompted to enter the number of tickets to be purchased. A block IF statement checks the NumTickets field of the desired concert. If the tickets are available, the value of the TicketCost field is multiplied by the number of tickets to determine the amount of money the user owes. The number of tickets being purchased is subtracted from the NumTickets field. This new value is written to the file by a PUT statement. If the tickets are not available, a "sorry" message is displayed.

To obtain a printout of all upcoming concerts, the user enters a 3. Notice the condition controlling the FOR...NEXT loop that prints the records:

```
FOR Count = 1 TO LOF(1) / LEN(Concert)
```

The LOF function determines how many bytes are in the file and the expression "LEN (Concert)" calculates the bytes per record. By dividing the first value by the second, we can determine how many records are currently in CONCERT.DAT. Because the GET statement accesses the file a record at a time, the resulting quotient determines how many times the FOR...NEXT loop should execute to print the entire file. LPRINT statements print the contents of each record.

If a value outside the 1 through 4 range is entered in response to the menu options, an error message appears and the menu is redisplayed. When the user enters a 4, a goodbye message is displayed, CONCERT.DAT is closed, and execution terminates.

FIGURE 10-12

Flowchart and
Pseudocode for Concert
Information Program

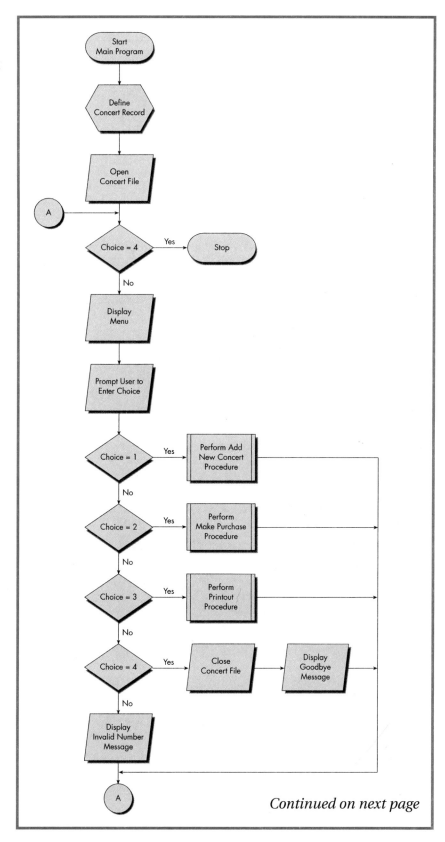

Continued on next page

FIGURE 10-12

Continued

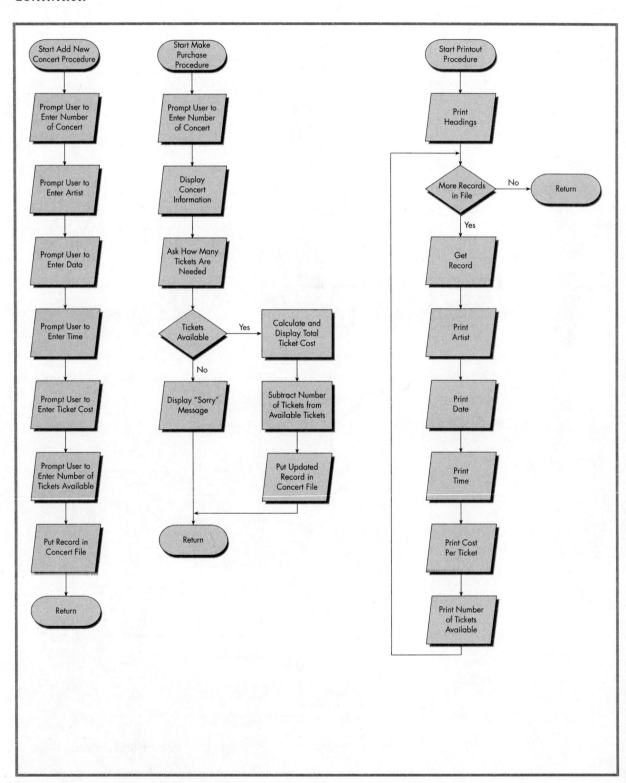

FIGURE 10-12

Continued

```
Begin main program
    Define concert record
    Open concert file
    Begin loop, do until choice = 4
        Display menu
        Prompt user to enter choice
        Choice = 1
            Perform add new concert procedure
        Choice =2
            Perform make purchase procedure
        Choice = 3
            Perform printout procedure
        Choice = 4
            Close concert file
            Display goodbye message
        Choice is invalid
            Display invalid number message
    End loop
End main program

Begin add new concert procedure
    Prompt user to enter concert number
    Prompt user to enter artist
    Prompt user to enter date
    Prompt user to enter time
    Prompt user to enter cost per ticket
    Prompt user to enter number of tickets available
    Write record to concert file
End add new concert procedure

Begin make purchase procedure
    Prompt user to enter concert number
    Display concert information
    Ask how many tickets are to be purchased
    If tickets are available
        Then
            Calculate and display total ticket cost
            Subtract number of tickets from available tickets
            Write updated record to concert file
        Else display "Sorry" message
    End if
End make purchase procedure
```

Continued on next page

FIGURE 10-12

Continued

```
Begin printout procedure
     Print headings
     Begin loop, do until end of file
          Get record
          Print artist
          Print date
          Print time
          Print cost per ticket
          Print number of tickets available
     End loop
End printout procedure
```

PROGRAMMING HINTS

- When declaring a record, remember that all string fields must be a fixed length. This means you must determine the maximum number of characters needed for the field and declare the string to be of that length.

- When using the DIM statement to declare a variable, you cannot include symbols such as $ and % in the variable's name.

- Make sure a file is closed when it is no longer being used. This step prevents data being lost.

- Be careful to always refer to the correct file number when referencing a file. Check back to the OPEN statement to determine the file number.

- When specifying a mode, remember that OUTPUT mode is used for writing data to a file and INPUT mode is used for reading data from a file.

- To add new records to the end of an existing sequential file, be careful to use the APPEND mode. Using the OUTPUT mode will destroy the previous records.

- When opening a random-access file, use the LEN function to determine each record's length.

- Be careful when specifying the record number in a PUT statement; using the incorrect number can cause a record to be accidentally overwritten.

Figure 10-13

Concert Information Program

```
DECLARE SUB AddRecord (Concert AS ANY)
DECLARE SUB MakePurchase (Concert AS ANY)
DECLARE SUB Printout (Concert AS ANY)

'***                      Gateway Concert File                    ***

'*** This program maintains a random file of concert records. Each ***
'*** record has the following fields:                             ***
'***      Artist        Name of the performer or group           ***
'***      Date          Date of the concert                      ***
'***      Tme           Time of the concert                      ***
'***      TicketCost    Cost per ticket                          ***
'***      NumTickets    Number of ticket available               ***
'*** The user can perform the following tasks:                    ***
'***      1. Add a new record                                    ***
'***      2. Purchase tickets                                    ***
'***      3. Obtain a printout of upcoming concerts              ***
'*** File User:                                                   ***
'***      CONCERT.DAT  Random file containing concert information ***
'*** Major variables:                                             ***
'***      Concert       Record variable of type ConcertRecord     ***
'***      RecNum        Record number at which a record is stored  ***


'*** Define the fields for ConcertRecord. ***
TYPE ConcertRecord
    Artist AS STRING * 20
    Date AS STRING * 8
    Tme AS STRING * 8
    TicketCost AS SINGLE
    NumTickets AS INTEGER
END TYPE


'*** Declare a record variable. ***
DIM Concert AS ConcertRecord


'*** Open CONCERT.DAT as a random file. ***
OPEN "CONCERT.DAT" FOR RANDOM AS #1 LEN = LEN(Concert)
```

Continued on next page

Figure 10-13

Continued

```
'*** Allow user to perform as many operations as necessary. ***
Choice = 0
DO WHILE (Choice <> 4)
    CLS
    PRINT "Welcome to Gateway Concert Hall Computerized Ticket Service"
    PRINT
    PRINT "1  Add a new concert"
    PRINT "2  Purchase tickets"
    PRINT "3  Obtain a printout of all upcoming concerts"
    PRINT "4  Stop"
    PRINT
    INPUT "Enter the number of your choice: ", Choice

    '*** Call correct procedure, depending on selection. ***
    SELECT CASE Choice
        CASE 1
            CALL AddRecord(Concert)
        CASE 2
            CALL MakePurchase(Concert)
        CASE 3
            CALL Printout(Concert)
        CASE 4
            CLOSE #1
            PRINT "Goodbye."
        '*** If user enters invalid choice, display error message. ***
        CASE ELSE
            PRINT
            PRINT "Invalid choice."
            INPUT "Press <Enter> to continue.", Go$
    END SELECT
LOOP

END

SUB AddRecord (Concert AS ConcertRecord)
    '*** This procedure prompts the user to enter concert data and    ***
    '*** writes it to the specified record number.                    ***

    CLS
    '*** Prompt user to enter concert information. ***
```

FIGURE 10-13

Continued

```
   INPUT "Enter concert's number: ", RecNum
   INPUT "Enter name of the artist: ", Concert.Artist
   INPUT "Enter the date of the concert: ", Concert.Date
   INPUT "Enter the time of the concert: ", Concert.Tme
   INPUT "Enter the cost per ticket: ", Concert.TicketCost
   INPUT "Enter the number of tickets available: ", Concert.NumTickets

   '*** Write record to the location indicated by the concert's number. ***
   PUT #1, RecNum, Concert


END SUB

SUB MakePurchase (Concert AS ConcertRecord)
   '*** This procedure allows the user to enter a record number,      ***
   '*** displays that record, and asks how many tickets are to be     ***
   '*** purchased. This number of tickets is subtracted from the      ***
   '*** NumTickets field and the cost of the tickets is displayed.    ***

   CLS

   '*** Prompt user to enter concert number. ***
   INPUT "Enter the record number of the concert"; RecNum

   '*** Display information on the concert. ***
   GET #1, RecNum, Concert
   PRINT
   PRINT "Artist:     "; Concert.Artist
   PRINT "Date:       "; Concert.Date
   PRINT "Time:       "; Concert.Tme
   PRINT "Ticket Cost "; Concert.TicketCost

   '*** Ask user how many tickets are to be purchased. ***
   PRINT
   INPUT "How many tickets do you wish to purchase"; Number

   '*** If this many tickets are not available, display "Sorry" message. ***
   IF Number > Concert.NumTickets THEN
      PRINT "Sorry, this quantity of tickets is not available for this concert."
   '*** Otherwise, display cost and update available tickets. ***
   ELSE
      Format$ = "\                        \ $$#,###.##"
      PRINT USING Format$; "Total cost of tickets is"; Concert.TicketCost * Number
```

Continued on next page

FIGURE 10-13

Continued

```
        Concert.NumTickets = Concert.NumTickets - Number
        PUT #1, RecNum, Concert
    END IF


    PRINT
    '*** Display information until user presses <Enter>. ***
    INPUT "Press <Enter> to return to main menu.", Go$

END SUB

SUB Printout (Concert AS ConcertRecord)
    '*** This procedure prints (on paper) information on all upcoming  ***
    '*** concerts.                                                     ***

    '*** Print headings. ***
    LPRINT
    LPRINT TAB(30); "Gateway Concert Hall"
    LPRINT
    LPRINT TAB(50); "Tickets"; TAB(62); "Cost per"
    LPRINT "Artist"; TAB(25); "Date"; TAB(37); "Time"; TAB(49); "Available";
      TAB(63); "Ticket"
    LPRINT STRING$(70, "-")
    LPRINT

    '*** Print each record in the file. ***
    FOR Count = 1 TO LOF(1) / LEN(Concert)
        GET #1, Count, Concert
        Format1$ = "\            \  \     \  \      ####
          $$##.##"
        LPRINT USING Format1$; Concert.Artist; Concert.Date; Concert.Tme;
          Concert.NumTickets; Concert.TicketCost
    NEXT Count

    '*** Tell user that the list is being printed and allow user ***
    '*** to return to main menu.                                 ***
    CLS
    PRINT
    PRINT
    PRINT "The listing is being printed."
    INPUT "Press <Enter> to return to main menu.", Go$

END SUB
```

FIGURE 10-13

Continued

```
Welcome to Gateway Concert Hall Computerized Ticket Service

1   Add a new concert
2   Purchase tickets
3   Obtain a printout of all upcoming concerts
4   Stop

Enter the number of your choice: 1
```

```
Enter concert's number: 1
Enter name of the artist: Working Stiff
Enter the date of the concert: 11/18/98
Enter the time of the concert: 8:00p.m.
Enter the cost per ticket: 32.50
Enter the number of tickets available: 450
```

```
Welcome to Gateway Concert Hall Computerized Ticket Service

1   Add a new concert
2   Purchase tickets
3   Obtain a printout of all upcoming concerts
4   Stop

Enter the number of your choice: 5

Invalid choice.
Press <Enter> to continue.
```

Continued on next page

FIGURE 10-13

Continued

```
Welcome to Gateway Concert Hall Computerized Ticket Service

1   Add a new concert
2   Purchase tickets
3   Obtain a printout of all upcoming concerts
4   Stop

Enter the number of your choice: 1
```

```
Enter concert's number: 2
Enter name of the artist: Astrofly
Enter the date of the concert: 1/14/99
Enter the time of the concert: 7:30p.m.
Enter the cost per ticket: 24.00
Enter the number of tickets available: 650
```

```
Welcome to Gateway Concert Hall Computerized Ticket Service

1   Add a new concert
2   Purchase tickets
3   Obtain a printout of all upcoming concerts
4   Stop

Enter the number of your choice: 2
```

FIGURE 10-13

Continued

```
Enter the record number of the concert? 1

Artist:      Working Stiff
Date:        11/18/98
Time:        8:00p.m.
Ticket Cost  32.5

How many tickets do you wish to purchase? 2
Total cost of tickets is      $65.00

Press <Enter> to return to main menu.
```

```
Welcome to Gateway Concert Hall Computerized Ticket Service

1   Add a new concert
2   Purchase tickets
3   Obtain a printout of all upcoming concerts
4   Stop

Enter the number of your choice: 4
```

SUMMARY POINTS

■ QBasic allows you to use the TYPE statement to define record types. Each data item in a record is called a field. Each field's name and data type must be listed. A DIM statement can then be used to declare a variable of this record type.

■ Files organize large amounts of data. Because they are kept in secondary storage, they solve the problem of limited space in the computer's primary storage unit.

■ A given file can be accessed by many different programs.

■ Sequential access retrieves a record based on the record's sequential order within the file. If it is necessary to access the fifth record, for example, the first four records must be accessed first.

∎ The following statements are used with sequential files:

- The OPEN statement accesses an existing file or creates a new one. OUTPUT mode is used to write to a file, INPUT mode is used to read a file, and APPEND is used to write new data to the end of an existing file.
- When processing on a file is completed, the CLOSE statement must be used to close it so that its contents are not lost.
- The WRITE# statement places data items in a file.
- The INPUT# statement reads data items from a file. The EOF function can be used to check for the end of the file.

∎ The following statements are used with random-access files:

- The TYPE statement is used to define the record type and the DIM statement then declares a record variable of that type.
- The OPEN statement accesses an existing file or creates a new one; it also specifies the record's name and length.
- PUT writes the contents of a record to a specified record location.
- GET reads the contents of a specified record location to a record variable.
- When processing is completed, all files must be closed to store their contents permanently on disk.

KEY TERMS

Access method – 366
Buffer – 368
Control break – 377
Control total – 377
Field – 359
File – 364
File position pointer – 367
Random access – 366
Record – 359
Sequential access – 366

REVIEW QUESTIONS

1. How are double-precision variables different from single-precision variables?

2. What will be output by the following program segment?

```
DIM Tree AS STRING * 10
DIM NumTrees AS INTEGER
   .
   .
   .
   .
Tree = "White Birch"
NumTrees = 4 + 26
PRINT Tree
PRINT NumTrees
```

3. Write a TYPE statement that declares a record type named PlayerRecord with the following fields:

Player
Number
Position
Batting Average

Assign an appropriate data type to each field. Then use a DIM statement to create a record variable named Player.

4. Explain how you can use the DIM statement to create an array of records. How are values assigned to the individual record fields?

5. What is a data file?

6. What is a buffer, and how is it used?

7. In using sequential files, what are the three modes of the OPEN statement, and how is each used?

8. What are the general steps in reading data from a sequential file?

9. Why must a file be closed?

10. What is a control break? Explain how control breaks can be used when creating summary reports.

11. What must be contained in the OPEN statement for a random-access file?

12. What is the purpose of the GET statement?

13. How are records inserted into a random-access file?

14. Can random-access files be accessed sequentially? How?

15. List some differences between random-access and sequential files.

DEBUGGING EXERCISES

Locate any errors in the following programs or program segments, and debug them.

1.
```
'*** Append data to end of file recipe. ***
OPEN "RECIPE.DAT" FOR APPEND AS #1
INPUT Ingredient, Quant
WRITE #1 Ingredient, Quant
INPUT Ingredient, Quant
WRITE #1 Ingredient, Quant
CLOSE #1
END
```

2.
```
'*** Read the contents of file BOARD.DAT and print data. ***
OPEN "BOARD.DAT" FOR INPUT AS #3
INPUT #3, Member$, Address$
PRINT Member$, Address$
INPUT #3, Member$, Address$
PRINT Member$, Address$
'*** Reopen file to append new data. ***
OPEN "BOARD.DAT" FOR APPEND AS #2
INPUT "Name, Address: ", Member$, Address$
WRITE #2, Member$, Address$
CLOSE
END
```

3.
```
TYPE Motel
    RoomNumber AS INTEGER
    Occupants AS INTEGER
    Charge AS SINGLE
END TYPE

OPEN "MOTEL.DAT" FOR RANDOM AS #1 LEN = LEN (Motel)

'*** Enter the guest's room information. ***
INPUT "Enter the room number"; Motel.RoomNumber
INPUT "Enter the number of guests"; Motel.Occupants
INPUT "Enter the room's cost"; Motel.Charge

'*** Place information in record number 3. ***
PUT #1, 3, Motel
        .
        .
        .
```

4.
```
TYPE CountryRecord
    Nme AS STRING
    Capitol AS STRING
    Population AS LONG
    SqMiles AS SINGLE
END

DIM Country AS CountryRecord

OPEN "COUNTRY.DAT" FOR RANDOM LEN = LEN (Country)

'*** Access record 6 and display its contents. ***
GET #1, 6, Country
PRINT "Name"; TAB(20); "Capitol"; TAB(35);
    "Population"; TAB(50); "Square Miles"
PRINT Country.Nme; TAB(20); Country.Capitol; TAB(35);
    Country.Population; TAB(50); Country.SqMiles
```

PROGRAMMING PROBLEMS

Level 1

1. A new mail-order company, Horizons, needs a program to create and maintain its mailing list. You are to write a program that allows the user to enter customer records to a sequential file (the records need not be alphabetized when they are entered). The sample data used to test the program is as follows:

Browning, M.	223 State St.	Toledo OH
Reed, R.	78 Eighth St.	Lansing MI
Crosby, D.	1098 Walnut Ave.	Richmond VA
Bell, G.	298 29th St.	New York NY

2. Horizons now needs a program that allows the user to add records to the existing mailing list (from Problem 1) and to display the newly updated list. The records to be added are as follows:

McKinniss, S.	167 Campbell Rd.	Raleigh NC
Keeler, J.	97 Forest St.	Atlanta GA

The list should be formatted as follows:

Name	Address
Browning, M.	223 State St., Toledo, OH

3. Write a program that creates a random-access file named PEOPLE.DAT with the following fields: each person's account number (4 characters), last name (10 characters), first name (10 characters), sex (1 character), city (10 characters), and

state (2 characters). Allow the user to enter the data at the keyboard.

4. Write a program that accesses the file PEOPLE.DAT from Problem 3 and displays a particular record when that person's account number is entered.

5. Write a program that accesses the file PEOPLE.DAT from Problem 3 and counts the number of males, the number of females, and the number of people who live in Ohio. At the end of the program, display these totals.

6. Write a program that accesses the file PEOPLE.DAT from Problem 3 and displays all of its records in alphabetical order by last name.

Level 2

1. Write a program to create a sequential file containing employee payroll data. Use the following sample data:

Name	Hours	Hourly Wage
Greenbill	30	8.00
Henderson	42	7.50

2. Use the file created in Problem 1 to create a second file containing the name, hours worked, gross pay, and net pay for each employee. The net pay is calculated by subtracting taxes withheld, using a tax rate of 25 percent. The total gross pay of all employees should also be calculated as each record is processed and added to the end of the second file. Then create a report containing the contents of the second file. This report should be displayed on the screen.

3. The Hoytville Citizens' Bank is holding an employee election to determine a proposed employee insurance policy change. The bank has a main office and two branches. You have been asked to write a program that will create a sequential file containing the following election data:

Location	Total Employees	In Favor	Opposed
Hoytville	53	37	14
Rudolph	20	15	5
Custar	12	4	6

Use this file to generate a report listing the office locations, the number of votes in favor, the number of votes opposed, and the percentage of employees who voted (print these to two decimal places). Also display the total number of votes for both decisions. The output should appear as follows:

```
Location        % Voted       In Favor       Opposed
XXXXXXXXX       XX.XX            XX             XX
    .             .              .              .
    .             .              .              .
    .             .              .              .
Totals:                         XXX            XXX
```

4. The school library needs a program to create a random-access file that is named LIBRARY.DAT to keep track of student fines. Each record should contain the following fields:

   Student's name
   Title of book
   Type of book (should be either *1* or *2*)
   Days overdue

   The user should be prompted to enter the data at the keyboard and be allowed to enter as many records as needed.

5. Now the school library needs a program to access the file created in Problem 4, display the contents of each record, and calculate and display the amount of each fine. There are two types of books. If the type of book is 1, the fine rate is 25 cents a day, and if the type is 2, the rate is 40 cents a day.

Challenge Problems

1. The Mudhens' Baseball Club is in the process of computerizing its operation. The owner would like a program to keep track of the payroll.

   Input:

   The user should be prompted to enter the following data for each player:

   a. Player's number
   b. Player's name
   c. Address
   d. Gross pay

   Use the following data to create the file:

Number	Name	Address	Salary
6	Sam Slugger	275 Sax Ave.	$25,000.00
2	Bob Debench	6292 Lily Dr.	10,500.00
4	Semore Flies	5432 Brookside Rd.	12,000.00
1	Casey Jones	51 Strike St.	18,000.00
9	Mickey Hitcher	756 Horton Rd.	25,800.00
5	Jeff Spibol	281 Ball Park Lane	19,500.00
8	Sidney Shorter	111 Mandalay Rd.	15,000.00
7	Lenny Leadoff	276 Wooster St.	21,000.00
3	George Slider	1822 Brookside Dr.	24,300.00

Processing Requirements:

a. Each record should be stored in a random-access file. The player's number should be used as the record number.

b. The user should be able to enter a new record.

c. The user should be able to enter a player's number and have that record displayed on the screen.

d. The program should be able to create paychecks when instructed to do so. Each player's record should be accessed and net pay should be calculated according to the following:

(1) Subtract 28 percent for federal taxes

(2) Subtract 6 percent for state taxes

The value of net pay does not have to be stored in the file. It is merely output with the other paycheck information.

Output:

The payroll information should be printed on paper. The payroll information for each player should be formatted as follows:

```
Name:      Casey Jones
Address:   51 Strike St.
Net Pay:   $11,880.00
```

2. Write a program that creates a sequential file that allows you to keep track of your personal expenditures. The program should allow you to print a summary report of all expenditures whenever you wish.

Input:

The user should be prompted to enter the following data for each expenditure:

a. Date

b. Type of expenditure

c. Amount of expenditure

Processing Requirements:

a. When you first access the program, you should be given the option of creating a new file or appending new expenditures to the existing file. This allows you to either start a new budget (for example, at the beginning of the month) or add more expenditures to an existing budget.

b. You should be able to enter as many expenditures as needed.

c. You should be able to obtain a monthly report listing expenditures whenever you wish. All expenditures of the same type should be added and only the totals should be printed in the report. However, you cannot assume that all expenditures of the same type will be grouped together. Therefore, before printing the report, you must go through the file and total all expenditures of each type. These totals will be used to create the report.

Output:

The printed report should contain subtotals for each type of expenditure and a grand total of all expenditures. It should be formatted similar to the following:

```
              Budget Report
Expenditure                    Amount
Clothes                        $75.89
Food                           $80.50
Books                          $49.65
Entertainment                  $24.15
Gas                            $12.30
Miscellaneous                  $26.08

- - - - - - - - - - - - - - - - - - - - - - - - - - - - - - -

Total Expenditures:            268.57
```

Graphics and Sound

Outline

Objectives

After studying this chapter, you will be able to:

▌ Define text mode and graphics mode.

▌ Explain how a system's graphics adapter is related to the graphics screen modes that can be used with that machine.

▌ Create graphics images using the SCREEN, LOCATE, PSET, PRESET, DRAW, LINE, CIRCLE, COLOR, and PAINT statements.

▌ Create bar charts to illustrate program output.

▌ Create sound using the BEEP and SOUND statements.

▌ Create music using the PLAY statement.

INTRODUCTION

Text mode *The mode in which text characters are displayed on the screen.*

Graphics mode *A mode in which illustrations can be displayed on the screen. The screen is divided into small dots, called pixels, that can be turned off and on.*

Pixel *Short for "picture element." A dot of light that can be turned on or off to create images. In graphics mode, the entire screen is divided into a grid of pixels.*

The monitor screen accepts two types of images: text images and graphics images. So far in this book, our programs have used only **text mode**. In text mode, characters (letters, numbers, and special symbols such as $) are displayed on the screen. When **graphics mode** is used, the entire screen is divided into tiny dots, called **picture elements** or **pixels**. These dots can be turned on and off to create images. Many kinds of interesting illustrations can be created using graphics. If your computer system is capable of displaying color, you can even create color graphics. However, even if you have a monochrome monitor, you can create attractive graphics. Monochrome monitors display only two colors: for example, black and white, black and amber, or black and green.

Sound is used sparingly in most programming applications. Ordinarily, it is used to alert the user that he or she has entered invalid data. However, the personal computer can produce more music than the single, rude beep we commonly hear. In this chapter, you will learn to write programs that generate both graphics and sound.

GRAPHICS

Text Mode

The overwhelming majority of programs are written in text mode. In text mode, the screen display usually consists of an 80-column by 25-row grid. When you first enter QBasic, you are automatically in text mode. Figure 11-1 demonstrates how you can display up to 2,000 (80 × 25) characters on the screen in text mode.

There are 256 characters that can be displayed on the screen. The first 128 make up the *standard ASCII* character set. The second 128 characters are defined as the *IBM extended character set*. Many of the characters, such as the digits, letters of the alphabet, and special symbols such as # and *, can be displayed by typing them on the keyboard. You can use the CHR$ function to display other characters. Recall from Chapter 8 that the CHR$ function returns the character assigned to the argument. For example, when this statement is executed:

```
PRINT CHR$(14)
```

the following is displayed:

♫

Although the easiest way to enter letters, numbers, and symbols is to type them on the keyboard, you can also use a CHR$

FIGURE 11-1

Text-Mode Display Grid

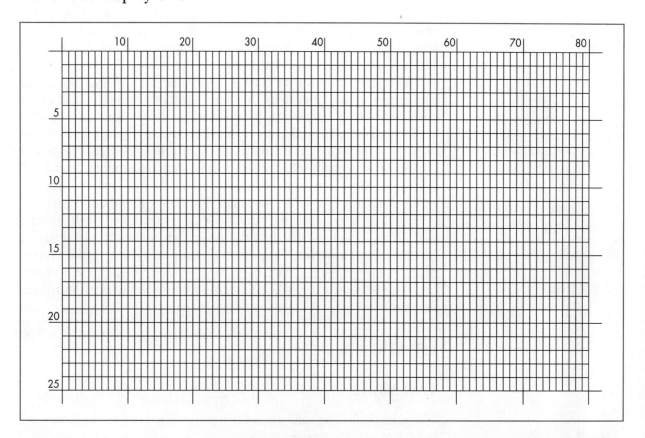

statement to display them. For example, PRINT CHR$(109) causes the letter *m* to be displayed. Figure 11-2 contains a simple QBasic program that displays those text-mode characters with ASCII values 1 through 6. Appendix C contains the complete ASCII codes. Some of the ASCII values do not output a character; instead they perform an action. For example, the ASCII code 13 is a carriage return, which moves the cursor to the beginning of the next line. ASCII 7 is "displayed" but does not appear on the screen; its "character" is a beep.

Graphics Modes

If your computer has a graphics adapter card that allows the screen to switch from text to graphics mode, you can create and display all sorts of interesting illustrations. Before your system can display graphics, it must be switched to graphics mode. Several graphics modes can be used in QBasic. The SCREEN statement is used to switch from one mode to another. Its format is

```
SCREEN (mode)
```

where mode is an integer value. Mode 0 is text mode. If you are in a graphics mode and want to switch back to text, enter

```
SCREEN 0
```

The modes available in QBasic are 0, 1, 2, 3, 7, 8, 9, 10, 11, 12, and 13. The modes you can use depend on the type of graphics adapter card contained in your computer system. The graphics adapter cards supported by QBasic are Hercules, CGA (color graphics adapter), EGA (enhanced graphics adapter), and VGA

FIGURE 11-2

QBasic Program to Display the Characters with ASCII
Values 1 through 6

```
'***            ASCII characters          ***

'*** This program displays the ASCII      ***
'*** characters for codes 1-6.            ***

CLS

LOCATE 8, 5
PRINT USING "\          \    \            \"; "ASCII Code"; "Character"
PRINT STRING$(30, "=")
FOR Code = 1 TO 6
   PRINT USING "          ###              \ \"; Code; CHR$(Code)
NEXT Code


END
```

```
        ASCII Code   Character
        ==============================
            1            ☺
            2            ☻
            3            ♥
            4            ♦
            5            ♣
            6            ♠
```

(video graphics adapter). Table 11-1 shows which modes are available for each type of card.

Mode 1 is commonly referred to as medium-resolution graphics mode and mode 2 as high-resolution graphics mode. Because VGA graphics adapters are by far the most widely used today, we will be using mode 12 for many of the programs in this chapter. If mode 12 does not work on your computer system, try using mode 2; it works with any system except those using Hercules graphics adapters.

TABLE 11-1 GRAPHICS SCREEN MODES

Note: Screen Mode 0 (text mode) is available with all graphics adapters.

Screen Mode	Resolution	Number of Available Colors
Modes Available for VGA (Video Graphics Adapter)		
1	320×200	two palettes available, each having four colors
2	640×200	16 choices, only two available at a time
7	320×200	16
8	640×200	16
9	640×350	64 choices, only 16 available at a time
10	640×350	None†
11*	640×480	256K colors; only two available at a time
12*	640×480	256K colors; 16 available at a time
13*	320×200	256
Modes Available for CGA (Color Graphics Adapter)		
1	320×200	Two palettes available, each having four colors
2	640×200	16 choices, only 2 available at a time
Modes Available for EGA (Enhanced Graphics Adapter)		
1	320×200	Two palettes available, each having four colors
2	640×200	16 choices, only two available at a time
7	320×200	16
8	640×200	16
9	640×350	64 choices, only 2 available at a time
10	640×350	None†
Modes Available for Hercules (or Hercules-Compatible) Graphics Adapter‡		
3	720×348	None

*When using screen modes 11–13, you can only specify a foreground color. The background will always be the default color.

†This mode is designed to be used with monochrome (black-and-white) screens. The screen shows output in different attributes, for example, by highlighting specified output or having it blink on and off.

‡If you are using a monochrome monitor with a Hercules graphics adapter card, a special program, named MSHERC.COM, must be executed at the system prompt before you enter QBasic.

The SCREEN Statement

Flowchart Symbol	Statement Format
	SCREEN mode

As previously mentioned, when in graphics, the screen is divided into pixels. The exact number of pixels on the screen varies depending on the screen mode you are using. For example, in mode 12, the screen is divided into a 640×480 grid. In general, the more pixels, the higher the screen's resolution. **Resolution** refers to the quality of the images. Screens with more (and therefore smaller) pixels tend to be able to display smoother, more defined images.

Resolution *The clarity with which output is displayed on the screen. Generally, the more pixels contained on the screen, the better the resolution.*

The coordinate systems for both text and graphics modes start in the upper-left corner of the display; however, there the similarities end. In text mode, the coordinate system references *character cells*. Eight-row by 8-column squares of pixels define each character. These characters are referenced in the order (row, column), and numbering starts at (1, 1). To write to the fourth character in the third row, you would reference text-mode coordinate (3, 4). In graphics mode, however, the coordinate system defines pixels; the pixels are referenced in the order (column, row); and numbering starts at (0, 0). Therefore, the pixel in row 10, column 50 is (50, 10). You will need to practice referencing characters and pixels to become comfortable with the coordinate systems. Figure 11-3 shows the range of coordinates in each of the available resolutions.

Mixing Text and Graphics

An unlabeled graph is useless. For that reason, the PRINT and PRINT USING statements are often used to clarify graphics. These statements behave the same way in both text and graphics modes.

Learning Check 11-1

1. Until this chapter, all programs have been written in _____ mode.

2. The _____ statement is used to switch the screen to different display modes.

3. True or False? The PRINT statement cannot be used in graphics mode.

4. In graphics mode, the screen is divided into a grid of tiny dots called _____.

FIGURE 11-3

Display Grids for Different Graphics Modes

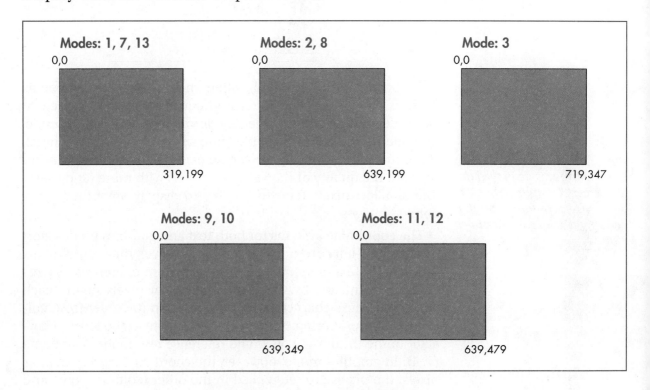

GRAPHICS COMMANDS

The following section describes three commonly used statements: LOCATE, LINE, and CIRCLE. Three more statements are added for flexibility: PSET, PRESET, and DRAW.

The LOCATE Statement

You already know how to use the LOCATE statement to position the cursor in a specific row and column on the screen. However, the LOCATE statement actually can perform three different functions:

- It moves the cursor to the specified location on the display.
- It tells the cursor to blink.
- It allows you to determine the size of the cursor.

The format for the LOCATE statement is as follows:

```
LOCATE [row][, [column][, [cursor][, [start][, stop]]]]
```

where

- *row* is the row number on which to place the cursor and must be from 1 through 25.
- *column* is the column number in which to place the cursor and must be from 1 through 80.
- *cursor* specifies whether to display the cursor or not. Zero turns it off; all other values turn it on.
- *start* is the line to start building the cursor and must be from 1 through 31.
- *stop* is the line to stop building the cursor and must be from 1 through 31.

Notice that all parameters in the LOCATE statement are optional. If you do not wish to change the current setting of a parameter, omit it, but leave a comma in its place. The following statement turns off the cursor and causes an exclamation point to appear in the center of the screen:

```
LOCATE 12, 40, 0
PRINT "!"
```

This statement changes the cursor into a large box:

```
LOCATE , , 1, 0, 14
```

while the next one changes the cursor into a narrow line.

```
LOCATE , , , 13, 13
```

You will need to experiment with the start and stop values to learn how they affect the size of the cursor. The greater the difference between the two values, the larger the cursor.

The LOCATE Statement

Statement Format

LOCATE [row][, [column][, [cursor][, [start][, stop]]]]

The PRESET and PSET Statements

The PRESET and PSET statements turn off or on a single pixel on the screen. The coordinates can be either in absolute or relative form. The absolute forms of these statements are:

```
PRESET (c, r)[, color]
PSET (c, r)[, color]
```

The relative forms are:

```
PRESET STEP (c-increment, r-increment)[, color]
PSET STEP (c-increment, r-increment)[, color]
```

where

- (*c, r*) are the column, row coordinates of the desired pixel.
- *color* is the color of the pixel.
- (*c-increment, r-increment*) are the column and row offsets to add to the previous PSET or PRESET statement's coordinates.

Some examples follow. This statement turns on the pixel at (20, 30):

```
PSET (20, 30)
```

To turn off the pixel at (10, 10) use the following statement:

```
PRESET (10, 10)
```

The following statement turns on the pixel 9 rows directly beneath the last pixel referenced:

```
PSET STEP (0, 9)
```

The next statement turns on the pixel 3 columns left of and 50 rows above the last pixel referenced:

```
PSET STEP (-3, -50)
```

The PSET Statement	**The PRESET Statement**
Statement Format PSET [STEP] (c, r)[, color]	Statement Format PRESET [STEP] (c, r)[, color]

The LINE Statement

The LINE statement draws a line or a box on the screen. As with the PSET and PRESET statements, the LINE works only in graphics mode. The format for the LINE statement is as follows:

```
LINE [(c1, r1)] - (c2, r2)[, [attribute][, B[F]][, style]]
```

where

- (*c1, r1*) is the starting coordinate of a line, or one corner of a box. The starting coordinate is optional; if it is omitted, the last point referenced is used instead. After a LINE statement is executed, the ending coordinate becomes the last point referenced.

- (c2, r2) is the ending coordinate of a line, or the corner opposite (c1, r1) when drawing a box.

- *attribute* defines the color and intensity of the line. For more information, see the section on the COLOR statement.

- *B* specifies that a box is to be drawn.

- *F* specifies that the box is to be filled in.

- *style* is a number specifying the desired pixel pattern, or line style, to display. For convenience sake, these numbers are usually expressed in hexadecimal notation (base 16). You need not understand these numbers, but can simply locate the line style you want and then use the corresponding number. For a summary of the available line styles, see Table 11-2.

The following program segment draws a diagonal line across the screen:

```
SCREEN 12
LINE (0, 0)-(639, 479)
```

The following program segment draws an empty box on the screen:

```
LINE (100, 120)-(200, 180), , , B
```

TABLE 11-2 LINE STYLE EXAMPLES

LINE (60, 4)-(319, 4), , , &H1	. . . .
LINE (60, 12)-(319, 12), , , &H1010	....
LINE (60, 20)-(319, 20), , , &H1111	....
LINE (60, 28)-(319, 28), , , &HAAAA	-----------------------------
LINE (60, 36)-(319, 36), , , &HFF08	-- -- -- -- -- -- --
LINE (60, 44)-(319, 44), , , &HFF24	--- --- --- --- ---
LINE (60, 52)-(319, 52), , , &HF248	--- -- -- --- -- --
LINE (60, 60)-(319, 60), , , &HF8F8	------------------------
LINE (60, 68)-(319, 68), , , &HFF00	- - - - - - - - -
LINE (60, 76)-(319, 76), , , &HFCFC	-----------------------
LINE (60, 84)-(319, 84), , , &HFEFE	-----------------------
LINE (60, 92)-(319, 92), , , &HFFFF	_____

In the next program segment, the first line draws a filled-in box. The last statement draws a horizontal line across the monitor screen in a dot-dash-dot-dash pattern.

```
LINE (100, 90)-(300, 190),,BF
LINE (0, 150)-(639, 150), , , &HFF08
```

The LINE Statement

Statement Format

LINE [(c1, r1)] – c2, r2)[, [attribute][, B[F]][, style]]

Learning Check 11-2

1. When using the LOCATE statement to position the cursor, the _____ coordinate is listed before the _____ coordinate.

2. The _____ statement can be used to draw lines from one coordinate to a second coordinate.

3. What two sets of coordinates are specified when using the LINE statement to draw a box?

The CIRCLE Statement

The CIRCLE statement is used to draw circles, ellipses, and pie slices on the screen. It works only in graphics mode. The format for the CIRCLE statement is as follows:

```
CIRCLE (c, r), radius[, [color][, [start], [end][, aspect]]]
```

where

- (c, r) are the column, row coordinates of the center of the circle.
- *radius* denotes the radius of the circle in pixels.
- *color* specifies the color of the circle. For more information, see the section on the COLOR statement.
- *start* and *end* are angles in radians defining where the arc of the circle is to begin and end. You can simplify this process by entering these values in degrees and converting to radians as follows: Radians = Degrees * 3.1416 /180. The values of *start* and *end* must be in the range of $-2 \times \pi \dots 2 \times \pi$. If the

value is negative, the ellipse is connected to the center point with a line, and the angles are treated as if they are positive.

- *aspect* defines the aspect ratio of the *x* radius to the *y* radius. The default ratio is 4:3. The value of the aspect ratio determines if the drawing is a true circle or an ellipse. You will want to experiment with this to determine how it works.

The following program segment draws a circle 40 pixels in radius on the screen.

```
SCREEN 12
CIRCLE (300, 200), 40
```

The third line in the following program segment draws a 270-degree arc at location (130, 130) with a radius of 50 pixels. The last statement draws an ellipse with the same center and radius.

```
SCREEN 12
DegreesToRadians = 3.1416 / 180
CIRCLE (130, 130), 50, , 0, 270 * DegreesToRadians
CIRCLE (130, 130), 50, , , , 5 / 3
```

The CIRCLE Statement

Statement Format

CIRCLE (c, r), radius[, [color][, [start], [end][, aspect]]]

The DRAW Statement

The DRAW statement is used to draw a figure. The format for the DRAW statement is as follows:

```
DRAW string
```

where *string* is a string expression containing the commands to draw the figure. See Table 11-3 for a list of DRAW commands.

Here are some examples of the DRAW statement:

```
SCREEN 12
DRAW "U20; L20; D20; R20"
DRAW "BM50,50; M+20,+0; M+0, +20; M-20,+0; M+0,-20"
DRAW "BM170, 150; M170, 170; M150, 170; M150, 150; M170, 150"
```

All three of the preceding DRAW statements draw identical boxes on the screen, but notice how differently the statements are constructed. The first DRAW statement starts at the last defined pixel coordinate; if this is the first one referenced, the default will be the

TABLE 11-3 DRAW STATEMENT COMMAND SUMMARY

Command	Description
Movement Commands: The following are relative movement commands; they begin movement from the current graphics position. Movement distance depends on the scale factor multiplied by *n*, where the default for *n* is 1.	
U*n*	Up
D*n*	Down
L*n*	Left
R*n*	Right
E*n*	Diagonally up and right
F*n*	Diagonally down and right
G*n*	Diagonally down and left
H*n*	Diagonally up and left
M *x, y*	Move absolute or relative and draw a line. To write this command in relative form, insert a + or – before *x*.
Prefix Commands: The following prefixes may be added to the above movement commands.	
B	Move, but don't plot any points.
N	Move, but return here when done.
A*n*	Set angle *n*, where *n* is in the range [0..3]. This command is used to rotate figures, where *n* represents the multiple of 90 degrees to turn (0=0 degrees, 1=90 degrees, and so on).
TA*n*	Turn angle *n*, where *n* is in the range [–360..360].
C*n*	Set color *n*.
S*n*	Set scale factor *n*, where *n* is in the range (1..255]. *n* is divided by 4 to derive the scale factor. The scale factor is multiplied by the distances given in the U, D, L, R, E, F, G, H, and the relative M commands to travel the correct distance. The default is 4.
x *string; variable*	Execute a substring. *string* contains movement commands.
P *paint, boundary*	Defines the desired color and filled-in pattern for a figure. *paint* is the desired color, and *boundary* defines the border color.

center of the display. This statement uses the predefined "up-left-down-right" commands, which move the specified relative distance in a right angle from the current position. The second DRAW statement uses the *M* command to move to coordinate (50, 50) without drawing a line (as instructed by preceding the *M* with a *B*). Then the statement makes *relative* movements across the screen, using the *M* command and inserting a + or a – before the x coordinate. The last statement draws a box using the *M* command and absolute coordinates.

The following program segment draws a triangle starting at pixel (100, 20):

```
DRAW "BM100, 20; F50; E50; L99"
```

This DRAW statement demonstrates how the different commands—*M*, *L*, and the commands that allow you to draw diagonal lines (*E* and *F*)—can be combined in one DRAW statement.

The DRAW Statement

Statement Format

DRAW string

Using Loops in Graphics

Graphics statements can be used in loops in the same way ordinary statements can be used. Loops are a simple method of providing animation to your graphics. Figure 11-4 shows an example of animation in which a FOR...NEXT loop controls a ball's height. Each time the loop executes, the ball moves closer to the ground, providing the illusion of a dropping ball.

Color Graphics

As you can see from Table 11-1, color graphics can be produced with CGA, VGA, and EGA graphics adapter cards. The computer must also be equipped with a color monitor. The number of colors available depends on the type of hardware being used. For example, when using mode 12 (which we have been previously using) you can specify only a foreground color. The background will always remains the default color. However, medium-resolution graphics mode (SCREEN 1) allows you to specify both a foreground and a background color. Therefore, we only discuss using color in the screen 1 mode.

You need to define two main colors before you start drawing your graphics: the background color and the foreground color. (The foreground color is the color of the image you are drawing.) In ordinary text mode, the background color of the screen is black, or off; the pixels are not lit. The colors available for the foreground and background are shown in Table 11-4.

The COLOR statement defines the current background color and the palette from which the foreground colors can be chosen. The format for the COLOR statement is

```
COLOR [background color][, [palette]]
```

where

- *background color* is a color selected from the background colors listed in Table 11-4. Background color must be in the range of 0..15.

- *palette* defines the foreground colors available from one of the two palettes listed in Table 11-4. Palette must be in the range of 0..1.

FIGURE 11-4

Animation Program Showing Falling Ball

```
'***                         Falling Ball                        ***

'*** This program uses animation to illustrate a falling ball. ***
'*** Major variables:                                          ***
'***      BallRadius     Radius of the falling ball            ***
'***      DustRadius     Area in which dust will fly when ball  ***
'***                       hits the ground                     ***
'***      VertLine       Center line of the falling ball       ***
'***      Height         Current height of falling ball        ***
'***
CLS
SCREEN 12
BallRadius = 50
DustRadius = 3
Frame = 1
Ground = 420
VertLine = 320

'*** The ball is falling...
LINE (0, Ground)-(639, Ground)
FOR Height = BallRadius TO (Ground - (BallRadius * 3 / 7)) STEP Frame
   CIRCLE (VertLine, Height), BallRadius
   CIRCLE (VertLine, Height - Frame), BallRadius, 0
NEXT Height
CIRCLE (VertLine, Height - Frame), BallRadius, 0


' *** Splat! ***
FOR Piece = 1 TO 25
   DustX = VertLine - BallRadius + INT(RND * BallRadius * 2)
   DustY = Ground - INT(RND * BallRadius)
   CIRCLE (DustX, DustY), DustRadius
NEXT Piece


END
```

TABLE 11-4 COLORS AVAILABLE IN MEDIUM-RESOLUTION GRAPHICS (MODE 1)

Color	Number	Color	Number
Background Colors			
Black	0	Gray	8
Blue	1	Light blue	9
Green	2	Light green	10
Cyan	3	Light cyan	11
Red	4	Light red	12
Magenta	5	Light magenta	13
Brown	6	Yellow	14
White	7	Bright white	15

Palette 0		Palette 1	
Color	Number	Color	Number
Foreground Colors			
Background (any color in 0–15 range)	0	Background (any color in 0–15 range)	0
Green	1	Cyan	1
Red	2	Magenta	2
Brown	3	White	3

Here is an example of the COLOR statement:

```
SCREEN 1
COLOR 2, 0
```

The preceding COLOR statement turns the background green (2) and selects palette 0, which permits foreground colors of green, red, or brown. If you draw a green object with a green background color, the object will be drawn but will be invisible. Figure 11-5 contains a program that generates a series of concentric circles. The random function is used to change the colors of the circles.

The COLOR Statement

Statement Format

COLOR [background color][, [palette]]

Filling Objects with Color

You can use the PAINT statement to fill an object with a specific color. The following statements show how the PAINT statement can be used:

```
SCREEN 1
COLOR 2,0
CIRCLE (100, 100), 40, 3
PAINT (100,100)
```

The CIRCLE statement creates a circle with a radius of 40 in color 3 of the current palette. The PAINT statement causes the circle to be entirely filled in with color 3. Notice that two coordinates are specified in the PAINT statement. These coordinates can be any point contained within the object that is to be filled. In this example, they happen to be the coordinates of the circle's center (100,100). However, they can be *any* coordinates within the object. In addition, the object to be filled must have a solid border. If it does not, the color will "leak out," and fill the entire screen. In addition, the coordinate cannot be on the object's boundary. If they are on the boundary, the object will not be filled.

The format of the PAINT statement is as follows:

```
PAINT [STEP] (x, y)[, paint][, bordercolor]
```

FIGURE 11-5

Program to Display Concentric Circles of Different Colors

```
'***                   Colorful Circles                    ***

'*** This program displays a series of concentric circles. ***
'*** The colors contained in each circle change randomly   ***
'*** as the graphic is displayed. The background color     ***
'*** also changes.                                         ***

CLS
SCREEN 1
RANDOMIZE TIMER

BallRadius = 50
COLOR 14, 1
FOR Outer = 1 TO 3
    COLOR RND * 15, RND * 1   'Determine current background and palette
    FOR Middle = 1 TO 300
       FOR Inner = 50 TO 1 STEP -1
           Front = RND * (3)    'Determine color of next circle drawn
           CIRCLE (160, 100), (BallRadius - Inner), Front
       NEXT Inner
    NEXT Middle
NEXT Outer

END
```

where

- *STEP* can be used to define the coordinates relative to the most recently plotted point.
- *(x, y)* is any set of coordinates inside the object to be filled.
- *paint* is the number of the color to be used.
- *bordercolor* is the number of the color to be used for the object's border.

The PAINT Statement

Statement Format

PAINT [STEP] (x, y)[, [paint] [, bordercolor]]

Learning Check 11-3

1. The *H* command in the DRAW statement draws a line in what direction?
2. The first value listed in the CIRCLE statement is the _____.
3. Write a DRAW statement that creates a square that is 40 pixels in length.
4. The _____ statement can be used to fill an object with a specified color.
5. What happens when the following statement is executed in medium-resolution graphics (SCREEN 1)?

```
COLOR 6, 1
```

SOUND

Three statements produce sounds on the PC: BEEP, SOUND, and PLAY.

The BEEP Statement

BEEP is the one most often used. Here is an example of how the BEEP statement might be used:

```
BEEP
PRINT "Invalid input. Try again."
```

The BEEP Statement

Statement Format

BEEP

The SOUND Statement

The SOUND statement allows you to generate sounds through the speaker. The format of the SOUND statement is as follows:

```
SOUND frequency, duration
```

where

- *frequency* is the desired frequency in Hertz (Hz). Frequency must be in the range of 37..32,767. The larger this number, the higher pitched the sound will be.
- *duration* is the duration of the sound in clock ticks. The computer has an internal clock that ticks 18.2 times a second. Duration must be in the range of 0..65,535. Therefore, the following statement generates a sound at 800 Hz for two seconds:

```
SOUND 800, 18.2 * 2
```

Figure 11-6 shows some examples of the SOUND statement. The second part of the program imitates the sound of a siren.

The SOUND Statement

Statement Format

SOUND frequency, duration

The PLAY Statement

The PLAY statement allows you to create a sequence of notes or tones—in short, to play music. Figure 11-7 gives two examples of coded music strings. Although they may look difficult to play, they are simple to code. The format for the PLAY statement is as follows:

```
PLAY string
```

where *string* is a character string composed of the special music commands. Figure 11-8 shows four octaves of notes. Table 11-5

FIGURE 11-6

Examples of the SOUND Statement

```
'***                Examples of SOUND Statements                ***

'*** Simple tones ***
FOR I = 300 TO 1200 STEP 100
    SOUND I, 8
    '*** Pause for effect ***
    FOR J = 1 TO 500
    NEXT J
NEXT I


'*** Pause between examples ***
FOR J = 1 TO 600
NEXT J

'*** Siren ***
FOR I = 1 TO 3
    FOR J = 450 TO 1200
        SOUND J, .1
    NEXT J
    FOR J = 1200 TO 450 STEP -1
        SOUND J, .1
    NEXT J
NEXT I


END
```

summarizes the music commands. Figure 11-9 shows how an excerpt from a Bach minuet could be translated into QBasic.

The PLAY Statement

Statement Format

PLAY string

FIGURE 11-7

Examples of Coded Music

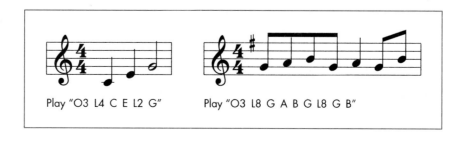

Play "O3 L4 C E L2 G"   Play "O3 L8 G A B G L8 G B"

FIGURE 11-8

Octaves 1 through 4

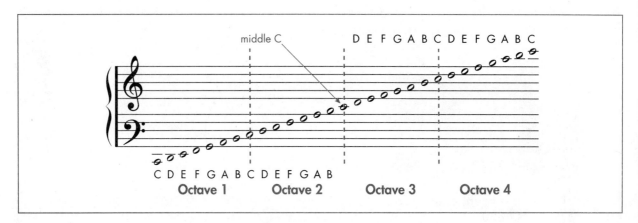

TABLE 11-5 PLAY STATEMENT COMMAND SUMMARY

Command	Description
A–G[#,+,–]	A through G are notes. The optional #, +, and – signs follow the note. The # and + signs both denote a sharp; the – denotes a flat.
L*n*	L defines the length of each note. *n* must be in the range [1..64]. This statement affects all the notes following it until the next L statement is encountered. Alternatively, for one note only, the length of the note may follow the note. *Example 1*: "L2 C D" denotes a half-note played at notes C and D. *Example 2*: "L4 C C C8 D8 C" denotes the first two Cs as quarter notes, the next C and D as eighth notes, and the last C as a quarter note.
ML	Music Legato. Each note plays the full period specified by L, so that the notes flow smoothly together.
MN	Music Normal. After this command, each note plays seven-eighths of the time determined by the last L (length command).
MS	Music Staccato. Each note plays three-quarters of the time specified by L. When playing staccato, the notes sound abrupt and quite distant from each other.
O*n*	Set the current octave. *n* must be in the range [0..6]; middle C is at the beginning of octave 3.
P*n*	Pause. *n* must be in the range [1..64], and indicates the length of each pause; for more details, see the L command.
T*n*	Tempo. *n* specifies the number of quarter notes (L4s) per minute, and must be in the range [32..255]. The default is 120.
.	A period following a note changes the duration the note is played (L) to 1½ times the original duration.
X*string*;	Play the substring *string*, where *string* is a variable assigned to a string of PLAY commands. This command is useful when a section of music must be repeated.

FIGURE 11-9

Music Excerpt, "Menuet," by J. S. Bach

```
'*** Excerpt from "Menuet", by Johann Sebastian Bach ***

DIM Measure$(1 TO 8)       ' Measure$ contains the notes to be
                           ' played in each measure.

Measure$(1) = "04 D4 03 ML G A B 04 C"
Measure$(2) = "04 D4 03 MN G4 ML G4"
Measure$(3) = "04 MN E4 ML C D E F#"
Measure$(4) = "04 G4 03 MN G4 ML G4"
Measure$(5) = "04 MN C4 ML D C 03 B A"
Measure$(6) = "03 MN B4 ML 04 C 03 B A G"
Measure$(7) = "03 MN A4 ML B A G F#"
Measure$(8) = "G2. MN"

CLS
PRINT
PRINT " ***  An excerpt from 'Menuet', by Johann Sebastian Bach  ***"

PLAY "T180 L8 03 MN"
FOR I = 1 TO 8
   PLAY Measure$(I)
NEXT I

END
```

Learning Check 11-4

1. True or False? The BEEP statement can generate sounds at different frequencies.

2. Write a statement that will play a 1200-Hz tone for four seconds.

3. In the SOUND statement, the duration is specified by _____.

4. Write a statement that causes the computer to beep if a value greater than 50 is entered for a variable TestScore.

5. Write a statement that plays the following music:

Mastering Program Development

Problem Definition

Graphics output is often used to create business charts. In this section, we will create a bar chart to illustrate monthly pizza sales for Smiley's Pizza Parlor. A bar chart is composed of horizontal or vertical bars of the same width but scaled in length to represent a quantity, in this case the number of pizzas sold over a 12-month period. The program should prompt the user to enter the number sold during each of the 12 months. The labeled chart will then be displayed. To make the chart more readable, we will insert horizontal and vertical "tick marks." Figure 11-10 contains a sketch showing how the final chart should look.

Solution Design

There are three basic tasks to be performed here:

1. Assign names to the constants used in creating the chart.
2. Prompt the user for the input.
3. Draw the chart.

In graphics programs, it is usually easiest to name constants that are used repeatedly in the program. Then, if a value needs to be

FIGURE 11-10

Sketch of Monthly Sales Chart

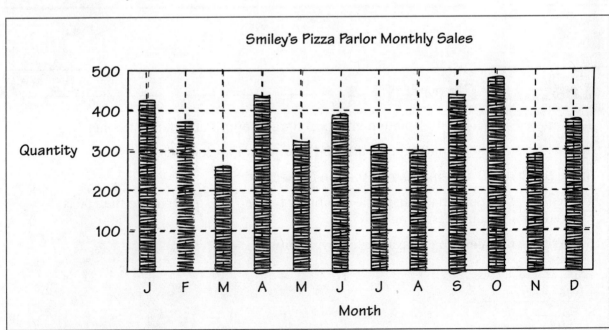

changed later, it needs to be changed in only one place, rather than everywhere it appears. Therefore, when this program is written, the first step is to assign variable names to the constants used in the program. The values contained in these variables will not be altered during execution.

Step 2 can be divided into two substeps:

2.A. Display the headings.

2.B. Prompt the user to enter the sales for each month.

Step 3 is the most complex and can be broken down as follows:

3.A. Draw the bar chart title.

3.B. Draw the vertical tick marks and labels.

3.C. Draw the horizontal tick marks and labels.

3.D. Draw the bar for each month.

The structure chart for this problem is shown in Figure 11-11. The flowchart and pseudocode for the solution are shown in Figure 11-12.

FIGURE 11-11

Structure Chart for Monthly Sales Chart Problem

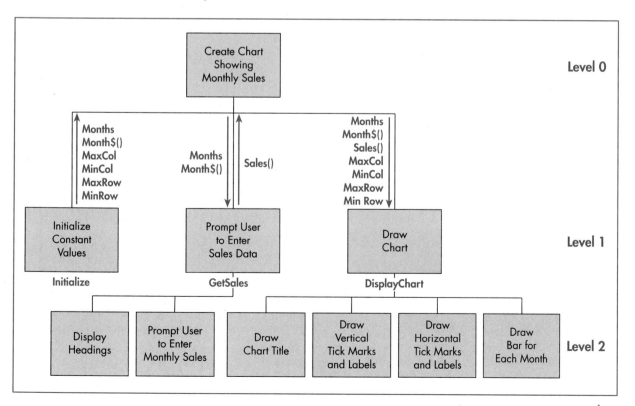

FIGURE 11-12

Flowchart and Pseudocode for Monthly Sales Chart Problem

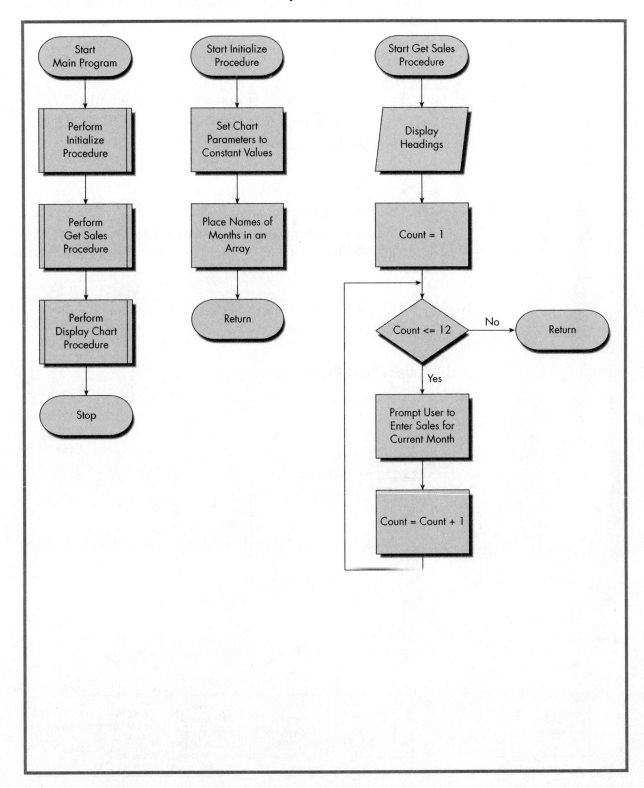

FIGURE 11-12

Continued

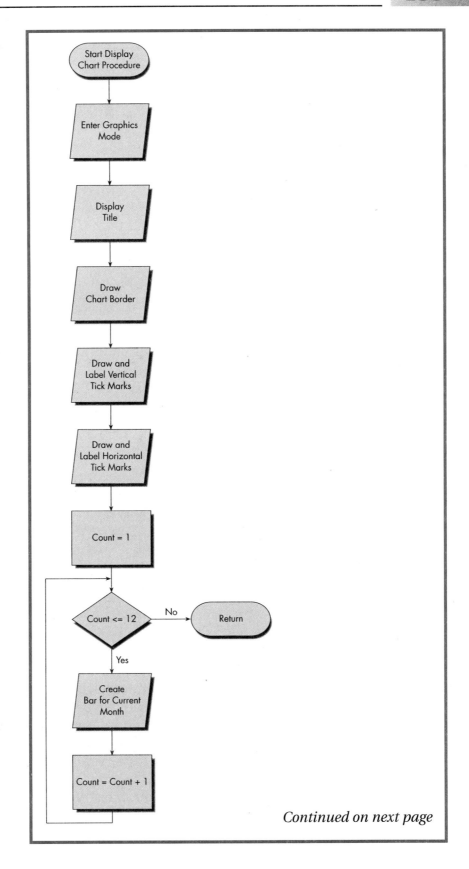

Continued on next page

FIGURE 11-12

Continued

```
Begin main program
    Call Initialize procedure
    Call GetData procedure
    Call DisplayChart procedure
End main program

Begin Initialize procedure
    Set chart size parameters to constant values
    Place names of months in an array
End Initialize procedure

Begin GetData procedure
    Display headings
    Begin loop; repeat 12 times
        Prompt user to enter sales for current month
    End loop
End GetData procedure

Begin DisplayChart procedure
    Enter graphics mode
    Display chart title
    Draw and label vertical tick marks
    Draw and label horizontal tick marks
    Begin loop; repeat 12 times
        Display bar for current month
    End loop
End DisplayChart procedure
```

The Program

Examine the program shown in Figure 11-13. Procedure Initialize is called first so that constants can be established. As previously mentioned, using constants simplifies altering the chart at a later time. A good example of this is MaxRow and MinRow, which indicate the upper and lower border of the graph. Suppose you decide to make this graph taller; you can do this by altering one or both of these values. Notice that the names of the months are assigned to array Month$. Later, when the name of a month needs to be displayed, the corresponding array element can be accessed.

The second procedure, GetData, prompts the user to enter the quantity of pizzas sold each month. These values will determine the height of each of the 12 bars.

Finally, the chart is drawn in procedure DisplayChart. The title is displayed at the top and then the chart's border is drawn. A FOR...NEXT loop is executed to draw the dotted vertical lines indicating the months. These marks are then labeled with the first letter of the corresponding month. Another FOR...NEXT loop draws the dotted horizontal lines for the quantities and also labels them. The values in the array Sales are then used to create each bar.

PROGRAMMING HINTS

- Check with your instructor or another designated source to determine what type of graphics adapter card your system contains. The type of graphics card determines what screen modes can be used in your programs.

- Remember that if your graphics program works on one system, it may not work on another. The second system may have a different type of graphics adapter card (or no card at all).

- The resolution of your screen depends on the kind of graphics adapter card, not the kind of monitor.

- When specifying a coordinate in text mode (for example, when using the LOCATE statement), the row is always listed before the column. However, in graphics mode, the column is always specified before the row.

- If your circles are more elliptical than round, try changing the aspect ratio in the CIRCLE statement.

- Using constants in graphics can simplify making edits in the future.

- When using the PAINT statement, make certain that the coordinates specified inside the statement are actually within the object to be filled. In addition, the object must have a solid boundary.

- Do not overdo your use of color. Keep the quantity of colors down to two or three.

- During the debugging stage of your drawing, concentrate on one small part of the picture and program at a time.

FIGURE 11-13

Program to Generate Monthly Sales Chart

```
DECLARE SUB Initialize (Months, Month$(), MaxCol, MinCol, MaxRow, MinRow)
DECLARE SUB GetSales (Months!, Month$(), Sales!())
DECLARE SUB DisplayChart (Months!, Month$(), Sales!(), MaxCol, MinCol, MaxRow,
MinRow)


'***                    Smiley's Pizza Sales                ***

'*** This program prompts the user to enter monthly sales   ***
'*** for Smiley's Pizza Parlor. A bar chart is then used    ***
'*** to display the sales for the previous 12 month period. ***
'*** Major Variables:                                       ***
'***       Months    Maximum of months that can be charted  ***
'***       MinCol    Minimum column, in pixels, of axis      ***
'***       MaxCol    Maximum column, in pixels, of axis      ***
'***       MinRow    Minimum row, in pixels, of the axis     ***
'***       MaxRow    Maximum row, in pixels, of the axis     ***
'***       Month$    A 12-element array containing names     ***
'***                 of the months of the year              ***
'***       Sales     A 12-element array containing the       ***
'***                 quantity of pizzas sold for each        ***
'***                 of the 12 months                        ***

Months = 12

DIM Sales(1 TO Months)
DIM Month$(1 TO Months)

CALL Initialize(Months, Month$(), MaxCol, MinCol, MaxRow, MinRow)


'*** Obtain sales data for each month. ***
CALL GetSales(Months, Month$(), Sales())


'*** Display the chart and the bar for each month. ***
CALL DisplayChart(Months, Month$(), Sales(), MaxCol, MinCol, MaxRow, MinRow)


END

SUB DisplayChart (Months, Month$(), Sales(), MaxCol, MinCol, MaxRow, MinRow)
   '*** This procedure displays the axes and the bars corresponding ***
   '*** to the pizza sales for each of the 12 months.               ***

   SCREEN 12    '***Switch to VGA graphics mode
```

FIGURE 11-13

Continued

```
'*** Center the title on the screen. ***
Length = (LEN("Smiley's Pizza Parlor Monthly Sales"))
LOCATE 5, 1
PRINT TAB((80 - Length) / 2); "Smiley's Pizza Parlor Monthly Sales"


'*** Label for vertical axis.
LOCATE 16, 1
PRINT "Quantity"

'*** Draw border around chart. ***
LINE (MinCol, MaxRow)-(MaxCol, MinRow), , B

'*** Draw vertical tick marks. ***
FOR Count = 130 TO MaxCol STEP 40
   LINE (Count, MaxRow)-(Count, MinRow), , , &H1010
NEXT Count

'*** Draw horizontal tick marks and label them. ***
Increase = 160
FOR Count = 160 TO MaxRow STEP 60
   LOCATE (Count / 16 - 3), 8
   Quantity = 500 - (Count - Increase)
   PRINT Quantity
   Increase = Increase - 40
   LOCATE (Count / 16 - 3), 12
   LINE (MinCol, Count)-(MaxCol, Count), , , &HF248
NEXT Count


'***Create each bar. ***
M = 0
FOR Count = 132 TO MaxCol STEP 40
  M = M + 1
   LINE (Count - 8, MaxRow)-((Count + 8), MaxRow - Sales(M) / 1.65), , BF
NEXT Count

'*** Label hatch marks for months. ***
FOR Count = 1 TO 12
   LOCATE 27, 12 + Count * 5
   PRINT LEFT$(Month$(Count), 1)
NEXT Count
```

Continued on next page

FIGURE 11-13

Continued

```
    '*** Print label for bars. ***
    LOCATE 29, 40
    PRINT "Month"


END SUB

SUB GetSales (Months, Month$(), Sales())
    '*** This procedure prints the headings for the data entry   ***
    '*** screen and prompts the user to enter the monthly sales ***
    '*** data.                                                   ***

    CLS
    PRINT TAB(22); "Smiley's Pizza Parlor"
    PRINT TAB(26); "Weekly Sales"
    PRINT TAB(22); "_____"
    PRINT

    FOR Count = 1 TO 12
        PRINT TAB(10); "Enter sales for pizzas sold in "; Month$(Count);
        INPUT Sales(Count)
    NEXT Count
    LOCATE 20, 10
    INPUT "Press enter to display the chart.", Temp$

END SUB

SUB Initialize (Months, Month$(), MaxCol, MinCol, MaxRow, MinRow)
    '*** This procedure initializes constants used by ***
    '*** the program.                                 ***


    Months = 12    '*** Data for 12 months will appear in chart

    MaxRow = 400
    MinRow = 100
    MaxCol = 600
    MinCol = 90


    Month$(1) = "January"
    Month$(2) = "February"
    Month$(3) = "March"
    Month$(4) = "April"
```

FIGURE 11-13

Continued

```
    Month$(5) = "May"
    Month$(6) = "June"
    Month$(7) = "July"
    Month$(8) = "August"
    Month$(9) = "September"
    Month$(10) = "October"
    Month$(11) = "November"
    Month$(12) = "December"


END SUB
```

```
                    Smiley's Pizza Parlor
                       Weekly Sales
                _____

        Enter sales for pizzas sold in January? 439
        Enter sales for pizzas sold in February? 380
        Enter sales for pizzas sold in March? 276
        Enter sales for pizzas sold in April? 462
        Enter sales for pizzas sold in May? 314
        Enter sales for pizzas sold in June? 395
        Enter sales for pizzas sold in July? 303
        Enter sales for pizzas sold in August? 297
        Enter sales for pizzas sold in September? 446
        Enter sales for pizzas sold in October? 478
        Enter sales for pizzas sold in November? 296
        Enter sales for pizzas sold in December? 381
```

Continued on next page

FIGURE 11-13
Continued

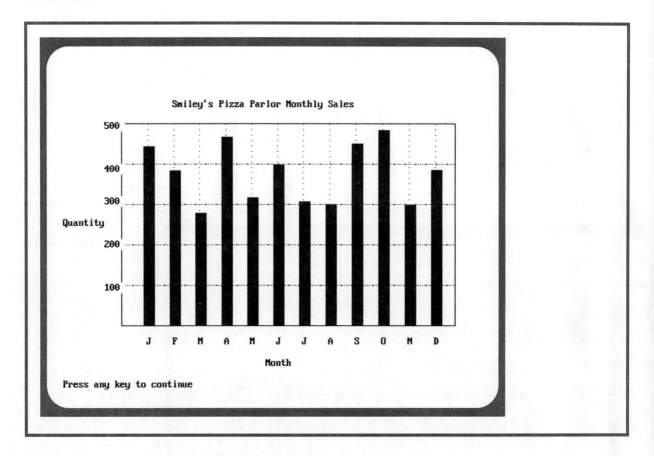

SUMMARY POINTS

▮ Text mode allows you to display characters on the screen whereas graphics mode allows you to turn pixels (dots) on and off to create images.

▮ The SCREEN statement allows you to place the screen in a particular mode. SCREEN 0 places the screen in text mode. All other modes place the screen in graphics mode. The modes you can use to create graphics depend on the type of hardware you are using.

▮ The LOCATE statement moves the cursor to a specified row and column in text mode. It can also be used to change the size of the cursor.

▮ PSET turns on a specified pixel and PRESET turns it off (that is, to the background color).

■ The LINE statement draws a line between two pixels. It can also be used to create a rectangle by specifying the upper-left and lower-right coordinates.

■ The CIRCLE statement creates circles and ellipses.

■ The DRAW statement allows you to draw a figure. Movement commands are placed in a string.

■ If your computer system allows you to display color output, you can specify background and foreground colors for your graphics.

■ The three statements that generate sound are: BEEP, SOUND, and PLAY. BEEP makes a single beeping sound and is often used to tell the user an error has occurred. SOUND allows you to determine the frequency and length of the tone. PLAY is used to create music.

■ The COLOR statement allows you to specify the background color of your screen and the color palette to be used in figures. The PAINT statement allows an object to be filled with a specified color.

KEY TERMS

Graphics mode – 415
Pixel – 415
Resolution – 419
Text mode – 415

REVIEW QUESTIONS

1. What happens when the following statement is executed?
```
PRINT CHR$(251)
```

2. What happens when the following program segment is executed? Why?
```
PRINT "Every character"
PRINT CHR$(13)
PRINT "has its own"
PRINT CHR$(13)
PRINT "ASCII value."
```

What happens if a semicolon is placed at the end of the first, third, and fifth PRINT statements as shown below?
```
PRINT "Every character";
PRINT CHR$(13)
PRINT "has its own";
PRINT CHR$(13)
PRINT "ASCII value.";
```

3. Write a program segment that displays the following:

   ```
   The value of π is approximately 3.1416.
   ```

4. What type of equipment is necessary to display graphics on a PC?

5. How are character positions referenced when using text mode?

6. Give two examples of how the ampersand character (&) can be displayed on the text-mode screen.

7. What is a pixel?

8. Write a statement that draws a line from pixel (10, 20) to pixel (40, 80).

9. What is the purpose of the aspect ratio in the CIRCLE statement?

10. Will the following statement draw an empty box or a filled-in box? Why?

    ```
    LINE (100, 80) - (200, 180), , BF
    ```

11. How is the SOUND statement different from the BEEP statement?

12. What is the most common use of the BEEP statement?

13. Explain how the PAINT statement works.

14. On a PC, an octave runs from note _____ to note _____.

15. The PC can play notes in _____ octaves, and they are numbered _____ through _____.

DEBUGGING EXERCISES

Locate any errors in the following programs or program segments, and debug them.

1.
```
'*** Display a title at the top of the screen. ***

SCREEN 12
LOCATE 50, 1
PRINT "The computer screen is now in graphics mode."
'*** Display a title at the top of the screen. ***
```

```
2.
'*** Draw two circles and fill them with color. ***
SCREEN 1
COLOR 11, 1
CIRCLE (100, 100), 110, 2
PAINT (100,100)    '***Fill in first circle
CIRCLE (200, 20), 10, 1
PAINT (20,200)     '***Fill in second circle
END

3.
'*** Draw a dashed line. ***
SCREEN 12
LINE (50, 50)-(150, 150),&HFF00

4.
'*** Play a little music. ***
PAY "03 L4 C E L2 G"
PLAY "03 L8 G A B G L4 A L8 G B"
```

PROGRAMMING PROBLEMS

Level 1

1. Write a program that draws a tunnel similar to the following:

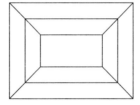

2. Write a program that creates a chain. For example:

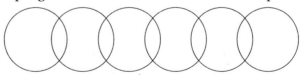

    Make your chain of any length. If you wish, you can make it twist around the screen.

3. Write a program in medium-resolution graphics mode that draws a house. Use color in your drawing.

4. Write a program that clears the screen, displays the word "Done!" in the center of the screen, beeps, and then erases the word.

5. Write a program that draws a series of four semicircles, similar in appearance to a rainbow. Make each semicircle a different color.

FIGURE 11-14

Busy Bee Honey
Company Logo

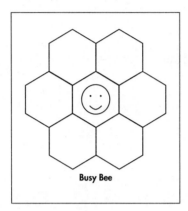

Busy Bee

6. Write a program that displays a single die on the screen. The program should generate a random number from 1 through 6 and then display that number of dots on the die.

Level 2

1. Draw a map that shows your route to school. Label any major streets or other important landmarks. Use color if you wish.

2. Create a program that displays your initials on the screen. Place the statements in a loop and alternate between the initials being the background color (so that they do not show up), and a foreground color of your choosing. This will make the initials appear to be flashing on and off. If you wish, you can make each initial a different color.

3. Write a program that draws the picture in Figure 11-14.

4. Write a program that plays the music in Figure 11-15.

5. Write a program that plays your school's fight song. You can use only a portion or the entire song. You will probably need to simplify the music before you can write the needed PLAY statements. If you have difficulties, try to get some help from someone who can read music.

FIGURE 11-15

Excerpt from "Yankee Doodle"

6. Write a program that displays a company logo of your choice. If you wish, you may want to create a drawing of your school's mascot.

Challenge Problems

1. You are writing a term paper on the lumber business in Michigan's Upper Peninsula. You would like to illustrate your paper with a bar chart showing the distribution of different types of trees within your city parks.

   Input:

   Prompt the user to enter the following data:

   Data:

Silver Birch	56
Quaking Aspen	44
Speckled Alder	25
Diamond Willow	21
Eastern Hophornbeam	14
Northern Red Oak	10
Paper Birch	6

   Processing Requirements:

   a. Create a title for the chart.

   b. Create a bar for each type of tree.

   Output:

   The bar chart should be displayed on the screen and appear as shown in Figure 11-16.

2. Mr. Long, a high school geometry teacher, would like a short computerized quiz of five or more questions to give to his students. Each question should display a geometric figure and ask the student to answer a question concerning that figure.

   Input:

   Prompt the student to enter the answer for each question.

   Processing Requirements:

   a. Display each multiple-choice question on the screen.

   b. After student answers each question, indicate whether the answer was correct or incorrect.

   c. Keep track of total number of correct answers.

   Output:

   A sample question is shown in Figure 11-17. After the student has completed the quiz, the total number of correct answers should be displayed.

FIGURE 11-16

Bar Chart Showing Tree Distribution Within City Park Areas

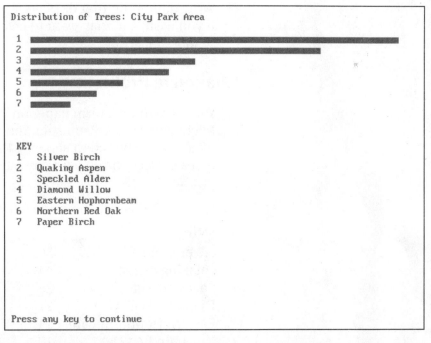

FIGURE 11-17

Sample Question for Geometry Quiz

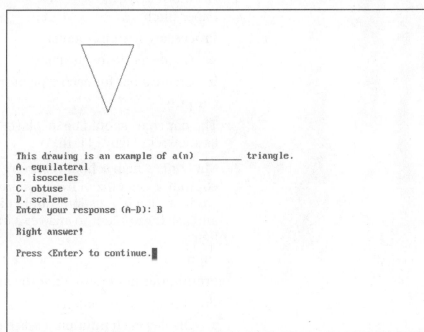

Keywords for QBasic

A

ABS
ABSOLUTE*
ACCESS
ALIAS†
AND
ANY
APPEND
AS†
ASC
ATN

B

BASE
BASIC†
BEEP
BINARY†
BLOAD†
BSAVE
BYVAL†

C

CALL

CALL ABSOLUTE
CALL INTERRUPT†
CALLS†
CASE
CDBL
CDECL†
CHAIN
CHDIR
CHR$
CINT
CIRCLE
CLEAR
CLNG
CLOSE
CLS
COLOR
COM
COMMAND†
COMMON
CONST
COS
CSNG
CSRLIN
CVD
CVDMBF
CVI
CVL

* Not a keyword in QuickBASIC 4.5.
† Keyword in QuickBASIC 4.5 only.

CVS
CVSMBF

D

DATA
DATE$
DECLARE
DEF FN
DEF SEG
DEFDBL
DEFINT
DEFLNG
DEFSNG
DEFSTR
DIM
DO
DOUBLE
DRAW

E

ELSE
ELSEIF
END
END IF
ENVIRON
ENVIRON$
EOF
EQV
ERASE
ERDEV
ERDEV$
ERL
ERR
ERROR
EXIT
EXP

F

FIELD
FILEATTR
FILES

FIX
FOR
FRE
FREEFILE
FUNCTION

G

GET
GOSUB
GOTO

H

HEX$

I

IF
IMP
$INCLUDE†
INKEY$
INP
INPUT
INPUT #
INPUT$
INSTR
INT
INTEGER
IOCTL
IOCTL$
IS

K

KEY
KEY(*n*)
KILL

L

LBOUND
LCASE$

† Keyword in QuickBASIC 4.5 only.

LEFT$
LEN
LET
LINE
LINE INPUT
LINE INPUT #
LIST
LOC
LOCAL†
LOCATE
LOCK
LOF
LOG
LONG
LOOP
LPOS
LPRINT
LSET
LTRIM$

M

MID$
MKD$
MKDIR
MKDMBF$
MKI$
MKL$
MKS$
MKSMBF$
MOD

N

NAME
NEXT
NOT

O

OCT$
OFF
ON
ON COM(*n*)

ON ERROR
*x*ON KEY(*n*)
ON PEN
ON PLAY
ON STRIG†
ON TIMER
ON UEVENT†
OPEN
OPEN COM
OPTION BASE
OR
OUT
OUTPUT

P

PAINT
PALETTE
PCOPY
PEEK
PEN
PLAY
PMAP
POINT
POKE
POS
PRESET
PRINT
PRINT USING
PRINT #†
PSET
PUT

R

RANDOM
RANDOMIZE
READ
REDIM
REM
RESET
RESTORE
RESUME
RETURN

† Keyword in QuickBASIC 4.5 only.

RIGHT$
RMDIR
RND
RSET
RTRIM$
RUN

S

SADD[†]
SCREEN
SEEK
SELECT CASE
SETMEM[†]
SGN
SHARED
SHELL
SIGNAL[†]
SIN
SINGLE
SLEEP
SOUND
SPACE$
SPC
SQR
STATIC
$STATIC
STEP
STICK
STOP
STR$
STRIG
STRING
STRING$
SUB
SWAP
SYSTEM

T

TAB
TAN
THEN

TIME$
TIMER
TO
TROFF
TRON
TYPE

U

UBOUND
UCASE$
UEVENT[†]
UNLOCK
UNTIL[†]
USING

V

VAL
VARPTR
VARPTR$
VARSEG
VIEW
VIEW PRINT*

W

WAIT
WEND
WHILE
WIDTH
WINDOW
WRITE
WRITE #[†]

X

XOR

* Not a keyword in QuickBASIC 4.5.
† Keyword in QuickBASIC 4.5 only.

QBasic Operators

ARITHMETIC OPERATORS

^	Exponentiation
*	Multiplication
/	Division
+	Addition
-	Subtraction

STRING OPERATOR

+	Concatenation

RELATIONAL OPERATORS

<	Less than
<=	Less than or equal to
=	Equal to
>=	Greater than or equal to
>	Greater than
<>	Not equal to

LOGICAL OPERATORS

NOT	Negates an expression
AND	Both combined expressions must be true for entire expression to be true
OR	One or both combined expressions must be true for entire expression to be true

457

HIERARCHY OF OPERATIONS

1. Evaluation of functions
2. Exponentiation
3. Multiplication and division
4. Addition and subtraction
5. Concatenation
6. Relational operators
7. NOT
8. AND
9. OR

APPENDIX C

ASCII Codes Table

ASCII Value	Character Displayed	ASCII Value	Character Displayed	ASCII Value	Character Displayed
0	(null)	24	↑	48	0
1	☺	25	↓	49	1
2	☻	26	→	50	2
3	♥	27	←	51	3
4	♦	28	(cursor right)	52	4
5	♣	29	(cursor left)	53	5
6	♠	30	(cursor up)	54	6
7	(beep)	31	(cursor down)	55	7
8	■	32	(space)	56	8
9	(tab)	33	!	57	9
10	(line feed)	34	"	58	:
11	(home)	35	#	59	;
12	(form feed)	36	$	60	<
13	(return)	37	%	61	=
14	♪	38	&	62	>
15	☼	39	'	63	?
16	►	40	(	64	@
17	◄	41	)	65	A
18	↕	42	*	66	B
19	‼	43	+	67	C
20	¶	44	,	68	D
21	§	45	-	69	E
22	▬	46	.	70	F
23	↨	47	/	71	G

ASCII Value	Character Displayed	ASCII Value	Character Displayed	ASCII Value	Character Displayed
72	H	110	n	148	ö
73	I	111	o	149	ò
74	J	112	p	150	û
75	K	113	q	151	ù
76	L	114	r	152	ÿ
77	M	115	s	153	Ö
78	N	116	t	154	Ü
79	O	117	u	155	¢
80	P	118	v	156	£
81	Q	119	w	157	¥
82	R	120	x	158	₨
83	S	121	y	159	ƒ
84	T	122	z	160	á
85	U	123	{	161	í
86	V	124	|	162	ó
87	W	125	}	163	ú
88	X	126	~	164	ñ
89	Y	127	(delete)	165	Ñ
90	Z	128	Ç	166	ª
91	[	129	ü	167	º
92	\	130	é	168	¿
93	]	131	â	169	⌐
94	^	132	ä	170	¬
95	_	133	à	171	½
96	`	134	å	172	¼
97	a	135	ç	173	¡
98	b	135	ê	174	«
99	c	137	ë	175	»
100	d	138	è	176	▒
101	e	139	ï	177	▓
102	f	140	î	178	█
103	g	141	ì	179	│
104	h	142	Ä	180	┤
105	i	143	Å	181	╡
106	j	144	É	182	╢
107	k	145	æ	183	╖
108	l	146	Æ	184	╕
109	m	147	ô	185	╣

ASCII Value	Character Displayed	ASCII Value	Character Displayed	ASCII Value	Character Displayed
186	‖	210	╥	234	Ω
187	╗	211	╙	235	δ
188	╝	212	╘	236	∞
189	╜	213	╒	237	φ
190	╛	214	╓	238	∈
191	┐	215	╫	239	∩
192	└	216	╪	240	≡
193	┴	217	┘	241	±
194	┬	218	┌	242	≥
195	├	219	█	243	≤
196	─	220	▄	244	⌠
197	┼	221	▌	245	⌡
198	╞	222	▐	246	÷
199	╟	223	▀	247	≈
200	╚	224	∝	248	°
201	╔	225	β	249	•
202	╩	226	Γ	250	·
203	╦	227	Π	251	√
204	╠	228	Σ	252	π
205	═	229	σ	253	²
206	╬	230	μ	254	■
207	╧	231	γ	255	(blank)
208	╨	232	φ		
209	╤	233	θ		

APPENDIX D

Microsoft QuickBASIC Version 4.5

GETTING STARTED

As you know, this textbook covers QBasic, which comes with MS-DOS. QBasic is a modified version of Microsoft's QuickBASIC 4.5. QuickBASIC contains a number of additional features. Fortunately, at the level of this textbook, these advanced features are generally not important. In reality, QBasic and QuickBASIC 4.5 are quite similar. Because of these similarities, you can begin to familiarize yourself with QuickBASIC by reading the section in Chapter 1 on getting started with QBasic. After this preparation, read the remainder of this appendix, which discusses several differences between the two languages. If you wish to learn about more advanced QuickBASIC features, refer to the documentation that came with it.

MENU DIFFERENCES

The menu titles are basically the same in QBasic and QuickBASIC. However, QuickBASIC has both short-menu and full-menu versions. When you start QuickBASIC, it is automatically in the short-menu version. This version contains all of the features you really need, although the full-menu version contains additional commands to make programming more efficient. We discuss only the short-menu version here. If you wish to examine the full menus, choose Full Menus from the Options menu.

Several minor differences exist between the QBasic and QuickBASIC menu lists. For example, when entering a new program in QuickBASIC, you select the New Program command, whereas in QBasic, you select the New command. Some commands, such as

Save, are available only when using full menus. However, you can use the Save As option in the File menu to perform the same function. We do not discuss all of these minor differences, because they are easy enough to figure out yourself.

ADDITIONAL HELP FEATURES

Online help is more extensive in QuickBASIC. For example, Figure D-1 shows the headings that appear across the top of the Help window for the PRINT statement. (This window is displayed when you move the cursor to the keyword PRINT and press `F1`). Notice the items listed across the top (QuickSCREEN, Details, Example, and so forth). These items are referred to as *hyperlinks* and allow you to access additional information on PRINT or related topics. For instances, if you position the cursor on Details and press `F1`, more information on the format of the PRINT statement is displayed. If you want more examples of the PRINT statement, press `F6` (move to next window) until you are in the window at the top of the screen. Then press `Tab↹` until Example is highlighted and press `F1`. The examples will appear on the screen. To return to the original Help screen, press `Alt`,`F1`. Press `Esc` to leave online help.

If you select Contents, QuickBASIC's help topics are listed. The Index hyperlink displays an alphabetized listing of QuickBASIC keywords.

If a help topic uses more than one screen, use `PgUp` and `PgDn` to read the entire item. To obtain a printout of a Help screen (if you

FIGURE D-1

Help Screen for the PRINT Statement in QuickBASIC

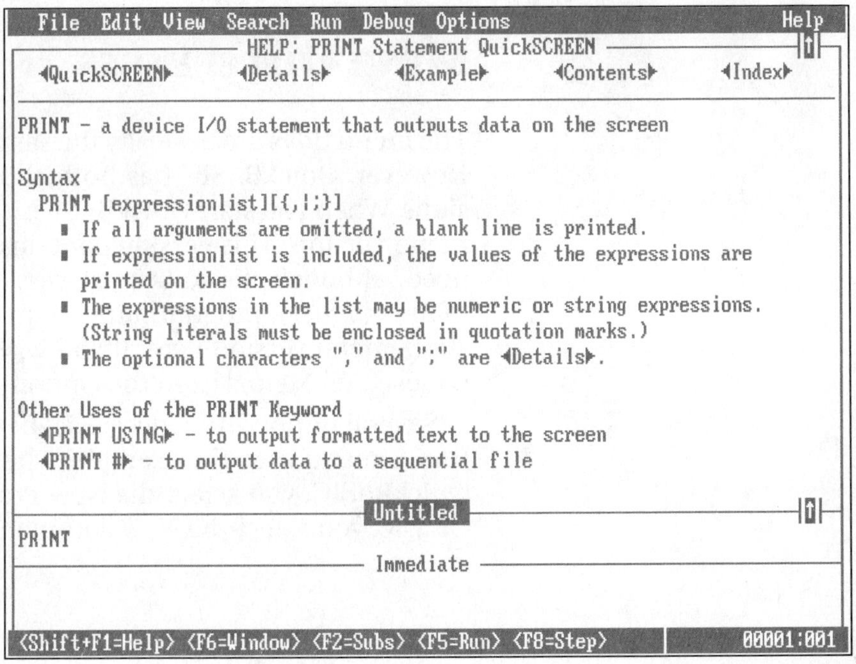

```
 File  Edit  View  Search  Run  Debug  Options                      Help
 ────────────── HELP: PRINT Statement QuickSCREEN ──────────────
 ◄QuickSCREEN►      ◄Details►      ◄Example►      ◄Contents►      ◄Index►

 PRINT - a device I/O statement that outputs data on the screen

 Syntax
   PRINT [expressionlist][{,|;}]
     ▪ If all arguments are omitted, a blank line is printed.
     ▪ If expressionlist is included, the values of the expressions are
       printed on the screen.
     ▪ The expressions in the list may be numeric or string expressions.
       (String literals must be enclosed in quotation marks.)
     ▪ The optional characters "," and ";" are ◄Details►.

 Other Uses of the PRINT Keyword
   ◄PRINT USING► - to output formatted text to the screen
   ◄PRINT #► - to output data to a sequential file

 ──────────────────────────── Untitled ────────────────────────────
 PRINT
 ─────────────────────────── Immediate ───────────────────────────

 <Shift+F1=Help> <F6=Window> <F2=Subs> <F5=Run> <F8=Step>        00001:001
```

have a printer hooked to your computer and ready to go), place the cursor on <QuickSCREEN> and press [Enter ←].

DEBUGGING FEATURES

The integrated debugger in QuickBASIC is somewhat more sophisticated than the QBasic debugger. Most of the features discussed in Chapter 8 are also present in QuickBASIC, but we discuss several differences and additions here.

There is no Step command in QuickBASIC. However, as with QBasic, you can repeatedly press [F8] to execute your program a statement at a time.

The major additional feature is the Watch command. Quick-BASIC's Watch command allows you to display the values of several variables continually during program execution. To select the variables you want to watch (or trace), press [Alt],[D],[A]. The screen shown in Figure D-2 appears. Type in the name of the variable to be traced and press [Enter ←]. Now use [F8] to step through program execution. As each statement is executed, the value of the watched variable appears at the top of the screen. To delete a watch, press [Alt],[D],[D], use [↑] or [↓] to highlight the name of the variable, and press [Enter ←]. The highlighted variable will be removed from the watch list.

COMPILING A PROGRAM

QBasic is an interpreter. This means that program statements are translated into machine language and executed a line at a time. However, this also means that "stand-alone" programs cannot be created. You must execute programs from within QBasic itself. Because QuickBASIC is a compiler, it does not have this problem. An entire program can be translated into machine code (that is, compiled), thus creating an object program. This object program is automatically saved on disk. You can then execute the program at the system prompt by simply typing in its name and pressing [Enter ←]. It is no longer necessary to use QuickBASIC to execute a program. This is especially important for software developers who

FIGURE D-2

The Add Watch Dialog Box

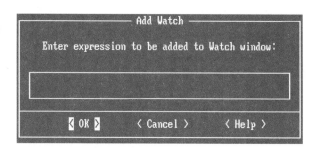

are creating programs to be used by others. Anyone can run a compiled program, as long as he or she has the correct hardware.

To compile a program, select the Make EXE File option under the Run menu. Leave QuickBASIC, and at the system prompt type in the name of the program. The program will run as usual and any output will appear on the screen.

Answers to Learning Check Exercises

ANSWERS TO LEARNING CHECK 1-1

1. speed, accuracy, ability to store and retrieve programs and data
2. hard disk drives; diskette drives
3. Data
4. input devices
5. hard copy

ANSWERS TO LEARNING CHECK 1-2

1. False
2. Mainframes
3. Supercomputers
4. networked

ANSWERS TO LEARNING CHECK 1-3

1. operating system
2. user interface
3. View
4. reference
5. [Alt]

ANSWERS TO LEARNING CHECK 1-4

1. The New option prepares QBasic to have a new program entered. Any program currently in main memory is erased.

2. Save As
3. bas
4. Print
5. Exit

ANSWERS TO LEARNING CHECK 1-5

1. Start
2. It resumes program execution where it had previously stopped.
3. Insert
4. Open

ANSWERS TO LEARNING CHECK 1-6

1. backed up
2. ethics
3. password
4. Public-domain software

ANSWERS TO LEARNING CHECK 2-1

1. Software
2. machine language
3. high-level languages
4. modules (or subprograms)

ANSWERS TO LEARNING CHECK 2-2

1. False
2. Define and document the problem
3. Design and document a solution
4. algorithm
5. False

ANSWERS TO LEARNING CHECK 2-3

1. Coding
2. desk checking
3. syntax
4. Debugging
5. False

ANSWERS TO LEARNING CHECK 3-1

1. numeric, string
2. variable
3. string
4. quotation marks
5. reserved words

ANSWERS TO LEARNING CHECK 3-2

1. CLS
2. by using REM or by using a single quotation mark (')
3. LET
4. a. `LET Age = 19`
   b. `LET Amount = 8 ^ 3`
   c. `LET Lunch = 100 + 65 + 305`
5. a. 14
   b. 16
   c. 81
   d. 6

ANSWERS TO LEARNING CHECK 3-3

1. False
2. literal
3. END
4. a. `PRINT "NAME", "ADDRESS"`
   b. `PRINT "____", "_____"`
   c. `PRINT City$, State$`
   d. `PRINT X + Y * Z`
   e. `PRINT A, B, A ^ B`
5. a. Valid
   b. Invalid

ANSWERS TO LEARNING CHECK 4-1

1. INPUT
2. prompt
3. False
4. comma

ANSWERS TO LEARNING CHECK 4-2

1. SPC; TAB
2. position or column

3. comma
4. c
5. 20
6. b

ANSWERS TO LEARNING CHECK 4-3

1. LPRINT
2. to insert a comma between each group of three digits in numeric values
3. row; column
4. In the first statement, the dollar sign will always be in the same column, whereas in the second statement it will "float" to the position immediately to the left of the number.
5. quotation marks

ANSWERS TO LEARNING CHECK 5-1

1. Control
2. END IF
3. Yes
4. False
5. Relational
6. 77

ANSWERS TO LEARNING CHECK 5-2

1. Menus
2. CASE ELSE
3. END SELECT
4. nested
5. a. 3
   b. 20
   c. 65

ANSWERS TO LEARNING CHECK 5-3

1. NOT; AND; OR
2. NOT
3. OR
4. NOT
5. a. False
   b. False
   c. True

ANSWERS TO LEARNING CHECK 6-1

1. SUB; FUNCTION
2. F2
3. CALL
4. END SUB
5. to the first statement after that procedure's CALL statement

ANSWERS TO LEARNING CHECK 6-2

1. arguments; parameters
2. False
3. value
4. pass by reference
5. local
6. side effect

ANSWERS TO LEARNING CHECK 6-3

1. Edit
2. False
3. Stubs
4. There is no maximum.

ANSWERS TO LEARNING CHECK 7-1

1. iteration
2. a. The loop control variable is initialized to a starting value.
   b. The program tests the loop control variable to determine if the loop should be executed.
   c. The loop body is executed.
   d. At some point, the loop control variable is modified to allow an exit from the loop.
   e. The loop is exited when the decision of Step b determines that the right number of repetitions have been made.
3. Boolean
4. three times
5. priming

ANSWERS TO LEARNING CHECK 7-2

1. DO UNTIL...LOOP
2. sentinel
3. EXIT
4. True

5. LOOP

ANSWERS TO LEARNING CHECK 7-3

1. a
2. four times
3. +1
4. the statement immediately following the NEXT
5. False

ANSWERS TO LEARNING CHECK 8-1

1. library
2. False
3. INT
4. RND
5. a. −1
   b. 4
   c. 1
   d. 1

ANSWERS TO LEARNING CHECK 8-2

1. Concatenation
2. LEN
3. 358
4. ASC returns the ASCII value of the first character of its argument. CHR$ performs the opposite function of ASC.
5. False

ANSWERS TO LEARNING CHECK 8-3

1. FUNCTION
2. A value must be assigned to the FUNCTION procedure.
3. user-friendly
4. END FUNCTION

ANSWERS TO LEARNING CHECK 9-1

1. subscript
2. DIM
3. False
4. False
5. `DIM Inventory$(1 TO 90)`

ANSWERS TO LEARNING CHECK 9-2

1. two-dimensional
2. row; column
3. `DIM Schedule(1 TO 30,1 TO 8)`
4.
```
FOR I = 1 TO 15
    ColumnTotals(I) = 0
    FOR J = 1 TO 10
        ColumnTotals(I) = Numbers(J,I)
    NEXT J
NEXT I
```

ANSWERS TO LEARNING CHECK 9-3

1. The array is sorted.
2. sequential search
3. five values
4. three values
5. False
6. no; yes

ANSWERS TO LEARNING CHECK 10-1

1. a. INTEGER
   b. DOUBLE
   c. STRING
   d. SINGLE
   e. SINGLE
2. True
3. END TYPE
4. by using the variable name, a period, and the field name

ANSWERS TO LEARNING CHECK 10-2

1. records; fields
2. Sequential; relative
3. False
4. cylinder

ANSWERS TO LEARNING CHECK 10-3

1. `OPEN "CUSTLIST.DAT" FOR OUTPUT AS #3`
2. `OPEN "ADDRESS.DAT" for OUTPUT AS #1`
3. pointer
4. CLOSE

ANSWERS TO LEARNING CHECK 10-4

1. INPUT
2. APPEND
3. ```
OPEN "BILLING.DAT" FOR APPEND AS #3
INPUT #3, "Bula Walcott", "713 Jefferson"
```
4. ```
OPEN "BILLING.DAT" FOR INPUT AS #3
INPUT #3, Nme$, Address$
PRINT Nme$, Address$
```
5. control

ANSWERS TO LEARNING CHECK 11-1

1. text
2. SCREEN
3. False
4. pixels

ANSWERS TO LEARNING CHECK 11-2

1. row; column
2. LINE
3. upper left and lower right

ANSWERS TO LEARNING CHECK 11-3

1. diagonally up and left
2. column that contains the center of the circle
3. ```
DRAW "U40;R40;D40;L40"
```
4. PAINT
5. Sets the background color to brown and selects palette 1.

## ANSWERS TO LEARNING CHECK 11-4

1. False
2. ```
SOUND 1200, 72.8
```
3. the number of clock ticks
4. ```
IF TestScore > 50 THEN
    BEEP
END IF
```
5. ```
PLAY "O3 L4 D E L2 F"
```

Glossary

A

Access method The way in which the computer transmits data between secondary storage and the primary storage unit.

Algorithm The sequence of steps needed to solve a problem. Each step must be listed in the order in which it is to be performed.

Alphanumeric data Any combination of letters, numbers, or special characters.

Argument An expression placed in parentheses in a CALL statement. It allows values to be passed between a procedure and the calling module.

Arithmetic/logic unit (ALU) The part of the central processing unit that performs arithmetic and logical operations.

Array An ordered group of related data items having a common variable name, all of the same data type.

Ascending order Items arranged so that they go from smallest to largest (in the case of numbers) or from *a* to *z* (in the case of letters).

Assembly language A programming language that uses symbolic names instead of the 1's and 0's of machine language. It falls between machine language and high-level languages in difficulty.

Assignment statement A statement used to assign a value to a variable.

Auxiliary storage *See* Secondary storage.

B

Backup A duplicate copy of data for use in case the original is damaged or destroyed.

Binary search A search that repeatedly divides a sorted array into halves, comparing the target to the middle element and eliminating the portion that does not contain the target.

Boolean expression An expression that evaluates as either true or false.

Bubble sort A type of sort in which adjacent list items are compared and, if they are out of order, switched. This process is repeated until the entire list is in order.

Buffer A reserved part of the primary storage unit used to temporarily store data that is being written to or read from a file.

Byte The amount of space required to store a single character.

C

CALL statement A statement that causes a SUB procedure to be executed.

Central processing unit (CPU) The "brain" of the computer, composed of two parts: the control unit and the arithmetic/logic unit.

Character string constant A group of alphanumeric data consisting of any type of symbols.

Code To write a problem solution in a programming language.

Collating sequence The internal ordering that the computer assigns to the characters it can recognize. This ordering allows the computer to make comparisons between different character values. The collating sequence most commonly used on microcomputers is ASCII.

Command-line user interface A user interface that requires the user to type in commands. MS-DOS is an example of a command-line user interface.

Commercial software Software developed with the intent of making a profit. The user must agree to follow the licensing agreement that comes with the software.

Complete program testing Testing all possible paths of program execution.

Computer An electronic machine capable of processing data in many different ways. Its speed, accuracy, and storage and retrieval capabilities make it extremely useful to people.

Computer ethics The standard of moral conduct applied to computer use.

Concatenate To join together two or more data items, such as character strings, to form a single item.

Constant A value that does not change during program execution.

Control break The situation that occurs when there is a change in the value of a specified variable.

Control structure A structure that allows the programmer to determine whether or not specific statements are executed.

Control total A subtotal that is output when the value of a specified variable changes.

Control unit The part of the central processing unit that governs the actions of the various components of the computer.

Counter A numeric variable used to control a loop. It is incremented (or decremented) and tested each time the loop is executed.

Counting loop A loop executed a specific number of times. The number of repetitions must be determined before the loop is first entered.

Cursor The blinking rectangle of light on the screen indicating where typing will appear on the screen.

D

Data Facts that have not been organized in a meaningful way.

Debug To locate and correct program errors.

Decision structure A structure in which a condition is tested. The action taken next depends on the result of this test.

Descending order Items arranged so that they go from largest to smallest (in the case of numbers) or from z to a (in the case of letters).

Descriptive variable name A variable name that describes the contents of the storage location it represents.

Desk check To trace through a program by hand in an attempt to locate any errors.

Documentation Statements that are used to explain a program to humans. Documentation is ignored by QBasic. Either the word REM or a single quotation mark (') can be used to indicate documentation.

Double-alternative decision structure A decision structure in which one action is taken if the specified condition is true and another action if it is false.

Driver program A program whose primary purpose is to call procedures; the actual processing of the program is performed in the called procedures.

E

Element An individual data item within an array.

E-mail Messages that are sent electronically from one computer system to another.

Error trapping The technique of writing a program in such a way that it "traps" or catches input errors, such as invalid data.

Execute To carry out the instructions in a program.

F

Field An individual data item in a record.

File A collection of related data kept in secondary storage.

File position pointer An imaginary pointer that indicates the next record to be processed.

Flowchart A graphic representation of the solution to a programming problem.

Function A subprogram designed to return a single value to the calling program. The two types are standard functions and user-defined functions. In QBasic, user-defined functions are written by using a FUNCTION procedure.

FUNCTION procedure A subprogram designed to return a single value to the calling program.

G

Gigabyte (GB) Approximately one billion bytes.

Graphical user interface (GUI) A visually oriented interface that allows the user to interact with the system by manipulating icons and selecting commands from menus. Typically a mouse is used to perform these actions.

Graphics mode A mode in which illustrations can be displayed on the screen. The screen is divided into small dots, called pixels, that can be turned off and on.

H

Hard copy Output printed on paper.

Hardware The physical components of the computer system, such as the central processing unit, printers, and disk drives.

Hierarchy of operations Rules that determine the order in which operations are performed.

High-level language A programming language that uses English-like statements that must be translated into machine language before execution.

I

Immediate mode The mode in which a QBasic statement is executed as soon as `Enter ←┘` is pressed. The statement is entered in the Immediate window.

Infinite loop A loop that executes indefinitely. This occurs because the condition controlling loop execution never reaches the value needed for the loop to stop executing.

Information Data that has been processed to make it meaningful.

Input Data that is entered into the computer to be processed.

Inquiry-and-response mode A mode of operation in which the system asks a question and the user types in a response.

K

Keyword A word that has a predefined meaning to QBasic.

Kilobyte (KB) Approximately one thousand bytes.

L

Library function *See* Standard function.

Literal A group of characters in a PRINT statement that contains any combination of alphabetic, numeric, and/or special characters.

Local variable A variable that is used only in a specific procedure. A local variable exists only while the procedure is executing and its value is not known to the calling module.

Logic error An error caused by a flaw in a program's algorithm.

Logical expression *See* Boolean expression.

Logical operator An operator that acts on one or more conditions to produce a value of true or false.

Loop body The statement(s) that are executed each time a loop repeats.

Loop control variable A variable used to determine whether a loop will be executed.

Loop structure A structure that allows a series of instructions to be executed as many times as needed.

Looping The process of repeating a series of statements as many times as needed.

M

Machine language The only instructions that the computer is able to execute directly; consists of combinations of 0's and 1's that represent high and low electrical voltages.

Main memory The component of the central processing unit that temporarily stores programs, data, and results.

Main storage *See* Main memory.

Mainframe A large computer system capable of quickly processing enormous quantities of data; mainframes are typically used by large companies and universities with enormous amounts of data processing.

Megabytes (MB) Approximately one million bytes.

Menu A list of functions a program can perform; the user chooses the desired function from the list.

Microcomputer The smallest and least expensive type of computer currently available; it is generally designed to be used by only one person at a time. The CPU typically is contained on a single chip, called the microprocessor.

Microprocessor A single chip that contains an entire central processing unit.

Minicomputer A computer with many of the capabilities of a mainframe, but is typically slower, has less memory, and is somewhat less expensive.

Module A subpart within a program; each module is designed to perform a specific task.

N

Network To join computer hardware components so that hardware, software, and e-mail can be shared.

Numeric constant A number contained in a statement.

Numeric variable A variable that stores a number.

O

One-dimensional array An array that contains a single list of elements.

Operating system (OS) A collection of programs that manages system resources, runs other software, and provides the user interface.

P

Parallel arrays Arrays in which the values in corresponding elements are related to one another.

Parameter A "dummy" variable placed in parentheses after a procedure's name. When the procedure is called, the value of the corresponding argument is placed in the parameter.

Pass by reference The process of passing an argument to a procedure parameter in which the address of the argument's storage location is passed to the parameter rather than the value itself.

Pass by value The process of passing a copy of an argument's current value to a procedure parameter. Any changes to the parameter are not returned to the calling program.

Pixel Short for "picture element." A dot of light that can be turned on or off to create images. In graphics mode, the entire screen is divided into a grid of pixels.

Primary storage *See* Main memory.

Priming read A statement used to initialize a loop control variable before the loop is entered for the first time.

Program A list of step-by-step instructions that a computer can use to solve a problem.

Programming language A language that a programmer can use to give instructions to a computer.

Programming mode The mode in which programs usually are entered and executed. Programs are not executed until the programmer instructs QBasic to execute them.

Programming process The steps used to develop a solution to a programming problem.

Prompt A statement telling the user what data should be entered at this point.

Pseudocode An English-like description of a program's logic.

Public-domain software Software that is made available to the public for use by anyone without paying a fee.

R

Random A term describing a group of values such as numbers, in which each value has an equal chance of occurring.

Random access A method of file access in which records are accessed directly, often by using their numbered locations in the file.

Record A group of related data items, not necessarily of the same data type.

Relational operator An operator used to compare two expressions.

Reliability The ability of a program to work properly regardless of the data entered to it.

Reserved word *See* Keyword.

Resolution The clarity with which output is displayed on the screen. Generally, the more pixels contained on the screen, the better the resolution.

Run-time error An error that causes a program to stop executing before its end is reached.

S

Scroll To change the portion of a document that is currently visible so that you can see items that were previously hidden from view.

Secondary storage device A device used to copy data to and from secondary storage.

Secondary storage Storage that is supplementary to the primary storage unit. It can be easily expanded. The secondary storage most commonly used with microcomputers is floppy or hard disks.

Selective program testing Testing a program by using data with specific characteristics, such as being at the edge of the range of acceptable data.

Sentinel value *See* Trailer value.

Sequence A group of statements that are executed in the order in which they occur in the program.

Sequential access A method of file access in which data is accessed in the order in which it is physically stored in the file.

Sequential search A search that examines array elements, from the first to the last, until the specified value is found or the end of the array is reached.

Shareware Software that is copyrighted but can be distributed free of charge to anyone. If, after trying out the software, an individual plans to use it on a regular basis, the program's author expects a nominal payment for the software.

Shell sort A sort that groups elements separated by a chosen gap into sublists, ordering each sublist independently. The chosen gap is progressively diminished until the entire list is sorted.

Side effect An accidental change to a variable that is not local to the procedure.

Single-alternative decision structure A decision structure in which an action is taken if the specified condition is true. Otherwise, control continues to the next statement.

Soft copy Output displayed on a monitor screen.

Software A program or a group of related programs.

Standard function A function that is built into QBasic.

String variable A variable that stores a character string.

Structure chart A diagram that visually illustrates how a problem solution has been divided into subparts.

Structured programming A method of programming in which programs are constructed with easy-to-follow logic, attempt to use only the three basic control structures, and are divided into modules.

Stub A procedure that has yet to be written and consists only of SUB and END SUB statements and a PRINT statement indicating that the procedure was called. Stubs are used to test the calling program.

SUB procedure A module that is essentially a program within a program. It starts with the keyword SUB and ends with END SUB.

Subscript A value used to identify the position of a particular array element; it is enclosed in parentheses after the array name.

Subscripted variable A variable that refers to a specific element within an array.

Supercomputer The fastest type of computer currently available, it is very expensive and primarily used for tasks that involve large quantities of numerical processing.

Syntax error A violation of the grammatical rules of a language.

System unit The main component of the computer system; it contains the central processing unit, main memory, and possibly other hardware devices such as floppy disk and hard disk drives.

T

Terabyte (TB) Approximately one trillion bytes.

Text mode The mode in which text characters are displayed on the screen.

Top-down design A method of solving a problem that proceeds from the general to the specific. The major problems are dealt with first, and the details are left until later.

Trailer value A data value indicating that a loop should stop executing. It must be a value that would not ordinarily occur in the input data.

Two-dimensional array An array in which elements are arranged in both columns and rows.

U

Unary operator An operator, such as NOT, that is used with a single operand.

Unsubscripted variable A variable that refers to a single, independent storage location.

User friendly A term used to describe a program that is written to be as easy and enjoyable as possible for people to use.

User interface The part of a program such as an operating system that allows the user to interact with the system.

User-defined function A function written by a programmer to meet a specific need.

V

Variable A storage location whose value can change during program execution.

Variable name A name used to identify a storage location.

Index

PHOTO CREDITS